Recreating Japanese Men

Recreating Japanese Men

Edited by

SABINE FRÜHSTÜCK AND ANNE WALTHALL

University of California Press

BERKELEY LOS ANGELES LONDON

University of California Press, one of the most distinguished university presses in the United States, enriches lives around the world by advancing scholarship in the humanities, social sciences, and natural sciences. Its activities are supported by the UC Press Foundation and by philanthropic contributions from individuals and institutions. For more information, visit www.ucpress.edu.

University of California Press
Berkeley and Los Angeles, California

University of California Press, Ltd.
London, England

Library of Congress Cataloging-in-Publication Data

Recreating Japanese men / Sabine Frühstück and Anne Walthall, editors.
p. cm.
Includes bibliographical references and index.
ISBN 978-0-520-26737-4 (cloth, alk. paper) — 978-0-520-26738-1 (pbk., alk. paper)
1. Men—Japan. 2. Masculinity—Japan. 3. Men—Japan—Identity. 4. Sex role—Japan. I. Frühstück, Sabine. II. Walthall, Anne
HQ1090.7.J3R43 2011
305.38'895600903—dc22 2010052332

Manufactured in the United States of America

20 19 18 17 16 15 14 13 12 11
10 9 8 7 6 5 4 3 2 1

In keeping with its commitment to support environmentally responsible and sustainable printing practices, UC Press has printed this book on Cascades Enviro 100, a 100% post consumer waste, recycled, de-inked fiber. FSC recycled certified and processed chlorine free. It is acid free, Ecologo certified, and manufactured by BioGas energy.

Contents

Illustrations

FIGURES

TABLES

Acknowledgments

This volume began as a panel organized by Roger H. Brown and presented at the annual meeting of the Association for Asian Studies in 2006. With the encouragement of Kären Wigen, coeditor of the University of California Press series "Asia: Local Studies / Global Themes," an international workshop at the University of California, Santa Barbara, organized by Anne Walthall and Sabine Frühstück, followed in late January 2008. In addition to the contributors to this volume, the paper presenters included Roger Brown, Jason Karlin, and David Obermiller. We were also lucky to have Bishnupriya Ghosh, Dick Hebdige, David Howell, and Robert Nye participate as commentators and discussants.

Funding for the conference came from a number of institutions, including the Center for Asian Studies, the History Department and the International Center for Writing and Translation, UC Irvine; and the Chancellor, the Executive Vice Chancellor, the College of Letters and Science, the Division of Fine Arts, the Division of Social Science, the Interdisciplinary Humanities Center, and the departments of History, Anthropology, Sociology, and East Asian Languages & Cultural Studies at UC Santa Barbara.

In addition to the participants and audience at the workshop, we extend special thanks to Kirsten Ziomek, who ably assisted us in organizing the workshop, and to Matthew Mewhinney and Jeremy Pavy, who served as interpreters for Nagano Hiroko and Sakurai Yuki. Amy Stanley and another reviewer for UC Press provided insightful comments on the manuscript. We are most obliged to Reed Malcolm, who ushered it through the publication process.

Introduction

Interrogating Men and Masculinities

Sabine Frühstück and Anne Walthall

Shoguns, hunters, merchants, pundits, soldiers, shop clerks, labor union members, anime producers and their creations, techno-geeks, homeless people, members of village youth organizations, hermaphrodites, rock climbers, and robots. Insofar as they are designated male, all embody some form of masculinity, yet all are readily distinguishable one from the other, not just because they lived or live at different times and occupy different spaces, but because each lays claim to a specific notion of what it means to be a man. From the status-based differences of early modern Japan to the occupation- (or joblessness-) based identities of the present, the connotations of masculinity have varied widely.

Depending on their topic and discipline, the authors in this volume have taken diverse approaches to questions of how to study masculinity while remaining sensitive to gulfs between different periods, from earlier ages to the present. If shoguns, merchants, farmers, or store clerks in the seventeenth through the early nineteenth centuries had been asked what it takes to be a man, such a self-evident question would likely have been met with a blank stare. In our contemporary world of overly determined identities, it can elicit a detailed response. Men in the past (that is, before modernity) conceived of masculinity primarily in terms of maturity while taking their manhood for granted. In other words, the history of *masculinity* before the late nineteenth century is primarily one of *maturity* envisioned, struggled for, fallen short of, or achieved. Just as Gregory Pflugfelder demonstrated that taking the premodern manifestations of sexual practices into account provides the essential background for modern discourses on same-sex desire, juxtaposing Sawara shop clerks to the techno-geeks of Akihabara provides us with a similar perspective on how premodern manifestations of manhood interlock with modern and contemporary ones. Both clerks and geeks live in a world of asymmetrical power relationships in that men can inhabit spaces apart from women, but spaces for women only are created by men. It is much easier for men to move from male-only space to heterosocial space than it is for women to accomplish a similar feat, and this is true whether we speak of premodern village youth or today's rock climbers.

Our approach of juxtaposing masculinity formations at different periods prompts us to reexamine the notion of "hegemonic masculinity," a phrase coined by R. W. Connell.[1] Connell notes that "hegemonic masculinity" is not a fixed character type, always and everywhere the same: "It is rather the masculinity that occupies the hegemonic position in a given pattern of gender relations, a position always contestable." In his view, hegemony is a "historically mobile relation"; it is the "successful claim to authority" and likely to be established only "if there is some correspondence between cultural ideal and institutional power, collective if not individual." The mechanics of marginalization, of dominance and subordination between groups of men, and of the complicity of men who do not embody "hegemonic masculinity" but gain from its patriarchal dividend work to reconfirm "hegemonic masculinity" at various moments in time.[2] Connell's vocabulary has achieved broad currency in the field of masculinity studies; while accepting his main point that hegemonic masculinity is mobile, we examine not figures who represent hegemonic masculinity itself, but those who in one way or another offer alternative perspectives. Or, to define our project in another register, we focus not on iconic masculinities but on masculinities at the margins.

This volume strives to overcome scholarly boundaries currently in place in the field of Japan studies. Hence the essays are characterized by significant disciplinary breadth and draw from textual, numerical, oral, and visual materials. Whether historians, sociologists, anthropologists, or practitioners of cultural studies, most authors in this volume have tried to combine two or more such registers in order to ask what forms of difference, what kinds of identities, and what subject positions are constructed within the framework of a given cultural, ideological, or discursive formation.[3] Some are inspired by the Foucauldian concept of power as permeating and being inscribed on bodies. Others pay close attention to living bodies and listen to people doing things in a given historical moment, past or present.[4] Together, the contributors are interested in how actual male figures, modes of manhood, and styles of masculinity reinforce and undermine a sense of gender as authentic and stable and how different meanings of masculinity are produced in a number of different sites. After all, as Sherry Ortner has noted,

> One of the central games of life in most cultures is the gender game, or more specifically the multiplicity of gender games available in that time and place. The effort to understand the making and unmaking of gender, as well as what gender makes, involves understanding the workings of these games as games, with their inclusions and exclusions, multiple positions, complex rules, forms of bodily activity, structures of feeling and desire, and stakes of winning, losing, or simply playing. It involves as well the question of how gender games themselves collide with, encompass, or are bent to the service of other games, for gender is never, as they say, the only game in town.[5]

The essays in this volume address both of these insights—the multiplicity of "gender games" and the interconnectivity of gender games with "other games."

In short, we seek both to interrogate what it meant to embody manhood in the past and what it means today, and to present an array of possible methodologies for attacking the problem. Constructing masculinity has always been contingent on a host of factors, and for historians, anthropologists, and literary theorists, the ways to approach its study are equally varied. What holds this volume together is the common effort to analyze categories assigned to men based on the theoretical implications found in the concept of gender. While recognizing that the concept is overused, subject to abuse, and easily misunderstood, we present four interlocking strategies that draw on existing theoretical work, expand its implications, and promise to shed new light on men and masculinities as made in Japan from the seventeenth to the twenty-first century.

MASCULINITY IN CRISIS

The study of gender has contributed greatly to our knowledge of history while challenging preconceived notions of sociocultural phenomena and processes in Japan and elsewhere.[6] As one of the many effects of these studies, we almost universally agree today that femaleness does not automatically produce femininity and maleness does not automatically produce masculinity. In the field of Japan studies, the effects of disassociating sex from gender in the arena of women, femaleness, and femininity have been examined in substantial and fruitful ways too numerous to recapitulate here, ranging from Gail Lee Bernstein's influential volume *Recreating Japanese Women* (1991) to Kathleen Uno's and Barbara Molony's *Gendering Modern Japanese History* (2005).[7] Similarly, the "performativity" of femininity has come to be acknowledged and understood as transferable, mobile, and fluid by a wide range of scholarly studies in anthropology, history, and theater studies.[8]

Men, manhood, and masculinity, by contrast, seem to have an altogether different relationship to performance, the real, and the natural. Besides the tendency toward "ethnocentric, Eurocentric, race-blind, and imperialist" views in historical scholarship, it appears to be far more difficult to pry apart maleness and masculinity than femininity and femaleness, particularly in premodern times. To quote Judith Allen, "As the dominant sex in patriarchal culture, and historically the dominant practitioners of history, men as a group have not proved especially curious about men as a sex."[9] However, some important steps have been taken.[10] In Japan, journals such as *Jendā Shigaku* (Gender history) and *Modan Masukyurinitiizu* (Modern masculinities) spearheaded this new area of intellectual inquiry together with such pathbreaking volumes as Nishikawa Yūko and Ogino Miho's *Danseiron* (On men, 1999) and Itō Satoru, Murase Yukihiro, and Asai Haruo's *Nihon no otoko wa doko kara kite, doko e iku no ka* (Where did Japanese men come from? Where are they going? 2001), as well as a steadily increasing number of similar collective attempts at staking out the territory of inquiry.[11]

James Roberson and Suzuki Nobue's *Men and Masculinities in Contemporary Japan: Dislocating the Salaryman Doxa* (2002) and Kam Louie and Morris Low's *Asian Masculinities: The Meaning and Practice of Manhood in China and Japan* (2003) launched anglophone analyses of men, maleness, and masculinities in Japan.[12] Contributions in these volumes on transgender practices, male beauty work, popular culture, the marriage market, the new "family man," working-class masculinity, day laborers, domestic violence, gay men, and fatherhood and work, among other subjects, successfully make the point that in the early twenty-first century a significant number of Japanese men no longer embody or desire to fulfill the ideal of the salaryman. Young men comment on this sense of crisis in their own, in some cases radical, ways; they spend billions to retain the bodies and hair of their youth, going well beyond the rationale of good health, ordinary vanity, or even the practical requirements of being competitive in the sex market.[13] In 2008, from tens of thousands to more than a million young men were estimated to be "shut-ins," individuals who refuse to engage with the physical social world around them.[14] This particular crisis of masculinity, namely the struggle with or resistance to growing up, is a global phenomenon. Today in Japan the nexus between mature manhood and a white-collar lifestyle, which had seemed naturalized and even institutionalized for decades, appears to have broken down for a large portion of the younger generation. No day passes without social critics in Japan and elsewhere noting what U.S. historian Gary Cross recently called "the making of modern immaturity," the strange phenomenon of boys no longer being eager, able, or willing to grow up.[15]

As Judith Allen has pointed out, masculinity is not just in constant crisis but is inherently a "crisis-bound formation."[16] But we also believe that this is a particularly salient moment for conversations about men and masculinities in Japan. "Japanese masculinity is in crisis," claimed the sociologist Itō Kimio recently.[17] He also suggested that the present is the beginning of an era marked by a series of distinct "men's problems": the inability of many men to get married despite a desire to do so; the rising divorce rate among middle-aged and older couples; and a number of role-strain phenomena because conventional roles are no longer perceived to bring the customary rewards whether with respect to individual fulfillment, material gain, or social respect. As Sabine Frühstück shows in this volume, soldiers of the Self-Defense Forces face their own crisis in that the once natural connection between military and manhood is neither exclusive nor intact.

To assume that today's crisis is new, however, is a product of historical amnesia. Eiko Ikegami argued in *The Taming of the Samurai* that sixteenth-century warlords strove to civilize the brutal cruelty that marked both their own behavior and that of their men, a goal achieved not without challenge in the seventeenth century.[18] As Luke Roberts points out in his close reading of the journal written by a well-to-do merchant in Kawagoe from that same era, a proclivity for honor violence and the desire for renown in martial prowess also marked the merchants' culture of masculinity. In the early Meiji period bureaucrats and intellectuals discovered a crisis of masculinity in trying to craft a new code for gentlemanly behavior that fitted international norms of civility while leaving room for crudity and violence.[19] At the end of the nineteenth century, students at the higher schools developed "rites of masculinity" and promoted an "athletic school spirit" aimed at constructing men fit to lead the nation.[20] The early twentieth century saw more symptoms of crisis, first represented by Tokutomi Sōhō's castigation of "rich men's sons, soft and spoiled," and then epitomized in left-wing students, who in 1918 founded the New Man's Society (Shinjinkai) to sweep away their elders' "wickedness, vulgarity, and lack of principle."[21] In contrast to a socially engaged masculinity, the modern boy of the interwar years sought individual fulfillment by getting in touch with his feminine side in a display of androgyny that horrified government officials and social critics.[22] The exigencies of war brought a hiatus to debates over what it meant to be a man. When the salaryman took on the characteristics of hegemonic masculinity, a new sense of crisis emerged. Beginning in a television series in 1967–69, the Tora-san film series of forty-eight installments capitalized on the theme, "it's tough being a man" by portraying a comic alternative to the salaryman in a peripatetic peddler.

Another trajectory also needs to be acknowledged. Our attention as scholars as well as debates in Japan's public sphere on the roles of men and masculinities in most of the late twentieth century have focused, for the most part, on what the late Pierre Bourdieu in a slim book titled *Masculine Domination* proposed to be a political question: "Can we neutralize the mechanisms through which history is continuously turned into nature, thereby freeing the forces of change and accelerating the incipient transformations of the relations between the sexes?"[23] Discussion surrounding this central gender question has recently shifted to replicating the interwar outcry over men's weaknesses, shortcomings, and failures that appears to portend a collapse within normative concepts of masculinity altogether, as Ian Condry notes in his carefully nuanced study of the connection between technology and geeks. However, this decline of masculinity is proclaimed in spite of a major backlash against feminism and only mild modifications to the gendered order of power in Japanese society.[24] Hence, while not offering a definitive answer to Bourdieu's question, this volume is a collective attempt to take a close look at these very mechanisms and to pay ample attention to currents and undercurrents.

The sense of crisis of masculinity has been expressed in the formation of new men's organizations, self-help groups, and publications. In 1991, for instance, a group calling itself Men's Lib arose in Osaka. A few years later it took a new name, Men's Center Japan, and began to publish a bimonthly newsletter, *Men's Network.* In 1996, Itō Kimio published *Danseigaku nyūmon* (Introduction to men's studies). In 1999, in response to rapidly increasing divorce rates, a magazine editor in Fukuoka founded the National Chauvinistic Husbands Association in order to help middle-aged men save their marriages by teaching them how to be more respectful of their wives.[25] In the same year, the curiously rapid approval of Viagra by the health authorities prompted a wave of critical (feminist) comments about the failure to otherwise keep male power and (sexual) potency intact. Other observers saw the old guard holding onto power (and potency) while a substantial number of young men were no longer interested in engaging politically, socially, or sexually.

MEN AGAINST MEN

Many essays in this volume explore how distinct modes of masculinity become visible only if pitched against an actual or imagined Other. In some cases this Other is an imaginary "feminine" against which the masculine can be aspired to and achieved. Jennifer Robertson analyzes how roboticists both reflect and struggle against a proclivity to gender robots female. Even the prototype for Tetsuwan Atomu was a girl robot. In such configurations that have been central to debates on gender for most of the late twentieth century, the female emerges as a radical opposite, complementary or subordinate to the male and masculine. Occasionally this has meant the erasure of the masculine element. Whether in debates about "professional housewives" *(sengyō shufu)*, "education mamas" *(kyōiku mama)*, the "flying women" *(tonderu onna)* of the 1980s, or the (mostly female) current-day "parasite singles" *(parasaito shinguru)*, men and masculinities remained largely silent. By the same token, sometimes the Other is envisaged as another mode of masculinity, typically that of a more/less powerful group of men. As in China, socially marginal men can be regarded as "more of a threat to legitimate, heterosexual male power than were any categories of women."[26] Even within the same social or political circle, whether the community of seventeenth-century merchants, early nineteenth-century shop clerks, or the fraternity of rock climbers today, men measure themselves against other men.

It is worth noting the troubles that emerge from men competing with other men over the order of prized masculinities. We believe that this competition has structured the construction of masculinity from premodern times to the present. Anne Walthall examines guns as signifiers of masculine status and largely symbolic tools of authority in an age more usually identified with glorification of the sword. She asks how and by whom guns were used for hunting and what the hunt meant for rulers within a social and historical context, in which valorized masculinity had nothing to do with a female Other and everything to do with male-male competition over status. Roberts's analysis of a merchant diary also illuminates the writer's desire to achieve what doubles as character/masculinity through self-cultivation in competition with other men. As we see in Wolfram Manzenreiter's essay, throughout the modern period and to this day, technologies of masculinity have been perhaps nowhere as gender-consistent as in sports, in which men turn their own bodies into projects of fitness, health, work, and capital, thus in one way or another attempting to achieve normative masculinity by mirroring a male-male competition for skill and status.[27]

Today even the salaryman's world has become a field of struggle. An impressive number of books give advice on how to be a successful salaryman, even while the accusation that Japan is a "fatherless society," one that drives men away from their families and into a premature death caused by too much work for and devotion to one's company, already lurks in many examples of collective Japanese social self-diagnoses. The *otaku* debate of the 1980s has given way to equally anxious debates about *furiitaa* (euphemistically termed "freelance workers") and NEET (not currently engaged in employment, education, or training), those fifteen- to thirty-four-year-olds who are unemployed, unmarried, not enrolled in school or engaged in housework, not seeking work or the technical training needed for work, and are entirely financed by their parents. The problem is attributed almost entirely to individuals' social withdrawal as well as to their middle-class parents' willingness to support them. The phenomenon of social withdrawal, or *hikikomori*, is seen not only as a crisis of masculinity but also as a symptom of Japanese working culture, in which the oppression of men by men is taken for granted.

CONSTRUCTING MASCULINITY

There is a third paradigm that studies of early modern Japan help to highlight: the other as child. Men across different historical periods have recognized the need to not (simply) be *masculine* but the importance of how to become and how to be a *mature* human being. While the current crisis of perceived immaturity worries (grown-up) observers, historical examples of the search for maturity can be found in the essays by Sakurai Yuki and Nagano Hiroko in this volume. Sakurai Yuki finds that in the minds of nineteenth-century shop clerks, achieving maturity and achieving manhood were intrinsically intertwined in a homosocial environment. Both ideals were only loosely related to biological age and required a twin effort pursued with determination and expressed in fashion. In the farm villages studied by Nagano Hiroko, masculine maturity was constructed through individual and communal effort, in large part through the political and physical subjugation and control of female villagers' sexuality by self-regulating organizations. Rural social mechanisms were hierarchically structured to produce men whose superior masculinity was based on their maturity. These mechanisms not only worked to exclude women but also to manage women as wives, mothers, and objects of sexual desire.

During the all-too-determined masculine (modern) nation and empire building of the late nineteenth and early twentieth centuries, the state intervened in the construction of masculine maturity. On the one hand it established institutions designed to mold future leaders. As Donald Roden documented in his book on elite higher schools, the students both accepted the training that turned them into men fit for lives as bureaucrats and developed their own culture in which seniors molded the behavior of underclassmen through harassment and communal bonding. On the other, in 1872 the state introduced compulsory elementary education for boys and girls as well as mandatory military conscription for the rank and file of men. Established within the twin pillars of modernization and militarization, a physical examination system began to name the markers of valorized manhood in new, social scientific terms. Military and school authorities accumulated a host of data, including pupils' and soldiers' height, weight, strength, lung capacity, and (the absence of) a host of diseases and conditions assumed to be inheritable, as well as such "conditions" as the levels of literacy and poverty.[28] In addition, the Imperial Military Reserve Association incorporated village youths into age-specific organizations that replicated the premodern communal effort in producing the masculine maturity analyzed by Nagano, but this time directed by a nationwide institution for national goals. Molded by his engagement with association-sponsored activism, the civilian soldier would practice the five manly virtues of "decorum, courage, loyalty, obedience, and bravery."[29]

These large shifts within the configuration of maturation/masculinity become visible through our historically deep and cross-disciplinary perspective, but they are not the only ones. A somewhat different mode of masculine maturity was at stake for blue-collar labor union activists in the 1960s. Christopher Gerteis tells us that labor union officials misjudged a particular crisis of masculinity then. For young working-class men who weighed the rigidity of the path of maturation within the labor unions against the promises of a bourgeois white-collar and, yes, a salaryman's life, the latter proved the more seductive.

Likewise, the "technologized masculinity" of the *otaku* in *Train Man* is permeated by a nostalgia for the modern fantasy that one could ever "just be oneself" and "be loved for who one is." As Susan Napier points out in her incisive textual-visual analysis of this iconic figure, behind the intense attachment to transitional objects emerges an idealized attachment to actual human beings that is couched in the equally idealized vision of marriage and living happily ever after. We also learn that new technologies provide new ways of communicating romance and desire, while the package of sentiments and their heterosexual, traditional containment has remained surprisingly conventional.

HEGEMONIC VERSUS ICONIC MASCULINITIES

At first glance, the attempt to pinpoint a "hegemonic masculinity" seems beside the point. After all, men and masculinities have taken on a variety of simultaneously active meanings and significances across the boundaries of historical, social, and class contexts. On the basis of this volume's collective *longue durée* perspective, we acknowledge the viability of a "hegemonic masculinity" during the modern period (i.e., the twentieth century), whereas in premodern and postmodern Japan, we propose to speak of numerous microcosms of "(hegemonic) masculinities," which render invisible (or make visible the absence of) hegemonic masculinities that a majority of men adhere to or benefit from. While locality, status, and class as well as the restrictions of mobility (social and geographical) were important for the formations of valorized masculinity within the domestic and physical framework of premodern times, the effects of globalization and digitization govern such phenomena today. Indeed, contemporary modes of masculinity in Japan, perhaps more radically than elsewhere in the postindustrial world, have diversified and shifted away from the most straightforward examples of modern hegemonic masculinity, namely those associated with the top levels of business, the military, and government.[30]

At the same time, every age has had its iconic figures that are not necessarily the same as the hegemonic. In early modern Japan, for example, the samurai (or, more accurately, the *bushi*) constituted the epitome of iconic masculinity. Although townspeople's culture celebrated merchant attitudes and values, it also lauded masculine characteristics associated with the samurai as well as tales of samurai valor. Collective organizations in villages may have provided the structure for the construction of masculinity, but headman families proudly traced their lineages back to samurai ancestors. And, as Michele M. Mason points out in her analysis of *bushidō*'s iterations in the twentieth century, although *bushidō* is meant to be the way of the warrior, it inevitably evokes the soldier. In the Meiji period the soldier replaced the samurai as the iconic masculine figure, a trend that intensified with the implementation of a "farm bushidō."[31]

In this volume we attend less to iconic masculine figures than to their other. We believe that analyzing non-iconic masculine figures runs less risk of reifying stereotypes, of assuming solidity where none in fact exists, and of repeating theoretical models derived from other contexts. For this reason Walthall places her emphasis not on the samurai's sword, but on the gun. Algoso analyzes the physical examinations endured by men under the conscription law, but rather than discuss the imperial soldiers who became masculine icons before the war she focuses on hermaphrodites, who troubled the smooth functioning of Japan's military conscription system. Instead of examining the salaryman phenomenon, Tom Gill studies how homeless men enact masculinity. Ever since First Higher School students defeated American teams in Yokohama at the end of the nineteenth century, the iconic masculine model for modern sports has been the baseball player, whether a high school student, a college student, or a professional.[32] Rather than take yet another look at this quintessential paradigm of men in sports, Manzenreiter has chosen to examine a new sport, indoor rock climbing, which sheds light on how the rhetoric of masculine self-cultivation has managed to survive the sport's comparatively androgynous practice.

For most of the second half of the twentieth century, a white-collar married man and breadwinner, the salaryman, who ideally was employed by a large corporation for a lifetime, marked the epitome of masculine maturity. Although less than 30 percent of gainfully employed Japanese men actually embodied this icon of post–World War II masculinity, many more aspired to it, tried to look and live it, soaked up television, manga, and anime series about it, and were affected by the crumbling of its validity toward the end of the twentieth century. While Japan scholars have discerned the salaryman's beginnings before the war in the development of Japan's new middle class based on bureaucratic as much as corporate employment, his heyday from the decade of high-speed economic growth through the bubble years of the 1980s, and signs of his disintegration in the decades since, we are still somewhat at a loss when it comes to describing what happens when men fail to achieve that kind of maturity.[33] In part this conundrum arises from the misfit between salaryman as icon and salaryman as hegemon.

Although in 1989 most of us would have pointed to the salaryman as Japan's masculine hegemon of his time, in 2011 this is no longer the case—not since philosopher Azuma Hiroki announced "game-ish realism" *(gēmuteki riarizumu)* and the "animalizing postmodern" *(dōbutsuka suru posutmodan)* to be the order of our postmodern days, dispensing with any claims to hegemonic masculinity as well as to a coherent and consistent self. In a way, the "techno geeks" or "database animals" have won. Between 2001 and 2007, the *otaku* forms and markets quite rapidly won social recognition in Japan. In 2003, Miyazaki Hayao won the Academy Award for his animated film *Spirited Away;* around the same time Murakami Takashi achieved recognition for *otaku*-like designs; in 2004, the Japanese pavilion in the 2004 International Architecture Exhibition of Venice Biennale featured *otaku*. In 2005, the word *moe* was chosen as one of the top ten "buzzwords of the year," a point that Condry emphasizes in his analysis of anime production and consumption. And Akihabara, a Tokyo district in which *otaku* gather, is now one of the most attention-grabbing districts of Japan.[34]

In the eyes of many pundits today, the continuing presence of salarymen on Japan's urban streets cannot change the fact that new roles for men have yet to materialize. Former prime minister Hashimoto Ryūtarō expressed this sense of a crisis of masculinity in his critique of Japanese men as incapable of caring for their families because they did not undergo military training.[35] It is constantly reinforced by the self-doubt expressed by some of Japan's most prominent men. Popular art icon Murakami Takashi proposed that Japanese men have never overcome the childlike condition attributed to them by Allied occupation commander General MacArthur,[36] while right-wing demagogue and Tokyo mayor Ishihara Shintarō is eager to turn Japan's Self-Defense Forces into a full-blown military and thus restore a "normal state" with "real men" in charge at a time when a demographic collapse promises to produce ever fewer young men who would staff that organization in the future.

In addition, ours is a moment at which a number of analytical opposites—including sex/gender, human/cyborg, body/mind—seem to be more resistant to dichotomization than ever before in ways that challenge notions of hegemony and erode the iconic status of previously existing figures. New technologies threaten to render these categories problematic, if not obsolete. Even now slippage between them challenges the banal male/female and heterosexual/homosexual binaries in new ways and provides the potential to rethink what once appeared as firmly established categories.

While each essay in this volume speaks from its own vantage point and conveys its own insights, our multi-tier approach that mixes paradigms also allows us to intervene collectively in the ongoing debates about men, manhood, and masculinity in a number of ways. It is our hope that in doing so we will build on a point about gender that Jennifer Robertson has recently made: it is the "composite character of gender," she wrote, that makes it fundamentally ambivalent and ambiguous. "Gender is capable of fluctuating between or being assigned to more than one referent or category." Masculinity can attach to social roles as well as identity, for example, when a soldier fit for combat engages in relief work. Masculinity is thus "capable of being read or understood in more than one way," as seen in homeless men who lay claim to a defiantly individual masculinity. "Such an excessive semiosis reflects an epistemology of *both/and* rather than *either/or*."[37] The reshuffling of categories and etiologies pervades most contributions to this volume, shedding light on the various positions an individual might occupy in the course of his lifetime on the continuum of, on one end, embracing categorization as "a way of creating places for acts, identities, and modes of being which otherwise remain unnamable"[38] and, at the other end, remaining suspicious of all categories, old and new.[39]

OUTLINING THE VOLUME

When taken together, the strategies outlined above allow us to collectively reexamine some of the most eulogized and mythologized masculine figures in Japanese culture from the perspective of those who were not, even as we also illuminate some men and modes of masculinity that have remained understudied and undertheorized in Japanese studies. We explore sites where formations of masculinity are devised, contested, and renegotiated in a dialectic response to historical transformations, including the impact of institutions that exert a normative influence, the production of new knowledge, and the social impact of new technologies from guns to robots. We have organized this volume into three sections, each exploring specific formations of masculinity: legacies of the samurai, marginal men, and bodies and boundaries.

In the late nineteenth and twentieth centuries the nation-state was arguably the overpowering frame of reference for manhood in Japan. The rise and fall of the soldier as one dominant paradigm of masculinity was partly informed by repeated efforts to appropriate "the way of the warrior" *(bushidō)* of a long-gone and mythologized past.[40] A massive "nationalization of male bodies"—the self-conscious, active, and aggressive interconnecting and amalgamating of individual male bodies and minds with the national body politic—provided fertile ground for appropriations of *bushidō*. Michele M. Mason traces how the concept was instrumentalized in the writings of Nitobe Inazō around 1900, appropriated by Mishima Yukio in the 1970s, and further vulgarized by the relatively obscure Hyōdō Nisohachi today. An important current in the modernizing, imperialist and militarist, and eventually pacifist nation-state of the twentieth century was the transition from the intimate entanglement of the male body with the body politic/nation-state in the early twentieth century toward their separation in the late twentieth century.[41] By the same token, *bushidō* has moved from politics to business and beyond to arrive at the current status quo, where it is easily evoked everywhere *except* in the military.

For the last half century, soldiers have found themselves caught between a state that has constitutionally severed the ties between itself and the military and an international environment in which more nation-states and their peoples are willing to condemn conventional armed conflict. By the same token, Japanese soldiers themselves no longer subscribe to the idea that "the way of the warrior is found in death."[42] How, then, asks Sabine Frühstück, do soldiers of the Self-Defense Forces lay claim to a distinct militarized masculinity given that the once-naturalized connection between the military and manhood is no longer exclusive nor intact? Such displacements of "militarized masculinity" and its accoutrements, however, have powerful historical precedents, as Walthall and Roberts demonstrate in their essays, the one examining guns as signifiers of masculine status, the other the escapades of a young merchant who desired renown in martial prowess.

At the beginning of the twenty-first century, many of us would agree that gender (and thus masculinity) is performed and achieved through a process of maturation. In her contribution to this volume, Sakurai Yuki demonstrates that for shop clerks, the process of achieving manhood occurred within a homosocial environment in which the goal of heterosexual family life was postponed until, for many, it came too late. Christopher Gerteis shows that blue-collar workers rejected the models of masculinity proposed by union leaders in favor of the iconic salaryman. As Susan Napier points out, even the "technologized masculinity" of the *otaku* in *Train Man* is permeated by a nostalgia for the modern fantasy of marriage and happiness forever. Most radical are the homeless men studied by Tom Gill who try to claim agency as members of society while also keeping a critical distance to power, asserting their self-reliance to the point of defiant individualism. From a Foucauldian perspective, they demonstrate how "power is not just repressive, it is also constructive; it moves people to act in ways they perceive as self-motivated and self-interested, even though their actions may end up reproducing their low status in the social order."[43]

The four essays in the section on marginal men suggest that they stand in a conflicted relationship to hegemonic masculinity. In some cases the realization of failure has been indistinguishable from the grandeur of resisting power, be it the power of the merchant house for early nineteenth-century shop clerks, labor unions for blue-collar workers, mainstream society for the aberrant *otaku,* or more diffuse capitalist forces for homeless men. Many of the men who run away, turn their backs, refuse to engage, or live in cardboard boxes self-consciously refuse to budge. The masculinities they live might be marginal when viewed from the vantage point of mainstream society, but they also remind us that the maturity (and masculinity) of one individual has always been the result of collective collusion.

While numerous observers have claimed a postmodern fragmentation of competing or coexisting masculinities, the five essays in this third section of our volume collectively work to complicate such global proclamations. By highlighting the various political dimensions to such "boundary work," they illuminate how the boundaries and demarcations of masculinity and gender more generally have been created, advocated, attacked, or reinforced. They show that such delineations often have had high stakes involved for the participants and carried with them the implication that such boundaries are flexible and socially constructed. Nagano Hiroko demonstrates how the hierarchical structure of rural social organizations privileged older men over younger ones, excluded women, and controlled women's sexuality. According to Teresa Algoso's analysis, anxieties about the infirmity of the nation and empire were mirrored in the socio-medical debate on hermaphrodites at the beginning of the twentieth century. Wolfram Manzenreiter focuses on the technologies of masculinity in sports to explore the shifting gender boundaries in the comparatively androgynous practice of indoor rock climbing.

We also have been witnessing a major transformation in the relationship between humankind and technology. Social modernity of the nineteenth century, noted historian Anson Rabinbach, was the "project of superseding class conflict and social disorganization through the rationalization of the body." The metaphor of the human motor proposed that the working body is a productive force capable of transforming universal natural energy into mechanical work and integrating the human organism into highly specialized and technical work processes.[44] But why not, when even robots (and robotics), believed to constitute the next technological revolution with the potential for enormous social impact, behave traditionally when it comes to (the transgression of) gender norms? Roboticists today, as Jennifer Robertson explains, make every attempt to create machines that resemble (conventionally gendered) human beings. Departing from earlier studies of representation, Ian Condry critically engages both creative production and creative adaptation of new modes of manhood in the realm of anime production and consumption.[45] On his walk on the wild side of where the actual and the virtual meet, he suspects that a "love revolution" lies at the heart of this project.

We hope that our readers will be inspired and seduced both to follow the frameworks and paths carved out by the individual essays as well as the structure of this book, *and* to read against the narrative grain, thus creating new insights on their own about the malleability of men, manhood, and masculinity, in Japan and elsewhere.

NOTES

1. Connell 1995, pp. 76–81.
2. Connell 1995, p. 77.
3. Ortner 1997, pp. 1–2.
4. Wacquant 1995, p. 65.
5. Ortner 1997, p. 19.
6. For an extensive international bibliography of manhood and masculinity studies, see Flood et al. 2007. Franz X. Eder has put together a bibliography of historiographies of German men and masculinity at http://wirtges.univie.ac.at/Sexbibl/. For a discussion of the state of the field of studies in the historiography of men and masculinity in the anglophone world, see Nye 2000. For an international compilation of the literature, see Janssen 2008 and Flood 2008 at http://mensbiblio.xyonline.net/.
7. For a broader overview of that field of scholarship, see Frühstück 2005.
8. See, for example, Robertson 2001 [1998]; Walthall 1998; and Kano 2001
9. Allen 2002, p. 192.
10. See the interview of Judith Halberstam at www.genders.org/g29/g29_halberstam.html.
11. The eight-volume series *Jendā shi sōsho,* published by Meiseki Shoten in 2009–10, has essays analyzing masculinity in each volume.
12. See Nishikawa and Ogino 1999; Asai, Itō, and Murase 2001; Roberson and Suzuki 2002; Janssen 2008; Sreetharan 2004; Schad-Seifert 2001 and 2007; and Cook 2005. The journal *Modern Masculinities (Modan Masukyurinitīzu)* is edited by Hosoda Makoto with the assistance of the Kindai Nihon Danseishi Kenkyūkai.
13. Cross 2008, p. 5; for Japan, see Miller 2003 and 2006.
14. McNicol 2003.
15. Cross 2008, p. 5.
16. Allen 2002, p. 204.
17. Itō 1993.
18. Ikegami 1995.
19. Roden 2005.

20. Roden 1980b, pp. 100, 115.
21. Smith 1972, pp. xi, 56.
22. Roden 1990.
23. Bourdieu 2001 [1998].
24. Yamaguchi 2006.
25. See http://justwoman.asiaone.com/Just+Woman/News/Women+In+The+News/Story/ A1Story20071107–34962.html.
26. Brownell and Wasserstrom 2002, p. 10.
27. Abe 2006; Chapman 2004; Light 1999a, 1999b, 2000a, 2000b, and 2003; and Manzenreiter 2006, among others. The following authors have taken this particular approach: Gill, Henwood and McLean 2005; Crossley 2005; Wacquant 1995.
28. For early analyses of the beginnings of social science in Japan, see Kawai 1994; Hein 2005; Barshay 2007.
29. Smethurst 1974, p. xvii.
30. Connell 1995, p. 77.
31. Havens 1974.
32. Roden 1980a.
33. Kinmoth 1981; Vogel 1963; LeBlanc 2009; Dasgupta 2000 and 2003.
34. Azuma 2007 and 2009 [2001].
35. Frühstück 2007, p. 89.
36. Murakami 2005, p. 152.
37. Robertson 2001 [1998], p. 40.
38. See the interview of Judith Halberstam at www.genders.org/g29/g29_halberstam.html.
39. Butler 1995, p. 172.
40. Connell 1995.
41. Frühstück 2003 and 2007; Cook 2005; Karlin 2002; Kinmoth 1981; Louie 2003; Low 2003; Mangan and Komagome 1999; Mason 2005; Roden 2005; Schad-Seifert 2001.
42. Yamamoto 1979, p. 17.
43. Brownell and Wasserstrom 2002, p. 24.
44. Rabinbach 1990, p. 289.
45. As Frühstück (2005) has noted, analyses of gender representations dominate within the larger field of gender studies of Japan. See also, for instance, Herman 1993; Itō 1994; Mackintosh 2008; Matsugu 2007; McLelland 2003; Nakamura and Matsuo 2003; Standish 2000; Yano 2002; Yoshinaga 2002.

REFERENCES

Abe Ikuo. 2006. "Muscular Christianity in Japan: The Growth of a Hybrid." *International Journal of the History of Sport* 23, no. 5: 714–38.

Allen, Judith A. 2002. "Men Interminably in Crisis? Historians on Mascu-

linity, Sexual Boundaries, and Manhood." *Radical History Review* 82: 191–207.
Aoyama Tomoko. 2003. "The Cooking Man in Modern Japanese Literature." In *Asian Masculinities.* See Louie and Low 2003.
Asai Haruo, Itō Satoru, and Murase Yukihiro. 2001. *Nihon no otoko wa doko kara kite, doko e iku no ka?* Jūgatsusha.
Azuma Hiroki. 2007. *Gēmuteki riarizumu no tanjō: Dōbutsuka suru posuto modan 2.* Kōdansha.
———. 2009 [2001]. *Otaku: Japan's Database Animals,* trans. Jonathan E. Abel and Shion Kono. Minneapolis: University of Minnesota Press.
Barshay, Andrew. 2007. *The Social Sciences in Modern Japan: The Marxian and Modernist Traditions.* Berkeley: University of California Press.
Bourdieu, Pierre. 2001 [1998]. *Masculine Domination.* Stanford: Stanford University Press.
Brownell, Susan, and Jeffrey N. Wasserstrom, eds. 2002. *Chinese Femininities / Chinese Masculinities: A Reader.* Berkeley: University of California Press.
Butler, Judith. 1995. "Melancholy Gender—Refused Identification." *Psychoanalytical Dialogue* 5: 165–80.
Chapman, Kris. 2004. "*Ossu!* Sporting Masculinities in a Japanese Karate *Dōjō.*" *Japan Forum* 16, no. 2: 315–35.
Connell, R. W. 1995. *Masculinities.* Berkeley: University of California Press.
Cook, Theodore F. 2005. "Making 'Soldiers': The Imperial Army and the Japanese Man in Meiji Society and State." In *Gendering Modern Japanese History.* See Molony and Uno 2005.
Cross, Gary. 2008. *Men to Boys: The Making of Modern Immaturity.* New York: Columbia University Press.
Crossley, Nick. 2005. "Mapping Reflexive Body Techniques: On Body Modification and Maintenance." *Body & Society* 11 (March): 1–35.
Darling-Wolf, F. 2004. "Women and New Men: Negotiating Masculinity in the Japanese Media." *The Communication Review* 7, no. 3: 285–303.
Dasgupta, Romit. 2000. "Performing Masculinities? The 'Salaryman' at Work and Play." *Japanese Studies* 20, no. 2: 189–200.
———. 2003. "Creating Corporate Warriors: The 'Salaryman' and Masculinity in Japan." In *Asian Masculinities.* See Louie and Low 2003.
Flood, Michael, Judith Kegan Gardiner, Bob Pease, and Keith Pringle, eds. 2007. *International Encyclopedia of Men and Masculinities.* London: Routledge.
Frühstück, Sabine. 2003. *Colonizing Sex: Sexology and Social Control in Modern Japan.* Berkeley: University of California Press.
———. 2005. "Genders and Sexualities." In *Companion to the Anthropology of Japan,* ed. Jennifer Robertson, 167–82. London: Blackwell.
———. 2007. *Uneasy Warriors: Gender, Memory, and Popular Culture in the Japanese Army.* Berkeley: University of California Press.
Gill, Rosalind, Karen Henwood, and Carl McLean. 2005. "Body Projects and

the Regulation of Normative Masculinity." *Body & Society* 11 (March): 37–62.

Havens, Thomas R. H. 1974. *Farm and Nation in Modern Japan: Agrarian Nationalism 1879–1940*. Princeton: Princeton University Press.

Hein, Laura. 2005. *Reasonable Men, Powerful Words: Political Culture and Expertise in Twentieth-Century Japan*. Berkeley: University of California Press.

Herman, Vivian. 1993. "Phallus, Image, Other: Reading Masculine Desire from Japanese Representations of Asia." In *Translations/Transformations: Gender and Culture in Film and Literature, East and West: Selected Conference Papers*, ed. V. Wayne and C. N. Moore, 82–98. Honolulu: University of Hawai'i and the East–West Center.

Ikegami, Eiko. 1995. *The Taming of the Samurai: Honorific Individualism and the Making of Modern Japan*. Cambridge, MA: Harvard University Press.

Itō Kimio. 1993. *"Otokorashisa" no yukue : Dansei bunka no bunka shakaigaku*. Shinyōsha.

———. 1994. "Images of Women in Weekly Male Comic Magazines in Japan." *Journal of Popular Culture* 27, no. 4: 81–96.

Janssen, Diederik F. 2008. *International Guide to Literature on Masculinity: A Bibliography*. Harriman: Men's Studies Press.

Kano, Ayako. 2001. *Acting Like a Woman in Modern Japan: Theater, Gender, and Nationalism*. New York: Palgrave.

Karlin, Jason G. 2002. "The Gender of Nationalism: Competing Masculinities in Meiji Japan." *Journal of Japanese Studies* 28, no. 1: 41–77.

Kawai Takao. 1994. *Kindai Nihon shakai chōsashi*. 3 vols. Keiō Tsūshin.

Kinmonth, Earl H. 1981. *The Self-Made Man in Meiji Japanese Thought: From Samurai to Salary Man*. Berkeley: University of California Press.

LeBlanc, Robin. 2009. *The Art of the Gut: Manhood, Power, and Ethics in Japanese Politics*. Berkeley: University of California Press.

Light, Richard. 1999a. "High School Rugby and the Construction of Masculinity in Japan." In *Making the Rugby World: Race, Gender, Commerce*, ed. T. J. L. Chandler and J. Nauright. London: F. Cass.

———. 1999b. "Learning to Be a Rugger Man: High School Rugby and Media Constructions of Masculinity in Japan." *Football Studies* 2, no. 1: 74–89.

———. 2000a. "Culture at Play: A Comparative Study of Masculinity and Game Style in Japanese and Australian School Rugby." *International Sports Studies* 22, no. 2: 26–41.

———. 2000b. "A Centenary of Rugby and Masculinity in Japanese Schools and Universities: Continuity and Change." *Sporting Traditions* 16, no. 2: 87–104.

———. 2003. "Sport and the Construction of Masculinity in the Japanese Education System." In *Asian Masculinities*. See Louie and Low 2003.

Louie, Kam. 2003. "Chinese, Japanese and Global Masculine Identities." In *Asian Masculinities*. See Louie and Low 2003.

Louie, Kam, and Morris Low, eds. 2003. *Asian Masculinities: The Meaning and Practice of Manhood in China and Japan.* London: Routledge.

Low, Morris. 2003. "The Emperor's Sons Go to War: Competing Masculinities in Modern Japan." In *Asian Masculinities.* See Louie and Low 2003.

Mackintosh, Jonathan D. 2008. *Homosexuality and Manliness in Postwar Japan.* London: Routledge.

Mangan, J.A. and T. Komagome. 1999. "Militarism, Sacrifice and Emperor Worship: The Expendable Male Body in Fascist Japanese Martial Culture." *International Journal of the History of Sport* 16, no. 4: 181–204.

Manzenreiter, Wolfram. 2006. "Fussball und die Krise der Männlichkeit in Japan." In *Arena der Männlichkeit: Über das Verhältnis von Fußball und Geschlecht,* ed. Eva Kreisky and Georg Spitaler, 296–313. Frankfurt: Campus.

Mason, Michele M. 2005. "Manly Narratives: Writing Hokkaido into the Political and Cultural Landscape of Imperial Japan." Ph.D. diss., East Asian Languages and Literatures, University of California, Irvine.

Matsugu, Y. 2007. "Cosmo Girls and Playboys: Japanese Femininity and Masculinity in Gendered Magazines." Ph.D. diss., University of Arizona, Tucson.

McLelland, Mark. 2003. "Gay Men, Masculinity and the Media in Japan." In *Asian Masculinities.* See Louie and Low 2003.

McNicol, Tony. 2003. "'Shut-ins' Turn Backs on Japan: 'Hikikomori' Make a Fresh Start in Foreign Climes." *Japan Times,* December 16.

Miller, Laura. 2003. "Male Beauty Work in Japan." In *Men and Masculinities in Contemporary Japan.* See Roberson and Suzuki 2002.

———. 2006. *Beauty Up: Exploring Contemporary Body Aesthetics.* Berkeley: University of California Press.

Molony, Barbara, and Kathleen Uno, eds. 2005. *Gendering Modern Japanese History.* Cambridge, MA: Harvard University Press.

Murakami Takashi. 2005. "Superflat Trilogy: Greetings, You Are Alive." In *Little Boy: The Arts of Japan's Exploding Subculture,* ed. Murakami Takashi, 150–63. New York: Japan Society.

Nakamura, Karen, and Hisako Matsuo. 2003. "Female Masculinity and Fantasy Spaces: Transcending Genders in the Takarazuka Theatre and Japanese Popular Culture." In *Men and Masculinities in Contemporary Japan.* See Roberson and Suzuki 2002.

Nishikawa Yūko and Ogino Miho. 1999. *Kyōdō kenkyū: Danseiron.* Kyōto: Jimbun Shoin.

Ortner, Sherry. 1997. *Making Gender: The Politics and Erotics of Culture.* Boston: Beacon Press.

Rabinbach, Anson. 1990. *The Human Motor: Energy, Fatigue, and the Origins of Modernity:* Berkeley: University of California Press.

Roberson, James E., and Suzuki Nobue, eds. 2002. *Men and Masculinities in Contemporary Japan: Dislocating the Salaryman Doxa.* London: Routledge.

Robertson, Jennifer. 2001 [1998]. *Takarazuka: Sexual Politics and Popular Culture in Modern Japan.* Berkeley: University of California Press.

Roden, Donald. 1980a. "Baseball and the Quest for National Identity in Meiji Japan." *American Historical Review* 85, no. 3: 511–34.

———. 1980b. *Schooldays in Imperial Japan: A Study in the Culture of a Student Elite.* Berkeley: University of California Press.

———. 1990. "Taishō Culture and the Problem of Gender Ambivalence." In *Culture and Identity: Japanese Intellectuals During the Interwar Years,* ed. J. Thomas Rimer, 37–55. Princeton: Princeton University Press.

———. 2005. "Thoughts on the Early Meiji Gentleman." In *Gendering Modern Japanese History.* See Molony and Uno 2005.

Schad–Seifert, Annette. 2001. "Samurai and Sarariiman: The Discourse on Masculinity in Modern Japan." In *Can Japan Globalize? Studies on Japan's Changing Political Economy and the Process of Globalization,* ed. Sung–Jo Park and Arne Holzhausen, 119–212. Heidelberg: Physica Verlag.

———. 2007. "Dynamics of Masculinities in Japan—Comparative Perspectives on Men's Studies." *Gender Dynamics and Globalisation: Perspectives from Japan within Asia,* ed. Claudia Derichs and Susanne Kreitz-Sandberg, 33–44. Münster: LIT.

Smethurst, Richard J. 1974. *A Social Basis for Prewar Japanese Militarism: The Army and the Rural Community.* Berkeley: University of California Press.

Smith, Henry Dewitt II. 1972. *Japan's First Student Radicals.* Cambridge, MA: Harvard University Press.

Sreetharan, C. S. 2004. "Students, Sarariiman (pl.), and Seniors: Japanese Men's Use of 'Manly' Speech Register." *Language in Society* 33, no. 1: 81–107.

Standish, Isolde. 2000. *Myth and Masculinity in the Japanese Cinema: Towards a Political Reading of the "Tragic Hero."* Richmond: Curzon.

Vogel, Ezra. 1963. *Japan's New Middle Class: The Salary Man and His Family in a Tokyo Suburb.* Berkeley: University of California Press.

Wacquant, Loïc J. D. 1995. "Review Article: Why Men Desire Muscles." *Body & Society* 1: 163–79.

Walthall, Anne. 1998. *The Weak Body of a Useless Woman: Matsuo Taseko and the Meiji Restoration.* Chicago: University of Chicago Press.

Yamaguchi Tomomi. 2006. "Jendaa furii ronsō to feminizumu undo no ushinarawareta jūnen." In *Bakkurashu! Naze jendaa furii wa tatakareta no ka,* ed. Ueno Chizuko et al., 244–82. Sofusha.

Yamamoto Tsunetomo. 1979. *Hagakure: The Book of the Samurai,* trans. William Scott Wilson. Kodansha International.

Yano, Christine R. 2002. "The Burning of Men: Masculinities and the Nation in Japanese Popular Song." In *Men and Masculinities in Contemporary Japan.* See Roberson and Suzuki 2002.

Yoshinaga, S. 2002. "Masculinist Identifications with 'Woman': Gender Politics in Postwar Japanese Literary Debates." *US-Japan Women's Journal* 22: 32–63.

PART I

Legacies of the Samurai

1 Do Guns Have Gender?

Technology and Status in Early Modern Japan

Anne Walthall

In the fall of 2006 I happened to be a visiting researcher at the National History Museum in Sakura when it held an exhibition on the sixteenth-century introduction and diffusion of guns in Japan. While planning a conference on gender and museums, my sponsor teased me by saying that the gun exhibition had nothing to do with gender. Like many people, he identifies the term *gender* with women, and since women did not participate in Japan's early modern gun culture, he considered gender irrelevant to the topic as well. More significantly, he saw the gun as an example of technology. Disengaged from their social context, guns indeed have no gender. But by asking which men used guns, under what circumstances, and how guns functioned in relation to other weapons, it is possible to analyze the history of guns for multiple factors that conditioned what it meant to be a man in early modern Japan.

Among the items at the exhibition were guns owned by the first Tokugawa shogun, Ieyasu, and his heir, Hidetada. Manufactured at Sunpu (present-day Shizuoka) in 1607, Ieyasu's favorite gun is an exquisite 1.4 meters long. According to the catalog, he was a proficient marksman, and Hidetada was not his inferior.[1] Given that in the Tokugawa period guns were usually associated with lowly foot soldiers and hunters, I was surprised to see them in the hands of shoguns. Both Ieyasu and Hidetada were seasoned warriors, yet they fired guns not in battle but against game. Throughout the seventeenth century and sporadically in the eighteenth, their descendants, who never fought a war, continued to demonstrate their mastery of firearms in the hunt. To understand Japan's gun culture, it is thus necessary to compare what it meant for men at the apex and at the bottom of the social hierarchy to use guns.

How is it possible to argue that the gun can be identified with masculinity? Female palace guards in Southeast Asia impressed eighteenth-century Europeans with their skill at musketry.[2] In India, the emperor's wives and concubines shot deer with guns, as did Elizabeth I of England.[3] In the United States, Molly Pitcher, Annie Oakley, and images of the Prairie Madonna challenged the American ideal that guns were for men.[4] Japanese women were no strangers to weapons, either; in the late twelfth century, Tomoe Gozen rode and fought with Kiso Yoshinaka. To the end of the Edo period samurai women famously carried daggers and practiced fighting with halberds *(naginata)*. So far as I have been able to ascertain, however, women in early modern Japan did not fire guns. It would be easy to assume that this was because guns quickly became identified with the masculine pursuit of war, and, unlike in the small mounted forces of the 1100s, women had no place in sixteenth-century infantry troops numbering in the scores of thousands. This assumption overlooks both the roles found for guns in arenas other than war (ceremony, the hunt) and the way that notions regarding the use of guns entered Japanese culture; it is because these spaces and ideas associated with them came to be constructed as masculine that guns became so identified with men as to appear unremarkable. Judith Allen has noted that because men are the dominant group, their attributes remain "unmarked, transparent, unscrutinized," and that is certainly true in Japan's history of guns.[5] In their use of these and other weapons, men of different statuses measured their masculinity against each other in ways that have nothing to do with women as the Other.

To analyze the connection between guns and masculinity in Japan it is important to situate the desire for guns in historical, social, and cultural contexts. Unlike in Europe or the Americas, in Japan guns supplemented rather than replaced the hawk and bow. In teaching the appropriate attributes of manly behavior, manuals on gunmanship advocated mental preparation similar to that for other martial arts. Despite documents that identify projectiles as the cause of most battlefield deaths and wounds, hand-to-hand combat represented the epitome of male-inflected bravery.[6] The sword, not the gun, symbolized the soul of the samurai. Nonetheless, guns became more than a technical expedient. Whether in gift exchanges, hunts, or parades, warlords and shoguns incorporated guns into their panoply of self-representations. Guns figured in the skills through which they proved their manhood and in the practices they used to construct their masculinity for public consumption ("public" here means other male members of the military). Not all shoguns mastered this weapon, proof that their gender identities had to be constructed and remained unstable.

I plan to use guns as a lens on the cultural elaboration of the masculinity dominant in sixteenth-century Japan—that of the warlord—and analyze how it is affirmed, rejected, and reconstituted in the seventeenth and eighteenth centuries. I begin with the politically charged history of the matchlock's introduction in 1543, the prestige it acquired as a gift item, the part played by male religious practitioners who dramatized their control over fire by mastering the gun, and its ubiquitous role in militarized ceremony. I then examine manuals that defined the physical and moral attributes necessary to master the art of gunmanship. Rather than join the debate on whether guns transformed warfare in sixteenth-century Japan, I will concentrate on the complicated connection between guns and status in the seventeenth and eighteenth centuries. In particular, by examining how and by whom guns were used for hunting and what the hunt meant for rulers, I demonstrate how the early Tokugawa shoguns both modeled and exceeded definitions of warrior masculinity through their prowess at arms and uncover the different ways their successors contested and celebrated that legacy.

THE INTRODUCTION OF GUNS

The earliest document on the introduction of guns to Japan is "Record of the Musket" ("Teppōki"), written in 1606 for Lord Tanegashima Hisatoki, ruler of a small island by the same name.[7] According to it, on the twenty-fifth day of the eighth lunar month of 1543, a storm-damaged ship arrived in a bay on the other side of Tanegashima from the castle town. Among its crew were Portuguese who carried unusual weapons. As soon as Hisatoki's ancestor Tokitaka saw these weapons in action, he realized their promise for hunting and warfare. He learned to shoot, he bought the guns, and he set a retainer to learn the secrets of making gunpowder. In addition to sending one of his guns to a priest at Negoro temple in Kii (present-day Wakayama), he had blacksmiths make copies. These Tokitaka distributed to warlords to curry favor. Other guns from Tanegashima reached eastern Japan when the ship in which they were transported was blown off course. To sum up, the first guns arrived in Tanegashima carried by exotic foreigners, they were first manufactured on that island, and they spread across Japan from that location.

Historians in Japan have recently revisited the question of how guns entered Japan and how they were diffused thereafter. Based on an examination of the earliest guns still extant and manuals describing their use, they have both complicated and clarified the process by which guns came to be employed and even prized. But in discounting "Record of the Musket," they have not asked what purpose it served beyond the immediate political interests of the Tanegashima family. In order to assess why this account gained such general acceptance, let us examine what scholars now think regarding the gun's arrival.

Scholars have produced two types of evidence for challenging the Tanegashima account. Suzuki Masaya points to other documents and archaeological evidence that place guns in Japan before 1543.[8] Udagawa Takehisa has analyzed guns produced around the same time. In particular he notes that Satsuma guns had a cover over the spring for the firing mechanism, in contrast to Tanegashima-derived guns. If Japanese gunsmiths based their products on foreign guns, the only way to explain this difference is to assume that they used different models. The shortness of the butts of the earliest muskets to reach Japan suggests to Udagawa that they were not made in faraway Portugal but in Southeast Asia. The men who first brought them to Japan were less likely to be Portuguese than the ethnically mixed crews of traders, smugglers, and pirates known as *wakō*.[9] Kenneth Chase and Carlo Cipolla point out that Chinese were manufacturing matchlocks in Siam (Thailand) before the arrival of the Portuguese in 1511. In a seventeenth-century letter to the king of Siam, Tokugawa Ieyasu wrote, "Guns and gunpowder are what I desire more than gold brocade."[10]

Before we dismiss the "Record," let us ask why it matters. How did it gain such widespread currency that the eighteenth-century historian of Japanese weapons, Arai Hakuseki, incorporates it practically verbatim?[11] As Japanese historians have pointed out, reading the document in the context of sixteenth-century maritime trade between Japan and Southeast Asia suggests that although the "Record" calls the two Portuguese gunmen "leaders among the traders," they were probably merely members of the crew, or at most adventurers on a vessel captained by Gohō (Ch. Wu-feng), a famous merchant/smuggler. Given his dubious occupation, once Gohō was blown off course between Siam and China, he might have preferred to land far from a center of authority such as a castle town. By adding respectability to the exotic (turning Portuguese into leaders), the "Record" puts guns not in the hands of pirates but describes them as wonders of foreign manufacture suitable for rulers. In short, it not only served the interests of the Tanegashima lords in their quest for recognition out of proportion to the size of their domain, but it also helped to legitimize guns as prestige items to be exchanged among warlords.

Although the part played by traders and gunsmiths in the diffusion of guns beyond southern Kyushu should not be ignored, it is important to mention the enabling roles played by religious practitioners and warlords because of the way they connected guns to military men. The "Record" emphasizes that the first purchaser of a gun outside Tanegashima was from the esoteric Shingon temple Negoro, attesting to the contribution made by religious establishments to sixteenth-century warfare. Other religious figures, *yamabushi* (mountain shamans) in particular, contributed to the spread of guns to eastern Japan. One was the younger brother to Hōjō Ujitsuna of Odawara, Muneaki (d. 1582), who found his calling in the Shingon school and served as temple administrator *(bettō)* as well as a gunnery expert. The Tanegashima lord's status as quasi-subordinate to Ōtomo Sōrin of Bungo in Kyushu makes it unsurprising that Sōrin not only acquired guns early but also disseminated them to other lords. Guns probably spread to Tosa on Shikoku through a marital connection between the Ōtomo and the Ichijō; the Kano in Iyo were Ōtomo friends. Historians have noted how, when guns were rare, they functioned as exchange items between warlords anxious to prove their goodwill to potential allies or to reassure a suspicious overlord of a subordinate's support.[12]

Made valuable by their rarity, guns, especially those manufactured abroad, readily circulated as gifts calculated to bestow benefit on the giver. Cipolla has noted that Europeans habitually presented guns to local rulers in exchange for special permissions or privileges,[13] a practice followed by Catholic missionaries in Japan as well. In 1552 shogun Ashikaga Yoshiteru wrote a letter to Yokose Narushige, a minor warlord in Kanto, offering him a gun in hopes of winning Yokose's ally, the powerful Uesugi Kenshin, to his side. From the time he exiled his father and became the Ōtomo chieftain, Sōrin sent swords, money, and horses to Kyoto in his quest to be made military governor in Kyushu. He brought Yoshiteru's patronage with the gift of a foreign gun in 1554; later, when his governorship was expanded to two more provinces, he sent Yoshiteru a gun made in Tanegashima and a bronze breach loader from Southeast Asia. Yoshiteru later gave one of the guns he had received from Sōrin to Uesugi upon the latter's promise of help.[14]

In Japan gifts assumed a gender depending on the gender of their recipient, and guns were no exception. In the Tokugawa period the shogun's wife received manuscript copies of classical literature in famous calligraphy; Ieyasu, too, collected such texts, but for the most part shoguns accepted tea utensils, horses, and swords, whose value depended upon who had made the objects and who had owned them. Shoguns delighted in receiving guns from the Dutch and other foreigners,[15] and they accepted guns from important daimyo as well.[16] Guns that had been owned by Ieyasu were distributed to his sons and to favored daimyo with the understanding that they would be treasured by the family for generations.[17] To this day the Tokugawa Art Museum in Nagoya displays guns bestowed by Ieyasu on his son Yoshinao, who founded the Owari Tokugawa house; and a huge exhibition at the Tokyo National Museum in fall 2007 on the Tokugawa legacy included swords, armor, and guns distributed to Ieyasu's heirs.[18]

Individual guns figured as gifts; guns manufactured in quantity became part of the paraphernalia displayed in parades. When Ieyasu sent his seven-year-old granddaughter Senhime to marry Toyotomi Hideyori in 1603, he had the daimyo line the banks of rivers between Fushimi and Osaka with bowmen and gunmen. They did the same in 1611 when Hideyori and his mother reluctantly went to Kyoto to pay their respects to the emperor and Ieyasu. Held in silence at night, Ieyasu's funeral procession in 1616 was led by standard-bearers followed by five men carrying bows and then five men carrying guns. More weapons, including guns, brought up the rear.[19] Their presence on such a solemn occasion suggests that they had become naturalized and, like bows, their efficacy against evil extended to the invisible realm of spirits.

For the duration of the Tokugawa period, shoguns and daimyo placed guns in processions. Parades for weddings, funerals, and memorial services coursed through Edo streets, the chief participants hidden in palanquins while their majesty was displayed through the accompanying weapons. Status and sex mattered: the memorial service in 1658 for the fourth shogun Ietsuna's birth mother, a mere concubine, featured neither mounted guards nor bows nor guns, whereas the memorial services for Hidetada's official wife (and Ietsuna's grandmother) earlier that same year and at the fiftieth anniversary of her death in 1675 went on for days, with retainers summoned to position guards at the castle gates armed with bows, guns, and spears.[20] When daimyo performed their duty of going from their castle town to Edo where they waited upon the shogun, their processions mimicked military campaigns. The vanguard carried guns on their shoulders wrapped in special cases, followed by spears and bows.[21] The most magnificent displays of weaponry were reserved for the shoguns' pilgrimages to Nikkō to worship Ieyasu's incarnation as the great shining eastern avatar of the Buddha. On these occasions daimyo as well as housemen accompanied the shogun's palanquin in processions that stretched for miles.[22]

It is not surprising that the Tokugawa shoguns, chieftains of a military regime founded on conquest, recalled their heritage in parades of weapons. These performances both neutralized the potential for violence that weapons represented for the military and reminded spectators that they had no legitimate claim on either weapons or violence.[23] Yet it is important to maintain a distinction between the guns exchanged among warlords as gifts and those carried by foot soldiers in processions. Treated as rarities of great value, guns enhanced their owners' prestige and contributed to a cultural symbol of masculinity for the elite; distributed in quantity to foot soldiers, guns marked their bearers' low status. In order to uncover another dimension of the gun's multiplicity of meanings, let us turn to the secret transmission of gunmanship.

THE CONSTRUCTION OF MASCULINITY IN SECRET TEXTS

It would be easy to attribute the connection between esoteric Buddhism and instruction in gunmanship to the well-attested tendency in the history of Japanese culture for experts to keep their knowledge secret. Especially during sixteenth-century warfare, when aristocrats survived by claiming mastery over arcane bodies of information, the only knowledge worth possessing was that unattainable on the open market. This factor alone, however, does not explain why early specialists might be *yamabushi*. For this we need to remember the *yamabushi*'s long-standing mastery of fire. Given the fuse cord used in the firing mechanism for muskets and the notorious tendency for gunpowder to explode when handled incautiously, their ability to control fire could have functioned as a prerequisite for earning the trust of potential pupils. As *yamabushi* proclaimed, the gun was dangerous if one did not respect its connection to powerful unseen forces.

The mystification of gunmanship reflected elite sensibilities regarding the valuation of knowledge. Oda Nobunaga, for example, learned to shoot from a marksman named Hashimoto Ippa. This does not mean that he submitted to the discipline imposed by specialists who founded schools. Instead, he, like other warlords, had trustworthy attendants master occult teachings in order to prove that their skill in handling this rare and precious commodity surpassed that of ordinary warriors denied the opportunity to reach the deepest possible understanding of gun lore. Even after the mass manufacture of guns and their usefulness in warfare put them into the hands of foot soldiers, men at the apex of the military hierarchy continued to hone their skill with guns, and instructors continued to sell secrets.

One school imbued with esoteric Buddhism was called Kishinowada. It originated with a merchant who learned gunmanship from a hunter in Kyushu and codified his teaching in a secret text. A 1594 copy provides instructions for how to aim, breathe, pull the trigger, and hit a target at a distance as well as rules for gun etiquette. It describes six shooting positions, each illustrated, and included illustrations of gun sights and targets. At the same time, it puts technique in the service of religion: "When you hit a living being with a gun, you should recite this sutra. No matter what you hit, the efficacy of this sutra means that it will become a Buddha." Furthermore, "When appearing on the target range, you should have your gun in your right hand, the fuse cord in your left. The gun is the weapon that displays Fudōmyōō's wisdom, and the fuse cord has the virtue of frightening away demons and evil spirits. Guns originated in the age of Sakyamuni [the original Buddha] to pacify evil for the sake of Buddhist teachings."[24] The enraged, red-faced Fudōmyōō, a frequent presence in Shingon temples, was known for dispelling disasters and transforming enemy curses into good fortune. He thus made a fitting metaphor for the argument that it was precisely because guns inflicted harm by belching smoke and projectiles that they had the potential to bring peace to war-stricken Japan.

By the last decade of the sixteenth century and the beginning of the seventeenth century, secret texts handed down in various schools competed for clients by teaching not only the physical movements required to shoot a gun but the mental attitude as well. The texts also contained vast amounts of experimental data on gunpowder recipes appropriate for various kinds of weather and different types of bullets and their uses. By providing information on everything imaginable related to guns, they can be seen to have functioned as encyclopedias. In that guise they paralleled the proliferation of schools based on secret transmissions related to the practice of swordsmanship and archery, and they also contributed to what Mary Elizabeth Berry has called a seventeenth-century information revolution. She argues that maps, novels, and compendia of all sorts organized the information needed to become a civilized and conversant member of urban society, though the continuing emphasis on secret traditions in the martial arts reminds us that this information was not uniformly available to everyone.[25] Only by being accepted as a disciple or, in the case of warlords, hiring an instructor could the pupil learn the secrets of how to fire a gun, and only high-ranking members of this military society could expect to receive gold-embossed, hand-illustrated copies of the secret texts.

Illustrations in the secret texts embody the connection between guns and masculinity. The 1618 copy of the Nanban school secret text shows a man with his legs spread wide, squatting on tall wooden sandals as if he had waded into a rice paddy to shoot birds. In another image a grace-

Figure 1.1. Young boatman; his patron (not shown) is shooting at a duck. From the *Inatomi ryū hidensho,* 1612, held at the New York Public Library.

ful youth prepares to raise his gun to his cheek. An illustration from the Tabuse scroll of 1636 shows a youth sighting a gun. He wears formal attire, with his pants draped over his feet. The attention given to the clothing and the model's youthful appearance suggest that the drawings conveyed an erotic charge.[26]

The connection between clothing and sexuality is even more apparent in the Inatomi school secret texts. A 1612 copy in the New York Public Library contains thirty-two lavishly colored illustrations of the various stances for shooting a gun, from crouching on the ground with the gun placed across a gun rest, to firing from horseback, to shooting a duck from a boat.[27] What is particularly notable about the Inatomi illustrations is that the models are shown practically naked, wearing only a colorful loincloth, in order to show the proper alignment of torso, hands, and feet, yet the bodies are outlined simply, with no more attention given to the musculature than in erotic prints *(shunga)* of the same period. Whereas *shunga* lavished detail on the genitals, in the Inatomi scrolls the exquisite draftsmanship focuses attention on the gun. The only fully clothed individual is a plump young boatman (figure 1.1). Meant for a male audience, these texts depict the male body, sexier clothed than unclothed, engaged in the manly art of shooting.

Founded by Inatomi Ichimu (1552–1611), a gunnery expert employed by

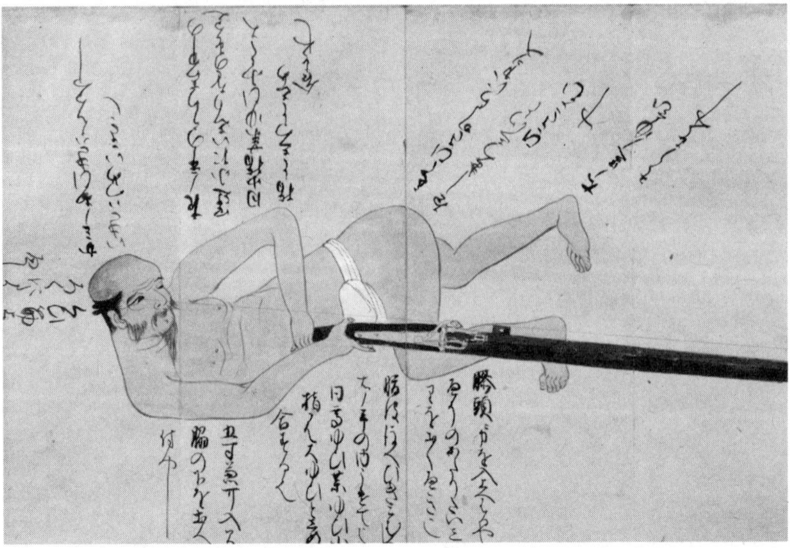

Figure 1.2. Man flinging himself to the ground while shooting a gun. From the *Inatomi ryū hidensho,* 1612, held at the New York Public Library

Ieyasu, the Inatomi school drew on traditions associated with the martial arts. Warriors were expected not only to attain competence in everything from archery to swordsmanship, but also to recognize nonfunctional flourishes that differentiated one school from another and transformed drill into art *(gei),* to learn not mere gunnery, but the discipline of gunmanship more suited to the target range than the battlefield.[28] John Michael Rogers lambastes the Inatomi for forcing students to "master strained acrobatic postures," and the 1612 text indeed shows a man shooting while flinging himself to the ground (figure 1.2).[29] More ubiquitous and, I argue, more typical of symbolic distinctions is the way the left hand typically holds the barrel, leaving the ring and little fingers free. Given that guns weighed around eight pounds, this posture would have required considerable strength, even when the gun was held straight. When, as depicted in one image, the gun was pointed at the ground (figure 1.3), the pose becomes impossible. This suggests that this secret text did not provide a transparent representation of how adherents of the Inatomi school fired guns. Unlike outsiders, initiates knew how to read it, not how to imitate it. In contrast to modern military manuals, the Inatomi text constituted a highly stylized memento that marked its owners as masters of masculine military arts.

In secret texts, the embodiment of masculinity extended to mind as well as body. In addition to esoteric Buddhism, the texts drew on Confucianism,

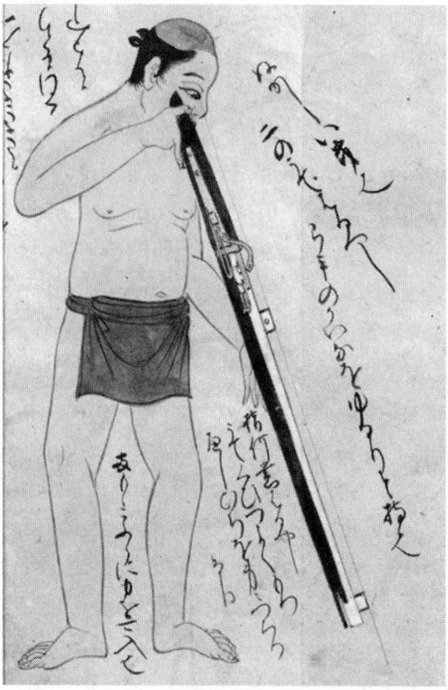

Figure 1.3. Man shooting at the ground. From the *Inatomi ryū hidensho,* 1612, held at the New York Public Library.

Zen, Daoism, the balance of the opposing and complementary forces of yin and yang, pressure points and the circulation of humors in Chinese medicine, and belief in the potency of native deities. A pledge to Inatomi Ichimu signed in 1606 by a retainer assigned to Tokugawa Yoshinao promises that if he betrays the school's teachings he will accept punishment by all the myriad deities.[30] A 1608 text from the Uta school describes how a prince in China had prayed to the merciful Kannon for a means to drive away a demon plaguing his land. That night he dreamed that an old man instructed him in mixing gunpowder, loading a gun, and pulling the trigger. Upon awakening, the prince did as he was told and drove the demon away. The Yasumi school secret tradition dated 1599 states, "Guns have spread widely throughout the world. Many enjoy them regardless of their ability, although none can be called exceptionally skilled. This is because they do not practice the appropriate techniques until embedded in their hearts and bodies. . . . When your heart is disordered, you will forget to aim when you shoot. . . . [I]n order to reach a higher level, you must not let anything bother you, and if you let your heart be itself, you will lack for nothing." This last is an allusion to the Broom Tree chapter of *The Tale of Genji.*[31] The famous classic is cited not because it opened a window on the tenth-century courtly world of women but because it provides a lesson for regulating masculine behavior.

Secret traditions were not for the dilettante. The first volume of the Isenokami school's teachings on measurement insists that "you should sincerely receive your teacher's tradition, devote yourself to it as though to a parent, and practice making every moment count. . . . If you focus your undivided attention on the way, you will as a matter of course achieve discernment based on natural morality. To first set your heart on the correct path, I herein discuss the measurement of distance and gunpowder."[32] The idea behind the transmission of secret traditions is that they went only to men who had demonstrated an earnest seriousness of purpose and dedication to physical and mental improvement. In other words, one purpose of pursuing gunmanship was to build character. Amy Ann Cox argues that guns in America were associated with "a range of often masculine values, especially liberty, freedom, and independence."[33] Insofar as gunmanship schools in Japan contributed to ridding the samurai of the honor violence that distinguished masculine behavior in the sixteenth and (as Roberts shows elsewhere in this volume) the early seventeenth centuries, they promoted the values of bravery, perseverance, equanimity, and discipline.

Most secret texts have colophons that trace their transmission by naming teacher and pupil, neither of whom were warlords. Pupils received such documents only at the end of arduous training and a commitment to the master's discipline that no commander of armies was likely to make. Warlords could not afford to specialize; instead they needed knowledge of all the martial traditions, from horseback archery to sword fighting to gunnery. Nonetheless, documents prove that warlords received instruction in guns from the same experts who crafted the secret traditions, and, like the experts, they too believed in the importance of training body and mind to build a moral military character gendered male.

GUNS AND STATUS

By focusing on the implications of guns for sixteenth-century warfare, historians have overlooked their more ubiquitous role in hunting and their complicated imbrication with the early modern status system. Because guns were associated with low status hunters and foot soldiers in the Tokugawa period, it is often assumed that they started out as low status items in the arsenals of war. Udagawa believes that the first guns to arrive in Japan were hunting guns, and secret texts deal with how to kill game, not wage war.[34] As we have seen, guns first circulated among warlords before being modified and manufactured in sufficient quantity to equip soldiers.[35] Ascertaining who used guns and under what circumstances shows that they continued to appeal to military men after the end to warfare in 1615, albeit under carefully circumscribed conditions.

To explore the connection between guns, masculinity, and status during the Tokugawa period, let us examine the various meanings of the hunt. Thomas Allsen argues that across Eurasia the royal hunt ennobled the hunter because it enabled him to demonstrate his command over hundreds or even tens of thousands of participants and to kill vast quantities of game for pleasure, for recreation, for sport.[36] As Emma Griffin has said, "the less any given society depended upon hunting for subsistence, the more potent a symbol of wealth and leisure it seemed to become."[37] In contrast, men who hunted out of necessity, usually alone, either to keep vermin away from their fields or to supplement a meager diet, were scorned as primitive. In Japan, as well, hunters, hunting, and the hunting gun occupied a social margin, with the same significant exception. Tools of daimyo and shoguns with entourages that sometimes numbered in the thousands, the hawk and the hunting gun displayed the ruler's ability to rule, his authority, and his majesty. The contrast with hunters who occupied the opposite end of the social compass suggests that guns had not only a gendered component but also reflected the hierarchy of values associated with the status system.

Guns troubled the Tokugawa shogunate more than other weapons. In 1645 it banned personal ownership in urban areas, instead urging samurai to become proficient in archery, horsemanship, and swordsmanship.[38] Guns circulated more widely in the countryside, although rulers tried to restrict their use to hunters. Only hunters had rights to the meat and skin of animals they killed; nonhunters had to bury the corpse intact. Even during the infamous wild boar famine of 1749 in Hachinohe, the daimyo posted guards over boars' graves lest the starving poach the meat.[39] Tsukamoto Manabu has argued that so far as peasants were concerned, guns were simply tools for expelling vermin from their fields. The status of guns sank along with that of hunters, who were seen as polluted because they handled dead animals. In the late seventeenth century, Tsunayoshi's efforts to verify the number of guns in the countryside as part of his laws of compassion had the further effect of degrading the status of hunters.[40]

No one better captures the debasement of hunters in the Tokugawa status system than Kanpei, one of the ill-fated warriors featured in the *Kanadehon Chūshingura*, a tale of forty-seven loyal retainers. Having neglected his duty to his lord by dallying with his wife and thus bearing the blame for En'ya Hangan having been forced to commit suicide, Kanpei takes refuge with his wife's peasant parents. Unsuited to tilling the soil, he becomes a hunter. One night he shoots at what he thinks is a boar, only to discover that he has killed a man carrying fifty *ryō*. (Unbeknownst to him, his victim, Sadakurō, had earlier killed Kanpei's father-in-law, who had gotten the fifty *ryō* by selling Kanpei's wife into prostitution.) Kanpei had hoped to use the money to pay for his lord's memorial service and thereby gain reinstatement in the retainer band. Instead, mistakenly believing that he had killed his father-in-law and rejected by other members of the warrior band for offering tainted money, he commits suicide.

Kanpei's story highlights the difference between sword and gun in the popular imagination of the time. So long as Kanpei works as a hunter, he wears the rough straw raincoat of a peasant over a short, loose kimono. When he thinks he is going to be restored to warrior status, he lays aside his gun, changes to a tightly wrapped long kimono, and sticks his swords in his belt. At that point he is suitably dressed to commit suicide in time-honored samurai fashion: hair flying, hand held to a knife in his gut, body rocking back and forth in agony. In contrast to the thief Sadakurō, who was taken by surprise by a shot in the dark, Kanpei chooses the moment of his death. Dying by his own sword, he epitomizes samurai masculinity.

Written in 1748 for the puppet theater and quickly adopted for kabuki, *Chūshingura* has never gone out of style.[41] Whether parodied or performed straight, it delimits the ligaments of military morality under impossibly trying circumstances. Even though it highlights the characteristics of the warrior—loyalty, autonomy, and self-sacrifice—it does so in a society in which the military display of these virtues is increasingly irrelevant. Ignored are the weapons that had once been carried by warriors, especially the bow, and the marker of the greatest difference among them, the horse. By sharpening the distinction between gun and sword, *Chūshingura* speaks to the warrior's anxieties about his status in a time of peace and his fear that the gulf between hunter or foot soldier and himself could be crossed with only a change of clothes. In this way it reifies not only martial virtues but also weapons.

Surrounded by weapons of all sorts, shoguns both modeled and exceeded military masculinity. In ceremonies that marked the New Year, they inspected their armor, wrote poetry *(renga)*, rode horseback, watched archery contests, and went hawking. Whenever they walked from one part of the palace to another or when they sat in meetings and audiences with the daimyo, they wore swords and had a page carry their great sword. Given the centrality of the blade to their ceremonial gift exchanges with daimyo, we might be forgiven for assuming that they identified exclusively with it and hand-to-hand combat. Yet they learned gunmanship for pleasure and to demonstrate mastery over arms.

Neither Ieyasu nor Hidetada nor their descendants used guns to kill people. On the other hand, although the first two shoguns fought battles, they did not kill people at all. Ieyasu warned his descendants that a general should not kill men in battle but should keep himself out of danger, nor should he waste his energy in cutting people down.[42] During the sieges of Osaka castle in 1614 and 1615, Ieyasu and Hidetada faced hails of bullets while they leisurely inspected the front lines in a display of bravery designed to intimidate their enemies and hearten their supporters, yet they never fired a shot.[43] How did they achieve a reputation for prowess with arms?

The answer is the hunt. Throughout his life, but especially following his retirement in 1606, Ieyasu spent weeks at a time hunting around Sunpu and across the shogunate's home territories in Kanto. Whenever he visited Edo he enjoyed the hawking grounds established around the city. He even went hunting on his way to and from Osaka, perhaps as a way to demonstrate his confidence in the outcome of the battle ahead. Hunting provided an opportunity to check on local conditions and talk to people in the hinterland. Hunting was a privilege. Daimyo hunted in their domains, but only the shoguns and the collateral houses were allowed to hunt in the provinces around Edo. Weapons used in the hunt were the bow and the gun. Shoguns particularly prized the hawk, a weapon that was itself a projectile.

Hawking had been the sport of emperors since at least the eighth century, and the shoguns made sure it continued to be monopolized by the ruling class. After Ieyasu revoked the emperor's hawking privileges, he and his descendants sent cranes caught by their hawks to the court in a display of militarized authority. In Morioka, only the daimyo, men he assigned to hawk in his name, or men granted special privileges flew birds; his heir had to content himself with guns.[44] In the rest of Eurasia the spread of guns resulted in the decline or disappearance of hawking,[45] but perhaps because of hawking's close association with high status in Japan, there it coexisted with guns.

Ieyasu's skill with the gun was legendary. While hunting near Mount Asama in 1611, he hit his target whenever he fired his gun. Shooting at three kites, he killed two and wounded the third. Anecdotes about his shooting of birds inevitably compare him favorably to his attendants and suggest that as a marksman he had no equal. From the time he was a youth until he was more than seventy years old, his daily regimen included horseback riding, firing his gun, and target practice with a bow and arrow. In 1612 he organized a deer hunt that mobilized five to six thousand men armed with guns and bows, and he shot at a wild boar himself.[46]

Like his father, Hidetada hunted frequently and ranged widely in search of game. Four years after having received investiture as shogun in 1606, he employed twenty thousand beaters for a hunt in Mikawa in central Japan and bagged deer, wild boar, foxes, and rabbits. "The sound of shouts added to the guns and arrows reverberated through the mountain valleys like thunder" in a fitting display of martial majesty. Hidetada and his attendants slaughtered even more game two weeks later. Once, while hunting, he was going to send his hawk after a goose, but he shot it with a gun instead. Upon his return he pointed out the importance of flexibility in choosing weapons and doing the unexpected.[47]

The hunt started to change under the third shogun, Iemitsu. Unlike his father and grandfather, he never had the opportunity to demonstrate his prowess in battle; instead he tried to prove his skill at arms by mastering the sword and hunting. His sword teacher, Yagyū Munenori, said, "Using Zen you can improve your technique; using your technique, you can improve governance," a classic statement connecting the martial arts and the ability to rule.[48] Although Iemitsu was an enthusiastic hunter, he usually stayed near the castle. After the day's ceremonies were over, he often had himself carried in a palanquin to a nearby river to pursue birds using hawks, bow, gun, and sword. He also enjoyed watching displays of horsemanship, gunnery, and fireworks at the homes of the senior councilors. As a young man hunting deer, Iemitsu shot one with a gun, pierced two with spears, and cut off the head of a fourth with his sword.[49] In a practice followed by rulers across Eurasia, he held banquets for the men who accompanied him on his hunting expeditions at which he served the game that they had bagged. Among the guests were the hawk masters, sword carriers, and gun loaders.[50] In a social imaginary in which those at the top mirrored those at the bottom, the game that degraded hunters featured in gifts from shogun to daimyo and the imperial court.[51]

The connection between shogun and guns faded over the next four generations. When Iemitsu died in 1651, his heir, Ietsuna, was only ten years old. Ietsuna's affinity for the martial arts was decidedly weaker than his predecessors', and his advisors discouraged unscripted expeditions outside the castle. Even after he started hawking, he was more likely to watch others fly the birds than do so himself. That was also his preference for shooting, archery, and sword fighting. In summing up his reign, *Tokugawa jikki* recounts that Ietsuna studied sword fighting and horseback riding and often listened to lectures on all the military techniques, including bird guns. Whenever he had a moment to spare from his duties he observed his retainers performing martial arts, but he preferred tea ceremonies, painting with ink and brush, watching dance, and listening to *Tale of the Heike*.[52]

The reign of the fifth shogun, Tsunayoshi (1680–1709), ushered in a reformulation of what it meant to be a military man. Tsunayoshi is famous for his laws of compassion designed to protect the lives of birds, game, horses, and especially dogs, with rare exceptions for wild boar and deer that ravaged fields or wolves that attacked men. Although the shogunate continued to send gifts of dead cranes to the court in Kyoto in accordance with the precedent established by his ancestors, Tsunayoshi never hunted after becoming shogun. Supply officers received instructions to keep guns in working order, and archers on horseback performed for officials, but Tsunayoshi devoted himself to other tasks.[53] The martial arts, including gunmanship, fell into abeyance. At the same time, Tsunayoshi tried to model himself on the Confucian gentleman, to transform a military regime into a benevolent bureaucracy, and, through his lectures on the Confucian classics addressed to warriors across the status spectrum from daimyo to guards, to civilize the samurai by inculcating new standards of manly behavior that focused on literary arts instead of martial ones.

The first three shoguns had understood the way of the warrior to encompass both the literary and martial arts, and they had modeled masculine military prowess through their mastery of weapons. Tsunayoshi and his immediate successors showed little to no interest in the martial arts. Surrounded by councilors intent on wrapping the shoguns in a cocoon of ceremony, they traveled around Edo not to hunt but to be entertained at the mansions of their favorites. By rejecting the identification of shogun with weapons, they contested a masculinity that had defined manliness in warrior society. In response, critics complained that Tsunayoshi preferred banquets to hunting, had loose sexual habits, and practiced various amusements as though he were a foolish child.[54] It is little wonder that, as Kurushima Hiroshi has said, military specialists became teachers of etiquette.[55]

Adopted into the Tokugawa main line in 1716 after it had failed to produce an heir, Yoshimune took immediate steps to reassert a militarized masculinity. As a young man and daimyo of Kii in what is now Wakayama, he had enjoyed hunting and killing game. Now, in accordance with Confucian principles, he rectified personal norms of behavior associated with the shogun by reviving the position of hawk master and reestablishing hawking grounds. He put his family in order by issuing a series of regulations governing the women's quarters in the Great Interior. In 1717 he went hunting for the first time as shogun and shot two cormorants, a feat that surprised his attendants, and he continued to hunt frequently throughout his career. Particularly notable are the many boars he shot, including two in Aoyama, not far from the castle.[56]

In addition to hawking and shooting in the Edo environs, Yoshimune also revived the large-scale hunts staged by his ancestors. In 1718 he employed three thousand peasants as beaters to flush pheasants and quail while he and his retinue chased them on horseback with bows. He enjoyed this exercise so much that he did it repeatedly, summoning larger and larger numbers of troops and beaters, whose movements he directed with a complicated system of flags that turned the hunt into a war game. He had deer hunts organized east of Edo in 1725 and 1726, the first time such large expeditions had been arranged since the days of Iemitsu. For these occasions Yoshimune dressed himself in the style of Minamoto no Yoritomo, invested with the title of shogun in 1192. The hunt began with a drum roll, and then thousands of troops attacked the game in the order established in advance. At the end, everyone received sake and meat before Yoshimune returned to the castle late that night. The next day he ordered the court painter to create pictures advertising the hunt as a military exercise.[57]

In addition to honing his skill at the martial arts himself, Yoshimune encouraged their practice among the warriors as a class. On his first hunting expedition as shogun he had two men take turns shooting at a cormorant with bird guns. Starting in 1718 he ordered inspectors to test the troops' gunnery skills, established a prize for the unit that turned in the best performance, and encouraged the troops to perfect their marksmanship through the lavish distribution of bonuses and rewards. Occasionally master gunners and their subordinates had the opportunity to display their skills before Yoshimune, and he was known to make surprise inspections of the guns carried by guards at the castle gates. He watched guard units ride horseback, he developed a new school of archery on horseback, and he ordered his second son, later called Tayasu Munetake, to perpetuate it.[58]

Yoshimune is known for his efforts to reform the shogunate, especially in matters of finance following the profligacy of his immediate predecessors, but equally noteworthy was his attempt to reinvent the shogun's persona as a military man. After his death his retainers recounted tales of his courage—not in battle, because he never had to fight, but during the hunt. Faced with a wounded wolf, he calmly reloaded and shot again. In Shinagawa he stopped a wounded boar in its tracks with a small gun. He also tried to instill martial values in his attendants and guards by having them practice swimming, horseback archery, sword fighting, and gunmanship. Sometimes he would divide them into teams to compete against each other, and once he had them fight on horseback with bamboo swords. He studied books on military science and paid special attention to training soldiers. When he died, his favorite swords, spears, and guns were displayed in the funeral procession.[59] In short, by personal example and leadership, he tried to return the shogunate to its roots by glorifying military masculinity.

Yoshimune's heroic efforts to restore martial arts to the shogun's performance of masculinity lasted only as long as his line. Under his watchful eye, his heirs Ieshige and Ieharu hunted and practiced shooting and watched their attendants do the same. Ieharu became a noted marksman, hunted regularly, and supervised gunnery and horseback archery for his attendants and guards. Within six months of his son's birth, Ieharu had a new bird gun made for him. It was said that Ieharu's favorite practical jokes were to startle his attendants by shooting arrows at them in the garden or firing a gun unexpectedly.[60] After his son died from a fall while out hunting, Ieharu adopted Ienari from the Hitotsubashi house to be the next shogun. Although Ienari continued the New Year's rituals of riding horseback, displaying his armor, writing poetry, hawking, and watching archery contests, *Tokugawa jikki* contains only one mention of him ever having killed a deer. The link between shogun and firearms had at last been broken.[61] Instead the people of Edo lauded him as a god of good fortune because he fathered fifty-five children.

Considering the relationship between military men and guns in premodern Japan requires careful periodization and attention to status markers. For the first twenty or so years after their introduction, guns served as objects of exchange between warlords and in the hunt. Once they came to be produced in large quantities, they found a lasting place in Japanese armies, and so long as armies remained a measure of a daimyo's might, guns continued in that capacity as well, even when locked in castles. To the extent that armies continued to perform ceremonial functions after the establishment of the Tokugawa regime, so did guns.

Guns carried different symbolic values depending on who handled them. When used to earn one's livelihood, guns were associated with foot soldiers of low status or, worse, degraded hunters. To borrow Cox's phrasing, guns served as tools that assisted in the performance of masculine tasks, not as cultural symbols of masculinity.[62] Although warriors enjoyed shooting guns at targets and in recreational hunts, to have the gun associated with one's profession risked a loss of status, something that was always a source of anxiety during the long Edo peace. Men at the top of the pyramid, however, suffered no such qualms. In direct converse to their followers, for the shoguns and daimyo to shoot guns at game enabled them to project competence in masculine pursuits, to demonstrate masculine virtues, and to enhance their authority as rulers.

NOTES

For help in understanding gunmanship, I thank Wilson J. Walthall, David Love, and Benjamin Froidevaux.

1. Kokuritsu Rekishi Minzoku Hakubutsukan 2006, p. 65.
2. Andaya 2008, pp. 23, 31.
3. Allsen 2006, p. 130; Griffin 2007, pp. 78–79.
4. Browder 2006, pp. 1, 15, 233.
5. Allen 2002, p. 192.
6. For the sixteenth century, see Suzuki 2007, p. 179; for the fourteenth century, see Conlan 2003.
7. For an English translation of this text, see Lidin 2002, pp. 36–42.
8. Suzuki 2007, pp. 154–56.
9. Udagawa 2007, p. 18.
10. Cipolla 1965, p. 110; Chase 2003, p. 138.
11. Arai 1993, pp. 72–75.
12. Udagawa 2007, pp. 46–48.
13. Cipolla 1965, p. 109.
14. Udagawa 2007, pp. 29–34.
15. *Tokugawa jikki* 1, p. 629; 2, pp. 187, 304; 4, pp. 136, 208; 8, p. 222.
16. In 1615 Shimazu Iehisa presented ten guns with gunpowder and fuse cords to Hidetada. *Tokugawa jikki* 2, p. 49.
17. *Tokugawa jikki* 2, pp. 207, 275. Ieyasu distributed his guns to the sons who founded the *sanke*, the three collateral houses set up as an inner line of defense for the main family and to provide a supply of heirs should the main family run out.
18. See *Dai-Tokugawa ten* 2007, pp. 28–29.
19. *Tokugawa jikki* 1, pp. 85, 546; 2, p. 96.
20. Compare *Tokugawa jikki* 4, p. 287 with 4, p. 277 (1658) and 5, pp. 218, 220.
21. Sugawa 1991, p. 1; Vaporis 2008, p. 95.
22. *Tokugawa jikki* 3, p. 536; 4, p. 336, 457; 8, pp. 435, 437, 467.
23. Ben-Ari and Frühstück 2007, pp. 187, 196.
24. Udagawa 2006, p. 217; Udagawa 2007, pp. 132–35.
25. Berry 2006.
26. Nye 2007, p. 435 argues that in the West, "sports photos were shot with an eroticism that denies it is erotic."
27. Kokuritsu Rekishi Minzoku Hakubutsukan 2006, pp. 17, 26, 27, 30.
28. Rogers (1998, pp. 152–53) dates this trend to the late seventeenth century, but given its long history in polite accomplishments such as poetry writing, I suspect it was coeval with the founding of the martial arts schools.

29. Rogers 1998, p. 189.
30. Kokuritsu Rekishi Minzoku Hakubutsukan 2006, p. 31.
31. Kokuritsu Rekishi Minzoku Hakubutsukan 2006, pp. 172, 175.
32. Kokuritsu Rekishi Minzoku Hakubutsukan 2006, p. 177.
33. Cox 2007, p. 142.
34. Udagawa undated.
35. Allsen 2006, p. 21 argues that "missile and projectile weapons were first developed for the hunt and later modified for war, while shock and thrusting weapons—the spear, sword, and mace—were typically specialized for war."
36. Allsen 2006, pp. 8–9. See also Baer 2008, pp. 179–87 for a study of Ottoman sultan Mehmed IV as a hunter.
37. Griffin 2007, p. 6.
38. Rogers 1998, pp. 23, 118–20.
39. Endō 1994, pp. 248–52. See also Walker 2001.
40. Tsukamoto 1993 [1983], pp. 9, 71, 74, 127. See also Howell 2009, pp. 67–68.
41. Smith 2003.
42. *Tokugawa jikki* 1, p. 352. In 1600 a retainer chided Mogami Yoshiaki for leading his forces in battle, saying, "A general ought not lightly risk his life in the vanguard" (Katagiri 2007, p. 82).
43. *Tokugawa jikki* 1, pp. 262, 735, 740, 744.
44. Endō 1994, pp. 80, 166.
45. Tsukamoto 1993 [1983], p. 106.
46. *Tokugawa jikki* 1, pp. 351, 354, 363.
47. *Tokugawa jikki* 2, pp. 285, 292.
48. *Tokugawa jikki* 3, p. 713.
49. See, for example, *Tokugawa jikki* 3, p. 196.
50. See, for example, *Tokugawa jikki* 3, p. 211.
51. See, for example, Endō 1994, pp. 56, 160, 238, 253.
52. *Tokugawa jikki,* 4, pp. 101, 193, 201; 5, pp. 344, 351.
53. *Tokugawa jikki* 6, pp. 20, 47, 169, 338, 464. For a laudatory account of Tsunayoshi and his era, see Bodart-Bailey 2006.
54. Such complaints surfaced soon after Tsunayoshi's death. See Walthall 2007.
55. Kurushima 1986, p. 288.
56. *Tokugawa jikki* 8, pp. 1, 29, 36, 44–45, 59, 71, 596.
57. *Tokugawa jikki* 8, pp. 8, 105, 132, 265–66, 284, 400–402.
58. *Tokugawa jikki* 8, pp. 72, 118, 119, 197, 221, 303, 378, 428, 493, 610, 651.
59. *Tokugawa jikki* 9, pp. 136, 262, 265, 270, 541–42.
60. *Tokugawa jikki* 9, pp. 769–70; 10, pp. 1, 111, 594, 840.
61. Decades after he had renounced the office of shogun in 1867, Yoshinobu had himself photographed in Western-style hunting garb carrying a gun. He participated in modern hunts with beaters numbering in the handful rather than mobilizing thousands of men, as had his ancestors.
62. Cox 2007, p. 141.

REFERENCES

Allen, Judith A. 2002. "Men Interminably in Crisis? Historians on Masculinity, Sexual Boundaries, and Manhood." *Radical History Review* 82: 191–207.

Allsen, Thomas T. 2006. *The Royal Hunt in Eurasian History.* Philadelphia: University of Pennsylvania Press.

Andaya, Barbara. 2008. "Women and the Performance of Power in Early Modern Southeast Asia." In *Servants of the Dynasty: Palace Women in World History,* ed. Anne Walthall, 22–44. Berkeley: University of California Press.

Arai Hakuseki. 1993. *Honchō gunki kō.* In *Kojitsu sōsho,* vol. 21, ed. Kojitsu Sōsho Hensanbu. Meiji Tosho Shuppan Kabushiki Kaisha.

Baer, Marc David. 2008. *Honored by the Glory of Islam: Conversion and Conquest in Ottoman Europe.* Oxford: Oxford University Press.

Ben-Ari, Eyal, and Sabine Frühstück. 2007. "The Celebration of Violence: A Live Fire Demonstration Carried out by Japan's Contemporary Military." In *Open Fire: Understanding Global Gun Cultures,* ed. Charles Fruehling Springwood, 178–98. Oxford: Berg.

Berry, Mary Elizabeth. 2006. *Japan in Print: Information and Nation in the Early Modern Period.* Berkeley: University of California Press.

Bodart-Bailey, Beatrice M. 2006. *The Dog Shogun: The Personality and Policies of Tokugawa Tsunayoshi.* Honolulu: University of Hawai'i Press.

Browder, Laura. 2006. *Her Best Shot: Women and Guns in America.* Chapel Hill: University of North Carolina Press.

Chase, Kenneth. 2003. *Firearms: A Global History to 1700.* Cambridge: Cambridge University Press.

Cipolla, Carlo M. 1965. *Guns, Sails, and Empires: Technological Innovation and the Early Phases of European Expansion 1400–1700.* New York: Pantheon Books.

Conlan, Thomas. 2003. *State of War: The Violent Order of Fourteenth-Century Japan.* Ann Arbor: Center of Japanese Studies, University of Michigan.

Cox, Amy Ann. 2007. "Arming for Manhood: The Transformation of Guns into Objects of American Masculinity." In *Open Fire: Understanding Global Gun Cultures,* ed. Charles Fruehling Springwood, 141–52. Oxford: Berg.

Dai-Tokugawa-ten Shusai Jimukyoku, ed. 2007. *Dai-Tokugawa-ten.* Dai-Tokugawa-ten Shusai Jimukyoku.

Endō Kimio. 1994. *Morioka han onkari nikki: Edo jidai no yasei dōbutsushi.* Kōdansha.

Griffin, Emma. 2007. *Blood Sport: Hunting in Britain since 1066.* New Haven: Yale University Press.

Howell, David L. 2009. "The Social Life of Firearms in Tokugawa Japan." *Japanese Studies* 20, no. 1: 65–80.

Katagiri Shigeo. 2007. "Mogami Yoshiaki no gassen: kenkyū saizensen." *Rekishi dokuhon* 817 (August): 74–83.

Kokuritsu Rekishi Minzoku Hakubutsukan, ed. 2006. *Rekishi no naka no teppō denrai: Tanegashima kara Bōshin sensō made.* Sakura: Kokuritsu Rekishi Minzoku Hakubutsukan.

Kuroita Katsumi, ed. 1931. *Shintei zōho kokushi taikei,* vols. 38–47: *Tokugawa jikki,* vols. 1–10. Yoshikawa Kōbunkan.

Kurushima Hiroshi. 1986. "Kinsei no gun'yaku to hyakushō." In *Nihon no shakaishi* 4, ed. Yamaguchi Keiji, 273–317. Iwanami Shoten.

Lidin, Olof G. 2002. *Tanegashima: The Arrival of Europe in Japan.* Copenhagen: Nias Press.

Nye, Robert A. 2007. Review Essay: "Western Masculinities in War and Peace." *American Historical Review* 112, no. 2: 417–38.

Rogers, John Michael. 1998. "The Development of the Military Profession in Tokugawa Japan." Ph.D. diss., Harvard University.

Smith, Henry Dewitt II. 2003. "The Capacity of Chūshingura." *Monumenta Nipponica* 58, no. 1: 1–42.

Sugawa Shigeo. 1991. *The Japanese Matchlock: A Story of the Tanegashima.* Published by the author in Tokyo; distributed by Kogei Shuppan.

Suzuki Masaya. 2007. *Sengoku jidai no daigokai.* PHP Kenkyūjo.

Tokugawa jikki. See Kuroita Katsumi.

Tsukamoto Manabu. 1993 [1983]. *Shōrui o meguru seiji: Genroku no fōkuroa.* Heibonsha.

Udagawa Takehisa. 2006. "Tōkoku e no teppō denpa to Kishinowada ryū: hōjutsu no ryūkō." In *Sengoku shikihō-ki no shakai to girei,* ed. Futaki Ken'ichi, 212–38. Yoshikawa Kōbunkan.

———. 2007. "Teppō denrai no jitsuzō." In *Teppō denrai no Nihonshi: Hinawajū kara raifurujū made,* ed. Udagawa Takehisa, 2–27. Yoshikawa Kōbunkan.

———. Undated. Available at www.rekihaku.ac.jp/e-rekihaku/126/rekishi.html.

Vaporis, Constantine Nomikos. 2008. *Tour of Duty: Samurai, Military Service in Edo, and the Culture of Early Modern Japan.* Honolulu: University of Hawai'i Press.

Walker, Brett L. 2001. "Commercial Growth and Environmental Change in Early Modern Japan: Hachinohe's Wild Boar Famine of 1749." *Journal of Asian Studies* 60, no. 2: 329–51.

Walthall, Anne. 2007. "Histories Official, Unofficial, and Popular: Shogunal Favorites in the Genroku Era." In *Writing Histories in Japan: Texts and their Transformations from Ancient Times through the Meiji Era,* ed. James C. Baxter and Joshua A. Fogel, 175–99, Kyoto: International Research Center for Japanese Studies.

2 Name and Honor

A Merchant's Seventeenth-Century Memoir

Luke Roberts

Enomoto Yazaemon (1625–86) began his autobiography with descriptions of his male ancestors.[1] The first "was a man who had been wounded in eighteen places." The second "had the strength of eight men. He could pull up by the roots a bamboo four or five inches around. Once, when the wooden bridge at Takazawa ward was destroyed, the head of a rusty eight-inch spike was sticking up, and he easily pulled it out with his bare hands." His father (the third generation) was "also a big, brave man." Yazaemon emphasizes the physical strength and martial toughness of each ancestor, both traits that a student of Tokugawa Japan might expect from a member of the warrior class. Yazaemon and his forebears, however, were wealthy salt merchants.

The author of this text was a successful merchant in the castle town of Kawagoe (a city about forty kilometers northwest of Edo), a wealthy landowner, and a purveyor to the daimyo's family. Having kept diaries from as early as 1636, he completed a draft of his autobiography in 1680 and added to it until 1684. His preface states that he composed it to instruct his son and heir on how to bring up children. It was a family document to be shown to descendants as a testament to Yazaemon's values and a life lesson on how to achieve character through self-cultivation. Between 1653 and 1660 Yazaemon also kept a more random miscellany, "Yorozu no oboe," which contains much more information on his business activities and the events of his world. Together with scroll portraits of himself and his wife that Yazaemon commissioned, his descendants have preserved the original autobiography and miscellany.

The scholars who composed the early nineteenth-century regional history *Shinpen Musashi Fūdoki* knew these documents, but they have not been widely utilized by historians.[2] One article by Ōno Mitsuo on

Yazaemon's commercial practices and environment and another by Nagura Tetsuzō on the development of merchant family ideology constitute the only modern studies.[3] This is regrettable because the autobiography in particular provides a rare, and perhaps unique, window onto the lives of seventeenth-century merchants. To my knowledge, the only other remotely similar document of merchant self-representation from before the Genroku period (1688–1703) is the three-year diary written from 1663 to 1665 by a merchant youth, Katsurai Soan (1652–1706), in the castle town of Kōchi in southern Japan.[4] Until now research on merchant lives and ideologies has drawn on documents produced from the end of the seventeenth century, such as Ihara Saikaku's tales of merchants and the 1728 *Chōnin kōkenroku* by the Osaka merchant Mitsui Takafusa. It presents already-established cultural distinctions between the status groups of merchant, samurai, peasant, and others, each seemingly in possession of a distinctive way of life and set of values appropriate to the peaceful middle period of the Tokugawa era.[5] Yet to be explored is how these status groups developed culturally and socially during the changes of the seventeenth century as the era of civil war disappeared from living memory.

The issue of self-representation by people from commoner classes is important because dominant samurai-generated discourses of merchanthood emerge from an ideological desire to monopolize in the samurai class certain characteristics of status identity. For example, Daidōji Yūzan's influential *Budō shoshinshū*, a popular primer for young warriors written in the early eighteenth century, posits a key difference between samurai and members of other status groups as the samurai's constant readiness to confront danger. He writes in graphically physical terms that essentialize this difference in the bodies themselves: "A samurai who fastens swords at his waist but does not hold the spirit of battle in mind is no different than a merchant or farmer wearing a warrior's skin."[6] The naturalization of a distinctive samurai masculinity has likely blinded us to social and cultural changes that occurred in the merchant class and substantially affected the construction of merchant masculinity in the seventeenth century.

The larger goal that I pursue here is to modify Eiko Ikegami's notion of the "taming of the samurai" by suggesting that seventeenth-century pacification involved a much more general "taming of masculinity."[7] We need to rethink this era as a time for men of many statuses to restrict a culture of honor violence and redefine their roles according to the reshaped status order in ways befitting the Tokugawa "Great Peace." In a second move, I question the related, commonly recurring trope of the "samuraization" of the populace. For example, the doyen of merchant studies, Miyamoto

Mataji, relates in his book on merchant values that the samurai valuing of name and reputation "in time was transferred to the merchant class," yet Yazaemon's account depicts a merchant society already highly devoted to these concepts.[8] Thus, I will suggest that this trope is nothing more than an illusion of elitist samurai ideology.[9] Instead of envisioning a process of the adoption of the samurai ideals by all social classes, it seems more accurate to speak of a core set of values espoused by all men of lineage and property. This is not to say that samurai and merchants were the same in the seventeenth-century Kanto region, but rather that their notions of "manly behavior"—bravery, an ideology of self-restraint, and a devotion to lineage and household—were in fact largely indistinguishable.

Yazaemon's exercise in self-representation presents the voice of a successful mid-seventeenth-century merchant. I will focus on the two issues of honor violence and family headship as I follow his life through four stages, characterized as wild youth, learning restraint, midlife crisis, and paterfamilias. Throughout his career Yazaemon was concerned with gaining worldly respect, and the achievement of a secure inheritance in competition with his younger brother is the main drama of his life story. The issues that controlled his narrative interest—what might be called his problems of identity—changed over time. The first two stages of his life involved honor violence and gaining the respect of his parents; the latter two stages centered on control over his household and were tied to problems with his health and psychological vigor. Challenging the conventional notion that only the warrior class praised as manly virtues physical strength, bravery and such, I examine in this chapter the rhetoric of masculinity within the merchant class to the extent it emerges from Yazaemon's autobiography and the scarce sources from his time.

WILD YOUTH

Yazaemon's autobiography is particularly engaging because he chooses to present himself in terms of his journey of personal development from childhood to old age rather than as a finished product. He regards personal cultivation as a process that includes self-understanding and self-denial, and his goals include health, social well-being, and household longevity. In his preface, composed in early 1680, he describes himself in the third person:

> The fourth-generation Enomoto Yazaemon Tadashige is now in his fifty-sixth year. His childhood name was Ushinosuke. He is here writing out all the good and bad in himself from when he was a child year by year to leave this record to the fifth-generation heir of this

> household so that he may raise descendants who discern their inborn nature and raise them neither with hardship nor difficulties and without selfish indulgence.[10]

Yazaemon reveals numerous personal struggles resulting from his "inborn nature": he began as a timid, fearful, and self-indulgent child who gradually learned to become brave and later learned self-restraint and mastery over illness and depression. The narrative leads to the goal of his life course, the moral authority to control his family and to instruct his descendants. However, the autobiography is structured to be introspective by revealing faults to be overcome. Even his moral achievements are unstable, as a reference to himself discloses anxiety about the validity of his autobiographical project: "Until a man dies you do not truly know whether he is good or bad" (pp. 71–72).

His reflective autobiographical enterprise and his emphasis on the need for self-restraint is rooted in a persistent distrust of himself and others. He describes himself as aware of his own inauthenticity even at age six. In this year the overlord Tokugawa Iemitsu had come to Kawagoe to hunt with many fierce hunting dogs. As they barked and fought noisily through the nearly empty streets, young Yazaemon watched from his house's second-floor window. Upon seeing his father in the road he cried and called for his father to come inside. He describes himself at that moment in the following way: "Half of my thought was for my father, and half of my thought was that my parents would think me virtuous, being so young and yet worrying about my father and calling to him through my tears." Perhaps he was just displaying a precocious presence of mind, but its application to such an apparently innocuous action seems to be an indication of his strong sense of the selfishness that he needed to learn to restrain. Questioning his motives is a trope that flows through the rest of the diary, especially during his youth, when he lies, gambles, and steals: "So many things I should be deeply ashamed of in light of honor," he writes, using the word *giri,* a term that in a samurai context is translated as "honor" or "duty" and is regarded as a moral force that overcomes selfishness.

Yazaemon's interpretation of other events reveals his equal lack of trust in the motives of others. He writes that if, when he was seven years old, people praised his singing, "I would think maybe my singing was bad and be ashamed." At age twelve he secretly took some of the family firewood to give to his reading and writing instructor, a poor, masterless samurai. When the man's wife thanked him, "she acted so happy that I thought she was manipulating me, and I became secretly angry." There are a number of possible origins for this debilitating distrust, but two legacies from the Warring States era played a role. The first was a culture of suspicion and violence, and the second was the competitive inheritance practice that had not yet shifted to the mid-Edo norm of primogeniture regardless of capacity.

Yazaemon situates his origins in "big," "brave," and "manly" ancestors,[11] but he describes the beginning of his own life in unpromising terms, writing, "I hated all dangerous things and clung to people." He was even fearful of and kept his distance from some everyday objects such as shelves and querns. He was also violent. At age eight he pushed a child off a dike and broke his leg. Knowing that he had enraged the child's elder brother, Yazaemon would run away whenever he saw him. Yazaemon gradually became more fearless and wild. At thirteen he beat up a samurai's son, and got into such a fight with another that they ripped out each other's hair.

Yazaemon did not consider violence alone to be manly. Yazaemon describes himself as beginning to act "like an adult" only when he put his martial valor in the service of his household at age fourteen. During a large fire in Kawagoe his family had removed belongings from their house and set them in an open space. Yazaemon was left alone to guard the family's possessions from thieves. He writes, "I stood on top of the biggest trunk and brandished a spear to protect our goods. When a thief tried to take some luggage, I went after him brandishing the spear. He fled without taking anything. In this way I did the work of an adult. We ended up losing only one long-handled umbrella." In the same year Yazaemon also used violence to protect his honor when a twenty-five-year-old *otokodate* punk bullied and humiliated Yazaemon by rubbing black ink all over his face.[12] Yazaemon then ran home to get a short sword and hunted down the bully in a rented room in a wealthy merchant's house. Sword drawn, Yazaemon challenged him to a fight, saying, "You have shamed me and I cannot forgive it. Come out and we will fight to the death!" The punk apologized, and Yazaemon gained face for his threat of violence. This was a signal year for Yazaemon in achieving "manliness," for he also describes himself as beginning to eat as much as an "adult man" at that age.

Over the next few years Yazaemon repeatedly deployed his capacity for violence to protect his masculine honor. At age fifteen another *otokodate* punk, a tobacco merchant named Gonjūrō, tried to beat Yazaemon and perhaps even to rape him, for he ordered Yazaemon to take off his clothes. He had led Yazaemon out of town to the woods to "play" when he suddenly ordered Yazaemon to strip. Yazaemon promised to fight back and insulted his foe's masculinity, saying, "If you cannot keep up [trading punches] with me then you cannot be called a man!" Gonjūrō relented. He felt so humiliated that a month later he burst into a party at a merchant's house attended by Yazaemon and threatened to kill Yazaemon with his sword if Yazaemon tried to leave. Yazaemon jumped up, drew his short sword, and sliced Gonjūrō right across the forehead. Even worse would have happened had not a visiting monk-merchant named Keidenbō, whose arrival to sell hats and clothing was the occasion for the party, entered the fray. He pushed Yazaemon out of the room and, using martial arts techniques taught by the popular Bokuden school, twisted Gonjūrō's sword away with his bare hands. Gonjūrō fled and Yazaemon ran home, fearful that Gonjūrō might attack Yazaemon's father. A respected salt merchant and one of Kawagoe's town elders, Yazaemon's father ordered his son to the back of the house and sat at the entrance with his sword unsheathed, waiting for Gonjūrō to come. As it turned out, Gonjūrō did not appear because he had fainted from his wound.

This anecdote shows how a masculinity based on defending one's honor with violence was such a part of the seventeenth-century merchant world of Kawagoe that a number of merchants seem to have kept their swords handy, ready for use. Yazaemon's father could have locked the gates or called for help, but instead he chose to defend his house alone, making a statement about his confidence in his own martial skills. Even the monk-merchant Keidenbō, who used no sword, had trained in martial techniques. To Yazaemon's surprise, the quarrel ended up in court. He had not known about *kenka ryōseibai,* a prohibition against fighting that stipulated that both parties in a fight would be punished regardless of who was right and wrong. Yazaemon thought that fighting well would earn him respect in his community—a community, I will add, of merchants: "I did not know that if I had killed Gonjūrō it might have cost me my life. I just thought that if I could kill Gonjūrō it would be a sign of my martial skill, so I put my heart into my fighting. I thought that people would start calling me a great skillful fighter." The actual judgment was a lenient order to desist in the feud upon pain of family punishment, and Gonjūrō was placed in the custody of a local temple. Gonjūrō later went to work in Edo but repeatedly returned to Kawagoe intending to kill Yazaemon. Yazaemon wrote with bravado about remaining willing to fight until Gonjurō died: "In 1644 he fell ill and died at age twenty-five. I was finally able to stop worrying. For five or six years I lived in the world with a mortal enemy and was watchful day and night. I had decided to always be prepared to meet Gonjūrō at any moment and fight, and sometimes even asked around for him."

Not once in this or other accounts does Yazaemon describe himself as "like a samurai" or give any indication that he aspires to that status. Instead, at age twenty he wrote about himself that "all I could think about was commerce." The manliness for which he hoped was one that would be talked about and admired by his community of merchant peers. Nevertheless, the manliness that he describes as his own and pursues in the company of merchants is very like that which in time would be seen as the sole domain of the samurai. Even though the scholars mentioned in the introduction to this chapter assume that merchant masculinity always differed from that of the samurai, Yazaemon's notion of his own manliness suggests that in the seventeenth century notions of masculinity had yet to become differentiated in terms of status.

In that same year when Yazaemon was twenty, in 1645, he participated in another feat of arms that also speaks to a widespread culture of masculine violence in towns and villages. He and two merchant companions were on a pilgrimage to Mitsumine shrine when their hired guide mistakenly led them onto a village road not open to outsiders. Challenged by the villagers, one of Yazaemon's friends drew his sword. Yazaemon became embroiled when the villagers grappled with the merchants, and he boasted that because he was in those days studying armed and unarmed martial techniques he was able to wrest himself free. By this time a large crowd of villagers armed with "wooden swords, staves, spears, long swords, and short swords" had arrived to capture and punish the merchant who had drawn his sword. Fearing that he and his companions would be killed, Yazaemon threatened the crowd by drawing his sword. The village headman arrived and attempted to settle the argument. In the tense negotiations that followed the villagers accused the merchants of trespassing and starting the fight, while Yazaemon accused the villagers of thievery and his hired guide of incompetence. Finally Yazaemon and crew were made to take lodging in a neighboring town. Thanks to the headman's authority and Yazaemon's negotiating skills, the issue was settled a day later with apologies sent from the villagers. The people of the inn said, "What wondrous exploits!" using the word *tegara,* which we normally think of as being exclusive to samurai culture. When he returned to Kawagoe and told the story, his hometown friends were proud, saying to him in a way reminiscent of samurai tales of battle, "You have raised the name of Kawagoe!" From this instance and others in Yazaemon's autobiography, it becomes clear that despite the different lifestyles of the different classes, "true masculinity" could only be talked about in a language customarily identified with the samurai but was in fact more universal.

Yet another anecdote reveals how violent honor-bound manliness permeated villager and merchant society and how control of women was entangled in this behavior. Yazaemon first married the daughter of a village headman at twenty-one, but neither he nor his parents liked his wife, "who was large and clumsy and whose language was coarse." He summarily divorced her, sending her and a servant with his divorce statement to her family home. In doing so he insulted her family. When he had a chance to travel on business to her home village two years later, his mother said, "Your [former] father-in-law lives in the neighborhood. You have divorced your wife and made a mortal enemy out of him. Don't go!" Against her wishes, he became even more committed to going. After concluding business without seeing the father-in-law, he went to the front gate of his house and peered in. Hearing the sound of women weaving, he thought about entering, but instead he decided "it would not be wise to belittle and shame them too much." They were wealthy villagers, and he expected them to try to erase their dishonor with violence: "If they treat me as a mortal enemy, I don't care how many men attack me, just so that I could be satisfied by killing [her father] Shōemon" (p. 44). These last two incidents make it clear that violent honor-bound manliness was based not on samurai models but on more universal norms of masculine behavior that were a part of villager society in Yazaemon's world.

These anecdotes reveal that Yazaemon, his commoner friends, and his enemies participated in a culture of masculinity permeated by concern for honor violence and desire for renown in martial prowess with little to distinguish it from that of the samurai. Yet there also are signs that this kind of violent honor culture faced suppression. The law forbidding violent fights no matter who was at fault, described by Ikegami as a means to reduce samurai honor violence, also applied to townsmen.[13] The resolution of the "village road" conflict reveals how institutional authority represented by the headman worked to reduce violence even at the expense of honor. For Yazaemon, the main impetus for restraining his violent behavior was the pursuit of family approval.

LEARNING RESTRAINT

Yazaemon's closing observation about his visit to his first wife's village was "When I reflected back on all this at age thirty, I thought what a senseless idiot I was!" He had clearly changed much in the intervening years and regarded this as the fruit of many years of effort at self-improvement. Between the ages of nineteen and twenty-four he tried to refrain from talking down to people, to put his heart into commerce and taking a wife, and to become more truthful and less arrogant and indulgent. At age twenty-one he connected being unable to talk well about himself with his lack of respect for others. The next year he embarked on describing his bad qualities, but he also sometimes talked about his good decisions and intelligence. He quickly noticed that people respected him more as a result of these efforts.

One spur for self-improvement was Yazaemon's goal of acquiring the family inheritance. The pattern inherited from the highly competitive and unstable Warring States environment was that the eldest son was generally preferred as heir, but, in the interests of the effective management of the inheritance, the most capable son might be chosen instead. The decision was usually based on the father's express will. Inheritance also required acknowledgment by one's community of peers as well as, in the case of rich townspeople such as the Enomoto house, recognition by the samurai rulers.[14]

Born in 1593, Yazaemon's father, also known as Yazaemon during his family headship, grew up during the era of unification wars. His eldest son, Kahei, was born in 1615 just as the Tokugawa were cementing their authority with the siege of Osaka castle and the destruction of the Toyotomi clan. But just as Tokugawa Ieyasu did not choose his eldest son to inherit the Tokugawa house headship, so too the elder Yazaemon chose not to have Kahei inherit the family fortune. For reasons unrecorded Kahei was adopted into a different merchant house, leaving competition for inheritance of the Enomoto house to the second son, Ushinosuke (who became Yazaemon, our autobiographer), and the third son, Gorōbei, born in 1631. Their conflict continued until 1679, when our autobiographer was fifty-five and domain officials forced a rapprochement between them.

The people from whom Yazaemon most wished to earn respect were his parents, both for emotional reasons and for the inheritance, but achieving this respect was extremely difficult. Yazaemon found his father tough and distant and thought that his mother hated him. His personal cultivation appears to be a quest for regaining the parental acceptance he felt he had lost at an early age. He never gained his mother's full support on his own. Almost all of his stories regarding her relate how she treated him badly because she misunderstood him. For example, at age seven he once hit a young female servant. She struck him back, which he thought improper because she was both a girl and a servant. When he told his mother what had happened, the girl's mother retorted, "That child tells lies an adult would be ashamed of." Yazaemon was shocked and disappointed that his mother believed her. He lamented that he was unable to speak reason and had to put up with the injustice in silence.

Yazaemon's father seemed more willing to be impressed by him, but he was a harsh judge who demanded much. In response, Yazaemon worked hard at the family business. When he was seventeen, his efforts having enriched the house, Yazaemon's father showed his son his will, which named Yazaemon as heir. Moved by this display of approval, Yazaemon redoubled his efforts, but retaining his parents' favor continued to be complicated by the inheritance conflict with his younger brother. When he was twenty-four, Yazaemon wrote, Gorōbei "slandered me to my mother and made her hate me because he desired to steal my inheritance of the household. His ceaseless slander to my parents caused me great difficulty." Yazaemon remarried that year, but this did not soon improve his relationship with his parents, both of whom openly expressed their dissatisfaction. His father remained free to alter the will. At this point Yazaemon first became afflicted with the digestive problems that would plague him in varying degrees for the next two decades. Because of his parents' sour attitude, the next year he worried that he might develop a reputation around town as an unfilial son, which would be "just the same as being a beast."

To impress his parents Yazaemon made obeisance to them in everyday practice and ritual, began to exercise sexual restraint, and devoted himself single-mindedly to commerce, frugality, and household success. He became proficient at the family's salt business in Edo and Kawagoe and also expanded their business to include trade in other towns and other goods as the opportunity arose. His devotion to work consumed so much of his time that he occasionally feared for his own humanity. He noticed this when his elder sister died when he was twenty: "I was working in Edo when the messenger came. When I arrived at Kawagoe my parents were crying profusely. I wanted to shed tears as well, but I was born without a deep sense of attachment and no tears would come. It is a real pity. But there is something wrong with wanting to cry when one cannot. Maybe the truth is that all I could think about was commerce" (p. 40).

By age twenty-five he had restored the family funds that had been reduced to a mere sixty-three *ryō* when he started working at seventeen, yet, he claimed, "because of my brother's slander . . . I could say words of gold and my parents would not care." Yazaemon also began to try to refrain from extramarital sex, although he was not able to achieve this goal until he was twenty-nine. He does not specify the nature of his sexual activity, nor his motivation to quit. Given that he frequently touts frugality as a virtue, and his extramarital sex was probably with prostitutes, he could have seen paying for sex as a personal indulgence that wasted hard-earned money in addition to incurring his parents' displeasure.

Yazaemon felt he had fulfilled all reasonable demands of his position. He had restored the family fortune, he held the eminent office of purveyor to the lord's wife, and his reputation in town was good. Still unable to please his parents, however, he turned to religious confirmation of and support for his virtue. He made a pilgrimage to Ise to pray that he be made a filial son to both his parents. If he were not, he asked the deities to take away his life. The following year he worked harder at commerce and made a lot of money, but because Gorōbei and one of his uncles continued to talk badly about him to his mother, their relationship had not improved. He wrote, "I thought I should kill both Gorōbei and Uncle Jiemon, but I restrained myself out of fear of heaven's punishment." When he was twenty-seven, three samurai of the domain, seeking stability in the house of one of the town's leading merchants, helped repair his relationship with his father. However, his father said, "Your mother hates you very much, so you had better go apologize." Yazaemon asked why. His father answered, "You have done no crime, but she hates you." Out of desperation, in the following year, 1652, Yazaemon made another pilgrimage to Ise, this time asking that the deities kick him to death if he were not a filial son. In his autobiography he notes with laconic satisfaction, "They did not kick me to death." At last, after an additional pilgrimage to Zenkōji temple, his relationship with his parents finally improved, which he credited to the power of the deities. At twenty-eight his future inheritance seemed secure again. At this point he gave up the desire for commit violence against his younger brother or uncle, even though he continued to hate them for their slander, noting with satisfaction years later, "I am fifty-six and have not yet made them my mortal enemies."

Yazaemon practiced these forms of self-abnegation as part of his regimen of self-control in the service of his parents and his household. His emphasis on reining in desire to the point of self-immolation in the name of duty echoes the thought of the samurai Yamamoto Tsunetomo, author of *Hagakure,* who was famous for the phrase "The way of the samurai is found in death."[15] Both Yazaemon's prayers to the deities and Tsunetomo's thoughts suggest similar goals. One obvious difference, however, is that Yazaemon's primary duty is to his parents and family, whereas Tsunetomo says that a samurai's duty must be to his lord. Although the object of self-abnegation is different, the character of the person created in this context is similar. As with the transformation of samurai, Yazaemon also gradually tamed his violent impulses in part by turning them inward in exchange for stability.

The years between 1653, when Yazaemon was twenty-nine and his parents retired, and 1658 were the most successful of his life. He continued to be called by his initial adult name Hachirōbei and did not use his father's "Yazaemon" until domain officials encouraged him to do so, but he was given money and the family home. He traveled widely and successfully on business, and he saw evidence of receiving fortune's favor when he did not die during the great Edo fire of 1657. When the fire consumed the city he fled the flames wearing five layers of clothing. After he discovered that the outside layers were burning, he and an uncle took refuge by hiding inside a large cooking hearth, where he waited out the fire having placed a large ceramic pot over his head. He and his uncle escaped, "just like the saying 'emerging from the ashes.'" Gaining the inheritance allowed Yazaemon to begin practicing his role as paterfamilias. For the first time since a brief mention in 1648 that he "took a wife from Hachiōji," his second wife suddenly emerges in the account as the object of his management and advice. He began instructing her to be dutiful to his mother, noting that if she did so karma would see that she had a dutiful daughter-in-law herself. According to Yazaemon, "I taught her day and night how to behave pleasingly, and because of this I became well thought of too. From this time I no longer engaged in licentious sex."

Believing that overcoming hardship was the way to become successful and happy with oneself, Yazaemon continued many forms of self-restraint. The social rewards for a male such as himself were success in inheritance and business and the right to manage the household; his wife, through similar self-restraint, would earn the right to have an obedient daughter-in-law someday. The link between privation and happiness is best expressed in Yazaemon's description of his conversation at his father's deathbed in 1658. Stroking his father's hand, Yazaemon told him how as a child he had hated all of the difficult and degrading work that his father had made him do, and how he had almost run away from home to escape hardship. But now, Yazaemon confessed, he appreciated that hardship, which was "strangely now worth a thousand gold coins," because it had made him successful and happy. Yazaemon's father responded, "I am so happy that you did not run away then. But I regret that maybe if you had run away, overcoming hardship after hardship, you might even be happier now." Although this exchange may sound lugubrious, I think that Yazaemon viewed this moment of reconciliation as a quintessential expression of wisdom that linked emotionally distant parental love and training to personal hardship and success. As we shall see, in later years Yazaemon himself remained constantly dissatisfied with his eldest son and heir.

MIDLIFE CRISIS

The year 1658 began a period that would test this maudlin equation of hardship with happiness and success. Not only Yazaemon's father but also his mother fell ill and died that year. Yazaemon's wife cared for her mother-in-law faithfully without the reward of enjoying the womanly forms of household headship. Shortly after her mother-in-law's funeral, "like a bow that had been strung for too many years [and] suddenly weakens," Yazaemon's wife fell ill and died at the age of twenty-seven. The sudden loss of the three most important people in his recently successful life sent Yazaemon into years of depression and illness. "My power declined and I became helpless," he wrote. "It was hard for me to stand up or even to speak."

Yazaemon had difficulty engaging in work or handling his family affairs. As chance would have it, the cold, wet summer of 1658 was particularly bad for the production of salt and his business. He received a new wife from Edo by the end of the year, but his illness and unhappiness worsened. He had a hard time standing up, and he coughed all the time. He noted that his sexual desire declined, as did his desire to meet people. One of his two daughters from his second wife died in 1660. Including servants, nine household members had died since 1658. His younger brother again began stirring up trouble and gathering relatives into his camp, hoping, Yazaemon suspected, that he might benefit should his elder brother die. Whenever Yazaemon tried to argue he would begin coughing and be unable to speak. His servants, he said, "began to take me lightly and did not follow my orders." Yazaemon would get so angry that he would go deaf, and he cut off all relations with Gorōbei. To cure himself of the illness that he blamed for his business and family troubles, he became obsessed with his health and attempts at recovery. He watched his diet, consulted doctors, and took daily doses of medicine. He frequented the hot springs at Atami and began mental practices to balance his life energy and prevent it from rising to his head, which he saw as a cause of his illness.

ELDER WISDOM

Yazaemon entered a new stage in his life in 1664, at age forty. This period began with the recovery of his health, "after taking more than a thousand packets of medicine over six years." He felt as if his life force had increased and, thanks to this, he could effectively manage social relations again. Praise from two domain elders helped him in his recently worsening struggles with his relatives. By this time he thought that not only his younger brother but also his elder brother and two of his uncles were undermining his position in the hope of wresting the household inheritance away from him or his young son if he died. His improving health allowed him to deal with this threat to his leadership, even when they tried to disrupt the wedding he sponsored for his younger sister. The tide had turned. In the following year he wrote about his younger brother that "Gorōbei's evil dealings became known throughout Kawagoe, and I came to be known as genuine." At the same time Yazaemon secured more declarations of support from the most powerful samurai of the domain. People talked about him as "honest and unselfish, a person without bad intentions nor lascivious, a prudent person who observes decorum, and whose business is laudable." These qualities were certainly his ideal of the mature self and were indeed appropriate to the ideal of merchant masculinity as it came to be expressed in the eighteenth century. The rewards were substantial: in 1669 his business was "at its peak." At age fifty-two, in 1676, he rebuilt at great expense the family home and storehouses as a testimony to his success.

By reining in his behavior, Yazaemon gained both a sense of security within the domainal order and, in his own mind, the right to control the members of his family with the goal of preserving the Enomoto household for generations. His benevolent paternalism required everyone else in the household to act submissively, but of course this did not always happen. As master of the house he assumed that his wisdom was superior, and he even thought that he should instruct the women of the house in their work. His third wife was a particular trial, and in 1670 he complained to her father that she had not obeyed him for thirteen years. She became somewhat meeker as a result, and he decided not to retain his pent-up anger, because, he thought, she was just like a child who needed constant direction. The link in his mind between his wife's performance and the proper functioning of his own self is oddly revealed in his complaint about his lack of complete mastery: "She has gone against my directions for many years, and that is why I have declined so in health."

Despite the marital discord, Yazaemon's third wife bore him many children, and he took great interest in parenting and planning for the household's future. In 1679 he remodeled a store building for his eighteen-year-old son to live in and arranged for him a marriage with Omuku, the twelve-year-old daughter of another leading local merchant. Thinking his son, like his wife, was stubborn and hard to control, he wrote up a list of advice and presented it to him the next year. It is a curious document that combines his personal history ("I quit licentious sex at age twenty-nine") with instructions on frugal dress, the value of comporting oneself with dignity, and various injunctions: one should go to bed early and rise with the servants; one should raise children with neither hardship nor selfishness; one should stay away from gambling, prostitutes, and investments in gold mines. He gave a final warning against popular entertainments and songs, saying that they were full of lies and intriguing story lines that went against all proper reason. Yazaemon remained dissatisfied with his son and seems to have been as reluctant to give praise as his own father had been. In 1683 he wrote that he was happy with six of his seven children, but his eldest son and heir "is poor at business. I teach him, but he does not understand. He does not make use of my advice, and this is very troubling."

Yazaemon also instructed his daughters, with results that were more to his satisfaction. In 1680, when his fourteen-year-old daughter Otake was wed, he sent her off with a written statement outlining how a woman should behave. Perhaps remembering that he had indulged in licentious sex before age twenty-nine, he told her not to be jealous of her husband and also not to think about men herself. He told her not to lie and to be obedient to everyone. He even directed her on childcare, telling her to change diapers frequently, wash the children's kimonos regularly, and not feed them too much, because that was the source of most illness. His most charming piece of advice was on how to deal with life energy rising to the head, a health affliction that could be brought on by anger. "Close your eyes and calm your spirit. Then start thinking down at the bottom of your feet about the funniest things in your life. If you think of two or three, and the bottom of your feet are continually laughing, then your life energy will come down and you will avoid illness. Doing this every day is the best preventative medicine." He then told her he would give her seven books of learning, including the predictable *Mirror for Women* and *Imagawa Letter*, commonly used as a copybook, but also, less predictably, an early philosophical text by Kumazawa Banzan, *Yamato saimei*. This treatise contained extensive advice on good government and economic management, the sort of public affairs not generally considered the province of women at the time. He expected her to read them but not become proud, and he recommended that she ask her husband to explain them to her. If that coda were not enough to reveal his belief in a generalized male superiority, he also wrote that even men in their forties would not stand up to much scrutiny of their wisdom, so all the more some "young girl will not accord with reason." In sum, she should not even consciously aim to please people but just be obedient. Being fifty-three now and beyond what he saw as the dubious forties, he must have thought himself in accord with reason, because he wrote that she should have all her future children copy his sheet of advice and to cherish the original as a memento of her father. He liked his advice so much that later he presented a copy to his other daughter, Osan, on her betrothal.

Yazaemon had achieved the role of paterfamilias, a fine place in the new order, thanks to key support from senior domain officials. He achieved his crowning moment of security in 1668, when he had his first private audience with the domain lord. To this mark of distinction government officials added the recommendation that he begin using his father's name, Yazaemon. Not surprisingly, Yazaemon began writing in effusive support of the order that treated him so well. In 1682 he had his son copy a proclamation by Tokugawa Tsunayoshi and then wrote, "In my humble opinion, he is a great holy man of Japan. We are so grateful to have this shogun!" He decried people who criticized Tsunayoshi as "stupid."

Yazaemon also began recording his and others' opinions on a merchant morality designed to promote the stability of the end-of-the-century status system. On the one hand, nothing was more important than that merchants should be devoted to the family occupation. On the other, they should live free from ostentation and luxury. He ecstatically quoted a wealthy merchant's pronouncement on the dual way of his status group: "Townspeople should not give up the desire for profit. That is their family occupation. They should not succumb to pride and luxury. No matter how wealthy, they should not depart from being townspeople. You should hang these two principles around your neck and never forget them. Yesterday Isoda Chōemon, a man worth a hundred thousand *ryō*, said this." Yazaemon added with satisfaction, "Yes, this is the enlightened way of the merchant, as if the *kirin* has appeared!" referring to the beast of Chinese myth, so holy that it killed nothing but still lived for a thousand years. Longevity within the order was the goal, and the pursuit of profit and personal frugality, the dual way of the merchant, would preserve it. For well-off townspeople of the late seventeenth-century order, as for the samurai, personal restraint and respect for order were increasingly important.

Yazaemon's autobiography speaks in the rare voice of a seventeenth-century merchant concerning daily life and culture. It suggests that we need further enquiry into the character of pacification and the role of status in the seventeenth-century transition to stable Tokugawa rule. It also opens for future investigation the question of how representative it might be of commoner masculinity cultures in other parts of Japan. Yazaemon's record is that of a wealthy merchant and thus speaks little to less well-off townspeople. After all, people lower in the hierarchy of security and power were less likely to produce or desire to hold to the ideals of the advantaged.

The autobiography also suggests that by the end of the seventeenth century notions of manliness were becoming more differentiated along status lines as the division of labor in hereditary households also stabilized. According to the samurai dual way of arms and letters, warriors were to continue to profess adherence to honor violence and military skills, even if increasingly severe restrictions on the use of such violence meant that they rarely or never used it during the Great Peace, while merchants were to practice the pursuit of profit and manifest frugality and humility. Hence, Yazaemon looked back on his youthful violent defense of his honor as the actions of a "senseless idiot," while an eighteenth-century samurai youth might have continued to be trained to threaten and possibly enact such behavior.

The stabilization of the division of labor into hereditary households permitted or required by the peace and stability of the seventeenth century led to differing ideals of masculinity along status lines toward the end of that century. Centuries of instability and the sixteenth-century civil war had doubtless created a type of man appropriate to that age: adaptable, competitive, and ready to act violently to protect or advance his interests. The Warring States era had its notions of status difference, but the obscure and common origins of so many seventeenth-century daimyo and samurai houses, and the "samurai" origins of so many seventeenth-century commoners, are a testament to the instability of ascribed status identities at that time, as Yazaemon hints in his depiction of his ancestors—tough fighters and merchants both.

Following the wars of unification at the end of the sixteenth century and the fall of Osaka castle in 1615, political stability began to take hold, but the associated cultural changes in masculine behavior for villagers, townsmen, and samurai likely took generations, a process that paralleled Yazaemon's maturation. All statuses were subject to seventeenth-century policies of cultural pacification that aimed at taming violent honor-bound masculinity. Hideyoshi's sword hunt and his "realm at peace" edicts constitute early manifestations. Various daimyo—and later Tokugawa—injunctions against fighting were also part of this promotion of a culture of masculine civility. The separation of warrior and peasant is a theme in the historiography of this era, but perhaps it should not be narrowly recounted only in terms of policies of sword confiscation, pulling samurai out of the villages, and putting them into cities, because this separation also required an ideological transformation of masculinity into differently gendered status identities.

The seventeenth century thus appears less as the era of the taming of the samurai than an era of the taming of masculinity. Two centuries later, the Meiji-era efforts at socializing males into a nationalist and imperialistic masculinity invoked a rhetoric of samuraization. An endless list of scholars since has contributed to the naturalization of the seductive notion that there had to be an intrinsic relation between samurai culture and essential "Japaneseness."[16]

My analysis of Yazaemon's autobiography shows that distinctions between the masculinities of different status groups developed by the eighteenth century were the ideological products of powerful members in each status group who strove to secure their advantageous position in the hereditary status order. Yazaemon lived during a transitional period and wrote revealingly of changes that he experienced in his lifetime. Subsequent writers, by contrast, tended more often to naturalize and dehistoricize differences created in the course of the seventeenth century.[17] For that reason, Yazaemon's autobiography reminds us that the masculinities produced by status distinctions were not natural but constituted over time, and they had to be constituted under pressure—political, social, and economic.

NOTES

1. "Mitsugo yori no oboe," found in Enomoto 2001, pp. 15–120. Yazaemon's childhood name was Ushinosuke, and he took the name Hachirōbei at his coming-of-age ceremony at age twenty. He took his father's name, Yazaemon, when he was forty-four. For convenience I will refer to him as Yazaemon throughout.

2. From Ōno's introduction in Enomoto 2001, pp. 4–9.

3. Ōno 1969; Nagura 1980. I am indebted to Ōno's work for a basic understanding of this difficult text, and to Nagura for his thoughtful exploration of Yazaemon's family ideology.

4. Collections such as the thirty-volume *Nihon shomin seikatsu shiryō shūsei* (1968–84) and the ten-volume *Nihon toshi seikatsu shiryō shūsei* (1975–77) include no seventeenth-century merchant diaries or autobiographies, with the exception of Katsurai Soan's diary in volume 3 of the latter series. Katsurai, at the time known as Negoroya Matasaburō, wrote this surviving portion when he was only eleven to thirteen years old. It reveals the life of the intellectually precocious son of a wealthy castle town sake merchant.

5. Miyamoto 1977 [1941]; Miyamoto 1982; Hayashi 1992, pp. 43–88, 209–62.

6. Inoue and Arima 1905, vol. 1, p. 289.

7. Ikegami 1995.

8. Miyamoto 1982, p. 21.

9. I explore this general phenomenon in detail in Roberts 1998, esp. pp. 117, 132, 178, 193.

10. Enomoto 2001, p. 17. Because the autobiography is brief and is organized by year and his age, hereafter I will not cite page numbers when the year or his age is noted. Page numbers, when provided, will appear in the text.

11. Enomoto 2001, pp. 17, 134.

12. A type of misfit identity common in the early seventeenth century, *otokodate* were youths who liked to dress outlandishly and pick fights. More common terms for them were *datemono* and *kabukimono*. See Ikegami 1995, pp. 203–11.

13. Ikegami 1995, pp. 141–45, 206, 211.

14. Nagura 1980, p. 32; Ōtake 1974, pp. 26–28, 33–35.

15. Yamamoto 1979, p. 17; Saiki, Okayama, and Sagara 1974, p. 220.

16. For example, see Miyamoto 1982 and Kasaya Kazuhiko's work on samurai culture and its relation to "Japaneseness" (Kasaya 1993), although the list of works is nearly endless.

17. This is why it is dangerous to take eighteenth-century documents, such as Mitsui Takafusa's famous *Chōnin kōkenroku* of 1728, as reflecting the values of the earlier eras it discusses.

REFERENCES

Enomoto Yazaemon (Ōno Mitsuo, ed.). 2001. *Enomoto Yazaemon oboegaki: Kinsei shoki shōnin no kiroku.* Heibonsha.

Hayashi Reiko, ed. 1992. *Nihon no kinsei 5 Shōnin no katsudō.* Chūo Kōronsha.

Ikegami, Eiko. 1995. *The Taming of the Samurai: Honorific Individualism and the Making of Modern Japan.* Cambridge, MA: Harvard University Press.

Inoue Tetsujirō and Arima Sukemasa, eds. 1905. *Bushidō sōsho,* vol. 1. Hakubunkan.

Kasaya Kazuhiko. 1993. *Samurai no shisō: Nihongata sōshiki, tsuyosa no kōzō.* Nihon Keizai Shinbunsha.

Miyamoto Mataji. 1977 [1941]. *Kinsei shōnin ishiki no kenkyū.* Kōdansha.

———. 1982. *Nihon chōnindō no kenkyū: Akinaigokoro no genten o saguru.* Kyoto: PHP Kenkyūjo.

Nagura Tetsuzō. 1980. "Shōninteki 'ie' ideorogii no keisei to kōzō: Enomoto Yazaemon Oboegaki ni tsuite." *Nihonshi kenkyū* 209: 30–68.

Nihon shomin seikatsu shiryō shūsei. 1968–84. 30 vols. San'ichi Shobō.

Nihon toshi seikatsu shiryō shūsei. 1975–77. 10 vols. Gakushū Kenkyūsha.

Ōno Mitsuo. 1969. "*Enomoto Yazaemon oboegaki* ni tsuite: Sono shōkai to kare no shōgyō katsudō yori mita kinsei zenki no shijo kōzō no kentō." *Shiryōkan kenkyū kiyō* 2: 59–132.

Ōtake Hideo. 1974. "Nihon." In *Kōza kazoku,* vol. 5, *Sōzoku to keishō,* ed. Aoyama Michio et al. Kōbundō.

Roberts, Luke S. 1998. *Mercantilism in a Japanese Domain: The Merchant Origins of Economic Nationalism in 18th-Century Tosa.* New York: Cambridge University Press.

Saiki Kazuma, Okayama Taiji, and Sagara Tōru, eds. 1974. *Mikawa monogatari, Hagakure.* Iwanami Shoten.

Yamamoto Tsunetomo. 1979. *Hagakure: The Book of the Samurai,* trans. William Scott Wilson. Kodansha International.

3 Empowering the Would-be Warrior

Bushidō and the Gendered Bodies of the Japanese Nation

Michele M. Mason

The Japanese warrior's powerful hold on the social imagination persists despite the vast and growing temporal, political, and cultural distance between the eras of samurai rule and today.[1] At the turn of the twenty-first century, for instance, with the millennial crossroads inspiring reflection on past and future, Japan witnessed something of a "*bushidō* boom." In certain circles this invigorated discussions about the state of the nation, the importance of "the Japanese spirit," and the usefulness of "samurai values." The centerpiece of this boom was a new Japanese translation of Nitobe Inazō's (1862–1933) *Bushidō: The Soul of Japan* on the occasion of its hundredth anniversary.[2] A newer treatise on the subject, *Why Bushidō Now? (Ima naze bushidō ka)* was ranked among Yaesu bookstore's top ten books of 2000. *New Bushido (Atarashii bushidō)*, by Hyōdō Nisohachi (1960–), joined the growing collection in 2004, and one book with a less obvious title, 2005's *Our Country's Dignity (Kokka no hinkaku)*, promoted the idea of "*bushidō* over democracy."

Underpinning much modern writing on *bushidō* is a premise that assumes a symbiotic relationship between individual and national bodies, the condition of one determining the other. Sometimes this is articulated as a physical and spiritual inheritance that is proof positive of Japan's strength and moral rectitude. More often, unfavorable habits or weaknesses in individual bodies serve as the barometer of decline or crisis in the national body, and problems plaguing the nation-state register as symptoms of deeper troubles within the citizenry. The cure, the authors suggest, rests on a prescription of *bushidō* that promises to fortify and heal both. Sabine Frühstück's work on sexological discourse in the modern era emphasizes this assumption of an inexorable connection between citizens' bodies and the national body. Her discussion of the fact that the emerging health system focused in large part on men's bodies and that "the condition of the 'Japanese nation's body and soul' . . . seemed critical in relation to both the defense against Western colonial powers and the handling of East Asia" is particularly instructive in that it contextualizes the construction of masculinity within a complex domestic and international sociopolitical history.[3]

Below I examine works addressing *bushidō* by three figures who, in decidedly different but clearly gendered ways, shaped images of both the body politic (the Japanese nation-state) and the ideals of physical bodies (modern Japanese "samurai"/citizens) as they responded to their changing historical, political, and social environments. The first and most famous is Meiji-era (1868–1912) author, educator, politician, and diplomat Nitobe Inazō, whose legacy can be found in many of the central arguments of twenty-first-century reworkings of *bushidō*. The long-lasting renown of Nitobe, a man of considerable influence during Japan's modernizing period, is attested to by the fact that his visage graced the five-thousand-yen note for twenty years (1984–2004). Next, Mishima Yukio (1925–70), the famous writer of fiction and drama, actor, and provocative public personality, offers us a postwar articulation of the "samurai." Mishima, a serious contender for the Nobel Prize for Literature, who had more than ten major works translated into English before his stunning suicide in 1970, was, like Nitobe, well known at home and abroad. Finally, I turn to one of the contemporary "Bushido boom" writers, Hyōdō Nisohachi, a self-proclaimed military theorist who has neither the influence nor the reputation of Nitobe or Mishima. Still, because Hyōdō's interpretation of *bushidō* represents a strain of contemporary politics that promotes a remilitarization of Japan—one of the most contentious debates in Japan today—it deserves critical attention.

The elusive object of my study, *bushidō* demands some words of clarification. Notions of *bushidō* have necessarily always been complex, changing, and contradictory idealizations of an ostensibly fixed and universally practiced ethical code of the samurai. Writers commonly point to an exemplary model of a remote historical moment while lamenting the failings of morals, society, and governance in their own age. Yet none of the samurai "house codes" *(kakun)*, philosophical treatises, and moral guidebooks produced during the centuries of samurai rule, taken together or separately, can be said to illustrate a comprehensive and consistent articulation of *bushidō*. Most do not use even use the term. In fact, B. H. Chamberlain's provocative statement about Nitobe's *Bushidō: The Soul of Japan* of 1900 reads like today's critique of an invented tradition.

> So modern a thing is it that neither Kaempfer, Siebold, Satow, nor Rein—all men knowing their Japan by heart—ever once allude to it in their voluminous writings. The cause of their silence is not far to seek: Bushido was unknown until a decade or two ago.
>
> *The very word appears in no dictionary, native or foreign, before the year 1900.* Chivalrous individuals of course existed in Japan, as in all countries at every period; but Bushido, as an institution or a code of rules, has never existed. The accounts given of it have been fabricated out of whole cloth, chiefly for foreign consumption. (italics in original)[4]

The debates about and mystifications of the "origins" of *bushidō* continue to this day precisely because *bushidō* has invariably been a dynamic constellation of ideals and not an immutable, coherent doctrine.

In their respective times, Nitobe, Mishima, and Hyōdō perceived "crises" and constructed concepts of *bushidō* that fused, in unexpected ways, national and gender identities. Contrary to received notions about *bushidō* as a wholly masculine trope, their writings demand that we recognize the strategic use of "femininity" in visions of *bushidō* and, by extension, Japan's national identity. The construction of gender invariably involves a process that dichotomizes masculinity and femininity, making their signification possible. Thus, any notion of manliness is unintelligible outside its opposition to and/or interplay with a feminine "other." Given the unequal power relations embedded within gender constructions, articulations of masculinity typically equate a perceived disempowerment or debasement of men with their "feminization." A lack of hegemonic male/masculine traits, whether in individuals or nations, regularly represents a lamentable fate, evidence of decline, or a symptom of illness. However, these writers express a gamut of strategic gender representations that offer both "negative" and "positive" portrayals of femininity and masculinity and conflate and color gendered characteristics in unusual ways. Thus, in addition to the predictable hyper-masculinized warrior, a reader discovers Nitobe's description of the highest form of *bushidō* as "feminine" and "innocent," Mishima's advocacy of "manly beauty," and Hyōdō's depiction of the Emperor as an "older sister."

Nitobe, Mishima, and Hyōdō's fluid, ambivalent, and even contradictory repertoires of *bushidō* must be considered within equally fluid, ambivalent, and contradictory domestic and international discourses on manliness, civilization, and national identity. Here I stress that these three men's constructions of *bushidō* are no less stable or authentic than any other trope of masculinity. Because all versions of masculinity (and *bushidō*) are shaped by and shape complex networks of social, economic, and political power, the usefulness of analyzing representations of masculinity lies in what specific formulations of masculinity reveal about how they interpreted their dynamic historical moment.

When Abigail Solomon-Godeau, the provocative scholar of feminist theory and French visual culture, cautions us not to accept a monolithic or static version of masculinity, she directs us toward a productive approach to both masculinity and *bushidō.* She asserts that "masculinity, however defined, is, like capitalism, *always* in crisis. And the real question is how both manage to restructure, refurbish, and resurrect themselves for the next historical turn" (italics in original).[5] An examination of the ways Nitobe, Mishima, and Hyōdō attempt to "restructure, refurbish, and resurrect" *bushidō* affords us provocative examples of how the "instability" of gender reflects the continually shifting grounds of national identity formation within domestic and international power politics.

BUSHIDŌ: THE MODERN JAPANESE INHERITANCE AND THE MOTOR FORCE OF THE NATION

It is often repeated that as a youth Nitobe Inazō proclaimed it his mission to be a "bridge across the Pacific." To that end he spent seven years abroad: three years in the United States, during which he became a Quaker and met his American wife, Mary, and another four years in Germany, where he earned a PhD. From 1901 to 1903 he served as a colonial administrator in Taiwan, and then he returned to Japan to hold various posts, including professor of law at Kyoto Imperial University, principal of the elite First Higher School, and the first chair of colonial policy at Tokyo Imperial University. Nitobe attempted to fulfill his self-appointed "duty" to foster communication between Japan and Western nations through his prolific writing as a journalist and as Under-Secretary-General of the League of Nations, a position to which he was appointed in 1920.

At the turn of the century, Nitobe produced numerous works on the samurai and his code of ethics, *bushidō.* Addressing the question of what Japan's moral system could possibly be, absent Christianity, Nitobe published *Bushidō: The Soul of Japan* in 1900. Written in English specifically for a Western audience, it gained best-seller status when it was reissued in 1905 on the heels of Japan's military triumph over Russia. In the early 1900s Nitobe also contributed numerous short English-language articles to the *Osaka Mainichi* (later collected and published as *Thoughts and Essays*) that reveal his perpetually changing stance as he repositions Japan vis-à-vis the West and its colonial possessions. Sometimes Nitobe casts

Japan as the virile protector of emasculated nations and sometimes as the "masculine" partner of the United States, while at other moments he describes "feminine" samurai as the apotheosis of civilization.[6]

In 1905 Japan could boast of multiple military victories, first in the Sino-Japanese War (1894–95) and then in the Russo-Japanese War (1904–5). Central to Japan's military success was the imperial project that deeply shaped Japan's political, economic, social, and cultural formation at the time. A mere five years into the new century Hokkaido's image as a foreign "frontier" was fading into the past and Okinawa's place in the nation was becoming ever more naturalized through anthropological discourses that sought there the origins of the Japanese "race." Taiwan was already ten years a colony. Assigned protectorate status, Korea was well on its way to becoming the Japanese empire's next colony.

Simultaneously, Japanese were keenly aware of their tenuous position and identity in relation to Western nations. After the Russo-Japanese War, Bishop William Awdry, a long-time resident of Japan, expressed discomfort with the new spotlight on Japan in the paternalistic and arrogant tone common to much of the writing on Japan by Westerners of the day: "The sudden revulsion of feeling has come when those who, not a generation ago, were thought of as pretty, interesting, artistic, little dolls or children, fantastic and whimsical, unsettled in purpose and loose in morals, dishonest in business, and cruel if you scratched through the skin, 'great in little things and little in great things,' have come out on the broad stage of the world."[7] It was precisely this kind of portrayal of Japan that had earlier provoked Nitobe to write his treatise on *bushidō.* He expected that *Bushidō: The Soul of Japan* might function not as a mere interpretation of Japanese society, but, more critically, as a rebuttal to the condescending Western discourse that depicted Japanese as childish, backwards, devious, and politically inept.

Nitobe proudly fixes the source of Japan's economic and military triumphs in a native tradition, "the way of the samurai," by crafting impressive, if "flowery," metaphors that equate *bushidō* with natural vegetation particularly suitable to the "environment" of Japan. He begins his argument with the following: "Chivalry is a flower no less indigenous to the soil of Japan than its emblem, the cherry blossom; nor is it a dried-up specimen of an antique virtue preserved in the herbarium of our history. It is still a living object of power and beauty among us; and if it assumes no tangible shape or form, it not the less scents the moral atmosphere, and makes us aware that we are still under its spell."[8] The Yamato spirit, he claims, is in its essence an "original, spontaneous outgrowth of our clime"

(1). Nitobe attributes the foundation and flourishing of the national soul to samurai ancestors. He writes, "What Japan was she owed to the samurai. They were not only the flower of the nation but its root as well. All the gracious gifts of Heaven flowed through them" (159–60).

Having planted the seeds of Japan's prosperity in *bushidō*, Nitobe argues that these knightly values still thrive, housed in the bodies of modern Japanese citizens. Once a doctrine of the elite samurai class, *bushidō* spirit now manifests itself corporeally in *all* Japanese citizens. Through the fuzzy logic of biological inheritance, the ethos of the samurai is "passed down" in the bodies of all citizens irrespective of their previous status affiliations or the temporal break with the past. Outwardly the powerful samurai code is invisible, but it remains, nonetheless, *"a law written on the fleshly tablets of the heart"* (5). "Scratch a Japanese of the most advanced ideas," Nitobe writes, "and he will show a samurai" (189). In a trickle-down system, *bushidō* acts "as leaven among the masses, furnishing a moral standard for the whole people" (163). Thus, the ancestors are passed on through Japanese bodies, regardless of status, class, or gender, and the legacy of their spirit resides in living flesh.

Bushidō, however, does more than simply uplift the common people and unify the country. Being thus embodied in national subjects, *bushidō* defines and propels the modern Japanese nation. The invisible essence of Japan's yesteryear guides the Japanese and Japan in concrete ways. "An unconscious and irresistible power, *Bushidō* had been moving the nation and individuals. . . . Unformulated, *Bushidō* was and still is the animating spirit, the motor force of our country" (171). It is to this "animating spirit" that Nitobe credits Japan's victory in the Sino-Japanese War. "What won the battles on the Yalu, in Corea and Manchuria, were the ghosts of our fathers, guiding our hands and beating in our hearts. They are not dead, these ghosts, the spirits of our warlike ancestors. To those who have eyes to see, they are clearly visible" (188–89). Nitobe's recurring theme is, thus, the ancient Japanese spirit dwelling in modern Japanese bodies. An invisible inner ethic dictates outward behavior and decisions. Regardless of whether the citizens are aware that a manly inheritance resides in their hearts, hands, and under their skin, it drives the nation on its course toward "civilization" and success.

As might be expected, one of the dominant tropes used to define *bushidō* is manliness. In the previous quotation, the "warlike ancestors," identified as "fathers," are clearly gendered as male. Even though Nitobe devotes a long chapter to women in *Bushidō: The Soul of Japan*, the models of "chivalry," both Japanese and Western, are always men. For Nitobe, manliness is predominantly defined and refined through vigorous training and the physical challenges of battle. In an essay entitled "Post-Bellum Work," published in 1905, Nitobe reminds his reading public that "peace is not in itself an absolute blessing. It is rather a condition of social and moral well-being. To attain higher ends, there must be strenuous effort and this is engendered by war."[9] In his earlier work, *Bushidō: The Soul of Japan,* he celebrates the martial spirit of the hardy warriors of the Warring States period as the epitome of manliness: "In Japan as in Italy 'the rude manners of the Middle Ages' made of man a superb animal, 'wholly militant and wholly resistant.' And this is why the sixteenth century displays in the highest degree the principal quality of the Japanese race" (21). Within the discourse of social Darwinism, the samurai of the sixteenth century comes to represent the perfection of Japanese men and the Japanese people. However, to posit the sixteenth-century soldier as the ideal Japanese male was not to imply that modern Japanese men and their nation were any less virile. Their virility had been proven through the victories in the Sino-Japanese and the Russo-Japanese wars. For Nitobe, what differentiated the modern Japanese male from his earlier counterpart was that he embodied the most elevated level of civilization while retaining the warrior core.

In this way Nitobe is not unlike his contemporary Theodore Roosevelt (1858–1919), who defined manliness through the notion of "strenuous life." For both men, manhood is cultivated and civilizations evolve only through the physical test of combat. If Roosevelt found his salvation in the image of the rough and rustic cowboy who honed his masculinity in battle with Indians on the Western frontier, Nitobe found it in the militant samurai of the Warring States era. Much like Roosevelt, who held that the ideal specimen of a male of the "American race" was a combination of conventional Victorian civility and restraint on the one hand and primordial virility on the other, Nitobe's definition of manliness rests on the balance between what scholar Gail Bederman denotes as "civilized manliness" and "primitive masculinity."[10]

Maintaining the balance between the two elements proved precarious. Evidence of "overcivilized decadence," often associated with a modern urban lifestyle, provokes grave concern. Even while lauding Japan's successes in *Bushidō: The Soul of Japan,* Nitobe senses an impending danger to *bushidō,* seemingly immanent in a rapidly changing society dominated by "quibbling lawyers and gibbering politicians" (185). On one page Nitobe laments that "knightly virtues" and "samurai pride" are fading away, and on the next he is close to despair, claiming, "Add to this the progress of popular instruction, of industrial arts and habits, of wealth and city-life,—

then we can easily see that neither the keenest cuts of samurai sword nor the sharpest shafts shot from Bushido's boldest bows can aught avail" (184). Yet overall the tone of *Bushidō: The Soul of Japan* is celebratory, positing Japan as a moral and political equal of the West.

Nitobe's configurations of *bushidō* both bolstered and were bolstered by notions of Japanese nationhood. Over the first decade of the twentieth century, they were nuanced according to how he positioned Japan vis-à-vis its colonial entities and the West. On the one hand there is the predictable emphasis on manliness. In several commentaries Nitobe rationalizes Japanese expansion and imperialism and promotes Japan's responsibility to the "less fortunate" nations through a civilizing mission. In "Post-Bellum Work" he makes an obvious reference to Rudyard Kipling's poem "The White Man's Burden" (1899) by coining the cumbersome phrase "the Brown Japanese Man's burden" to refer to Korea. In this essay Nitobe proposes seven goals on which the Japanese government and nation should set their sights in the days after the stunning victory over Russia. Urgent goal number two calls for the "settlement of Corea." Nitobe is convinced that Japan has a responsibility to "resuscitate" Korea and the Korean people, who lack masculine traits and skills: "A poor effeminate people, with no political instinct, with no economic 'gumption,' with no intellectual ambition, is become the Brown Japanese Man's burden. Something must be done to resurrect a dead nation."[11] By constructing Korea as Japan's feminized "other," Nitobe implies that Japan is *not* effeminate, but rather typically male, in other words, astute in politics, economics, and intellectual pursuits.

Moreover, Nitobe regularly attempted to resituate Japan outside the realm of potential "burden" in order to confirm Japan's newfound power, which he knew derived from its status as a colonizer rather than the colonized. In "Post-Bellum Work," he simultaneously readjusts Japan's place among advanced Western nations and portrays Japan as a beacon of civilization in Asia:

> Our political relations with foreign countries will become closer in every way. Russia, which has been in the habit of despising us, has now learned to do otherwise. Germany and France, which have never taken us seriously, will cease to look upon us as a joke. England and America, which have patronized us as a child-nation, will regard us as an adult. The whole of Asia, which has looked upon us with suspicion and condemned us as traitors to Asiatic tradition, will follow us as their guide.[12]

Nitobe bids farewell to hateful, condescending, and discriminatory treatment by Western nations. Instead, Japan is now "grown up" enough to take the mantle of leader of neighboring Asian nations. Thus, depictions of the manly Japanese nation dovetail with Nitobe's insistence that Japan, no longer a possible burden for white men, fully accepts its responsibility to benevolently take up its own "burdens."[13]

On occasion, a masculine Japan symbolized by the samurai and *bushidō* icon is enlisted to push beyond staking a claim to mere equality with the West. In "Samuraiism," Nitobe contrasts the Christian notion of love and Japanese *bushidō,* and this time Japan is overtly marked as masculine in opposition to a feminized West. Nitobe states, "True to its name, the morality of *Bushidō* was based on manhood and manliness. As the old Romans made no distinction between valor and virtue, so was *Bushidō* the apotheosis of strong manhood and of all manly qualities."[14] In this scenario, Japanese manliness stands on the same ground as that of the ancient Romans, who represent the origins of the modern Western world's symbolic power and moral superiority. In distinguishing love from *bushidō* Nitobe then asks, "Is it that the one [love] is eternally feminine and the other *[bushidō]* eternally masculine?"[15] If at the heart of Western society lie Christian morals crystallized in the one word *love,* which connotes tender affection and nurturing commonly associated with femininity, the Japanese ethics of the rough warrior class clearly falls into a masculine realm.

Still, Nitobe's *bushidō* was not static, and its masculine infusion is sometimes unexpectedly jettisoned. In 1906, less than a year after Japan's triumph over Russia, Nitobe wrote the essay "Ascent of Bushidō," in which he describes the paragons of *bushidō* as effeminate and childlike. Those qualities that Nitobe earlier associated with the purest form of *bushidō,* specifically military prowess and physical strength, are here relegated to lower levels. The crest of the "mountain of *bushidō*" is populated by samurai with characteristics hitherto associated disparagingly with the colonized "other." In this short piece, all below the crest are characterized by masculine traits and exemplified by occupations held by men only. For example, those who populate the lowest tier, the so-called "Boar samurai," have an "untamed spirit" and "undisciplined physical vigor" and brag about their brute force. They are epitomized by the "rank and file of the army during the war and the unruly element in peacetime." Military officers, governmental clerks, accountants, lawyers, and politicians consumed with petty power and cheap literature fill the various other levels. At the pinnacle, in contrast, one is greeted by "a gentler race of men—they are unsoldierlike and almost feminine in appearance and behavior. You would hardly suspect them to be samurai."[16] Furthermore, Nitobe observes,

"They play and laugh like children. . . . Their child-likeness makes a sinful conscience envious of purity."[17] Here the balance between "civilized manliness" and "primitive masculinity" is replaced by a hierarchy that privileges contained civilized femininity and innocence.

Clarity dawns at the end of this essay: "The zone where these [superior] samurai dwell is shared with the followers of Jesus."[18] This rendering of *bushidō* is Nitobe's strategic attempt to draw Japan closer to the West through Japan's connection to what we already know to be his feminized notion of Christian love. What at first seems an anomaly fits neatly into Nitobe's persistent repositioning of Japan vis-à-vis its relationships to and with the leading imperial nations of the West and its colonial possessions at the turn of the twentieth century. The various inflections of Nitobe's ideal forms of manhood, sometimes wild and masculine, sometimes masculine yet protective, sometimes feminine and childlike, are permeated with tensions arising from the need to constantly construct and reconstruct Japan's identity as it attempted to join the tail end of the age of imperialism.

However, we should not view Nitobe's lack of a consistent and coherent vision of manhood/nationhood as a failure. Nitobe's contradictory and ambivalent gendering of *bushidō* and Japanese national identity, articulated in extremely fluid configurations of masculinity/femininity, adult/child, and civilized/uncivilized, emerged within an equally contradictory and ambivalent larger international discourse on manliness, civilization, and imperialism. Through an ideology of Japan's colonial authority, Nitobe not so much resurrects as reinvents a conception of *bushidō* to refute the persistent Western discourse that defined Japan as a feminized, uncivilized, childlike country and to establish Japan as equal to the so-called advanced Western nations.

MANLY BEAUTY: THE CURE FOR JAPAN'S MODERN MALADY

Author, playwright, and actor Yukio Mishima also devoted an entire book to the subject of *bushidō*. *Yukio Mishima on Hagakure: The Samurai Ethic and Modern Japan* was published three years before his dramatic public ritual suicide in 1970. In this engagement with Yamamoto Tsunetomo's (1659–1719) Edo-period (1600–1868) text *Hagakure*,[19] Mishima attempts to offer an antidote for Japan's postwar emasculated state. Consumed with the ostensible "feminization of Japanese males today," Mishima identifies parallels to Yamamoto's time, which allows him to find the cause of emasculation in a deplorable lack of warfare. "When, breaking away from the rough-and-tumble masculinity of a nation at war, the Tokugawa *bakufu* had securely established its hegemony as a peaceful regime, the feminization of Japanese males immediately began."[20] The emasculation of men unable to hone their martial valor on the battlefield also threatens contemporary men in the "postwar" era. Despite the fact that Yamamoto prescribes "a cure too potent for the modern malady," his utopian "tale of an ideal country" (8) is, according to Mishima, worth pursuing.

Mishima's formulation of *bushidō* initially appears consistent with stereotypically masculine ideals, but because he asserts that constant, meticulous attention to one's outward appearance is the means by which one cultivates samurai virtues, he must contend with the associations of "cultivating beauty" as feminine practice. The desperate need for the remasculinization of Japanese individual bodies and the national body is understood within the framework of emasculation as a result of Westernization generally, and Americanization specifically. So, as with Nitobe, the conversation between masculinity and nation is always also a dialogue with the West.

For Mishima, Japan's shining ascent celebrated by Nitobe was long past. The path set by Japan's military victories at the turn of the century culminated in a crushing defeat in 1945. After the surrender, Mishima was tortured by the postwar ideology of peace and the "Americanization" of Japanese society, which he blamed for the emasculation of Japanese men and the Japanese nation. In *Yukio Mishima on Hagakure,* he anguishes over trends in historiography that depict Japan's role in World War II in an unfavorable light and finds hope in the "traditional" ethic of *bushidō* as formulated by Yamamoto. Mishima contends that *Hagakure,* widely read during the war but criticized and shunned in the postwar era, could serve as a "good lesson for our perverted day and age" (56). During the war *Hagakure*'s message was obvious and accepted, "like a luminescent object in broad daylight," but now, with Japan in a state of crisis, *Hagakure* promises to be a guiding beacon: "It is in pitch darkness that *Hagakure* radiates its true light" (5).

Echoing his predecessor Nitobe, Mishima insists that war best engenders masculinity, which is so crucial for the health of the nation. Yet, in postwar Japan, what Mishima considers the paragon of patriotism, the kamikaze pilots, are seen as mere tools for a deceitful and destructive wartime military regime. The modern educational system, to Mishima's chagrin, encourages philosophies of peace and creates peace-loving men, a clear symptom of the abyss into which Japan has fallen. Student protests against the United States–Japan Mutual Security Agreement brought the laudable Japanese fighting spirit to the fore, but only for a fleeting moment. After the signing of the treaty the agitators were suppressed, and the student movement died a disgraceful and dishonorable death.

As Mishima sees it, the cure for Japan's modern ills is a return to a traditional, manly samurai way of *life* that is defined first and foremost by an approach to *death*, most easily understood in terms of war, not peace. Mishima is particularly attracted to Yamamoto's phrase "The occupation of the samurai is death" (27). Since death is the primary mandate of the samurai, any fear of or attempt to evade death disqualifies the individual from that exalted rank. Peacetime Japan thus poses a serious threat to Mishima's notion of *bushidō*, which, as Roger T. Ames rightly points out, is formulated as a mode of action rather than an ethic.[21] Mishima writes, "In present-day Japan under a constitution that outlaws war, people who consider death to be their occupation objective—and this includes the National Defense Force—cannot exist, on principle" (27). In *Hagakure*, Yamamoto urges samurai to think of death morning, noon, and night and to be generous with the details with which they imagine their demise. While both Yamamoto and Mishima recognize that this is increasingly difficult in times of peace, the imperative remains to practice perpetual preparation for death. In Mishima's words, "One who in wartime employs rough and manly words appropriate to an age of war and in a time of peace words appropriate to peacetime, is not a samurai" (73).

Responding to this age of "degeneration," Mishima's argument rejects the "feminization" of Japanese society. Unlike Nitobe's conceptualization of masculinity, his emphasizes the external body. Only through the discipline and refinement of a man's outward appearance, a practice of cultivating "manly beauty," can he hope to foster a suitable inner morality. Just as Yamamoto was obsessed with various hygienic practices in the original *Hagakure*, Mishima exhorts each man to pay meticulous and exacting attention to his exterior presentation in a way that strengthens his resolve to face death bravely. A sharply dressed and groomed man thus proves that he has succeeded in accepting, even embracing, death. Irrespective of mundane obligations and despite the fact that it may be troublesome and time-consuming, this forms the central "occupation" of the samurai of yesterday or today.

Thus, death as an "occupation" for Mishima can be understood in terms of a *preoccupation* with death, constituted by daily rituals (regulated actions) that confirm a readiness to confront death. An important component of maintaining samurai valor, fastidiousness in dress and personal hygiene at first seems to be the very thing one would expect Mishima to eschew. He does, in fact, take particular umbrage at youths who talk of nothing but Cardin fashions and are obsessed with "cut[ting] a stylish figure," yet his brand of *bushidō* legitimates concern for personal appearance by connecting it to a samurai's training for death. In a section entitled "Man and Mirror," he suggests, "For a woman the mirror is a tool to be used in her daily toilette, but for a man the mirror is material for introspection" (66). What is a decidedly feminine practice, looking into the mirror, is thus transformed into a masculine mode of reflecting on the visible markers of his commitment to face death at any moment.

In a section entitled "A Morality of Appearances" Mishima contends that external appearances are a natural concern of the samurai who is "constantly mindful of his enemies." This entails grounding himself in the observant eyes of the opponent. By consistently assessing his outward appearance and manner from a vantage point outside his body, a man ensures that his honor and respectability will remain intact no matter the circumstances. A twist of logic allows Mishima to aver that the "essential characteristic is not an introspective morality but a morality concentrating on external reflection" (59–60). Thus, a samurai should always be impeccably dressed in case a discerning enemy cuts him down.

Within such a framework even cosmetics are not necessarily inconsistent with manliness. In fact, they separate the respectable samurai of old from the degenerate youths of the modern age. Mishima first cites the section in *Hagakure* on the use of cosmetics. "Men must be the color of cherry blossoms, even in death. Before committing ritual suicide, it was customary to apply rouge to the cheeks in order not to lose life color after death" (84). In order to assure the reader that attention to his appearance does not make a man feminine, he then clarifies, "It does not mean taking great care over clothing and becoming effeminate, but rather it brings together beauty and ethical goals in the greatest possible tension" (85). Constant readiness for death through attention to the physical body is what lent the samurai inner resolve. In summing up his vision of masculinity, Mishima claims, "What is beautiful must be strong, vivid and brimming with energy. This is the first principle; the second is that what is moral must be beautiful" (84). In an interesting twist on the conventional interpretation of *bushidō,* Mishima makes the external manifestation of the physical body define the interior of the samurai. One's moral fabric is thus maintained through outer garments and appearance. Mishima's manly "art of beauty" is akin to *kata,* the foundational formalized patterns of movement in martial arts that instill self-discipline and ultimately unify body and mind. To Mishima's mind, the idealized "movements" of a strict regime of hygiene and dress function simultaneously as training for and proof of a man's complete commitment to death, a perfect marriage of beauty and morality.

As is already suggested by Mishima's argument, emasculation is not articulated solely through concepts of enervated manliness, but it is also underwritten by the fear of men becoming indistinguishable from women. In Yamamoto's era this was, Mishima says, evidenced by woodblock prints in which one cannot distinguish between male and female bodies because of the similarity in their dress and hairstyle. He quotes an entertaining passage from *Hagakure* wherein a doctor claims that although the medical establishment formerly determined separate treatments for men and women due to their differing pulse rates, over time the distinction between male and female had become less clear, making it more and more difficult to know how to treat male patients. After discovering that treatments appropriate for men were no longer effective, he began applying women's treatments to them. Eventually the doctor concludes that "the world is indeed entering a degenerate stage; men are losing their virility and are becoming just like women" (18–19). Yamamoto and Mishima both lament that it seems impossible to find a "true man" anymore.

Mishima also laments that Japanese mothers have taken to spoiling their boys and turning them against their fathers. As a result, fathers are "ostracized, and the strict samurai instruction that is supposed to be handed down from father to son is completely neglected" (64). The weakening of the father's role is directly linked to the industrialization of Japanese society, which has turned fathers into machines. In Yamamoto's day increased bureaucratization of the samurai threatened their masculinity, and Mishima sees a parallel to this in his time. The Saga samurai criticized those who concentrated their energies on technical skill *(geinō)*, which Mishima interprets the following way: "What I think [Yamamoto] means is that a samurai is a total human being, whereas a man who is completely absorbed in his technical skill has degenerated into a 'function' [in English], one cog in a machine" (72). Similarly, in modern Japan "the father is reduced to a machine that brings home a paycheck" (64–65). Both men fear that male mechanization means the loss of control over their bodies to an entity outside the laws of *bushidō*.

The West, and especially the United States, figures prominently in Mishima's narrative of Japan's emasculation. Formulated in the postwar era, when Japan was not only coping with its defeat by the United States but was increasingly subjugated to the national interests of the United States, *Yukio Mishima on Hagakure* represents an attempt to conceptualize a Japanese national identity independent from Western intervention. For Mishima, his country's decline was evident in a society besotted by baseball and corrupted by Western democratic ideals, epitomized by the notion of "ladies first." Given that Mishima viewed Japan's "peace constitution" as imposed from the outside and loathed Japan's position as a junior partner, "protected" under the military umbrella of the United States, it is not surprising that he celebrates the riotous protests against the United States–Japan Mutual Security Treaty that incited the "death impulse" and invigorated his fellow citizens.

In lambasting the feminization/industrialization/Americanization of Japanese society and endorsing a mode of being that emphasizes outward appearances, Mishima perilously walks a discursive tightrope. Essentially he seeks to purify the practice of cultivating "manly beauty" from any possible associations with women or femininity. Here, Yamamoto's formulation of *bushidō* offers Mishima a masculine mode of living that not only includes mirrors, dapper dress, and rouge but can also be understood as indigenous to Japan before its dramatic confrontation with the West. So while Mishima's treatise is not a direct response to a particular challenge from a Westerner, as was the case for Nitobe's *Bushidō: The Soul of Japan*, it aims to define a manly national identity outside the sphere of influence of the United States and the West in general.

BUSHIDŌ REDUX

At first glance, Hyōdō Nisohachi seems a poor match for Nitobe and Mishima, both of whom have been recognized, studied, memorialized, and canonized.[22] Hyōdō, author of *New Bushidō*, has neither the stature nor the renown of these two men. He is a little-known self-professed scholar of military studies, author, and regular contributor to the martial arts newsletter *Budōtsūshin*. Yet Hyōdō's *New Bushidō*, whose dust jacket reads "Hey Japanese, become samurai!" is evidence that the idealized figure of the samurai and his ostensible code of ethics still have powerful appeal and offer us an opportunity to understand the ways in which *bushidō* continues to resonate in contemporary Japan. Highly cognizant of Japan's inferior position relative to the United States, Hyōdō forms a vision of *bushidō* that proceeds from a particular intersection of gender, age, and agency. Casting the emperor as "an older sister" who lacks "selfhood," symbolizing the feminized weakness of both Japan and its male population, Hyōdō defines his "new *bushidō*" as a path to the embodiment of masculine self-determination. The way of the samurai, at least as it is constructed in *New Bushidō*, is not anachronistic, historically removed, or of little consequence in modern Japan. Instead it promises a path toward individual and national empowerment. Hyōdō's assertion that until Japan possesses nuclear weapons it will not be a full-fledged (male) "adult" nation, moreover, brings *bushidō* to the center of the most pressing issues of the twenty-first century.

As can be expected, Hyōdō's articulation of *bushidō* differs in details since it addresses particular historical specificities. Yet it contains the kernels readily apparent in the works of his predecessors, namely a gendered conceptualization of the notion of *bushidō* and an engagement with Japan's place in the international arena. He directly addresses a male audience, offering them guidance for "how to live as men."[23] And if Nitobe and Mishima's works interpret internal and external embodiments of *bushidō*, Hyōdō's work lacks almost any reference to corporeality. Although the connection between the "physical and the mental" are sporadically acknowledged, the emphasis is placed on the latter. The physical body, he implies, is constituted through "selfhood" that, when healthy, serves as the basis for individual and national agency and pride. "Selfhood," however, is wholly lacking in modern Japan. Men are reduced to empty shells lacking the "honor" necessary to exercise their will, and the nation languishes in a vacuum of morals, unable to effect its own sovereignty. Awash in the headiness of Japan's victories against China and Russia in 1895 and 1905, Nitobe could afford to claim that *bushidō* was alive and well. But Hyōdō and Mishima, both in their own postwar moments, believe the values of the samurai to be "dead" or "dormant," and Japan suffers in its subordinate position to the West in general and the United States in particular. For Hyōdō, the enfeebled state of both the male population and the nation derives from Japan's dependency on U.S. military protection. His solution is to reinvigorate traditional samurai values and, notably, to acquire nuclear weapons.

Like Mishima, Hyōdō formulates his masculine conception of *bushidō* in opposition to the specter of the feminization of modern Japan. He couches his criticisms of contemporary Japan in gendered language that equates women with weakness and petty-mindedness. The term used throughout *New Bushidō* to describe the current mindset of Japanese men is the "housemaid temperament" *(jochūkonjō)*. This is first articulated in the preface, in which Hyōdō laments the unassertive attitude taken by contemporary youths toward Japan's possible need for defense against attack by neighboring countries. He abhors their casual acceptance of Japan's reliance on America and its Western allies for its security needs, claiming,

"If one is a real man *[ippashi no otoko]*, he detests such a manner of thinking" (4). By implication, "citizens" are assumed to be physically male yet compromised by their emotional femininity.

Hyōdō's attempts to engage his readers through direct challenges confirm that he offers his model of manly samurai to an explicitly male audience. Suggesting at one point that many readers might be frustrated that he has not yet offered concrete details about *bushidō* and its relevance to their lives, he guesses that they want to be told what exactly is "the path to live as men" *(otoko toshite ikiru michi)* (78). These male readers, Hyōdō imagines, are confused about why some people rule and others are ruled, or think to themselves, "I at least want to become a person who can't lose a fight" (49). Men seeking a proper way of being and acting as men should read on.

Hyōdō's conception of emasculated modern Japanese men and the nation rests on his explanation of "selfhood" *(jiga)*. He defines selfhood as "the way a person exercises reason according to unyielding standards and an unshakable moral compass regardless of objectively reasonable circumstances and power relations" (152). Not surprisingly, he stresses self-reliance and uncompromising determination. "Selfhood" means the opposite of following others blindly or forgetting one's personal mission when comparing oneself with others. For Hyōdō, this agency, most perfectly revealed in the lives of Edo-period samurai, is marked as an ideal masculine trait in contrast to a "housemaid's temperament."

Within Hyōdō's logic, the Japanese emperor, historically imagined as a father figure, is conceived of as an older sister *(ane)* (163). This designation suggests that the extent to which one might exhibit selfhood is manifested in particular intersections of gender, age, and agency. Hyōdō reasons that in a polytheistic religion the supreme being is commonly imagined as a "mother," while in a monotheistic religion it is a "father." The emperor, Japan's supreme religious figure, falls outside these categories; he cannot be seen as either mother or father. The relationship between the emperor and his subjects is still conceived in kinship terms, but he is "demoted" to that of elder sister. In this way Hyōdō emphasizes the emperor's lack of selfhood. The emperor necessarily cannot have selfhood since he, in his position as emperor, is forced to function as a puppet of the true wielders of power who exert their influence on matters of political importance. He is powerless to follow his own political desires and designs and he rules in name only (154–55).[24] The emperor's physical male body is not enough to guarantee him access to power, so he is cast neither as "father" nor as "older brother." The mother figure, while female and inferior to men, still represents some degree of agency in a way that eliminates her as a candidate. However, an older sister, even if protective and loyal, has little to no self-determination. Because he views the emperor as powerless, one might say impotent, Hyōdō relegates him to the lower echelons of the gendered family hierarchy.

According to Hyōdō, masculinity is not intrinsic to male bodies but emerges from a conscious activation of selfhood/agency. Cultivating the "spiritual values" of honor and bravery in the manner of samurai of Japan's past naturally leads to an autonomy that completes the physical male body and constitutes a "real man." One recognizes a complete man because he is master of himself and not the tool of others. He is a ruler, not ruled. Like bookends to his text, Hyōdō's preface and afterword emphasize the need to close the gap between the shameful mental state of Japanese and their magnificent *(subarashii)* physical condition. *New Bushidō* reads like a manifesto calling for Japan to "grow out of" the feminized (male) body and claim its true power through a proper realignment of its corporeal and spiritual inheritance.

The conceptualization of Japan as an effeminate dependent, symbolized by Hyōdō's gender reassignment of the emperor, is reinforced by where Hyōdō locates Japan in the global world order. Like those of Mishima, Hyōdō's concerns cannot be divorced from his understanding of Japan's relation to the West, and to the United States in particular. Japan's gross domestic product may be impressive, but to Hyōdō it signifies little in the face of Japan's inferior position as a military power. Japan's place as an economic superpower, second only to the United States, is irrefutable, but Hyōdō finds the term "economic superpower" absurd. The only benefit of economic ascendancy, and the only relevant criteria determining the difference between a super and a minor power, is the ability to invest in military protection. Japan, Hyōdō claims, is merely a "producer without sovereignty" (285). Having been misled by the "postwar educational system influenced by socialist and communist propaganda," Japanese live under the "small nation illusion" and do not demand that their nation fulfill its full sovereign potential (286).

Hyōdō concludes this line of thinking with the assertion that Japan must acquire nuclear weapons in order to manifest its proper national standing and put behind it the "housemaid temperament." "The spiritual power of a Japanese citizenry that does not attempt to possess nuclear weapons cannot satisfy the requirements of a strong nation and makes Japan a warped 'weak major power'" (285). The proof of Japan's autonomy will come when, rather than depend on the U.S. military umbrella for protection, it can negotiate its own "security" needs backed by nuclear weapons. Hyōdō asks Japanese to manifest their selfhood by both resolutely demanding that their nation obtain nuclear weapons and through the commitment and willingness to use them.[25] Only then can individual Japanese men know they are "real men" and Japan's military power equal its economic status.

Ultimately, the significance of Hyōdō's push for masculine selfhood through nuclear weapons lies not only in liberation from the United States, but also in redefining Japan's relations with Asian neighbors. In an eerie echo of the doctrine of the Greater East Asia Co-Prosperity Sphere of the 1930s and 1940s, Hyōdō suggests that the fate of other Asian nations/peoples is tied to Japan's. This sentence acquires an ominous tone when combined with his insistence on nuclear weapons. Moreover, Hyōdō takes umbrage at what he sees as China's overinflated sense of importance in that it expects certain foreign countries to use the flattering referential terms *chūgoku* and *chūka,* which mean "center of the world " and "magnificent center," respectively (171–73). According to Hyōdō, Japan's uncritical acceptance and continued use of these terms signifies its spiritual subjection through language and remains a stumbling block to regaining its honor. Encouraged by the West's "refusal" of these self-important appellations (it opts for "China" instead), Hyōdō insists on employing "Shina" (written in katakana script, which marks "foreign" words) throughout his book. The strategic use of "Shina," as with the acquisition of nuclear weapons, clears the way to reposition Japan vis-à-vis China (a nuclear state / security council member) and cure the inferiority complex Japan currently suffers.

Hyōdō's relatively marginal status does not warrant an easy dismissal. The relevance of his promotion of a "warrior spirit" and nuclear weapons must be contextualized within recent efforts to eliminate Article 9, the "no war" clause of Japan's "peace constitution." As conservative forces within Japan continue their attempts to abolish Article 9 and remilitarize, we need to be aware that *bushidō* ideology remains potent. Combined with other right-wing movements that continue to downplay Japan's imperial past and aggression during the Asia-Pacific War, it could potentially create even greater tension in the region and beyond.

Nitobe, Mishima, and Hyōdō each employ complex constructions of *bushidō* to create a narrative of an ideal past and posit its relevance to masculinity in his particular moment. Nitobe's reclamation of *bushidō* ideals was a means to boast of Japan's rapid advancement, to claim equal status with Western nations, and to highlight Japan's newfound power as an empire. In Nitobe's conception of *bushidō,* moral precepts such as courage and honor were the modern citizen's inheritance. These virtues naturally flowed in the bodies of all Japanese, and, understood as the foundations of a national consciousness, constituted the powerful if invisible force of the body politic. Mishima's and Hyōdō's works serve as clarion calls for the weakened postwar nation as it struggles to shape a new national identity under the weight of U.S. influence. For Mishima, *bushidō* is epitomized by fastidiousness with respect to one's appearance, always with an eye toward death, which produces the inner virtues expected of a samurai and modern man. The rituals devoted to the presentation of the body ensure manliness and a pure morality that could regenerate an ailing nation. Hyōdō claims that once Japanese men adopt the samurai ethic as a way of life, a newly gained "selfhood" will be embodied at the individual and national levels. Nuclear weapons, recommended as part of his "new *bushidō,*" are said to ensure Japan's full sovereignty, protect the national body/bodies from attacks by "neighbors," and secure international influence commensurate to its economic power. Whether promoted as secret tonic for military or economic potency or a panacea against national decline, each reiteration of *bushidō* is a product of original handiwork, forged within specific historical particularities with a unique mix of reappropriation.

Even though "the samurai" is an overworked cliché, its enduring popularity as a symbol of Japanese masculinity and national identity compels us to reconsider this powerful, if wholly overdetermined, icon. Associated with such virtues as honor, bravery, and sacrifice, the samurai commonly functions as a touchstone for Japanese masculinity. Yet a careful reading of these three writers confirms that constructions of *bushidō* strategically deploy "femininity" in both surprising and predictable ways. Nitobe's strategic gendering is by far the most elastic and unexpected of the three writers, even if his texts do not necessarily disrupt gender stereotypes. In his 1900 work, he emphasizes that the heyday of Japan's masculine soldierly code was forged during its era of unending war, at the same time that he postulates that all modern citizens embody *bushidō* regardless of gender. A few years later, as he jockeys about crafting Japan's identity vis-à-vis the West/United States and colonial Korea, his incarnations of *bushidō* sometimes include feminine and childlike traits linked with feminized Christian (Western) love and sometimes avoid any such references in order to argue that an "effeminate" Korea demands a masculine Japanese hand to rule it. Mishima and Hyōdō more consistently and overtly present the feminized citizen/nation in a negative light, highlighting it in opposition to their idealized masculine warrior model. On the one hand, Mishima derides young men who offer women public gestures of respect ("ladies first") and beautify themselves without a thought to a commitment to death. On the other hand, Hyōdō is contemptuous of Japan's "emasculated" citizenry with a "housemaid temperament" and a symbolic leader demoted to playing the "older sister." Their versions of *bushidō* reveal anxieties attending a perceived postmodern fragmentation of hegemonic masculinity, which are mapped onto their interpretations of the sociopolitical terrain.

The manner in which formulations of manliness and *bushidō* are, to repeat Solomon-Godeau's words, restructured, refurbished, and resurrected illustrates the complex ways the gendered bodies of the Japanese nation are deployed to negotiate international power politics. Generation after generation, promoters of *bushidō* hope to strengthen the moral fabric of the country and make a bid for expanded influence in domestic and U.S.- and Western-dominated global spheres. In our current historical moment it remains for us to keep a vigilant watch over the potential persuasive power of the new polish that authors such as Hyōdō give this well-used idea.

NOTES

1. Despite the vagueness of the English term *samurai*, I will use it in lieu of the more common Japanese word *bushi* when referring to those having hereditary military status prior to the Meiji period.

2. Nitobe's original work of 1900 was written in English.

3. Frühstück 2003, 18.

4. Powles 1995, 114.

5. Solomon-Godeau 1995, p. 70.

6. I employ the loaded term "emasculation" cautiously. While its articulation may suggest a concomitant feminization, I do not assume that this is always the case. Therefore, emasculation is not simply a synonym for feminization.

7. Ion 1995, p. 79.

8. Nitobe 1969, pp. 164–65. Subsequent reference to pages in this work are noted in parentheses in the text.

9. Nitobe 1909, p. 257. All of Nitobe's texts other than *Bushidō: The Soul of Japan* can be found in Nitobe 1909, a collection of commentaries entitled *Thoughts and Essays*.

10. See also Karlin 2002, pp. 41–77 for a discussion of "civilized" and "primitive" masculinity within the Japanese context.

11. Nitobe 1909, p. 255.

12. Nitobe 1909, p. 256.

13. See "Nitobe Inazō and Japanese Nationalism," which addresses Nitobe's nationalist and imperialist views (Oshiro 2004, pp. 61–79).

14. Nitobe 1909, p. 414.

15. Nitobe 1909, p. 423.

16. Nitobe 1909, p. 284.

17. Nitobe 1909, p. 285.

18. Nitobe 1909, p. 285.

19. The words of this samurai-turned-monk were actually written down by a follower, Tsuramoto Tashirō. Eiko Ikegami (1995, pp. 278–98) provides an important and nuanced contextualization of *Hagakure.*

20. Mishima 1978, p. 18. Subsequent reference to pages in this work are noted in parentheses in the text.

21. Ames 1995, p. 292.

22. Hyōdō Nisohachi is the pen name of Saitō Hiroshi. Hyōdō is a combination of the characters "soldier" and "head."

23. Hyōdō 2004, p. 78. Subsequent reference to pages in this work are noted in parentheses in the text.

24. For Hyōdō this has always been the case, as he claims that those emperors who sought true power/"selfhood" resigned and pulled political strings from behind the scenes *(insei)* (p. 154).

25. I understand every threat of the "use" of nuclear weapons to *be* a "use" of them in the same way that in an armed robbery, even if the weapon is not fired, it is still considered to have been "used" to perpetrate the crime.

REFERENCES

Ames, Roger T. 1995. "*Bushidō:* Mode or Ethic." In *Japanese Aesthetics and Culture: A Reader,* ed. Nancy G. Hume, 279–94. Albany: State University of New York Press.

Frühstück, Sabine. 2003. *Colonizing Sex: Sexology and Social Control in Modern Japan.* Berkeley: University of California Press.

Hyōdō Nisohachi. 2004. *Atarashii Bushidō.* Shinkigensha.

Ikegami, Eiko. 1995. *The Taming of the Samurai: Honorific Individualism and the Making of Modern Japan.* Cambridge, MA: Harvard University Press.

Ion, A. Hamish. 1995. "Japan Watchers 1903–1931." In *Nitobe Inazō: Japan's Bridge across the Pacific,* ed. John F. Howes, 79–106. Boulder: Westview Press.

Karlin, Jason G. 2002. "The Gender of Nationalism: Competing Masculinities in Meiji Japan." *Journal of Japanese Studies* 28, no. 1: 41–77.

Mishima, Yukio. 1978. *Yukio Mishima on Hagakure: The Samurai Ethic and Modern Japan,* trans. Kathryn Sparling. Tokyo: Charles E Tuttle.

Nitobe Inazō. 1909. *Thoughts and Essays.* Teibeisha.

———. 1969. *Bushido: The Soul of Japan.* Tokyo: Charles E. Tuttle.

Oshiro, George M. 2004. "Nitobe Inazō and Japanese Nationalism." In *Japa-*

nese Cultural Nationalism: At Home and in the Asia Pacific, ed. Roy Starrs, 61–79. Folkestone: Kent Global Oriental.

Powles, Cyril H. 1995. "Bushido: Its Admirers and Critics." In *Nitobe Inazō: Japan's Bridge Across the Pacific*, ed. John F. Howes, 107–18. Boulder: Westview Press.

Solomon-Godeau, Abigail. 1995. "Male Trouble." In *Constructing Masculinity*, ed. Maurice Berger, Brian Wallis, and Simon Watson, 69–76. London: Routledge.

4 After Heroism

Must Real Soldiers Die?

Sabine Frühstück

Warfare is only an invention, not a biological necessity.

MARGARET MEAD

In 2006 Japanese newspapers reported all Ground Self-Defense Force (GSDF) troops "safely home from their historic mission to Iraq," putting an end to two and a half years of the first deployment of the Self-Defense Forces to a war zone since their foundation in 1954, albeit for a noncombat, humanitarian operation.[1] The mission in Iraq increased Japan's international profile and strengthened ties with Japan's biggest ally, the United States. Suggesting that Japan had overcome the childlike state once attributed to it by General MacArthur, the international press claimed that the Iraq mission marked no less than Japan's transformation into a "grown-up nation" and a "normal state," and that its armed forces were on their way to becoming a "true military."[2] At least since the 1990s, a growing number of public figures in Japan have subscribed to this notion of normalcy as well, partly in response to the severe criticism Japan faced, particularly from the United States, for its purely monetary contribution to the Persian Gulf War. This notion of the "normal state" implies direct and close ties between a nation-state capable of waging war and a military masculinity based on individual men's ability to engage in combat. Modern military heroism, in other words, connotes the potential to kill and die in battle. In recent years, however, a number of scholars have challenged this notion of a "normal state" on two fronts: it has not universally applied to modern nation-states; and, since the end of the cold war, its sphere of influence has significantly decreased.

Japan's Self-Defense Forces both highlight these developments and complicate them: in Japan, Article 9 of the constitution and Self-Defense Forces laws and regulations disrupt the connection between soldiering heroism and death presumably normalized elsewhere. The exact wording of Article 9 is as follows: "Aspiring sincerely to an international peace based on justice and order, the Japanese people forever renounce war as a sovereign right of the nation and the threat of use of force as a means of settling international disputes. In order to accomplish the aim of the preceding paragraph, land, sea, and air forces, as well as other war potential, will never be maintained. The right of belligerency of the state will not be recognized."[3] The article forcefully disrupts the mutually reinforcing mechanisms of the potency of the state and the potency of its military men and women, creating a dramatically different framework for service members' negotiations of their militarized masculinity within a domestic, international, and historical setting. Members of the Japanese armed forces labor in the name of a state prohibited from waging war, creating service members who have come to embody a number of complex contradictions: they work, and occasionally risk their lives, in the name of a state that has declared their very organization illegal. While the civilian code prohibits the exercise of violence, the military trains its members for violent acts. Essentially, the military trains for battle so that it will not need to use those skills, prepares for war so that it will not happen, and ultimately proves its success if it remains unnecessary.[4] Thus in Japan the modern connection between proving oneself as a man and proving this manhood by success in organized killing, a definition that many societies have established for militarized manliness, seems obsolete. Despite this state of affairs that has characterized more than sixty years of recent Japanese history, the notion that full membership in the community of "real" men and the international community of "normal" states is contingent upon having a military with not only violent capabilities but also the willingness to use them in war remains powerful in international and some domestic debates about Japan's potential military roles.[5]

In this chapter I attempt to recover the discursive, institutional, and social practices implicated in contemporary anxieties about the normalcy of the state, the potency of its military, and the masculinity of its men. I examine the immediate repercussions of these anxieties regarding the normalcy of the Japanese state and its military for individual soldiers, for their sense of what constitutes a "normal soldier" and a "real man." Put more broadly, I ask questions about the cultural shaping of subjectivities within the military world, keeping in mind an issue that French philosopher Alain Badiou has recently addressed by asking, "Is there a place, in a disoriented world, for a new style of heroism? How can we find a heroic figure, which is neither the return of the old figure of the religious or national sacrifice, nor the nihilistic figure of the last man?"[6] As we will see in the pages that follow, in many ways, Japanese soldiers embody and live this set of questions.

For those Japanese men whose lives are permeated by military rules, values, and interests, an existential question has been how to negotiate their concepts of soldierhood given the complex and even contradictory demands of their military organization that trains them for war and exclusively engages them in operations that prohibit the exercise of violence. How do Japanese service members narrate those actions and experiences that constitute their professional identity as service members and contribute to their notion of a "normal" and "real" soldier? Perhaps more than service members anywhere else in the world, and certainly more than soldiers in Japanese history before them, Japanese service members are anxious about how to properly perform their soldierhood in order to be "real" *(honmono, futsū)* soldiers, and they often appear excruciatingly aware of their camouflaged identity as (trained) warriors and (practicing) humanitarians, saviors, engineers, construction workers, and handymen.[7]

I examine how individual soldiers in Japan navigate their militarized masculinity in conjunction with a set of contradictions associated with the notion of the "normal state." In other words, how do individual soldiers in their everyday lives negotiate the contradictory messages of the "normal" (state and military) while attempting to embody "real" soldierhood and manhood? How do they deal with the tensions between the combat training they receive (directed at inflicting and withstanding extreme forms of organized violence) and the risk taking required to save the lives of others (demanded of them in actual missions)?

DOMESTICATIONS

These tensions are apparent in soldiers' attitudes toward the possibility of engaging in combat. In addition to variations in motivations and expectations that depend upon the moment in post–World War II history at which young men join the Self-Defense Forces, every move that Japanese service members make has continued to attest to these men's anxiety about how to properly embody "normal soldierhood" without resorting to the violence traditionally associated with that concept of masculinity. After the 1995 Hanshin-Awaji earthquake, the most devastating since the Kantō earthquake of 1921, for example, a whole cohort of cadets entered the National Defense Academy dreaming not of bloody feats of daring, but of the gratitude they might one day reap by successfully engaging in disaster relief efforts as future officers of the Self-Defense Forces. Frustrated by the low social status of the Self-Defense Forces despite their demanding training and frequent deployment to disaster sites in Japan, one male officer close to his retirement at the age of fifty-one expressed his desire for public approval and the "recognition that any other working man in Japan can expect." Indicating a sense of contentment with his accomplishments and the scope of roles the Self-Defense Forces have engaged in for most of the postwar era, another male major sheepishly smiled when confessing his prayers for nothing to happen until after his retirement—hardly the hopes of a man who desires to experience combat. A new male recruit refused to acknowledge that the Self-Defense Forces are even a military, while dismissing questions about his thoughts on death and dying in the line of duty. One captain was proud of his status as "the mother of the squad," while another fretted that the men in the Self-Defense Forces were "not properly initiated into the concept of self-sacrifice for the sake of the nation."[8]

While men situate themselves along a continuum of masculinities once they are in the Self-Defense Forces, all of them articulate their various motivations to join and stay on with some reference to that dominant contender for hegemonic masculinity in postwar Japan, the "salaryman," or white-collar employee. First appearing as the antithesis of the soldier in Taishō Japan, the salaryman in a corporate environment that borrows military metaphors continues to be used as a foil by members of the Self-Defense Forces. He emerges from service members' narratives as a monolithic identity that renders invisible all other men outside the military. He signifies everything individual service members believe they are not or do not want to be. Thus, service members commonly refer to the salaryman with a rhetoric of loathing that casts him as unmanly, selfish, and weak. His professional life, characterized as "monotonous," "boring," and driven by profit making, stands in stark contrast to what they refer to as their own selflessness, individualism, and independence of spirit, albeit within the boundaries of the military.

Despite the common rejection of the salaryman as a figure of undesirable manhood, the reality of a soldier's life is not that far from that of a salaryman. A new twenty-five-year-old recruit had graduated from a university, worked as a sales clerk in a fishing equipment shop for several years, and eventually quit to enlist in the Self-Defense Forces. He was "bored with the day-in, day-out routine of his sales job," he "hated to have to be inside all day," and he "could not stand the idea of spending every single day for the next thirty-five years or so in the very same way."[9] As did many of his peers, he emphasized his expectation that he would be able to work outside, use his physical capabilities, participate in exciting and demanding training, and thus continue to challenge himself throughout his professional career. The irony of this service member's comment about the boring routine of a store clerk, in light of the repetitive exercises he engaged in the entire morning during mortar training, which consists of a handful of movements, seemed to escape him. During the previous few weeks he had also been required to get up, put on his military uniform, eat, and go to bed at precisely the same time as the other eight hundred men of his regiment, and—if he did indeed make the Self-Defense Forces his lifelong career—he would continue to do so for most of his working life.

Most officers find that they spend too many hours on clerical work despite their primary interest in being "in the field" and with other men. They express their frustration by making dismissive comments such as, "After all the training, I ended up living like a salaryman." Others believe that because the Self-Defense Forces are "not respected as a military, working as a service member comes down to being a salaryman." Yet others are content that, because they are service members, at least they have no need to "constantly prove their loyalty to a company by working as late as a salaryman."

The function of the salaryman as service members' main antihero defies written and unwritten rules that support efforts by the Self-Defense Forces to have their soldiers actually look (almost) like salarymen, or at least blend in with salarymen and mainstream society as much as possible, through a very specific management of dress codes, hairstyles, and body comportment. In pursuit of the "salarymanization" of the Self-Defense Forces, public relations officers mobilize the image of the salaryman in an effort to make the Self-Defense Forces appear almost like an organization that is populated by ordinary men (and women) who could just as well be found in any other male-dominated Japanese company, government agency, or organization, while at the same time instilling a sense that they work for a very special organization. A recruitment poster of 2005 (figure 4.1) is just one of many produced over the last few decades that underline this attempt. Two handsome young men and one woman, the latter dressed in casual, fashionable clothes that suggest a white-collar lifestyle, walk into the picture smiling. In contrast to the figures on the poster, who appear middle-class, the actual Self-Defense Forces recruits who join as enlisted men overwhelmingly come from a socioeconomically underprivileged background. Even officers (most of whom are graduates of the National Defense Academy) typically admit that they enrolled at the NDA because of the economic independence it offered them as cadets or that the NDA was their backup choice after they failed at the entrance exams for other universities.

Figure 4.1. Similar to many of its kind, this recruitment poster from 2005 has a distinctly civilian, middle-class look. It reads, "We [the Self-Defense Forces] appreciate young strength. There is a future to which I/we want to connect. There are people I/we want to help. There is a land I/we want to protect." Photograph by Jennifer Robertson.

The prominence of the salaryman figure in motivational narratives of members of the Self-Defense Forces is ironic for another reason. Until his loudly proclaimed death in tandem with the recession in the early 1990s, the salaryman played an important role in the formation of a militarized masculine identity among Japanese service members. Last glorified in popular media and the advertising industry both in and outside Japan as the "company warrior" in the 1980s, the salaryman had been an important prototype of post–World War II Japanese heroism.[10] Employing references to battle, victory, defeat, and death in portraying the white-collar employee's total devotion to his company, representations of salarymen in popular culture created an ideal image of the white-collar worker as a peacetime incarnation of a warrior at war. It is thus ironic that in wider society, the language of battle is most commonly associated with a warrior figure that many service members see as the antithesis of themselves—the salaryman or white-collar employee.

The notion of the warrior evoked by the salaryman is safely removed from modern war and thus remains untainted by unpleasant memories of aggression and defeat in recent Japanese history. The vulgarized and commercialized version of "the samurai of the twenty-first century" does not fight his battles in the field but at work. His loyalty is tied not to the clan but to the company. According to the promotional language of advertisements that informs popular wisdom, however, his militarized masculine spirit remains unchanged.

INTERNATIONALIZATIONS

> Let's not take the blame for America. Personally, I hate America. . . . As a service member of the Self-Defense Forces, however, as my profession, I would fulfill my duty. . . . If I go, I would definitely not let any of my subordinates die. I believe that that is an officer's duty. Besides, we need to do what we are told because this country was defeated.
>
> GSDF OFFICER on the Self-Defense Forces' involvement in Iraq, quoted in *Jieitai no Iraku hahei*

For some Japanese service members, constitutional restrictions have worked to highlight the ability of service members to do something more valuable than killing people. Others, however, articulate the effects of these restrictions on their professional lives as deficiencies, aberrations, and disabilities. These sentiments play out close to home, most painfully in direct encounters with members of the United States Armed Forces posted in Japan, soldiers who remain associated with the U.S. military that defeated and subordinated Japan, as the quotation above indicates. At the same time, members of the United States Armed Forces serve as the desirable link to the (imagined) "international community" of military establishments. With an eye on disabilities and performance anxieties of another kind, R. W. Connell notes that the "constitution of masculinity through bodily performance means that gender is vulnerable when the performance cannot be sustained."[11] In the case of Japanese service members, their gender is vulnerable even though the performance is sustained. In broader terms, the anxiety that permeates military subjectivity in domestic encounters with the U.S. military during combined exercises, and in encounters with international military establishments in the context of disaster relief or peacekeeping missions, for instance, drives a phenomenon that Clifford Geertz (regarding the Balinese cockfight) called the "dramatization of status concerns" and Erving Goffman once referred to as "status bloodbath."[12] It is not service members' lives that are at stake but esteem, honor, dignity, respect—in one word, status. These instances confirm the specific status of the Self-Defense Forces vis-à-vis the U.S. military and the rest of the world's military establishments. On the maneuver ground, for instance, hints at the status imbalance between U.S. and Japanese service members remain subtle but are nevertheless irritating to Japanese troops. One GSDF major granted that U.S. soldiers were "true professionals at war making." However, he also noted with impatience that the Self-Defense Forces must clean up after them because the Self-Defense Forces cannot afford to be accused of endangering civilians who might find cartridges or other dangerous pieces of weaponry that U.S. soldiers tend to leave behind. Nor can they risk suicides by troops or civilians who might find equipment that belongs to the Self-Defense Forces.[13]

Unequal power relations between Japanese and American service members emerge from off-base encounters as well. In August 2004 the crash of a U.S. Marine Corps helicopter onto a university campus near Futenma Air Base in Okinawa prompted immediate protests against the U.S. military. Some demonstrators also turned against the Self-Defense Forces, as they were seen deferring to the Americans running the crash site. The shouts of "Go back to Japan!" from some demonstrators served to recall not only the fact that U.S. soldiers occupied and controlled the site (and, by implication, Okinawa), but also the days of the Imperial Japanese Army (IJA), which had abandoned the Okinawan population, coerced many of them to commit suicide, and retreated to the mainland during the last months of World War II.[14]

More recently, the hierarchical U.S.-Japan relationship became clear when Japanese lawmakers were grappling with the difficult question of setting a date for the return of the troops from Iraq because they wanted "to avoid at all costs being the first country to announce its withdrawal."[15] Framed by a bilateral alliance that puts Japan in an inferior position vis-à-vis the United States, the deployment to Iraq had enormous symbolic and political significance for the Japanese state and for the status of the military within the state's apparatus. For Japanese service members, however, the Iraq mission primarily has highlighted and brought into the open some of the tensions that have been intrinsic to the lives of soldiers in

Japan's post–World War II military all along—the subordination to the United States and the overall sense of being different from other military establishments. These tensions have resided in Self-Defense Forces service members from the very beginning and have prompted them to constantly contest their subjectivities as soldiers, as professionals, and as men. Individual service members embody this unequal relationship, but they also critically reflect on it and occasionally resist it.

Today the primary manner in which members of the Self-Defense Forces directly encounter members of the U.S. military is through combined exercises in Japan and the United States, which function as important lenses for negotiations over valorized soldier figures and tests of their universality. Such encounters with the U.S. military shake Japanese service members' carefully nurtured notions of the military hero as a helper and savior rather than a warrior, an issue addressed in more detail in the following section. Here it is important to note that the concept of "the American soldier" in Japanese service members' imaginations is just as fraught with contradictions and tensions as the image of the salaryman. The American soldier personifies what some perceive as a more desirable military, but others view him as a permanent emasculating threat. However, international missions do more than simply articulate unequal power relations. Rather, participation in them serves as a kind of "sentimental education" for Japanese soldiers. These missions do not just generate and regenerate the gendered power relations between Japanese and U.S. armed forces; they are also positive agents in the creation and maintenance of a sensibility regarding these relations. At the heart of this sensibility, I would argue once again with Geertz, is a set of anxieties: anxieties about the fragility of the military's order and meaning within Japan mirror those regarding Japan in the world outside.[16]

The entanglement of contradictory sentiments regarding the U.S. armed forces can be traced to Japan's defeat and the post–World War II occupation era, when the belief that Americans would teach democracy to Japan became overpowering. This gesture of subordination and its rejection lingers among activists along the entire political spectrum, ranging from citizen movements that demand the removal of the U.S. bases in Okinawa on the left, to the political expression of radical right-wing organizations such as the Association to Honor the Spirits of the Fallen Heroes, a revisionist organization that is affiliated with the Japan Association of Bereaved Families. Their political goals and the Japanese state they envision as more desirable than the status quo differ radically, but they share a sentiment that has been expressed in this prayer posted at Yasukuni

Shrine: "May Japanese people one day be able to control this country. A Japanese citizen."

In Japanese service members' minds, the image of the U.S. military is juxtaposed with their own self-perceptions as a military that has helped build and rebuild infrastructure, including a sports stadium in Iraq; reconstructed remote roads that were washed away by typhoons; sorted through rubble in search of survivors after a variety of natural disasters such as the Kobe earthquake; and disinfected streets to prevent the outbreak of epidemics in Honduras. Today, the ideal soldier—a status that was once embodied by the combatant—is primarily associated with the conviction that only the Self-Defense Forces can successfully carry out these missions. Japanese service members' idea of the U.S. soldier tends to blend images of actual U.S. soldiers in Japan with those of American men in general in a singular, monolithic gender and model of military professionalism. The diversity of configurations of soldierhood within the U.S. military is rendered invisible and is amalgamated into a male, Caucasian combat soldier, even though many U.S. soldiers are non-Caucasian. This homogenization and singularization of U.S. soldiers has several important discursive effects: it facilitates Japanese service members' claim to a soldierhood (and masculinity) that is quite different from that in war-making armed forces; it furthers the stereotype of Japan's uniqueness that has currency beyond the boundaries of the Self-Defense Forces; and it allows for the establishment of a single normalized military rather than a more comprehensive understanding of the diversity of military establishments in other parts of the world.

Today, service members use the notion of a (highly fictional) American military as a template against which they measure their own organization, their level of professionalism, and their range of valorized configurations of soldierhood. The American soldier, however, also serves as the link to the international security world. Similar to how "internationalist women" view Caucasian American men as "linked to a kind of transnational social upward mobility" and the fetish objects onto which Japanese desires for inclusion into "global society" are projected, for Japanese service members the U.S. Armed Forces in Japan and the imaginary U.S. military more generally represent the promise of such an entry into the world of "normal" military establishments. American soldiers thus represent a military norm, and therefore service members accord American military men the authority to "pass" into the international sphere of respected and fully legitimate military organizations.[17]

The association with the U.S. military through a security alliance that puts Japan in a position subordinate to the United States carries a good deal of ambivalence for Self-Defense Forces service members, primarily in the context of combined exercises. In the eyes of some service members, U.S. troops personify military professionalism through their combat experience and the power they gain through their link to and prominence within the international security community. Since the first U.S.-Japanese combined exercises in 1984, several such exercises have been held every year in both Japan and the United States. In 2000 alone, Self-Defense Forces participated in twenty-one combined exercises. Service members comment on the high level of respect they accord to the U.S. Armed Forces in Japan and occasionally call them "truly professional" for how seriously they take their performance in training situations. But Japanese service members also occasionally view the American warrior masculinity negatively. U.S. troops are perceived as perpetrators of reckless behavior on Japanese and particularly Okinawan territory, including car accidents, violent crimes, and rapes, for which they have not or only very reluctantly been held accountable in Japanese courts. Service members note that some of the blame for such behavior has always been placed on the shoulders of the Self-Defense Forces because, first, the Japanese and U.S. militaries are often merged into one in the public view and, second, because the Self-Defense Forces are sometimes blamed for failing to protect civilians from the U.S. military.

In Japanese service members' eyes, the U.S. military figures as *the* Western military. Young officers in the Self-Defense Forces note with envy the uncomplicated status of the U.S. service members in wider society, as any U.S. military man's swagger and other physical expressions of confidence indicate. The Japanese troops desire to be incorporated into the uncomplicated militarism that the U.S. military represents for them. At the same time, however, they are aware that incorporation can be attained only by means of annulment of their constitutional framework and thus of the core of their self-understanding, which is, particularly in the Ground Self-Defense Forces, heavily and self-consciously marked by the legacy of their predecessor, the Imperial Japanese Army.

HISTORICIZATIONS

The Self-Defense Forces' historical ties to and roots in the IJA continue to feed the uneasiness with which service members construct their ideas about what a "normal soldier" and military heroism are. This ambivalence is most immediately apparent in their use of language, which was changed in order to disrupt any sense of connection to the old imperial structures, and particularly to IJA speech.[18] Carol Cohn points out that the language of U.S. defense intellectuals is packed with euphemisms that are "fun to say." They are "racy, sexy, snappy. You can throw them around in rapid-fire succession. They are quick, clean, light; they trip off the tongue. You can reel off dozens of them in seconds, forgetting about how one might just interfere with the next, not to mention with the lives beneath them."[19] Japanese military euphemisms, by contrast, are bulky, lengthy, and have a bureaucratic, objective sound to them. They are slow and easily twist the speaker's tongue. They are complicated and not easily understood by civilians, thus defeating the purpose of their invention, which was to signal a clear rupture between the IJA and the Self-Defense Forces. Furthermore, these euphemisms constitute one set of "technologies of the self" that have permitted Japanese soldiers to perform a certain number of operations on their own bodies (such as haircuts or body comportment), on their minds (self-perceptions), and on conduct that enables them to transform and modify themselves.[20]

Despite these careful attempts at dissociation, the imperial soldier is on service members' minds whenever international operations are on the agenda, precisely because these operations are loaded with symbolism regarding risk, heroism, and sacrifice in a tamed masculinity that enhances Japan's postcolonial moment. In the service members' minds, as is immediately evident in interviews with them, the imperial soldier is little more than a shadow, a caricature that is conjured not as a model but as a "serviceable identity narrative."[21] Elements that do not match the image of the sacrificial if failed heroism of Japan's imperial past need to be erased or repressed. Elements that allow members of the Self-Defense Forces to fashion themselves as opposite in conduct from the IJA but connected to their spirit of devotion to the cause are emphasized.

The imperial soldier is rhetorically mobilized in two directions, so that service members both differentiate *and* compare the risks they are willing to take on disaster relief or peacekeeping missions abroad to the violence that their predecessors perpetrated and are associated with in present-day service members' minds. In these schemes, imperial soldiers represent attack, aggression, war, destruction, death, and even massacres. Members of the Self-Defense Forces, by contrast, see themselves as committed to dealing with risks, whether those risks need to be taken at a the site of a natural disaster on behalf of civilians, such as the mission involving several thousand men after the 1995 earthquake in the Kobe area, or are taken following a conflict in order to prevent further conflict and maintain peace, such as the mission in Cambodia in 1992 and the mission to Iraq from 2003 through 2006.

In terms of masculinity, then, the transition from the Imperial Japanese Army to the Self-Defense Forces was not a restoration but a recasting from which a new set of tamed masculinities (that correspond to the "tamed militarism" of the German army) emerged.[22] According to the ideology of their time, members of the IJA fought in combat, killed, and died for the "Greater Japanese Empire." In the Self-Defense Forces, the will to sacrifice one's life has been transformed into the humanitarian ideal of performing a host of tasks for "the public." This redefinition of militarized masculinity from inflicting violence to taking risks lies at the very basis of Self-Defense Forces service members' present-day military conduct, which prescribes the avoidance of danger, although, as we have seen above, this causes tensions with the conflicting view that for a military man, not being able to kill is an aberration. In lieu of a battle cry, for example, officers are told to "value and respect their lives and the personalities and lives of others" in order to become good officers. As another example, the peacekeeping law demands that Self-Defense Forces withdraw if a violent situation emerges. International missions remain voluntary. Even if some Japanese service members speak of their "duty" to serve in Iraq, for instance, they can cite family and other reasons for not going. Hence, service members' concepts of militarized masculinity are established in actions that involve risk to their safety and well-being, even though these same service members attempt to save rather than violate the lives of others. They imagine an international mission not as the best alternative to the frontline experience of combatants but as precisely the same as combat. For Japanese service members, at least, combat has no essence.

The type of military heroism that emerges from service members' comments and contemplations as well as from the ways they have been conducting themselves is crisis-bound, malleable, and constructed. In their everyday negotiations of their roles and identities both within and outside the Self-Defense Forces, Japanese service members constantly oscillate between different kinds of heroism and soldierhood more generally. In their struggle to achieve a "military heroism" of their own, they re-create and fixate on a historic figure of militarized masculinity by attaching either nostalgic sentiments or complete repulsion to dramatically distorted notions of IJA soldierhood.

The struggle to define and successfully identify with a new idea of heroism remains compromised by an older notion that military heroism involves death, and that true heroes are dead men. Some service members, however, embrace the idea that, rather than killing and dying for the emperor, risking one's life for civilians is an attractive avenue toward an alternative kind of heroism. The separation remains incomplete in at least two ways. First, narratives about missions continue to be tied to the rhetorical framework of sacrifice and survival. The participation in high-profile disaster relief or peacekeeping missions, for instance—providing medical treatment to children, rescuing natural disaster victims, and rebuilding infrastructure—boosts individual soldiers' careers and is thus particularly attractive for career-minded service members. In individual soldiers' narratives, these international missions typically also double as frontline experience and are couched in notions of national identity.[23]

Second, similar to the idealists in the IJA who had imagined that the war would transform them and their society, service members in the Self-Defense Forces volunteer for international missions because, among other reasons, they long for an authentic experience of their own.[24] Maritime Self-Defense Force captain Abe Susumu, for example, felt that the importance of experience could not be exaggerated. He had returned from a six-month stint as a peacekeeper in Mozambique during the 1993–95 United Nations intervention there, an experience that had been the most disturbing of his career and left a deep impression on him. He and others like him are held in high regard as men with real experience. The desire to have some kind of genuine experience is evidenced in the relative unimportance that service members place on what, exactly, the goal of the mission is and what they do during that mission. These narratives are also framed as a journey toward becoming, serving as a reminder of the notion, frequently remarked upon, that the military is instrumental in enabling males to become men.[25] Japanese service members' tales of heroism suggest that they, too— just like the military as an organization and the Japanese state—think about their missions as rites of passage to adulthood.

Thus, as a narrative construct, military heroism has lived on in the Self-Defense Forces in the absence of war, while its meaning has changed dramatically, the ideal of dying for the emperor and nation giving way to that of risking one's life for the public. Tales of heroism continue to be narrated and renarrated, but this heroism borrows nothing but its rhetorical shell from the times and experiences of the soldier in the imperial armed forces. After all, most Japanese now live in what Edward Luttwak has called a "post-heroic" culture, composed of a citizenry that is no longer willing to buy into the once-presumed equation of military violence with proper masculinity.[26] Most Japanese, including Japanese service members, have also rejected that equation for most of the postwar era, and the Iraq experience suggests that this rejection is unlikely to change suddenly, precisely because the soldier mobilized for international peacekeeping missions has more in common with the (military) hero of a forest fire than with the soldier of conventional, modern nation-to-nation warfare. Neither aspires to kill or die for the nation, even though both might risk their lives.

Setting aside the differences between the three branches of the Self-Defense Forces, a soldier scholar and instructor at the Staff College in Tokyo conceded that some service members imagine the imperialist past as a simpler time when the place and status of the soldier stood unquestioned, his role was unmistakably clear, and the militarized masculinity he aspired to was singularly defined by his willingness to give his life. But for most soldiers, imperial nostalgia ends there. Reflecting on the dominant attitude toward Japan's role in World War II in the centers of military learning, he explained that during the late 1950s and the 1960s, IJA veterans were first excluded and then selectively integrated into the Self-Defense Forces, creating a continuity that seemed necessary then to build a functional military. He saw the main problem in viewing the IJA as a model for the Self-Defense Forces in the IJA's failure at executing their core expertise, war making. "That is the reason," he argued, "why it has been impossible to positively relate to the IJA and craft both a positive military history in which the history of the Self-Defense Forces could be incorporated and a model of soldierhood that service members could embrace and identify with."[27]

A colonel and director of the Office for International Collaboration within the Defense Ministry explained that "for the Self-Defense Forces, international deployments are important not only in order to accumulate experience in actual missions, but also to convince neighboring countries formerly under Japanese colonial rule that they have nothing in common with the IJA."[28] Hence, in many officers' imagination, the "imperial soldier" provides one cornerstone of their militarized masculine identity as service members, albeit one that does not primarily rest on the readiness to sacrifice their own lives but instead to take risks to save the lives of others. The imperial soldier represents an important configuration of militarized masculinity, both ambivalent and ambiguous, with which service members grapple. Even to this army that has always been at peace, the reference points for defining ideal masculinity are not women but other men.[29]

I would like to draw three conclusions on the basis of my examination of individual service members' struggles to embody a militarized masculinity that they do not perceive as lagging behind or falling short of what they imagine a "real" or "normal" military to be.

First, from their very beginnings, the Self-Defense Forces have been entrusted with the types of missions that many other military establishments—most notably the U.S. military—have only recently added to their list of actual and potential operations, including community works, fire fighting, disaster relief, and peacekeeping. Thus, Japanese soldiers epitomize the worldwide multiplication and diversification of military missions. Anthony Zinni, a retired general of the U.S. Marine Corps and former commander in chief of United States Central Command, speaks to the end of the kind of "real soldiering" that characterized the wars of the twentieth century. Spelling out his vision of the future of the U.S. military, and ostensibly the armed forces of other postindustrial, democratic countries, Zinni notes that U.S. military policy makers are still operating as if there were a "real adversarial demon" to be found that could be crushed, with an unconditional surrender to follow. Instead, he claims, military establishments will be "doing things like humanitarian operations, consequence management, peacekeeping and peace enforcement" as well as responding to environmental disasters. "The truth is," Zinni suggested, "that military conflict has changed and we have been reluctant to recognize it. . . . Odd missions to defeat transnational threats or rebuild nations are the order of the day, but we haven't as yet adapted."[30]

Second, returning to Margaret Mead's words in the epigraph of this chapter, war would be eliminated, she suggested in 1940, only if a method more congruent with today's institutions and feelings were invented. For war to give way to a better invention, Mead thought at least two conditions were necessary: a recognition of the defects of war, the old invention, and the creation of a new system. As a course of action she suggested propaganda against warfare and documentation of its terrible cost in human suffering and social waste. These strategies, she thought, would prepare the ground by teaching people to feel that warfare is a defective social institution, that social invention is possible, and that the invention of new methods would eventually render warfare out-of-date. She also cautioned, however, that a behavior becomes out-of-date only when something else takes its place. Thus, in order for war to become obsolete, people must believe that the invention of a new method is possible.[31] More than seventy years, several devastating wars, and an enormous body of propaganda, television footage, and other information on these wars later, one cannot help but acknowledge that we have yet to achieve the moment Mead envisioned in 1940.

Third, the meaning and significance of militarized masculinity is historical in two ways: It is affected by grander historical changes such as the rupture between the dissolution of the war-making imperial armed forces in 1945 and the foundation of the Self-Defense Forces in 1954. But it is also molded by the smaller histories of individuals such as the service members of the Self-Defense Forces. As I have argued, the concern with and anxiety about the "normalcy" of the Japanese state and its military reproduce an uneasiness and ambivalence within the service members, who struggle with what it means to be a "normal" and "true" soldier and with what it means to do one's duty. The anxieties that pervade military personnel are perhaps more pronounced in Japan, but they are not unique to the Self-Defense Forces.[32] After all, becoming a member of a military establishment always means becoming somebody else. As Paul Fussell notes, from the perspective of many service members, "one of the functions of military uniforms is precisely to assume a character not [one's] own."[33] For Japanese service members the military experience also seems to resemble what Frederic Jameson called a "fragmentation of the subject." Jameson suggested somewhat broadly that the postmodern subject "has been drained of subjectivity in the modernist sense."[34] Postmodern cultural forms, including those lines of cultural theory that posit the irrelevance or "death" of the subject, reflect this flattened subjectivity and at the same time heighten the subject's sense of disorientation. Thus Japanese soldiers' grappling with their military masculinity can be seen as attempts at "cognitive mapping" in the hope of eventually grasping their position as individual and collective subjects, as Jameson would have suggested, while Richard Sennett would have pointed out the importance of restoring their capacity for coherent self-narration that is constantly under assault in late capitalism more generally.[35] Both of these interpretations imply that the anxieties and conflicts I have briefly described in this chapter are not quite as exclusive to the military or Japan as some service members and social critics would like to suggest.

It remains to be seen whether the loss of the individual capacity for coherent self-narration (in Japan and elsewhere) might eventually be doing away with the modern equation between proving oneself a man and proving this by participation in organized killing. In the meantime, I believe it is important to note that most Japanese citizens, including service members, share the lack of willingness to buy into the once-accepted equation between the exercise of military violence and normal statehood. Recruitment figures have declined. Demographic projections suggest that yet fewer men will be eligible for military service. And, with the support for constitutional reform falling every year since 2005, constitutional reform is now once again effectively dead.

NOTES

I presented a shorter version of this paper at the annual meeting of the Association for Asian Studies, in San Francisco in 2006, during the panel "Reconfiguring Militarism in Postwar Japan." I thank my co-panelists Christopher Ames, Tanaka Masakazu, and Aaron Skabelund and discussant Harry Harootunian for invaluable comments. As this paper morphed into its current shape, Aaron Belkin, Tom Gill, David Leheny, Luke Roberts, and Jennifer Robertson provided important criticism and suggestions.

1. The *Japan Times* titled its report on 26 January 2006 "All GSDF Troops Safely Home from Historic Mission to Iraq."

2. The title of the article in the *Financial Times*, 14 April 2004, was "A Grown-up Nation? The Hostage Crisis in Iraq Sharpens Debate over Japan's Proper Role on the International Stage." The article in the 16 January 2004 issue of the *New York Times* was titled "Mission to Iraq Eases Japan Toward a True Military."

3. See Inoue 1991, p. 275. Consequently, the right of self-defense as well as newer legislation that provided the framework for international peacekeeping missions remain contentious. See, e.g., Pyle 2007; and "High Court: ASDF Mission to Iraq Illegal" 2008. Samuels (2007) describes a larger-scale security dilemma.

4. John Armitage (2003), for instance, writes that the democratization of war in the United States gave rise to the "routinization" of military charisma, whereby the charismatic hero endures as a celebrity, mostly in popular culture. Chris Hables Gray (2003) also finds that "most men have already abandoned war, or even military service, as a ritual defining masculinity although the playing at war is quite popular. While it is harder and harder to fill enlistment quotas, paint-ball and paramilitary groups seem to be everywhere. For these men, dressing up in camouflage drag for weekend games, masculinity is not what you do, it is how you look" (p. 220).

5. Meyer, Boli, Thomas, and Ramirez 1997.

6. Badiou 2007.

7. All of these professional labels were conveyed to me in interviews in which service members described how they saw themselves and their roles in the Self-Defense Forces and in Japanese society at large. See, for instance, Sheehan 2003, pp. 11–23, especially p. 17; and Frevert 2001, especially p. 351.

8. Individual interviews with the author, carried out between 1998 and 2004.

9. Interview with the author, July 2003.

10. Kinmonth 1981; Roberson and Suzuki 2002; Vogel 1963; Nakamaki and Hioki 1997; Osawa 1994.

11. Connell 1995, pp. 54, 56.

12. Geertz 1973 [1972], p. 437; Goffman 1961, p. 78.

13. Interview with the author, July 2003.

14. The memory of the IJA's prompt retreat from Okinawa once the Allied

forces had landed frequently fuels debates about criminal incidences by both Japanese and U.S. service members. See, for instance, Sakata 2002 [1942] and Angst 2003, pp. 135–57.

15. "SDF Still Looking for the Best Way to Make a Graceful Iraq Exit," *International Herald Tribune*, 20 May 2006.

16. Geertz 1973 [1972], p. 449.

17. Although the subordination of Japanese men to American men as one of the effects of defeat and occupation has been a common observation of scholars of postwar Japan, Kelsky (2001) first pointed to its continuing, much broader currency in present-day Japan. She suggests that Japanese women who in part pursue their careers abroad use their personal, professional, or romantic associations with typically Caucasian, Western men in order to pass into international society.

18. Public relations campaign materials consistently use the English term "the public" rather than "the nation" or even "Japan" to refer to the object of protection and defense. This choice of a foreign word can be read as a further technique used by the Self-Defense Forces to both distance themselves from the IJA and align themselves with other governmental institutions and civilian enterprises. For a more extensive discussion of the language of public relations campaigns, see Frühstück 2003, pp. 116–48.

19. Cohn 1987, p. 704.

20. Foucault 2007 [1997], p. 154.

21. Nye 2007, p. 437.

22. Nye 2007, p. 434.

23. The rhetorical conflation of heroism and sacrifice had been forcefully promoted during the first half of the twentieth century and reappropriated for the purpose of rebuilding Japan immediately after World War II. As I have shown elsewhere, the continuity of "heroism" and "sacrifice" as ideological technologies employed to reinforce national unity after the end of World War II is particularly apparent in books and magazines for children. See Frühstück 2007.

24. Ohnuki-Tierney 2002.

25. Mosse 1996, p. 111.

26. Sheehan 2009, p. 348.

27. Interview with the author, August 1999.

28. Interview with the author, September 1998.

29. Nye 2007, p. 438.

30. Urquhart 2004, pp. 28–33, especially p. 32. Proving Zinni's point, the U.S. military proposed an active-duty force for relief efforts after Hurricane Katrina had devastated New Orleans, according to Schmitt and Shankar 2005, p. A13.

31. Mead 1940, p. 405.

32. Gray 2003, p. 216.

33. Fussell 2002.

34. Jameson 1984, pp. 53–92.

35. Jameson 1984, p. 54; Sennett 1992, p. 98; Ortner 2006, p. 125.

REFERENCES

Angst, Linda Isako. 2003. "The Rape of a Schoolgirl: Discourses of Power and Gendered National Identity in Okinawa." In *Islands of Discontent: Okinawan Responses to Japanese and American Power,* ed. Laura Hein and Mark Selden, 135–57. Lanham: Rowman & Littlefield.

Armitage, John. 2003. "Militarized Bodies: An Introduction." *Body & Society* 9, no. 4: 1–12.

Badiou, Alain. 2007. "The Contemporary Figure of the Soldier in Politics." Talk presented at the UCLA Art Center in Pasadena, California. Available at www.lacan.com/badsold.htm.

Cohn, Carol. 1987. "Sex and Death in the Rational World of Defense Intellectuals." *Signs* 12, no. 4: 687–728.

Connell, R. W. 1995. *Masculinities.* Berkeley: University of California Press.

Foucault, Michel. 2007 [1997]. *The Politics of Truth,* trans. Lysa Ochroth and Catherine Porter, ed. Sylvère Lotringer. Los Angeles: Semiotext(e).

Frevert, Ute. 2001. *Die kasernierte Nation: Militärdienst und Zivilgesellschaft in Deutschland.* Munich: Verlag C. H. Beck.

Frühstück, Sabine. 2003. *Colonizing Sex: Sexology and Social Control in Modern Japan.* Berkeley: University of California Press.

———. 2007. "De la militarisation de la culture impériale." In *La societé japonaise devant la montée du militarisme: Culture populaire et contrōle social dans les années 1930,* ed. Jean-Jacques Tschudin and Claude Hammon, 109–22. Arles: Editions Picquier.

Fussell, Paul. 2002. *Uniforms and Why We Are What We Wear.* Boston: Houghton Mifflin.

Geertz, Clifford. 1973 [1972]. "Deep Play: Notes on the Balinese Cockfight." In *The Interpretation of Cultures.* New York: Basic Books.

Gibson, James William. 1994. *Warrior Dreams: Paramilitary Culture in Post-Vietnam America.* New York: Hill and Wang.

Goffman, Erving. 1961. *Encounters: Two Studies in the Sociology of Interaction.* Indianapolis: Bobbs-Merrill.

Gray, Chris Hables. 2003. "Posthuman Soldiers in Postmodern War." *Body & Society* 9, no. 4: 215–26.

"High Court: ASDF Mission to Iraq Illegal." 2008. *Japan Times,* 18 April. Available at http://search.japantimes.co.jp/mail/nn20080418a1.html.

Inoue Kyoko. 1991. *MacArthur's Japanese Constitution.* Chicago: University of Chicago Press.

Jameson, Fredric. 1984. "Postmodernism, or the Cultural Logic of Late Capitalism." *New Left Review* 146 (July–August): 53–92.

Kelsky, Karen. 2001. *Women on the Verge: Japanese Women, Western Dreams.* Durham: Duke University Press.

Kinmonth, Earl H. 1981. *The Self-Made Man in Meiji Japanese Thought: From Samurai to Salary Man.* Berkeley: University of California Press.

Konishi Makoto, Watanabe Nobutaka, and Yabuki Takashi. 2004. *Jieitai no Iraku hahei.* Shakai Hihyōsha.

Mead, Margaret. 1940. "Warfare Is Only an Invention—Not a Biological Necessity." *Asia XL*, 402–5.

Meyer, John W., John Boli, George M. Thomas, and Francisco O. Ramirez. 1997. "World Society and the Nation-state." *American Journal of Sociology* 103, no. 1: 144–81.

Mosse, George L. 1996. *The Image of Man: The Creation of Modern Masculinity.* New York: Oxford University Press.

Nakamaki Hirochika and Hioki Koichirō, eds. 1997. *Keiei jinruigaku kotohajime: Kaisha to sarariiman.* Osaka: Tōhō shuppan.

Nye, Robert A. 2007. Review Essay: "Western Masculinities in War and Peace." *American Historical Review* 112, no. 2: 417–38.

Ohnuki-Tierney, Emiko. 2002. *Kamikaze, Cherry Blossoms, and Nationalisms: The Militarization of Aesthetics in Japanese History.* Chicago: University of Chicago Press.

Ortner, Sherry. 2006. *Anthropology and Social Theory: Culture, Power and the Acting Subject.* Durham: Duke University Press.

Osawa Mari. 1994. "Bye-bye Corporate Warriors: The Formation of a Corporate-centered Society and Gender-biased Social Policies in Japan." *Annals of the Institute of Social Science* 19: 157–94.

Pyle, Kenneth. 2007. *Japan Rising: The Resurgence of Japanese Power and Purpose.* New York: Public Affairs.

Roberson, James E. and Nobue Suzuki, eds. 2002. *Men and Masculinities in Contemporary Japan: Dislocating the Salaryman Doxa.* London: Routledge.

Sakata Kiyo. 2002 [1942]. *Onna no mita senjo.* Nagoya: Arumu.

Samuels, Richard J. 2007. *Securing Japan: Tokyo's Grand Strategy and the Future of East Asia.* Ithaca: Cornell University Press.

Schmitt, Eric, and Thom Shankar. 2005. "Military May Propose an Active-duty Force for Relief Efforts." *New York Times*, 11 October.

Sennett, Richard. 1992. *The Fall of Public Man.* New York: W.W. Norton & Co.

Sheehan, James J. 2003. "What It Means to Be a State: States and Violence in Twentieth-century Europe." *Journal of Modern European* History 1, no. 1: 11–23.

———. 2009. *Where Have All the Soldiers Gone: The Transformation of Modern Europe.* Boston: Mariner Books.

Urquhart, Brian. 2004. "The Good General: Tom Clancy, with General Tony Zinni (Ret.) and Tony Koltz. Battle Ready. New York: Putnam." *New York Review of Books*, 23 September.

Vogel, Ezra. 1963. *Japan's New Middle Class: The Salary Man and His Family in a Tokyo Suburb.* Berkeley: University of California Press.

PART II

Marginal Men

5 Perpetual Dependency

The Life Course of Male Workers in a Merchant House

Sakurai Yuki

Translated by Anne Walthall

East of Edo (present-day Tokyo) lies Sawara, a town that served as an important node in water transport along the Tone River, not far from where it empties into the Pacific Ocean. In 1764, the owner of the clothing shop Naraya in Kyoto, Sugimoto Shin'emon, decided to make Sawara the location of his first branch store. His successor opened a second branch store nearby in Sakura. Unlike the large-scale Mitsui and Shirokiya enterprises, which placed their branches in Edo, Naraya is remarkable for having prospered in the provinces. Yet the principal management of Naraya, like that of its larger rivals, stayed in Kyoto. Its employees, too, came from western Japan and worked in the Kyoto office before being dispatched east. All were male. The Naraya records thus allow us to examine the world of all-male shop workers from the perspective of becoming a man.

A long history of research has produced an impressive body of materials about the branches established in Edo by main stores located in Ise, Ōmi, Kyoto, and other places. Most studies analyze the stores' management—the top-ranked men assigned specific duties—but leave the professional trajectories of most of the employees vague.[1] My reading of the Naraya documents, which cover almost all of the workers' working lives from 1800 to the end of the nineteenth century, allows me to outline the life courses of men who joined this closed male-only group. For a younger son from the countryside with no prospect of inheriting his family's farm and few other legitimate opportunities, this was a highly desirable career.

Modern people tend to think of maturity as a process experienced through the body; the term *puberty*, for example, refers to physical changes that make fathering or bearing children possible. In early modern Japan, however, the process had a significant social dimension. Everyone went through a coming-of-age ceremony, but what it meant depended upon the individual's sex and status. In this volume, Nagano Hiroko highlights entry into youth organizations as a crucial step toward manhood in farm villages. For the male shop clerks analyzed here, the maturation process was marked by travel and the acquisition of material possessions, chiefly clothing. Although the goal was the ability to stake out space as an independent businessman with a household and descendants, most never achieved this end. Their masculinity had to incorporate perpetual dependency on their employer's paternalism. The central irony is that the better a clerk performed, the more delayed was his chance to form his own household and open his own shop. Failure won personal freedom at the cost of abandoning the enterprise's finely woven safety net.

In this chapter I focus on crises surrounding transitions from one life stage to the another within the context of maturation as men and as merchant house employees, marked first by entry into the house, then by the coming-of-age ceremony, and thereafter by a series of trips to the main store. The merchant house played the role of benevolent parent for new recruits who were typically no older than ten or eleven. It established regulations to guide their behavior, supervised their demeanor and apparel, and shaped their masculine development to its own ends by enforcing a system of live-in employment. Neither the merchant house nor the employees always succeeded.

NARAYA AND ITS EMPLOYEES

Naraya's founder, the first Sugimoto Shin'emon, experienced many of the same vicissitudes as a youth that his workers later suffered. Born the sixth son of a farmer in Kayumi village, Itaka district, Ise, he went to work for the dry goods store owned by Naraya Kanpei in Kyoto at age fourteen. Naraya Kanpei went bankrupt when Shin'emon was twenty-one, so Shin'emon moved to a relative's shop, Naraya Yasubei. At Yasubei's he was put in charge of laying in stock, and he peddled dry goods in the eastern provinces of Musashi and Shimōsa. In 1743, at the age of forty, Shin'emon established an independent store in Kyoto. He then adopted his fourteen-year-old nephew as his successor. Having acquired valuable experience as a peddler traveling with his adoptive father, this second-generation Shin'emon launched Naraya's expansion with the branch store in Sawara. The third, Shinzaemon, opened Sakura store inland of Sawara in 1807. The Kyoto store retained control over the branches through visits by its head once or twice a year and by regulating both the laying in of stock and personnel affairs.

TABLE 5.1 New employees and retirements

Year	New employees	Retirements	Balance	Total
1763–1769	2	0	2	2
1770–1779	4	0	4	6
1780–1789	5	1	4	10
1790–1799	11	3	8	18
1800–1809	20	14	6	24
1810–1819	12	14	-2	22
1820–1829	23	20	3	25
1830–1839	31	20	11	36
1840–1849	24	28	-4	32
1850–1859	34	29	5	37
1860–1869	46	38	8	45
1870–1879	31	32	-1	44
1880–1889	31	33	-2	42
1890–1899	32	19	13	55
1900–1909	19	28	-9	45
1910–	0	1	-1	44

NOTE: This data tallies the numbers of men dispatched to Sawara and Sakura by the decade they received employment at the main store and the decade they quit (or died.)

Among the Naraya documents is the "Store Memo for the Provinces" ("Tanaju kuni oboe," hereafter referred to as the "Memo"), which records the origins and careers of the store's workers from 1802 to 1907.[2] From it we can obtain a chronological synopsis of about 330 workers. The "Memo" does not list aggregate numbers of employees; instead, it provides information about when they began their employment and when they left (table 5.1). Although the first entries of the "Memo" are from 1802, men who had worked for the store for a relatively long period before 1802 are also included in it, whereas both seasonal employees and those who worked for a short period and then resigned are possibly excluded.[3] At the time the Sakura store opened, the two stores together employed about twenty workers. During the 1830s to early 1840s, the number of workers increased to more than thirty. By the early twentieth century, the Sawara store had thirty workers and the Sakura store approached fifteen or sixteen, and in both cases all the workers were men.

In her analysis of Shirokiya's Edo store, Hayashi Reiko suggests that employment agencies assisted with finding workers.[4] In Naraya's case, the number of workers was not that large, and it apparently relied on local and kin connections operating first through the founding head and later through the workers themselves to find trustworthy employees. According to Nishizaka Yasushi, Mitsui Echigoya in Kyoto also depended not on employment agencies but on worker referrals. The shift in the point of origin for Naraya's workers to Kyoto, the location of the main store, came about through the creation of branch houses in the environs that provided referrals and sons.

In contrast to heirs to family farms, who were expected to spend their entire lives in their ancestral village, Naraya shop workers went through their maturation process far from their parents and their homes. Even most townspeople never suffered permanent separation from their home communities in the way that these workers did. Only a few boys from Sawara and Sakura worked in the store, and most of them were the eldest sons of branch houses or the sons of businessmen in the neighborhood who served apprenticeships. Of the approximately 330 employees recorded up to 1907, of those for whom their place of origin is recorded, 94 came from Kyoto, 88 from Ise, and 72 from Ōmi. These three regions, all in western Japan, comprised 80 percent of the total (table 5.2). Before 1868, the nucleus of employees came from Ise. Within Ise, Kayumi village, home to the first-generation head, sent at least 56 men, and Itaka district as a whole sent 64. Starting in the 1830s, the number of employees originating in Kyoto increased. The number of men from Kyoto came to dominate in the late nineteenth century until, by 1912, they numbered in the forties. Men from Ōmi as well started increasing in the 1840s, and in the Meiji period their numbers greatly surpassed those of Ise. Although Naraya's identity as a store with its source in Ise disappeared, its workers, whether they came from Ise, Kyoto, or Ōmi, still had to leave home as boys.

As at many branch stores established by merchants from western Japan, employees at Naraya started living in and working at the store at a young age. Between 1800 and 1909 most entered the store at between eleven and twelve *sai* (nine to eleven years old in today's terms). The youngest was nine years old. Rare were those fifteen *sai* and older, who were probably trainees for apprenticeships. One man who entered at age twenty-two *sai* was the son of a branch house who received special treatment. One man from Ise who entered in his thirties was a seasonal worker, unlike the young employees who took charge of supplies inside the shop. Broadly speaking, the age at which one began work was deemed to be the end of

TABLE 5.2 Change over time in points of origin for shop workers

Decade	*Ise*	*Kyoto*	*Ōmi*	*Eastern Japan (Kanto)*
1760s	1	—	—	—
1770s	2	1	—	—
1780s	3	—	—	2
1790s	6	1	2	1
1800s	11	4	—	3
1810s	8	—	1	1
1820s	12	1	2	1
1830s	14	8	4	3
1840s	10	1	9	—
1850s	12	8	7	—
1860s	9	20	11	1
1870s	—	20	5	—
1880s	—	15	7	4
1890s	—	9	15	—
1900s	—	7	9	—

childhood, after one finished elementary education. In the absence of a child labor law, which was implemented only in 1911, boys left their parents' home to become workers and typically did not return until after they had gone through a coming-of-age ceremony in their late teens or early twenties.

REGULATIONS FOR EMPLOYEES

Naraya took seriously its role in raising in loco parentis the boys it took far from home. To make them into men, it provided instructions on personal hygiene and morals, with the most elaborate rules focused on clothing, which significantly and visibly marked a series of steps toward adult manhood. The third-generation Shinzaemon at the main store in Kyoto wrote a set of house rules for Naraya known as "Kyōbunki" (Naraya's motto), which were directed to members of the household, the separate houses, and all shop employees. More than sixty regulations defined duties around the shop, with twenty-nine of these deemed "established practices" addressed to the managers, youths, and boys at Sawara.

The house rules reflected Naraya's extravagantly paternalistic attitude toward its employers. Workers were to take good care of their bodies, which they owed to their parents and ancestors. Avoiding physical pleasures, particularly the temptation to consume certain types of food, was central to this task: "Calamities issue from the mouth, and illnesses enter through the mouth. Enjoying varied foods is the first cause of ill health; misfortune and disloyalty also arise from this; and these foods are a cause for poverty, vileness, and shame." So to injure the body with the pleasure of food "is the worst of disloyalty and unfilial conduct. You should serve by taking your employment seriously without forgetting for a moment the depth of obligation you owe your parents, for it is true that your father and your mother's mercy begins with your birth." These injunctions admonish the employee to put his obligation to his master on the same level as his obligation to his parents and make loyalty and filial piety the way to repay this obligation throughout his employment. For the Sawara employees, becoming a man meant accepting these lifelong standards of responsible behavior.

Naraya's regulations instructed employees on how they were expected to comport themselves at the store and also defined good work habits. They directed the daily life of the employees, and included stipulations about taking precautions against fire, hints for laying in stock and making sales, rules about communications with the main store, instructions to channel communications with parents openly through the main store rather than seek clandestine routes, rules for relations with fellow workers, and encouragement to learn reading, writing, and accounting. Prohibited were gambling, all games of chance, business speculation, theater, songs, drinking, parties and other entertainment, making sales on one's own without permission, and leaving the store except when necessary for business.[5] The chief regulations, however, concerned the employees' attire.

CLOTHES MAKE THE MAN

Clothing was the chief marker of the stages in a shop employee's maturation to adult manhood. Upon entering the store, boys received uniforms twice a year, in the spring and fall, when they had important responsibilities during the biannual inventory. According to the reform of shop regulations in 1837, "For ordinary dress and for going to other places, clothing in both summer and winter is to be cotton with stripes, and the belt is to be of plain cotton. After coming of age, it is all right to put on underwear of plain cloth even when going to another place. Leather-soled sandals and *geta* [wooden sandals] are to be the same as before." This shows that clothing for boys was limited to striped cotton with a cotton belt.

More detailed regulations for livery appeared in 1875, but the intent was still the same—to maintain sumptuary distinctions based on years of service. In the spring boys received one unlined striped cotton kimono, one open-weave (Kokura-style) belt in pale blue, one set of underwear, one pair of leather-soled sandals, one pair of *geta,* three hand towels, one light blue cotton apron, and two ink sticks and five brushes to practice writing. In the fall they received one striped padded kimono, three pairs of white socks, one light blue cotton apron, and another two ink sticks and five brushes. Once they had gone through the coming-of-age ceremony they received an additional two pairs of white socks and two bleached cotton undergarments in spring and fall.

When the employee made his first trip back to Kyoto, he was supplied with clothing that allowed him to return in glory. In 1875 an employee who made this trip at seventeen *sai,* in his fifth year after starting work, received "a padded striped kimono in silk pongee, an unlined small-patterned silk jacket, one lined grayish-blue jacket in cotton, and an open-weave light blue belt." For the first time he was permitted jacket and silk, and we can assume that for a young man visiting his home village in such fine apparel, this must have been a moment of which to be proud.

Having completed the first trip back to Kyoto, the employee was considered a grown man. Every item of clothing worn thereafter reflected this new status and constituted his masculine capital. He no longer received livery; instead he was allowed to purchase clothing in the store at a discount as an advance against wages.

Although men had more freedom than boys in deciding what to put on their bodies, they were still subject to restrictions imposed by their employer to regulate their appearance both inside and outside the shop, day and night. According to the "Reform of Shop Regulations," issued in the seventh month of 1840, regular clothing consisted of striped cotton clothing summer and winter, with a plain open-worked belt. Clothing for outside consisted of a striped sateen or cotton-silk blend kimono with matching jacket, silk kimono, a jacket all in silk with a small pattern but no crest, and a plain belt woven of Chinese-style thread. Striped belts were allowed. After the first trip back to Kyoto, ordinary clothes changed from the Echizen stripe worn by boys to an Ōmi or Nara stripe. For going out the employee could show his elevation in rank by wearing a silk-cotton blend from Ōme or a sateen kimono as well as the jacket permitted for his first trip back to Kyoto. For accessories he was allowed a tissue holder of woolen cloth, a tobacco pouch for the sleeve, a brass pipe, black sateen for his undercollar, and so forth. There were also many things not permitted. It appears that the reform of 1840 was aimed at correcting customs inside the shop that tended toward showiness, and objects deemed useless were confiscated.

Clothing regulations for employees who had become regular clerks upon completing their second trip to Kyoto allowed for one degree more of grandeur. A sateen or a silk unlined kimono was permitted for ordinary wear, and when the employee went outside the shop, he was permitted to wear a thick silk or pongee jacket with a stripe in winter and a thin jacket with one crest on small-patterned linen or gauze in summer. His kimono could be a silk-cotton blend with a plain belt; a striped belt was not permitted. His tissue case could be felt, and his tobacco pouch was allowed to dangle from his belt. Also permitted were a thick silk small-patterned kimono without a crest and an unlined jacket in a double weave with a woven and printed pattern on the outside, plain on the inside. The wearing of hoods was permitted after the second trip to Kyoto. Silk became the standard attire, with woven and printed patterns on crested kimonos making for a showy appearance. Accessories, too, became fancier.

For the shop employee who managed to reach the top rank marked by a third trip back to Kyoto, his clothing became even finer, albeit still subject to regulation. His standard everyday attire was cotton, but when he went out, "he was allowed to wear whatever he owned, including a stripped belt." He was permitted a crested kimono with a woven and printed pattern, a three-crested jacket that was completely lined, or else a thin summer jacket. Objects that in 1840 had been confiscated by the shop as useless were returned to their owner upon this trip to Kyoto. Another reform was carried out in 1847. The regulations became even more detailed, with minute stipulations governing underwear as well as designs and background color for sleeve bands. Perhaps as the shop staff's clothing became showier, the regulations became stricter.

In early modern Japan, beautiful and luxurious clothing was a symbol of success. Kimonos reflected the wearer's rank in many ways. Their color (from lowly pale blue to brown or gray to high-ranking black), pattern (from stripe to plaid, and from a small print to a medium-size print), fabric (from cotton to linen or silk), weave (from plain to thick to pongee), and the number of crests all mattered. Even wearing a jacket was itself considered a privilege. This made clothing a valuable asset. Kimonos and belts often figured on lists of stolen goods compiled by magistrates' offices. Employees accumulated a considerable number of these objects during their years of service. Since these were their capital, when someone died or absconded, the goods that he left behind would be inventoried, with the list sent to his parents and the main store. Let us look at examples of what sorts of goods these men possessed.

Having started employment at twelve *sai* in the eleventh month of 1838 and arrived at the Sawara store a month later, Daitō Yasujirō was sent back to the main store in the intercalary first month of 1841 for being unsuitable. Having been in the store for just over two years, Yasujirō owned only "one striped, lined cotton kimono, one belt, fabric for one kimono, and one set of underwear."

Once an employee had completed his first trip back to Kyoto, the number of his possessions rapidly increased. Having begun work in 1814 at eleven *sai,* Saisuke completed his first trip to Kyoto in 1822, only to be dismissed for insolence in the first month of 1827. He was returned to his home along with his baggage, which included one padded kimono woven in Yūki, one padded variegated striped kimono from Ōmi, a Yūki full-weave jacket, an unlined jacket in patterned and figured cloth, a brown kimono in a Benkei pattern, a kimono in an Ōme stripe, two striped kimonos, a grayish-blue used belt, a grayish-blue belt in an arabesque pattern, a brown men's belt, one set of underwear with silk sleeves, some of medium size, and a long list of accessories. The remainder sent to the Kyoto store was comprised of one cotton and silk lattice-patterned kimono, one black Mooka kimono with crest, two lined kimonos in fine brown patterns from Yūki, two striped kimonos, one overkimono in an Echigo stripe, a vest in a Kawaka stripe, two sets of cotton underwear, and a grayish-blue man's belt in an arabesque pattern. These were the goods that he had acquired in barely thirteen years of employment.

Men who managed to pile up years of employment came to own large quantities of clothing. Having become a manager at the Sakura shop beginning in 1846, Yanagiya Shichirōbei found himself the next year put in the custody of his relatives on suspicion of not having followed regulations during his term in office. The list of his possessions totaled more than fifty-five items that had to be divided into three for shipment to Kyoto. He owned a great variety of clothing, including high-quality kimonos.

We can assume that men who successfully completed their terms as an employee owned many more items than did Shichirōbei, but no lists of possessions exist for them. Though accumulations of clothing constituted their assets, the outlay counted against the lump sum payments received at retirement. Offsetting the cost for splendid clothing and accessories meant that the amount of money received as wages was probably not that large either. In short, workers exchanged showy pretension for debt to the shop.

MARKING THE EMPLOYEE'S CAREER

In its role as the all-encompassing parental agent, Naraya punctuated each stage in an employee's career that allowed him greater finery with travel and promotions. Boys destined for the provinces were first brought from their parents' home to the main store in Kyoto. A contract probably specified the terms of employment, but these are no longer extant. Matsumoto Shirō has found in the Mitsui Osaka Money Exchange several contracts that were signed by the worker's guarantor and typically established a ten-year term of apprenticeship.[6] However, the attached condition that the worker could not retire until he had earned a lump sum that was larger than what could be acquired in ten years meant that in reality the worker was signing up for a lifelong apprenticeship. We can suppose that at Naraya, as well, apprentices had to work a lifetime if they wanted to retire successfully.

After training the boys at the Kyoto store for a period of between a few days and about a year, Naraya sent them to Sawara. Around the age of fifteen *sai* they went through the coming-of-age ceremony. This involved changing their names and hairstyles and receiving new clothing.[7] In recognition that they had achieved youth status, they were called "young men" *(wakaishu)*. After working as assistant clerks for about five years, they would be given the opportunity to make their first trip back to Kyoto and visit their parents. They made the trip via the main store, and the company paid all of their expenses, from their clothing to the souvenirs they took back to their hometown. Just as when they had first ventured to eastern Japan, they never traveled alone. Instead they traveled either with a supervisor or a director second to the supervisor in importance. This event was called *nobori* (going up to Kyoto), and through it the young workers established their identity as Naraya clerks. Dressed in their finest clothing, they distributed gifts to parents, families, and neighbors. Their homecoming not only brought glory to themselves, but it also might well have had an effect on boys in the village expected to be the next recruits.

These *nobori* marked important steps in the promotion process. A second trip to Kyoto would be permitted several years after the first. In the early years after the store's founding, an employee would return to the store and be promoted to manager upon his second trip to Kyoto. At the time of his third trip, he would retire. In later years, the third trip became a symbol of having achieved success. After successful retirement, the employee might work for two or three years inside the shop as a guardian to prove his gratitude to the store. At that point he might receive a portion of the store's customer base to set up as a branch house, be adopted into a different house (because they were a known quantity, adults were regularly adopted to ensure that the family enterprise continued from one generation to the next in the Edo period), begin his own business, or else remain in the shop in some sort of assistant capacity. For the first time he could have his own premises outside the store, which made it possible for him to marry and have children.

FAILING TO ACHIEVE A SHOP CLERK'S MANHOOD

Many men never finished the course laid out for them by Naraya. The first peak in dropouts came two to three years after starting employment, when boys, having come to a strange region from their faraway hometowns, had gradually become accustomed to the environment and the work. The next typically occurred in the five- to six-year range, after the boys had gone through their coming-of-age ceremony at which their status was changed to "youth." At this point they had culturally taken the first steps toward manhood, and their status in the store had risen to some extent. The third peak in dropouts came between the first and second visits home. Most of these men were entering their twenties, were working as regular clerks, and had the prospect of assuming a responsible office. The dropout rate dramatically decreased for men who lasted more than thirteen years at the store. If a man could pull through to this point, it seems likely that he would complete the ordinary life course for an employee.

The reasons for leaving employment varied from happenstance to individual initiative. According to the "Memo," the reasons included the following: death, illness, running away or absconding, inappropriate behavior, being unsuitable, taking leave (a neutral statement that does not disclose a reason), by request, a successful leave taking (through retirement or having completed a term of employment without incident), and completion of one's contract (see table 5.3).

The "Memo" also indicates that Naraya's extravagant paternalism extended to caring for boys and men once they had been employed and trained. Of thirty-nine men who died, thirty-seven died of illness and two by accident. Illness could become a reason for quitting in itself, but in many cases the patient would receive treatment from a doctor in the vicinity of Sawara or Sakura or else go back to Kyoto to receive medical treatment there at the store's expense. One case of treatment for illness

TABLE 5.3 Reasons for leaving employment

A. By decade

	Death	*Disease*	*Ran away*	*Unfit*	*Fired*	*Resigned*	*Retired*
1800s	3	—	—	6	1	—	—
1810s	—	1	2	1	5	—	2
1820s	2	—	4	7	1	1	1
1830s	3	1	—	11	—	1	—
1840s	3	—	4	9	1	3	—
1850s	7	1	2	9	1	6	—
1860s	6	5	6	13	—	2	1
1870s	5	—	8	5	—	8	1
1880s	3	1	15	1	1	4	3
1890s	2	—	4	1	3	2	3
1900s	4	2	7	—	1	5	—
1910s	1	—	—	—	—	—	—
unknown	—	—	—	—	1	—	—

NOTE: Differences in the reason for leaving depended heavily on length of service. Given the paucity of the data, it is difficult to draw conclusions, but it would appear that the first peak in departures occurred regardless of the era, the second peak showed the strongest definition in the 1860s and 1870s, and the third peak occurred chiefly after 1870.

clearly illustrates the store's sense of responsibility for its employees and their well-being. Nakanishi Sakubei from Ise started work at age thirteen *sai*. The "Memo" describes his case as follows:

> Since Sakubei had been sick for a long time, he went to Sakura to receive various medical treatments. None of them had any effect. Therefore, it was most fortunate that we gratefully received the instructions for him to take his third leave to go to Kyoto. At the main store in Kyoto he was handed over to Takenaka Shūkichi. In due course he became better, but then again he had a relapse, with a fever starting about the twentieth day of the sixth month. Even though we used doses of medicine prescribed by Takenaka Bunkei and Ema Choho, they had no effect at all. On the seventh day of the seventh month he died, ending his thirty-four years of life.

This record shows that Sakubei was deliberately moved to the Sakura store to receive treatment and thereafter sent to Kyoto, where three doctors tried to help him.

TABLE 5.3 *(continued)*

B. By term

Term (years)	*Death*	*Disease*	*Ran away*	*Unfit*	*Fired*	*Resigned*	*Retired*	*Contract expired*
0	2	—	—	—	—	—	—	—
1	3	1	1	3	3	1	—	—
2	3	1	1	6	2	—	—	—
3	4	—	2	7	—	3	—	—
4	2	—	4	4	—	3	—	—
5	1	3	4	7	—	1	—	—
6	4	—	5	6	1	2	—	—
7	3	2	6	4	1	3	1	—
8	2	—	2	4	—	3	—	—
9	1	—	6	2	2	2	—	1
10	1	1	7	5	1	2	—	—
11	2	1	3	5	—	1	—	—
12	1	—	1	3	1	6	—	—
13	4	—	3	2	1	1	—	1
14	1	—	1	1	—	1	1	—
15	—	—	1	1	—	1	1	2
16	1	—	3	1	—	—	1	2
17	—	—	—	1	—	—	1	—
18	1	—	—	—	—	1	1	1
19	—	—	1	1	—	—	1	4
20	—	—	—	—	—	—	1	9
21	1	—	—	—	—	—	—	3
22	1	1	—	—	—	—	—	4
23	—	1	—	—	—	—	—	6
24	—	—	—	—	—	—	—	4
25	—	—	—	—	—	—	2	11
26	—	—	—	—	—	—	—	5
27	—	—	—	—	—	—	—	1
28	—	—	—	—	—	—	—	—
29	—	—	—	—	—	—	—	1
unknown		—	1	—	1	1	—	—

Occasionally descriptions of illnesses also appear in the record. These include beriberi, diarrhea, lung disease, and kidney disease, as well as dizziness, dumbness, fainting, and other types of disease for which the cause remains unknown. Hayashi points out that the most common disease was beriberi, because workers in merchant houses ate better than ordinary villagers or townspeople, and thus enjoyed polished rice with their vegetables and fish. Rice polished to remove the bran was a symbol of luxury for the people of the Edo era, but it caused a deficiency in vitamin B1. In most cases, however, instead of describing the illness, the record simply states that an employee died.

Having the responsibility for its employees in loco parentis, the shop also took absconding seriously. Incidents of absconding increased in the early nineteenth century. In the 1870s and 1880s, twenty-three men ran away. Once it was discovered that someone had run away, the shop investigated. It immediately notified the man's guarantor (typically a parent), because the most likely destination for absconding young men was their hometown. Through arrangements with the man's supervisor, a search would be conducted, covering a broad area from criminal hangouts in Edo to the highways. Some men were discovered as soon as they turned up in their hometowns, but in many cases their whereabouts remained unknown. Probably because they had little knowledge of the lay of the land and little money in their possession, few boys ran away during the first three years of their employment. Perhaps they also lacked the endurance to make a long journey alone. A frightening example of what could happen to them was the case of Totsukasa Kikusaburō, who had arrived at Sawara in October of 1895. He ran away the following June at age fourteen *sai* and died on the road. Men were most likely to run away after they had been employed from four to ten years. They might go out on business and not return, visit a shrine and not return, or simply disappear suddenly one morning.

Genkichi from Kawamata in Ise, who entered the store in 1839 at the age of eleven *sai,* ran away two months after his coming-of-age ceremony in 1844. The circumstances are reported as follows:

> On the twenty-ninth day of the third month of 1844, Genkichi absconded together with Yohei early in the morning. We went immediately to request that the shopkeeper Kyūzō make inquiries. We pursued them as far as Yoshisato village and made inquiries as far as Shida. Having ascertained the direction they were going, we found them at Anzai. We told them what we thought of their behavior and tried to talk them into returning to the shop with us, but they

> refused to listen to anything we said. We could only tell them to give back their clothing as proof that we had found them. They were so insolent that we abandoned them as they were. On the third day of the fourth month we reported the incident to Kyoto and also to the boys' guarantors. Concerning the shop's funds, everything is as it should be [nothing stolen].

Within five days after the two men had run away the shop closed their case.

Another way in which one might fail to achieve the manhood offered by the merchant house employee path, being "inappropriate or unsuitable," was clearly determined by the store at its convenience. A man might not have the aptitude needed to be the employee of a dry goods store, he might commit an impropriety, or he might simply misbehave. Such a man was forcibly shipped back to the Kyoto store with the explanation that he was unsuitable, he did not conform to the ways of the store, he did not meet the store's standards, he was insolent, or he was dense. Thereafter he would be given permanent leave. Notations such as "unsuitable" or "not conforming to the ways of the store" were recorded for men who had worked a relatively short time, and some were sent back to Kyoto for one of these reasons less than a year after they had been dispatched to Sawara. Most notations for insolence and imprudence occurred for regular clerks after their first trip back to Kyoto. Naokichi from Kami Kayahara village in Ise, for example, had become a regular clerk, but "because he is unsuitable, he was found wanting in the sixth month of 1840, taken off the rolls, and turned over to his local guarantor." In this instance twelve years of employment were all for nothing. Yanagiya Shichirōbei, the manager at the Sakura store, was taken off the rolls because he had not maintained discipline. Even though he was an adult in terms of his age and experience, he suffered the indignity of being put in his parents' custody.

The reasons for "leave" remain unclear, but they must have reflected some defect in the worker's performance. Another set of reasons for quitting the store was categorized as "request" and was generally used for retirement based on amicable agreement owing to an appeal from the parents or guarantor before the years of employment had been completed. Such cases peaked around the twelfth year of employment, indicating that this must have been when a man began to see different life opportunities other than a long career as a store employee.

The successful "taking of leave" was for the sons of merchants in the vicinity of Sawara and Sakura who entered the shop to learn the business. Their period of training was determined upon their arrival, and they left when it was up. In the eyes of the shop owners, this kind of leave-taking reflected the man's and his parents' or guarantor's loyalty and sincerity.

A trend in the Meiji period was a decrease in the length of time men remained in the store, even when they completed the full course of employment. Along with heightened resistance to living in the store and an increase in the scale of business, fewer opportunities for regular clerks and those underneath them to rise in status probably contributed to the shortening of the term of employment. Cases increased of men who retired having completed their term but without having made manager, even though they had worked for long years. Perhaps to compensate, a second-in-command position was established along with its own employment track.

SUCCESS?

Completing a full term of employment did not necessarily mean escaping from Naraya's paternalistic grasp. As the following examples of successive managers' careers show, they were able to retire at a relatively young age, but that did not mean they could change employment. Instead, they continued to commute to work at the store even after they retired and lived in separate quarters. They needed the store's permission to marry. Only after a minimum of two or three years after their official retirement could they start their own businesses or be adopted into another family and continue its enterprise. Of the some 330 employees, only 70 became managers at either Sawara or Sakura or both. Since the scale of these establishments was not that large, this meant that the probability of becoming a manager was one in five for the men who began work there.

Remarkable about these managers is that despite the business training they supposedly received as apprentices and clerks, they seldom functioned well on their own. The first man to become a manager, Sakamoto Sōbei, was from Kayumi village, Ise province, the same village as the owner of Naraya. Sōbei began employment in 1763. Having become a manager in 1778 and worked for twenty-one years, he retired in 1783 and received a portion of the shop's customer base to open his own shop dealing in dry goods in Mito, north of Sawara. In 1802 he adopted Uhei, who had just completed his career as the fourth manager for Naraya, to continue his enterprise. In the end the business failed, and Naraya finally took back his entire remaining stock. Yoshida Buhei, also from Kayumi, became an employee of the Kyoto store in 1769. Later he came to Sawara, where he served as manager for three years starting in 1787 and then as guardian before retiring in 1792 to set himself up as a sake brewer. It appears that this new enterprise did not go well, because in 1800 he once again returned to the Sawara shop as a guardian. He must have managed to start a family, because he received ten *ryō* a year for their living expenses.[8]

Some managers succeeded on their own. Mohei started working in the Kyoto store in 1773 and went to Sawara in 1777. Having made two trips back to Kyoto, he became a manager in 1792 for four years and then spent another four years as guardian for live-out employees. In 1801 he set up a paper store in Kyoto. Two other men, Okada Chōbei, who entered employment in 1777 and became manager of the Kyoto store, and Kyūshichi, who was the manager of the Sawara store until 1864, opened their own businesses in Kyoto dealing in dry goods and piece goods following their retirement.

A special type of worker came from eastern Japan. Almost all of them were from Sawara or Sakura, with only a few from farther north, and the majority were the eldest sons of local branch houses or the sons of nearby merchants who worked as trainees. They did not go through the main store in Kyoto but instead went straight into employment in Sawara. Their trips home were not to Kyoto but to their families. Despite the advantage of remaining on their home turf, they too found a career in business to be a precarious proposition that had lifelong consequences for what it meant to be a man.

Two case studies show workers who continued to depend on their former employer. Coming from Fukuda village in Hitachi province, Asano Kyūbei started work at the Sawara store in the fourth month of 1787. In 1792 he was made manager of the Sakura Inn, possibly an earlier incarnation of the Sakura store, which would open in 1807. Having worked as manager until 1800, Kyūbei received a portion of the customer base in 1801 and opened his own business. In 1809 he borrowed 160 *ryō* from Naraya for business expenses. The son of Hamayado Seibei in Sawara, Yahei started working at the Sawara store in 1787. He moved to his own quarters in 1799 and began his own business. When it did not go well, he went back to work at the Sawara store as a commuting worker. In 1808 he again managed to start his own business, receiving an initial outlay of start-up funds from Naraya. Once again he failed. For a third time, he went back to work for the Sawara store in 1816. He took charge of provisions for the kitchen and worked as night watchman. At the end of 1824 he retired because of his advanced age. He then began a new business, but he failed yet again. Naraya continued to pay a small sum for his support until his death at age seventy-eight *sai*. Yahei spent years unsuccessfully trying to establish himself in an independent business. Despite his efforts, maturity for him meant relying on Naraya's support until the end of his life.

A counterexample can be found in the career of Okamoto Tsunekichi (later called Kinsuke). In 1796, at the age of fourteen *sai,* he started work for Naraya. The first time he had leave from the store, he went straight back to his parents in Sakura. After having worked for about fifteen years, in 1810 he took another leave. Since he was to set out on a pilgrimage in lieu of the trip to Kyoto, Naraya gave him his travel expenses to Kashima shrine and some more money for his clothes as well as souvenirs for his parents. Naraya's relationship with Tsunekichi's father justified this extraordinary outlay. Tsunekichi had satisfactory retirement. He succeeded to the Okamoto store in Sakura and probably achieved the full-fledged stature of an adult male, with family and descendants to match.

Naraya's practice of requiring its employees to remain single and live under its roof until they retired underwent modification over time. In the early nineteenth century, successful employees would begin work at the age of eleven or twelve *sai* and be promoted to manager in their late twenties or early thirties. Somewhere between their mid-thirties and the age of about forty they would end their live-in employment for the time being. Thereafter they could live in separate quarters with a family and commute to work. Around the middle of the nineteenth century, the managers started to get younger. In the late nineteenth century their age dropped to the mid-twenties at the Sakura store and to the late twenties at the Sawara store. This was reflected in a 1905 reform of store regulations, which specified that the period of compulsory residence in the store ended at twenty-one *sai.* This shortened the period during which men were required to live and work within the restricted confines of the shop and liberated workers to form their own families earlier. The reform also increased the relative length of time spent working following live-in employment and setting up a separate home, suggesting that Naraya had found it increasingly difficult to regulate the behavior of adult men when modernity increased their options.

Separated from their relatives and families at the age of eleven or twelve *sai,* the Naraya store employees in Sawara and Sakura went to a faraway region to spend twenty to thirty years in space defined by the shop. They might receive high wages comparable to other contemporary shop workers and wear sumptuous clothing, but so long as they were shop employees they could not get married, have children, or form their own households. Their lives were governed by strict regulations that required the permission of superiors even to go outside their androcentric space, which completely excluded women. The more earnestly they served, the longer the period during which they were confined to the store. Of course, if they worked the way they were supposed to, completed their three trips to Kyoto, and climbed to the summit of shop employees by becoming a manager or something similar, they were liberated from living in the shop and blessed with the opportunity to set up a branch house or be adopted by a different family, get married, and produce descendants.

It is unclear whether even successful managers were really able to establish their own bloodlines once they retired. The many opportunities for adoption into branch houses suggest that they could not. The irony is that the more successful an employee was—the more he rose through the ranks to become a manager—the longer he would have to defer achieving the merchant's masculine ideal of a home with a wife and children supported by his own enterprise.

The increase in men who absconded from the shop from the late Tokugawa period into the early Meiji era is, of course, in part a reflection of the greater number of employees. However, when we consider that their numbers increased after the men's first trip back to Kyoto, around the time they had been working for about ten years, it may reflect a spirit of resistance to confinement in the shop by youths in their mid-twenties. Perhaps in response to a perceived crisis, the 1875 reform set the compulsory period for boarders at a standard twenty-five years or until they reached the age of thirty-five *sai*. This, too, appears to have been too long, because the 1905 reform lowered the age of compulsory boarding to twenty-one *sai*. In this way it became possible for men to have a family while still continuing their lives as employees. Once employees who commuted to work came to have their own family units in the vicinity of the shop, their identity as sales clerks for the Naraya dry goods store included their family members as well.

In contrast to villages, where, starting in the seventeenth century, small households became the most effective units for farming rice and paying annual taxes, in urban areas small households were not necessarily needed. Multiple labor formations produced many single men, women, and family units not based on marital relations. This made it possible for groups of young, single men to exist apart from women and to participate in the accumulation of masculine capital represented by clothing and accessories.

NOTES

1. For the Mitsui store, see Matsumoto 1980; for the Mitsui moneychangers, see Hayashi 1983 and Matsumoto 1983. For Shirokiya, see Hayashi 1982

and 2003. In 2008, after a twenty-five-year hiatus, Nishizaka Yasushi published a big book about apprentices in Mitsui's Echigoya head store (Nishizaka 2008). Matsumoto, Hayashi, and Nishizaka based their work on materials in Mitsui Bunko. Records from Shirokiya provide good information on the lives of individual apprentices, but less on the total picture.

2. These ledgers are in the archives of the greater Tone (Ōtone) museum.

3. Figures for the first decade of the nineteenth century include workers at the Sakura store owing to its opening. Even though there are a number of men for whom the years they entered employment or quit are unknown or those who, because they returned to the main store in Kyoto in the middle of their careers, are not included in those who quit, the overall trends are clear. The Sawara store's size at the time it opened in 1764 is unknown, but since the Chiba store opened in 1909 with just five employees, we can assume that even at its height it had a small number of workers.

4. See Hayashi 1982 and 1983.

5. According to Hayashi, Shirokiya did not prohibit visits to brothels so long as they were not too expensive.

6. Matsumoto 1983.

7. For example, Fujimatsu became Shusuke, Yasumatsu became Chūhachi, Kikujirō became Bunshichi, and so forth. There do not appear to have been rules governing the change. A worker changed his childhood name to an adult name at the coming-of-age ceremony, and his next chance to alter his name was after the *nobori* (official trip to Kyoto). Hayashi says that Mitsui had strict rules for changing names. Childhood names ended in "-nosuke," plain clerks' names consisted of two Chinese characters, upper clerks used "-rō" "-suke," or "-bei/hei," managers "-emon," and the top manager's name was "-zaemon." Shirokiya had no such rigid rules.

8. Day laborers typically made one hundred *mon* a day; four thousand *mon* equaled one *ryō*. *Ryō* could be divided into four *bu* or sixteen *shu*. Unlike day laborers, apprentices received room and board from their employer, so their only expenses were incidentals and personal adornment.

REFERENCES

Hayashi Reiko. 1982. *Edodana hankachō*. Yoshikawa Kōbunkan.

———. 1983. "Ryōgaeten no hōkōnin." In *Mitsui ryōgaeshi*. Kabushiki Kaisha Mitsui Ginkō.

———. 2003. *Edodana no akekure*. Yoshikawa Kōbunkan.

Matsumoto Shirō. 1980. In *Mitsui Jigyōshi*, vol. 1. Mitsui Bunko.

———. 1983. "Ryōgaeten no hōkōnin to seikatsu." In *Mitsui ryōgaeshi*. Kabushiki Kaisha Mitsui Ginkō.

Nishizaka Yasushi. 2008. *Mitsui Echigoya hōkōnin no kenkyū*. Tōkyō Daigaku Shuppankai.

6 Losing the Union Man

Class and Gender in the Postwar Labor Movement

Christopher Gerteis

During the early decades of the postwar era, public and private institutions constructed social roles for blue-collar men that augured the reemergence of a common set of gender practices legitimizing the subordination of women to men and the dominance of some men over others. The resultant hegemonic masculine ideal for the blue-collar "working man" was nonetheless ideologically flexible: labor leaders found it useful as a means of mobilizing union militancy, corporate managers were able to deploy it to quell union militancy, and the state found it a useful symbol of Japan's economic success. By the mid-1960s, work had become the measure of citizenship, employment synonymous with manhood, and Japanese men the breadwinners of postwar society.

Higher wages overall also led to a significant change in workers' aspirations, and by the 1970s blue-collar workers increasingly dreamed of living a middle-class lifestyle. This chapter examines two aspects of this historical trajectory. First, it argues that higher wages had the unintended consequence of enabling working-class men of all ages to identify with middle-class notions of masculinity, from older men who wanted to buy cars to young men who wanted to go skiing. Second, it shows how a generational schism also developed within the rank and file as younger men increasingly rejected the union's hegemonic masculine "family man" norm while expressing bitterness that their wages did not allow them to access the familial and consumer trappings of middle-class life available to their older male co-workers. Some even found new outlets for militant activism, forming interclass relationships along generational lines by affiliating with their middle-class contemporaries rather than toeing the union line defined by their working-class elders.

This chapter narrates the generational contest to define working-class masculine identity that emerged during the era of global youth culture and radical political movements that characterized the 1960s and early 1970s. By analyzing the ways in which middle-aged male leaders of Japan's Old Left unions perceived politically active, young blue-collar men, the chapter shows how generational conflict influenced the ways in which an increasing number of blue-collar men of all ages identified with middle-class cultural and economic forms. One result was the fracturing of the Old Left's monopoly on class-based ideals of masculinity, which set the stage for a cascade of class and gender confusions that have shaped popular notions of "work" and "manhood" to the present day.

James Roberson and Nobue Suzuki's *Men and Masculinities in Contemporary Japan* broke new ground by staking out a field of diverse masculine ideals performed by blue- and white-collar workers previously dominated by the idea of a hegemonic salaryman persona.[1] Tom Gill's chapter in this volume transgresses the bounds of customary notions of work, workplace, and home by exploring the self-construction of masculine ideals among homeless men in the urban centers of contemporary Japan. This essay moves in a different direction by analyzing conflicting masculine ideals expressed by blue-collar workers during the first three decades of the postwar era, and the failure of the socialist labor movement to establish a well-defined blue-collar masculine ideal.

WAGE SYSTEMS

The sometimes violent confrontations between labor and management that characterized labor relations during the late 1940s and 1950s contributed to the creation of a postwar wage system premised on the notion that a blue-collar man was the sole breadwinner for his family, and set the stage for the increased standards of living that accompanied double-digit economic growth in the 1960s.[2] Developing alongside similar wage systems for white-collar workers, the blue-collar age- and seniority-based wage system can be seen as one cause of the alienation of young men that characterized youth culture of the late 1960s, because it left them lesser paid, despite individual skill and ability, and hierarchically subordinate to the older generation of male workers.

The socialist labor movement, which represented the majority of wage-earning men and women until the late 1980s, was no stranger to the use of gender norms as a means of mobilizing the working class. Labor propaganda had deployed gendered tropes since the early twentieth century, but the material basis for the postwar labor movement's reconstruction of customary gender roles fully emerged in the early 1950s. The Densan Wage System, named for the Electrical Utility Workers' Union (Nihon Denki Sangyō Rōdō Kumiai Rengō Kyōgikai, or Densan), which created it in the late 1940s, quickly became the basis upon which the socialist General Council of Trade Unions (Nihon Rōdō Kumiai Sōhyōgikai, or Sōhyō), a national federation of unions representing approximately six million wage earners, assessed target wages for the pattern bargaining campaigns in the 1950s, which consisted of contract negotiations between an industry-wide union and one employer during which the union focused all its resources on winning a favorable contract from that employer and then used the conflict and resultant agreement as a precedent to demand similar contracts from additional employers not otherwise bound by the original agreement. By the early 1950s, Densan had won several contracts that assessed worker wages based on the real cost of living as calculated by the union, not the government or management.[3]

A radical reconceptualization of the purpose of the workplace itself, the Densan Wage System ignored corporate profit (not a particularly pressing issue for a publicly owned utility) and privileged need by emphasizing that the purpose of work was to enable a worker to live the minimum cultured life guaranteed by Article 25 of the 1947 Constitution of Japan.[4] The Densan "market-basket" wage system established base wages based on the actual cost of food staples, housing, transportation, and medical care. Created to suit the needs of a majority male workforce, it was built on the premise that a male wage earner headed each worker household. By adopting the Densan market-basket ideal, Sōhyō promoted the demand for a family-centered wage for all Sōhyō workers. This resulted in a federation-wide wage system that privileged the male breadwinner as the economic goal central to union activism.[5]

In the mid-1950s, Sōhyō secretary-general Ōta Kaoru institutionalized the market-basket system by incorporating its premise that a workers' wages supported a wife and children at home into the way Sōhyō determined the base wage demanded during the annual Spring Wage Offensive (Shuntō). The Shuntō were jointly coordinated campaigns in which public and private sector unions collaborated in a series of direct actions in support of large-scale pattern bargaining for minimum increases in base wages. Both private and public railway unions played a central role in the success of the Shuntō because their ability to shut down the transportation nexus on command was crucial to Sōhyō's ability to engage in pattern bargaining with public and private officials. The Spring Wage Offensive provided a powerful, coordinated structure within which both private and public sector unions could ensure incremental wage increases during the high-speed double-digit growth of the 1960s, and it consequently dominated the collective bargaining arena until the late 1990s.[6]

With the launch of the first nationally coordinated Shuntō in 1956, the concept of a family wage gained hold through the federation's demand for base wages determined by the needs of a male worker's family implicit in the market-basket wage demanded by Densan in the early 1950s. At the heart of this system lay the fundamental assumption that women's wage-earning work merely supplemented the income of the male wage earner who presumably headed the Japanese household. What motivated workers belonging to Sōhyō-affiliated unions to join strikes coordinated by Sōhyō, even when their own unions had already reached a settlement with management, was the dream of a base wage that allowed a working man to support his family.[7]

Nationally coordinated strike actions to win contracts granting aggregate base-percentage increases in workers' wages worked. Aggregate hourly wages nearly doubled for all wage earners between 1955 and 1965. However, wage gains were not distributed equally. Women certainly bore the worst of this burden in the form of lower wages overall, but the wage gap between male blue-collar workers aged 20–24 and 30–34 also widened to 38 percent.[8] Later, the wage gap between male workers aged 20–24 and 30–34 narrowed to 34 percent from 1965 to 1975, while the wage gap for the cohort of men who were 30–34 years in 1975 (and in their early twenties in 1965) and men of the age cohort ten years older (40–44 years) also narrowed slightly to 12 percent, indicating a general flattening of age-based wage disparities that appeared to bode well for the wage-earning prospects of blue-collar men belonging to younger age cohorts. Although younger men still made two-thirds of that earned by older male co-workers, the difference was not as great as it had been just ten years previous.[9]

Blue-collar men were doing well, and union leaders heavily invested in schemes promoting social roles for blue-collar men that defined manliness in terms of work and wages as a means encouraging their own political agenda. Social expectations that a "real man" worked for his family increasingly became the norm. Yet many young men had reported to union officials a decade earlier their dismay that even by the age of thirty they did not make enough to marry, a predicament that threatened to become a self-perpetuating cycle—a man could not make enough to get married, but he would not be paid a high wage until he married.[10] Indeed, in addition to a wife, higher wages would also allow the acquisition of a host of consumer products recently arrived on the national scene, and in the minds of many blue-collar men the achievement of manhood had become tantamount to joining the middle class. Despite the narrowing of wage disparities between younger and older men, the rhetorical and material reality appear to have combined to create a wage and status hierarchy that subordinated male blue-collar youth.

Labor economist Ōmachi Keisuke thought that there was trouble brewing for the near future. Writing for the labor magazine *Monthly Sōhyō* in 1964, Ōmachi observed that the wage disparity between men in their twenties and men in their thirties (young and middle-aged) played a significant role in the "graying" of the labor movement. The majority of workers in the rapidly growing communications, transportation, and service sectors were aged twenty-five to thirty, but the average age of union members in those same sectors would soon reach thirty-five. Ōmachi argued that although workers under the age of thirty comprised more than half of the workforce, the rapid economic growth experienced during the preceding decade had facilitated a significant wage disparity between young and middle-aged men that was far worse in Japan than in Western Europe or the United States. Ōmachi warned of dire consequences for Sōhyō if the trend went unaddressed for much longer.[11]

Ōmachi's article pinpointed a problem that Sōhyō leaders preferred to ignore. Sōhyō unions had won contracts that secured better wages and faster promotion tracking for men in exchange for management schemes that, regardless of skill or ability, systemically relegated women and young men to the lower-paying base of the workforce. Sōhyō unions had agreed to contracts paying younger men and women less as a means of defraying the cost of higher wages for middle-aged men. Young workers, both males and females under the age of thirty, comprised a significantly larger percentage of the waged workforce than unions had on their membership roles. While the low rates of unionization among young workers resulted from a variety of causes, Ōmachi argued that the significant part of the problem lay with the wage disparity between younger and middle-aged men that underpinned the family wage model advocated by Sōhyō since the mid-1950s.

While union leaders did not at first agree with Ōmachi's assessment that the "graying" of union membership was an economic problem, the Sōhyō Youth Department nonetheless began to call for improved wages for younger workers, which seemed to result in a slight narrowing of the wage differential between younger and older men. That the average age of

Sōhyō members continued to rise (reaching thirty-three in 1970) suggests that despite a narrowed pay differential, Sōhyō unions continued to have a difficult time recruiting young members. Wage and union membership data offer only a glimpse of the economic basis of worker mentality, but it seems likely that the declining numbers of young blue-collar union members was in part the result of an emerging generational rift between blue-collar men.

YOUTH IN QUESTION

The nexus of gender and generation played a significant role in the way Sōhyō unions defined union militancy throughout the postwar period. In fact, the postwar period has been as much about conflicts of masculinities between men of different generations as about conflicts between men and women. The older generation of union leaders had come of age during the years immediately following World War II and embodied a manhood whose driving force was twofold: an interest in wages and a commitment to the political cause of the socialist party. While union propaganda of the 1950s and 1960s was constructed to mobilize union members for both political and economic agendas, union leaders understood worker militancy to be part and parcel of the union's ability to garner better wages for its membership.[12] The experience of war and defeat deeply influenced their political consciousness, and the economic desperation of the immediate postwar years combined with the conservative retrenchment that accompanied the onset of the cold war in Japan had precipitated their political radicalization. The younger generation increasingly rebelled not only against their fathers' generation but also against the ideal-type masculinity their fathers promoted.

During the 1950s, union leaders dreamed up ways in which union members could organize the ideal union family. "Family union" *(kazoku kumiai* or *katei kumiai)* literature promoted marriage between young union members. One 1950s issue of the monthly labor magazine *Railway Culture* even encouraged young railway men and women to marry and raise "union families" by reprinting love letters sent to the magazine by young "union couples" *(kumiai kappuru)* who had had a "workplace wedding" *(shokuba kekkonshiki)*. The magazine even went so far as to publish sample guest lists and wedding itineraries as templates for young union women to use as models for their own "union weddings."[13]

Many rank-and-file women who were loyal to the union, but unhappy with their secondary status within it, declared their opposition to becoming "union wives" within the pages of the same union magazines. When asked by organizers of a union roundtable, published by *Railway Culture* in 1956, whether she desired to marry a union man, twenty-two-year-old Kokurō member Kondō Masako replied that all she really wanted was fifteen thousand yen per month, which she was not going to see on her monthly pay stub if she married a union man. Despite many similar criticisms leveled by rank-and-file union women, Sōhyō and its member unions fashioned their national magazines into a forum aimed to persuade their female members to get behind the union's attempt to build a more family-oriented labor movement by supporting their male co-workers (and presumed future husbands) in their fight to win better wages.[14]

While the notions of marriage and child rearing appeared to have motivated the hard-working "soot-covered fathers" *(makkuro papa)* who had founded the railway workers' union in the mid-1940s, the "family union" trope no longer appealed to the generation of blue-collar men born after the war. Too young to remember the labor militancy that had won their unprecedented standard of living, Japan's generation of the 1960s had grown discontented with the political and cultural status quo and sought to destabilize the political establishment through cultural, intellectual, and even performative interventions such as experimental film, art installations, and theater productions.[15] Like their contemporaries in Europe and the United States, young men and women in Japan joined interrelated cultural and political movements at odds with institutions they perceived to be dominated by a petite bourgeoisie in league with a capitalist regime indifferently opposed by stolidly authoritarian socialist and communist movements.[16]

The countercultural and radical politics at the center of the youth movement during the mid- and late 1960s also had a significant impact on the labor movement. The growing unpopularity of the Vietnam War led Sōhyō secretary-general Ōta Kaoru to believe that the antiwar movement might provide the means to bring young workers back into the fold.[17] Despite Ōmachi Keisuke's warning about the potential consequences of Japan's age- and seniority-based wage system, Ōta blamed the divisive politics of the youth culture made popular by the radical student movement of the era, which he considered undisciplined and dominated by bourgeois students, for diverting young workers away from the labor movement's class-based political and economic agenda. Blaming the popularity of the so-called counterculture for a dearth of young people on union membership roles, in 1965 Ōta authorized Sōhyō to jointly fund, with the youth action group of the Japan Socialist Party (Shaseidō), the creation of the Antiwar Youth Committee (Hansen Seinen Iinkai, or Hansen). Ōta believed that

Hansen could become the means to reengage blue-collar youth by offering them an authorized alternative to the student movement.[18]

By embracing the anti-hierarchical, anti-authoritarian ideals espoused by the radical student movement, many Hansen chapters came into direct conflict with the Japan Socialist Party (JSP) and Sōhyō.[19] Having replaced Ōta as the head of Sōhyō in 1966, Horii Toshikatsu was frustrated by the trajectory Hansen had taken and expressed skepticism about the potential for future youth outreach programs. In 1967, Hansen broke with the JSP altogether, condemning the party for its authoritarian hierarchy and rigid doctrine. Ōta, who remained influential in the labor movement until his death in 1997, believed that "bourgeois radicals" had taken control of what was supposed to be a young worker's organization.[20]

Although Hansen did not break outright with Sōhyō, internal Sōhyō documents show that by 1968 the federation had little influence over the organization. Violent confrontations with police at Haneda Airport in October 1967, precipitated by radical student groups in collaboration with Hansen, further estranged Hansen and Sōhyō leadership. As a result, the Sōhyō Central Committee sponsored two directives, published as essays authored by the Sōhyō Youth Committee (none of whose members were under the age of thirty), which harshly criticized Hansen leadership for breaking away from the JSP and drawing too close to the radical student movement.[21] Condemned by the JSP, and in serious trouble with Sōhyō, the coalition of Hansen chapters declared the "Old Left" incapable of meeting the members' core demand for the right to determine their own political subjectivity.[22]

While Hansen had provided several thousand blue-collar men with an alternative forum for political activism, Sōhyō's attempt to harness the radical youth movement had failed. Indeed, the heads of several Young Workers' Departments of Sōhyō-affiliated unions had publicly argued in 1968 that young workers were likely to be further alienated unless the federation did a better job of adapting the labor movement to provide higher base wages and rapid promotion tracking. Charged with the responsibility of bringing young workers back into the fold of Sōhyō-led labor activism, Sōhyō representatives simply touted the federation line by asserting that young workers had a *duty* to devote themselves to the Spring Wage Offensive—and thus demonstrated that Sōhyō was still unable to adapt to accommodate the interests of a new generation of blue-collar workers.[23]

Perhaps most striking is that Sōhyō publications never presented young men in social roles that diverged from union orthodoxy. Throughout the radical 1960s, even as Sōhyō was funding Hansen's foray into radical youth politics, the labor press continued to deploy the trope of the "family man as union man" in its effort to stir up rank-and-file support. The paucity of young men's voices in Sōhyō publications and the lack of younger visions of socialist unionized manhood also underscores the issue: by failing to resolve the "youth question," Sōhyō and its member unions lost the struggle over blue-collar masculinity. Indeed, labor propaganda after 1965 offers next to no essays, poetry, or political cartooning credited as having been produced by men under the age of thirty. By the mid-1970s, union leaders stood at the head of an organization of middle-aged men unable to persuade their sons to engage with the unions they had founded. This generational divide marked a divergence in notions of masculine ideals to which the postwar labor movement seemed unable to adapt, and young workers appear to have been lost to the labor unions that sought to mobilize them.

DREAMING TO BECOME MIDDLE-CLASS

In the economically troubled years following the OPEC oil embargo of 1973–74, Sōhyō leaders were primarily concerned with stemming the impact of rising consumer prices and stagnant wages and no longer even tried to develop outreach programs for younger workers interested in alternative political and cultural modes of expression. Well before the radical youth movement began to wind down in the early 1970s, Sōhyō cut off funds for organizing young workers outside mainstream union halls. Union leaders also began to use the labor press to attempt to co-opt emerging middle-class expectations among the rank and file by providing a forum for them to explore their aspirations and reinvent what it meant to be a union man.

Nowhere was this reinvention of the union man more apparent than in the political cartoons included in the January 1975 issue of *Kokurō Bunka*. Selected by magazine editors for the 1975 New Year's special issue, two political cartoons by Suzuki Akuzō, an employee of the Japan National Railways at the Ōmiya Workshop, represent the growing generational tension within Sōhyō's flagship union.[24] Suzuki's cartoon (see figure 6.1) opened the segment with the ubiquitous depiction of the union man as a family man.[25] Central to this panel is a brief exchange between two young male children. Exclaims one to the other, "Only father and the postman work on New Year's!" The male railway worker the young boys are talking

Figure 6.1. "Only father and the postman work on New Year's!" Cartoon by Suzuki Akuzō of the Ōmiya Workshop, published in *Kokurō Bunka*, January 1975, p. 67.

about, the ticket puncher to the right of the frame, who presumably is also the father of the cheeky child, swings his head around with a surprised look on his face. The motive for his surprise is unclear, but the truth of the matter probably hit home with the intended audience of railway workers who had also likely worked more than one national holiday. Only he and the postal worker are forced to work on the most important family holiday of the year.

Suzuki's cartooning relied on the "family man as union man" trope, common in labor's political cartooning (manga) since the 1950s, to connect with his intended audience. However, the panel featured in figure 6.1 also depicts a growing undercurrent of resentment within the railway workforce by providing the intended reader the opportunity to explore its displeasure that management and union had agreed to longer work hours in exchange for higher monthly wages. By the early 1970s transportation workers were averaging 35 percent more hours per month than they had worked a decade earlier, and, although the hours were for the most part evenly distributed between age groups, wages were not.[26] Indeed, Kumazawa Makoto argued that the national trend was the result of a tacit agreement between union leadership and management to seek ways to improve worker productivity, by and large through longer work hours, in trade for higher aggregate monthly wages. While this was an overt process in many of the industrial unions outside Sōhyō, productivity arrange-

Figure 6.2. "New Year's Temple Visit." Cartoon by Suzuki Akuzō of the Ōmiya Workshop, published in *Kokurō Bunka*, January 1975, p. 73.

ments also accounted for a measurable percentage of the annual-base wage increases won by Sōhyō member unions since the early 1960s.[27]

Suzuki Akuzō's cartoon depicted in figure 6.2, also included in the January 1975 issue of *Railway Culture*, offers additional insight into the rank-and-file consciousness of Kokurō workers of the mid-1970s by illustrating an image of union roles for men and women that demonstrate how middle-aged men had failed to adapt to the changing interests of young workers. Entitled "New Year's Temple Visit," the panel was published as part of the occasional series "JNR Manga Collective," which magazine editors used to groom artists thought to show potential to become regular contributors. A panel divided into eight frames, Suzuki's vignette depicts a small group of union men out visiting on New Year's Day.

In the first frame, the men step into the entryway of the home *(genkan)* of the chief of their local union chapter while calling out their New Year's wishes to the union leader's wife. She greets them in the entryway but is surprised that they and even her husband have come to visit her. The men explain that their union secretary had almost been disinherited by his family because of the amount of time required by his union duties, but once his wife had realized what the family was up to she was able to convince them to back down by explaining that without the union he and his family would have nothing. In gratitude for her intervention, the union leaders elected to visit all their wives in order to convey their New Year's wishes. "We have resolved that at the start of the New Year we should visit the wives [*kami-san*, which is a homonym for both "wife" and the "god" of a shrine] of our union members instead of shrines and temples." "Mother," the woman's husband and union chief announces, "the Shuntō is coming soon; we would be grateful for your support."

The cartoon, meant as a reminder of normative gender roles for women and men, echoes prescribed roles for men by reinforcing the supportive role that married women were expected to play in union affairs. It illustrates a union orthodoxy that precluded the emergence of social roles at odds with gender norms established in the 1950s. While such kinds of social roles continued to appeal to men over the age of thirty-five, every year after 1960 fewer men under the age of thirty joined Sōhyō-affiliated unions, which suggests that the institutional culture of Sōhyō did not appeal to the majority of young blue-collar workers, male or female. The issue seemed to be changing notions of personal self-identification.

Making more money than ever before, blue-collar men, young and old, increasingly imagined themselves to be middle-class. Importantly, the January 1975 issue of *Railway Culture* also marks an increased interest in the trappings of middle-class life expressed by union leaders and rank-and-file members. Since the late 1940s, editors had featured works of fiction and prose submitted to the magazine by union workers.[28] Most submissions were selected to reflect the theme of a particular issue, and it should come as no surprise that the majority expressed the positive impact union activism played in the life of Japanese workers. Shinagawa-based passenger car attendant Yamada Akihiko's "The Union Badge" explored the pride felt by those men who earn a railway union pin (merit badge) through dedication and hard work for union causes. Stolid in its adherence to the "union line," Yamada's essay is a classic example of the literary productions preferred by union leadership and also accurately reflects the purpose of the magazine—to provide a regular forum for pro-labor propaganda.[29]

Despite the general emphasis on union-authorized propaganda, labor magazines allowed other perspectives as well. One essay by Okayama Station attendant Onimaru Hiroyuki introduced a new form of rank-and-file expression—the travel essay. Onimaru explored the historic sights and sounds of rural rail travel in and around the city of Kyoto, romantically intertwining modern rail travel with an ancient landscape.[30] Onimaru's dreamlike journey illustrates an emerging desire among blue- and white-collar workers for more leisure time, further developed in a short essay submitted by Railway Credit Union clerk Ōki Kiyoshi. Ōki's "Ski Area of the Future" narrates his personal dream of skiing mountain slopes like the Olympic athletes he and millions of Japanese had watched during the televised Winter Olympic Games hosted by the northern city of Sapporo in 1972, during which Kasaya Yukio and two other Japanese nationals swept the top three places in the ski jump event.[31] While sports and leisure travel were common tropes for establishing a masculine ideal in the socialist lexicon of Western and northern Europe, skiing requires expensive gear—skis, boots, poles—not customarily owned by blue-collar Japanese men. The essays by Ōki and Onimaru are not simply stolid nods to socialist ideals; they illustrate the emergence of a middle-class consumer consciousness among male blue-collar workers who wanted to enjoy the increased standards of living possible only since the mid-1960s. Writing in the mid-1970s, and in their early thirties, Ōki and Onimaru both expressed their dream of middle-class life outside the union-authorized trope of the "working man as family man."

While the leaders of Sōhyō unions were still deeply invested in constructing a socialist subjectivity for Japan's working class, by the mid-1970s the "railway man" greatly differed from the *makkuro papa,* the soot-covered craftsman who founded the union in the mid-1940s. He still dreamt of providing for his family, but he also wanted leisure time to spend on his own pursuits such as travel, sports, and perhaps owning his own automobile. The railway man of 1975 did not dream of class liberation, he dreamt of being middle-class, and the question that plagued Sōhyō leaders for the remainder of the decade was whether there was a role for socialist unions in a middle-class society.

The cover story of the January 1975 issue of *Railway Culture* provides evidence that influential members of the inner circles of Sōhyō were increasingly ambivalent toward, if not confused about, the impact that the changing class identity of blue-collar workers might have on the future of the labor movement. In "The Struggle with Inflation," Kokurō Central Committee chairman Sakai Ichizō and labor economist Kamakura Takao examine the extent to which the double-digit inflation that followed the 1973 "oil shock" threatened to erode the hard-won wage gains of the 1960s.[32] Interestingly, Sakai and Kamakura dedicate a significant portion of their jointly written essay to discussing the rapidly increasing cost of gasoline. Given that they were writing for an audience of unionized railway workers, the authors could easily have crafted their comments as an admonishment against overreliance on private automobiles. Instead, they offered reassurances that gas prices might yet stabilize enough to allow car travel to become affordable for most railway workers and their families. Automobile ownership, the first of the "three C's" (car, cooler, and color TV), was the primary consumer symbol of the middle class.[33] That Sakai and Kamakura felt compelled to offer an optimistic assessment of the chances that blue-collar workers like those of the Japan National Railways (JNR) could soon afford to drive their own automobile is a good indicator of the increasing cultural significance that blue-collar workers assigned to the material goods associated with middle-class life. But in embracing the dream of affluence, labor leaders somehow failed also to persuade Japan's blue-collar workers of the continued importance of union militancy in securing the wages that paid for it all.[34]

During the first three decades of the postwar era, leaders of Japan's socialist unions deployed notions of the "family man as bread winner" predicated on economic and cultural systems that relegated younger men and women of all ages to the lower tiers of a wage economy that privileged older family men. During the peak economic boom years of the 1960s, some six million workers belonged to unions affiliated with Sōhyō, making it appear that the gendered and class-based notion of the "family man" portrayed by socialist unions in the 1960s and 1970s appealed to middle-aged male union members and their families. However, the notion of the "union man as family man" did not have the same appeal to the young blue-collar men who came of age amid the countercultural and political movements of the 1960s. It did not benefit them much either.

The postwar wage system that excluded wage-earning women and disadvantaged young men was nonetheless responsible for an unprecedented improvement in the economic status of nearly all Japanese. Contemporary writings about Japan report that the vast majority of Japanese consider themselves to be "middle-class." Japan's labor unions played a significant role in the process of winning the wages that enabled this self-perception, but becoming middle-class also had serious consequences for the militant unions that spearheaded the wage struggles of the postwar period. By elevating blue-collar Japanese into the middle class, their economic success may have undone their own organizing base.

Sōhyō's flagship union, Kokurō, was disemboweled by the privatization of JNR during the late 1980s, which encouraged managers and government bureaucrats nationwide to redouble propaganda campaigns promoting a company-centered workforce. Perhaps in the face of a weakened labor movement, but also because of their gendered understanding of a changed economic status, men working blue-collar jobs represented by the militant unions that had defined the early postwar era increasingly thought of themselves as company, not union, men.

The "graying" of Sōhyō and its member unions continued until its dissolution in 1989, and while the socialist agenda of many labor unions did not die with the federation, its successor Rengo (Nihon Rōdō Kumiai Sōrengōkai) was never able to garner the organizational strength needed to stop, or even slow, the layoffs and wage cuts that characterized the 1990s. When the economic retrenchment in the post-bubble economy of the early 1990s led to the first mass layoffs since the early 1950s, Japan's labor unions were too weak to fulfill their fiduciary duty to resist the worst effects of downsizing. Hundreds of thousands of blue-collar men lost their jobs, contributing to what politicians and business leaders would later refer to as a national crisis of masculinity. While union membership was not a prerequisite to being a blue-collar man, the wages won by Japan's postwar labor movement were, and the dissolution of Sōhyō was the closing chapter to the era of union militancy that had won the wages at the root of the postwar masculine ideal. In many ways losing the union man also meant losing the economic basis of blue-collar manhood in postwar Japan.

NOTES

I wish to thank the Japan–United States Education Commission and the AAS Northeast Asia Council (NEAC) for generously funding the field and archival research that made this article possible.

1. Gordon Matthews, "Can a 'Real Man' Live for His Family?: Ikigai and Masculinity in Today's Japan"; James Roberson, "Japanese Working-Class Masculinities: Marginalizing Complicities"; Tom Gill, "When Pillars Evaporate: Structuring Masculinity at the Japanese Margins"; and Masako Ishii-Kuntz, "Balancing Fatherhood and Work: Experience of Diverse Masculinities in Contemporary Japan," all in Roberson and Suzuki 2002, pp. 109–25; 126–43; 144–61; and 198–216, respectively.

2. Kumazawa 1996, p. 52; and Gordon 1998, pp. 163–68.

3. Nihon Rōdō Kumiai Sōhyōgikai 1964, pp. 362–73.

4. The 1947 Constitution of Japan, available online at http://history.hanover.edu/texts/1947con.html (accessed 20 June 2008).

5. Women were not presumed to head a household, and job categories customarily held by women were subsequently excluded in the contracts that resulted from the pattern bargaining campaigns of the early and mid-1950s. See Gerteis 2009, pp. 82–85.

6. Kume 1998, pp. 73–106; and Weathers 2008, pp. 177–97.

7. Nihon Rōdō Kumiai Sōhyōgikai 1964, pp. 362–73; and Tōkyō Chihō Rōdō Kumiai Hyōgikai 1980, pp. 491–511.

8. Ōmachi 1964, pp. 65–73; and Nihon Tōkei Kyōkai 1975, pp. 398–99.

9. Men aged 20–24 holding manufacturing jobs earned 68 percent of the wages earned by men aged 30–34, while transportation and communication sector workers earned 71 percent. Male utility workers aged 20–24 earned 64 percent, and male service sector workers, which included government employees and teachers, 65 percent. Nihon Tōkei Kyōkai 1975, pp. 70–75, 398–99.

10. Gerteis 2009, pp. 129–30.

11. Ōmachi 1964, pp. 65–73.

12. Gibbs 2000; Kume 1998; and Carlile 2005.

13. Kokutetsu Rōdō Kumiai Seinenkyōiku 1956, pp. 26–28, 30–34. See Gerteis 2009, pp. 122–58.

14. Gerteis 2009, pp. 128–29, 122–58.

15. Marotti 2006, pp. 606–18.

16. Takami 1968.

17. Havens 1987; Takagi 1985; and from notes filed in the folder labeled "Hansen, 1965.7–1969.5," in the papers of Sōhyō Organizing Department, Ōhara Institute for Social Research, Hōsei University.

18. "Hansen, 1965.7–1969.5," in the papers of Sōhyō Organizing Department, Ōhara Institute for Social Research, Hōsei University.

19. Takami 1968, pp. 132–84.

20. "Hansen, 1965.7–1969.5," in the papers of Sōhyō Organizing Department, Ōhara Institute for Social Research, Hōsei University; and Mizuno 2002.

21. Sōhyō Seitai Iinkai 1968, pp. 18–27; and Enda 1968, pp. 28–38.

22. Takami 1968, pp. 132–84.

23. Sōhyō Seinenbu 1968, pp. 39–71.

24. The Ōmiya facility, which serviced rolling stock for half a dozen

major railway lines, was, despite appearances, the heart of Kokurō's cultural and political enterprises intended to promote concepts and ideals thought to help build a socialist consciousness among rank-and-file workers. Wes Sasaki-Uemura more fully explores how the hard-working *makkuro papa* (soot-covered fathers) of a similar JNR workshop in the 1950s composed their poetical expressions of work, life, and union. Sasaki-Uemura 2001, pp. 81–111.

25. The magazine does not tell us the actual work that Suzuki did at the Ōmiya Workshop.

26. Nihon Tōkei Kyōkai 1949–, 1975 edition, p. 71.

27. Kumazawa 1996, pp. 125–58.

28. Like their prewar predecessors, Japan's postwar unions were also in close collaboration with sympathetic artists and intellectuals to create what they hoped would become the basis of a socialist national culture for Japan. Shinoda 2005a, pp. 1–16; Shinoda 2005b, pp. 13–31; and Kokumin Bunka Kaigi 1995, pp. 3–15.

29. Yamada 1975, pp. 3–4.

30. Onimaru 1975, pp. 2–3.

31. Kasaya's gold medal was the first won by a Japanese national. Ōki 1975, pp. 4–5; and www.olympic.org/uk/games/past/index_uk.asp?OLGT=2&OLGY=1972 (accessed 18 June 2008).

32. Kamakura and Sakai 1975, pp. 8–19. The railway workers' union Kokurō was far weaker than it had been at the start of the postwar period. In part precipitated by the rise of the trucking industry, conservative factions in government and management initiatives to break the union had for all intents and purposes ended the railway union's primary means of wielding political power—the ability to control the nation's primary transportations modes—and split the railway workplace into three distinct bargaining units. Weathers 1994, pp. 621–33.

33. See Partner 1999, pp. 44–106.

34. Kamakura and Sakai 1975, pp. 8–19.

REFERENCES

Carlile, Lonny E. 2005. *Divisions of Labor: Globality, Ideology, and War in the Shaping of the Japanese Labor Movement.* Honolulu: University of Hawai'i Press.

Enda Genzō. 1968. "Seinen rōdōsha to shaseidō no tachiba." *Gekkan Sōhyō* 4: 28–38.

Gerteis, Christopher. 2009. *Gender Struggles: Wage-Earning Women and Male-Dominant Unions in Postwar Japan.* Cambridge, MA: Harvard University Asia Center.

Gibbs, Michael H. 2000. *Struggle and Purpose in Postwar Japanese Unionism.* Berkeley: Institute of East Asian Studies.

Gill, Tom. 2002. "When Pillars Evaporate: Structuring Masculinity at the Japanese Margins." See Robertson and Suzuki, 2002a.

Gordon, Andrew. 1998. *The Wages of Affluence: Labor and Management in Postwar Japan.* Cambridge, MA: Harvard University Press.

Havens, Thomas R. H. 1987. *Fire Across the Sea: the Vietnam War and Japan, 1965–1975.* Princeton: Princeton University Press.

Ishii-Kuntz, Masako. 2002. "Balancing Fatherhood and Work: Emergence of Diverse Masculinities in Contemporary Japan." In *Men and Masculinities in Japan.* See Robertson and Suzuki, 2002a.

Kamakura Takao and Sakai Ichizō. 1975. "Infure to tatakau." *Kokurō Bunka* 1: 8–19.

Kokumin Bunka Kaigi. 1995. *Kokumin bunka kaigi no yonjūnen.* Kokumin Bunka Kaigi.

Kokutetsu Rōdō Kumiai Seinenkyōiku. 1956. "Rabururetaa konkuru." *Kokutetsu Bunka* 4: 26–28.

Kumazawa, Makoto. 1996. *Portraits of the Japanese Workplace: Labor Movements, Workers, and Managers.* Boulder: Westview Press.

Kume, Ikuo. 1998. *Disparaged Success: Labor Politics in Postwar Japan.* Ithaca: Cornell University Press.

Marotti, William. 2006. "Political Aesthetics: Activism, Everyday Life, and Art's Object in 1960s' Japan." *Inter Asia Cultural Studies* 7, no. 4: 606–18.

Matthews, Gordon. 2002. "Can a 'Real Man' Live for His Family?: Ikigai and Masculinity in Today's Japan," in *Men and Masculinities in Contemporary Japan.* See Robertson and Suzuki, 2002a.

Mizuno Aki. 2002. *Ōta Kaoru to sono jidai: "Sōhyō" rōdō undō no eikō to haitai.* Dōmei Shuppan Sābisu.

Nihon Rōdō Kumiai Sōhyōgikai. 1964. *Sōhyō jūnen-shi.* Rōdōjunpōsha.

Nihon Tōkei Kyōkai. 1949–. *Nihon tōkei nenkan* (Japan statistical yearbook). Nihon Tōkei Kyōkai.

Ōki Kiyoshi. 1975. "'Chōmirai' no sukōbai." *Kokurō Bunka* 1: 4–5.

Ōmachi Keisuke. 1964. "Seinen wo gisei to shite keizai ha seichō shita—kōdo-seichō to teichingin." *Gekkan Sōhyō* 3: 65–73.

Onimaru Hiroyuki. 1975. "Roppyaku nen to yonhyaku nen." *Kokurō Bunka* 1: 2–3.

Partner, Simon. 1999. *Assembled in Japan: Electrical Goods and the Making of the Japanese Consumer.* Berkeley: University of California Press.

Roberson, James E., and Nobue Suzuki, eds. 2002. *Men and Masculinities in Contemporary Japan: Dislocating the Salaryman Doxa.* London: Routledge.

Sasaki-Uemura, Wesley Makoto. 2001. *Organizing the Spontaneous: Citizen Protest in Postwar Japan.* Honolulu: University of Hawai'i Press.

Shinoda Toru. 2005a. "'Kigyōbetsu kumiai o chūshin toshita mindō kumai to ha' (jo)." *Ōhara Shakai Mondai Kenyūjo Zasshi* 561: 1–16.

———. 2005b. "'Kigyōbetsu kumiai wo chūshin toshita mindō kumai to ha' (ge)." *Ōhara Shakai Mondai Kenyūjo Zasshi* 565: 13–31.

Sōhyō Seinenbu. 1968. "Seinenbu katsudō no genjō to mondaiten: zadankai." *Gekkan Sōhyō* 4: 39–71.
Sōhyō Seitai Iinkai. 1968. "Hansen tōsō to seinen rōdōsha no yakuwari." *Gekkan Sōhyō* 4: 18–27.
Takagi Masayuki. 1985. *Zengakuren to Zenkyōtō.* Kōdansha.
Takami Keishi. 1968. *Hansen Seinen Iinkai.* San'ichi Shobō.
Tōkyō Chihō Rōdō Kumiai Hyōgikai. 1980. *Sengo Tōkyō rōdō undō shi: Tōkyō chihyō nijūgonen.* Rōdō Junpōsha.
Weathers, Charles. 1994. "Reconstructing of Labor-management Relations in Japan's National Railways." *Asian Survey* 34, no. 7: 621–33.
———. 2008. "Shunto and the Shackles of Competitiveness." *Labor History* 49, no. 2: 177–97.
Yamada Akihiko. 1975. "Kōsekishō." *Kokurō Bunka* 1: 3–4.

7 Where Have All the Salarymen Gone?

Masculinity, Masochism, and Technomobility in Densha Otoko

Susan Napier

The 2005 hit television series *Densha Otoko* begins with the following memorable scenes. A flying saucer manned by skeletal aliens zooms through outer space while the loud strains of the American pop group Styx's "Mr. Roboto" (originally released in 1983) begin to play. The opening lyrics are in Japanese:

Dōmo arigatō, Mr. Roboto
Mata auō hi made
Dōmo arigatō, Mr. Roboto
Himitsu o shiritai

Thank you Mr. Robot
Until the day we meet again.
Thank you Mr. Robot.
I want to know your secret.

The flying saucer crash-lands on the Japanese archipelago. The scene shifts to contemporary Akihabara, the Tokyo center for all things *otaku* (geek) related. Styx sings:

You're wondering who I am—machine or mannequin
With parts made in Japan I am the modren *[sic]* man
So if you see me acting strangely, don't be surprised
I'm just a man who needed someone and somewhere to hide

The chorus "dōmo arigatō" returns, followed by the words, "I've got a secret, a secret, secret."

All the while scenes of Akihabara flash in front of the viewer. The obvious icons of *otaku* culture appear in claustrophobic close-up shots. Dolls and action figures encased in plastic cubicles loom. An array of brightly lit television screens blinks out of a shop window. Young men wearing ill-fitting sweatshirts stare longingly at sexy miniature female figurines. A tidal wave of cameras clicks at the performance of a comely anime voice actress. Girls dressed as French maids pose in the street. Rows and rows of anime DVDs and manga stand ready for purchase. An *otaku* clasps a plastic bag full of anime paraphernalia lovingly to his chest. A mélange of shots of famous electronic stores such as Laox and Ishimaru flicker in and out.

Abruptly the camera cuts to a wide-angle shot of the roof of a building above Akihabara, where a young man stands. The music dies and we see that he is crying while attempting to sing "Happy Birthday to me." Cramming a piece of shortcake into his mouth, the young man heads for the high fence surrounding the roof and puts his foot on it, still sobbing. He starts to climb. Will he jump?

Of course the young man does not jump, for he is the "hero" of the series, the Densha Otoko, or Train Man, but these opening scenes encapsulate core elements of what might be called *otaku* culture. This is a culture that in some ways may be seen as the masculine answer to the *shōjo*, or young girl, phenomenon, a female consumerist culture that, as Tamae Prindle puts it, "nestle[s] in a shallow lacuna between adulthood and childhood, power and powerlessness, awareness and innocence."[1] The *shōjo* is essentially nonthreatening, characterized by her presumed charm and sweetness and her attraction to "cute" goods such as stuffed animals and pretty, feminine accessories that smack of nostalgia for childhood. Whereas *shōjo* culture is seen in a generally positive light, as comforting and cute compensation for an increasingly fragmented and deterritorialized world, until recently Japanese commentators saw the *otaku* in darker colors.[2]

While there are specific reasons (discussed below) for Japanese society's uneasiness with *otaku* culture, it is also probably a result of the new and increasingly pervasive technologized culture to which *otaku* are strongly linked. While the *shōjo*'s adoration of cute and cuddly objects still partially connects her with a recognizable material world, and the salaryman's ethos can be viewed as having links with traditional Japan, the complex, amorphous, and nonrepresentational world of the techno-geek (what Scott Bukatman has characterized as "terminal identity," an identity based on the computer terminal rather than on material phenomena) has raised cultural hackles among any older and more mainstream Japanese.[3]

As I show in this chapter, *Densha Otoko* can be read as an artistic and commercial attempt to present what might be called the "technologized masculinity" of the *otaku* in as comfortable and appealing a form as possible. Exploring both the "hardware" and "software" facets of *otaku* culture, *Densha Otoko* presents the reader/viewer with a vision of *otaku*-dom that is largely lighthearted and entertaining. At the same time, it manages to capture some of the more disturbing and distancing aspects of the technologized lifestyle. Ultimately, with its conventional romantic resolution, achieved both through the powers of technology and of the human heart, *Densha Otoko* allays the audience's fear of the technologized masculinity emblemized by the *otaku*, showing that technology can help support and sustain romantic love, one of the most fundamental human emotions. At the same time, through its use of appealing and nonthreatening *otaku* characters, and its upbeat version of the Internet and computer technology, *Densha Otoko* helps lay to rest the fear that these characters are truly Other, lost in an all-encompassing cyberworld that separates them from "normal" Japanese.

What is an *otaku?* Although the English word *geek* captures some of the term's resonance, the two are not synonymous. In his 2001 novel *Idoru* the cyberpunk novelist William Gibson rendered the word into English as "a pathological-techno-fetishist–with-social-deficit," and this translation felicitously captures the several dimensions of what might be called "*otaku*-ism." As Japanese commentators point out, *otaku* are in some ways the inevitable expressions of a postindustrial society where technology has replaced community, and media products and electronic gadgets have become the main objects of desire. As the critic Azuma Hiroki points out in *The Animalizing Postmodern (Dōbutsuka suru posuto-mōdan)*, the *otaku* are at the cutting edge of contemporary culture, and, to some extent, there is a bit of the *otaku* in all members of industrialized nations. Nevertheless, for many years the word *otaku* has been a term of opprobrium in Japan, even described as a "problematic word" *(mondai kotoba)* on the national television channel NHK.

The most obvious reason for this is the so-called Miyazaki incident, which occurred in the mid-1990s when a young man named Miyazaki was arrested for murdering several little girls. Upon investigating his apartment, police found an enormous number of pornographic anime videos and manga, supposedly beloved of the *otaku*-type personality. A media moral panic ensued during which *otaku*—socially inept young men who tended toward loner hobbies such as watching anime, playing video games, collecting action figures, or indulging in any slightly outré pursuit—were considered likely to be dangerous deviants. Even before the Miyazaki incident, *otaku* were unlikely to be appreciated, since their antisocial and driven personalities seemed to encapsulate the worst aspects of contemporary Japanese society. The stereotypical *otaku* was badly dressed, physically unattractive, frightened of people in general and women in particular, and likely to spend a lot of time in the Akihabara area, the Tokyo electronics and entertainment center variously dubbed the *otaku* "mecca" or "fortress."

Thus, if the *shōjo* are the bright and appealing (if superficial) side of Japan's mammoth consumer culture, then *otaku* are its dark, secret side. Styx's "Mr. Roboto," with its invocations of shame ("I've got a secret, a secret, secret"), is, therefore, a peculiarly appropriate song to open a drama that centers on *otaku* culture. The song also suggests an awareness of difference from the mainstream—"if you see me acting strangely don't be surprised"—and a deep sense of alienation and isolation, summed up in the need for "somewhere to hide." The fact that the song is by an American rock group but concerns the "modern man / with parts made in Japan" both relates to the Japanese origin of the *otaku* and suggests its global reach. The opening montage for the television series, with its male gender coding, fetishism of commercial and technological products related to the feeling of *moe* (obsessive love for images and objects) experienced by *otaku,* and evocation of the brightly lit but somehow grimy spaces of Akihabara also beautifully encapsulates the distinctive world of *otaku.* At its most negative this is a world of unlovable men who can only buy connection in the form of what I have termed (following the psychologist H. D. Winnicott) "transitional objects," such as the toys, figures, and technological paraphernalia with which they surround themselves.[4] In the case of the *otaku,* however, these transitional objects, paradoxically, usually have a permanent basis. Although they may be replaced by other objects of the same type, such as the latest anime show or manga or a new *moe* figurine, they typically do not serve as the building blocks to human connection as does the classic transitional object.

As with the *shōjo* phenomenon, all of these elements are part of a transient media culture of electronics, plastic, and constantly shifting images. Also like the *shōjo,* the *otaku* phenomenon implicitly raises questions of sexuality, although it does so in a darker form. And yet both subcultures are marked by a sense of unreality when it comes to sexual matters. As seen in works by writers such as Yoshimoto Banana, the *shōjo* world is essentially a fantasy or dream world in which the physical demands of desire are subsumed in airy romances or worked through by way of appealing material objects, such as the little bell given by the protagonist to her lover in Yoshimoto's novella *Moonlight Shadow.* As for the *otaku,* rather than deal with flesh-and-blood human beings or the mutual physicality of lovemaking, many prefer the less threatening space of the Internet, or the bloodless give-and-take of video games, many of which feature strong sexual references. While Hello Kitty and the brightly lit realm of department stores and cute cafés may characterize *shōjo* culture, the invisible world of cyberspace frames *otaku* culture. If the Internet is its soul, Akihabara is its physical heart, so it is not surprising that *Densha Otoko,* in all its manifestations, begins in Akihabara, while much of the work's actual action takes place on the Internet.

In certain respects the story is a conventional one, mixing the traditional story of a romantic courtship with the new *otaku* identity of the Internet and other electronic media. *Densha Otoko* tells the story of an *otaku* who moves from his transitional objects and the fantasyscapes of Akihabara and the Internet to genuine connection with another human being in the confusing and challenging but ultimately more satisfying outer world of contemporary Japan. Originally a best-selling book published in 2004, *Densha Otoko* became a hit film, a manga, and finally the immensely popular television series discussed here. Along the way it helped to change Japanese perceptions of *otaku,* ushering in an arguably new vision of contemporary Japanese masculinity, one that includes some of the most salient manifestations of *otaku* culture, from comic book conventions to maid cafés. This new vision, it should be noted, embraces certain traditional elements, such as stoicism, endurance, sacrifice, and sincerity and even, I would suggest, masochism. At the same time, this masculinity is also deeply embedded in the wired culture of contemporary techno-Japan, embracing a community of techno-connection emblemized by the enormous online community 2channel, the most popular online forum in Japan. Although women certainly participate in 2channel (and there are women *otaku* as well), the majority of the members appear to be male. In the *Densha Otoko* texts, the site comes across as a refuge from outside pressures, a space in which males feel free to reveal their weaknesses, desires, and fantasies, especially concerning women, in a world that seems increasingly alienating and hopeless.[5]

It is worth reemphasizing the importance of the "wired" nature of *otaku* culture in relation to masculinity. I have called the *otaku* persona a kind of "technologized masculinity." The traditional salaryman was defined primarily through his relationship to his company (the bigger the firm the more security and prestige it offered), his relations with his colleagues (both in the office and during postwork socializing), and his clothes (conservative dark suit, shiny briefcase). In contrast, while clothes (grungy) and relationships (informal and often relegated to cyberspace) are certainly part of the *otaku* persona, he is recognized particularly for his expertise with all facets of computer-era technology, from hardware to arcane software to cyberspace in general. Thus, in all its versions *Densha Otoko* contains a hardware-related narrative thread in which the hero spends hours looking through computer catalogues to advise his romantic interest on what kind of computer she should buy. It is clear that in this wired world, at least, the *otaku* is a dominant masculine presence, comfortable in a realm that remains mysterious to many. On the software side, in an early scene the protagonist shows off his knowledge of the classic technogeek film *The Matrix,* and throughout all three versions of the story the protagonist and his friends make constant informed references to anime, manga, and video games, thereby expressing their expertise in the form of the subcultural capital that earns them the most prestige in the *otaku* world.

With regard to cyberspace technology, one of the most fascinating and unique features of the book version of *Densha Otoko* is its literal embodiment of 2channel, or more specifically a particular thread that supposedly occurred on the forum over a two-month period in 2004. This thread contained postings about a developing romance by a young man who became known as Densha Otoko, or Train Man, and the diverse reactions to each post by a variety of 2channel members. In a extensive range of messages, the members advise, encourage, and occasionally criticize Densha's courtship, offering him everything from tips on what clothes to wear on his first date, to heartfelt condolences when things appear to be going badly, to a final explosion of congratulations when his courtship finally succeeds. These posts were then collected (with, apparently, some summarization at various points) and turned into a book that was marketed as a true story by an anonymous collective author known as Nakano Hitori, which can be roughly translated as "one person in a group."

No doubt the possibility that this was a true story contributed to the book's immense popularity, but it is also clear that its unique narrative structure played an important role in its appeal. Written entirely in the form of Internet postings, the book is challenging even for some Japanese to read. The postings contain a wide variety of "in group" words and phrases, which include deliberate distortions (for example, the male pronoun "ore" is written "more" or "melt"), abbreviations, arcane references to anime and other pop cultural products, many emoticons (such as smiling faces and the more culturally specific image of someone bowing in apology), and even full-scale pictures created entirely using a computer keyboard. Furthermore, since the events play out over a two-month period, as Densha reports in and the other members react, the reader has the almost voyeuristic pleasure of feeling like a lurker on 2channel, watching a drama involving real people unfold across "real time" (or *"rearu taimu,"* as the members of 2channel themselves sometimes put it). It is also clear in all versions of the story that those involved in the thread are largely male and, if not all full-fledged *otaku,* still possess many *otaku*–like characteristics.[6] These include, most ubiquitously, self-styled *doku-otoko* (poisonous bachelors), anime fanatics, train buffs, military fans, and even *hikikomori* (shut-ins) and drug users. *Densha Otoko* therefore introduces the reader to a rich and intriguing subcultural community in which a variety of anonymous, largely male voices reveal themselves. As such it almost perfectly embodies contemporary techno-Japan.

It should be emphasized, however, that *Densha Otoko* offers more old-fashioned pleasures as well. Most obviously, it is a deeply satisfying and fairly conventionally structured love story, complete with a romantic, even melodramatic, initial encounter, a hesitant courtship stocked with the usual uncertainties and twists and turns, and, finally, an extremely romantic and remarkably innocent denouement in which the hero wins the girl and the lovers hold hands, exchange soft kisses, and tell each other about their love at copious length. What gives this rather hackneyed story its freshness is not only its 2channel structure in which we see all these events as if we were reading Internet postings but also the fact that the drama plays out from the point of view of the rather hapless male character who is supported by his group of anonymous Internet friends. In a sense, *Densha Otoko* may be seen as a modern-day Cinderella story, with the crucial difference that this time Cinderella is a man and his help comes not from fairy godmothers and magical creatures but from his anonymous 2channel friends and the contemporary magic of the Internet. All three texts—book, movie, and television series—are wish-fulfilling fantasies from the point of view of the male, specifically the male *otaku* who feels shunned by society in general and by women in particular.

Unlike the *otaku* characters, Hermes, the object of Densha's obsession, and the women friends around her are largely conventional. Hermes in particular seems to embody a particularly traditional male wish-fulfillment fantasy of the well-brought-up young woman from a good household. Women in this fantasy are naturally important, but they come across, especially in the book, largely as objects of mystery and obsession. Throughout their postings Densha and the 2channel members refer to the object of his affections as "Hermes," a nickname they give her because early in the story she sends Densha an expensive and elegant pair of Hermès-brand teacups. "Poisonous bachelors" in particular also see women as objects of fear and disappointment. In a number of comments members mention that they have never even had a meal with a woman. Some further describe times when women have ignored or rejected them or simply broken their hearts. It is perhaps no accident that a great deal of military technology appears in the book, as members speak of "attacking" or "bombing" Hermes. Although this terminology suggests some of their obsessions, it also promotes a worldview in which the genders are increasingly sundered and alien to each other.

Densha Otoko thus plays on the increasing sense of deterritorialization—the increasing sense of dislocation and alienation from local culture—as well as the emasculation and contradictory yearnings that make contemporary Japanese masculinity and Japanese society in general a peculiarly complex site of male-female interaction. In all of its forms, the work is an illuminating exploration of millennial Japanese society, both as a text and in the heartfelt reactions to the text. It encompasses consumer culture, from the Hermès brand of teacups, to the fancy clothing that Densha buys in order to pursue his romance, to the latest in technology. It even implicitly involves the question of class, since Hermes is clearly depicted as occupying a wealthier and more refined strata than Densha, who in the television series lives with his family in an old-fashioned house next to the bicycle shop they own. The popularity of all three versions of the story is both interesting and unsurprising; the narrative confronts crucial social issues, but it explores them in generally light-hearted and entertaining ways and offers a sense of hope or even salvation to both men and women caught up in a destabilized and threatening culture. For male readers and viewers, it suggests the possibility of outside affirmation of their innermost souls. For women, the work offers a different vision of masculinity that, although initially unappealing, ends up revealing itself as an increasingly attractive alternative to the driven salaryman culture that has long epitomized postwar Japan. The work thus offers something fresh for both genders. As the popularity of *Densha Otoko* took off, there were increasing media reports that women were rethinking their earlier disgust with *otaku,* discovering in their sincerity and simplicity an appealing alternative to the slickness of more conventionally popular male types.

Although women play an important role in the story, and especially in the television series, *Densha Otoko* provides a particularly revealing glimpse into one type of Japanese masculinity at the turn of the millennium. Although the book offers a fascinating example of a unique publishing event, the remainder of this chapter will focus on the film and

TV versions, especially the television show, whose eleven episodes add much more to the initial drama and allow for intriguing examinations of contemporary male-female relationships in Japan. The series includes a wide variety of dramatic, affecting, and sometimes bizarre scenes in which contemporary Japanese masculinity is explored, problematized, and even deplored. In this latter regard it touches on an impulse that can genuinely be described as masochistic, creating scenes that are excruciating for both character and viewer. Although the television series does not change the book's basic narrative arc, it adds many episodes that flesh out what might be called the *otaku* personality, some of which, especially in the beginning, are extremely negative.

This is clear from the opening scenes of the television series, which display a range of contradictory impressions. I have already mentioned the use of Styx's "Mr. Roboto." There is no question that the lyrics of the song are eerily appropriate for *otaku* culture, with their reference to "robots," "secrets," "hiding behind a mask," and "too much technology." These lyrics, however, can hardly be considered laudatory. The use of an American pop song to comment on a Japanese subculture is in itself intriguing, suggesting a consciousness of the *otaku* as a uniquely Japanese phenomenon, or, as the song puts it, "with parts made in Japan." The shift to a young man seemingly about to commit suicide above the streets of Akihabara gives an abrupt glimpse into the alienation at the heart of this culture. At the same time, the catchy music and the bright, rapidly shifting images of Akihabara express a sense of exhilaration, and even joy.

This celebratory vision of the *otaku* is canceled in a scene created specifically for the television series. The protagonist, known in the series as Yamada (but referred to hereafter as Densha, in accordance with the name used in the novel and movie), is shown returning from an Akihabara shopping trip and rushing to catch a train. When he bumps into an attractive young woman, his bag falls open, scattering DVDs and toys down the steps to her apparent horror. Even worse, their encounter has dislodged a makeup brush, which he picks up and attempts to return to her. She recoils in disgust and runs away, leaving him staring blankly in miserable embarrassment. In this scene the *otaku* persona is shown as essentially an object of abjection, something to be expelled as quickly as possible from the social body. The *otaku* is seen as weak, clumsy, and even feminized in his clutching of the makeup brush. It will turn out that the young woman in this encounter is actually the best friend of Hermes, the woman Densha falls in love with.

Densha's apparent odiousness having been established, the scene shifts to the encounter with Hermes with which both the book and the film begin. Densha has settled himself on the train and is discreetly ogling a beautiful young woman reading (in English) Dan Brown's *Angels and Demons.* A drunk appears on the train and starts hassling various passengers. In typical urbanite fashion, everyone looks down, hoping he or she will not be bothered. Eventually the drunk approaches the beautiful young woman (hereafter known as Hermes) and begins to touch her. Clearly to his own surprise, Densha gets up and stutters at him to quit. The drunk turns on him and they begin to tussle. A salaryman comes to Densha's aid, giving a group of middle-aged women passengers the opportunity to get the conductor. The conductor pacifies the drunk but asks Densha, the middle-aged ladies, and Hermes to come to the police office to make a statement. As Densha is leaving the office, the ladies and Hermes ask for his address so that they can send him a thank-you gift in appreciation of his bravery. Densha goes home and writes a message on 2channel describing his exciting encounter, his first time posting on the site after lurking for some years.

This simple but melodramatic opening is worth examining more closely. Although it should be remembered that this is supposedly a true story, the events described effectively play into conventional male and female wish-fulfillment fantasies. As Hermes later recounts to Densha, both she and the older women are deeply impressed by his bravery—so unusual in today's society, as she points out several times—and talk about it among themselves after he leaves the police office. Later in the narrative Hermes frequently makes a point of saying how she feels safer just knowing that someone like Densha still exists. From the women's point of view, Densha is an echo of a more gentlemanly past. This is particularly obvious in the television series, where the scene with the drunk goes on for a painfully long time and the camera lingers on the other male passengers' blasé or cowardly reactions.

To the women, Densha's willingness to take action, even at risk to himself, makes him a larger-than-life figure in a modern world characterized by reduced expectations and fear of involvement. Interestingly, when Hermes later describes the encounter to two friends, one of them suggests that Densha must be like Tom Cruise. When Hermes gently points out that her rescuer was Japanese, the friend then likens him to Watanabe Ken. This conversation is a clear reference to the film *The Last Samurai,* an American movie that attempted to encapsulate the traditional samurai virtues in a way that few products of contemporary Japan's more cynical cinema would dare to do. The movie's popularity in Japan suggests that nostalgia for "samurai values" (cinematic or real) still exists. While the comparison between the short, weak-looking Densha and Watanabe Ken may seem forced, as the television series continues it is obvious that Densha indeed exemplifies certain traditional values that exercise a distinctive spell on at least some of the women he encounters.

From the male point of view, especially that of Densha and all the members of 2channel who respond with excitement to his story, his deed is the chance to show that an *otaku* can be manly, even heroic, "saving" a beautiful young girl from unwanted attention in a manner that smacks of traditional romance. When old norms are fragmenting, new role models are hard to develop, and women seem less and less dependent on men, Densha's newly heroic character and actions seem to hint at an alternative form of masculinity that combines both the valorous ethos of the samurai and the contemporary "sensitive" *otaku*.

In this regard, the transient presence of the salaryman who helps Densha fight off the drunk is particularly intriguing. Erased in the movie, probably because of time constraints, he clearly, if briefly, appears in both the book and the television series. He is the only one involved in the fracas not invited to come along to the police station. His disappearance may have a reasonable explanation—perhaps he is the only one who has to go to work—but it a symbolically significant absence. It is as if the salaryman is being erased as the dominant masculine presence in today's Japanese society, a society in which, judging from the varied appearance of the other passengers on the train—from a louche-looking young man in a bright yellow muscle shirt to Densha in his disheveled "Akiba" attire (the style worn by Akihabara habitués)—he has less and less of a place. Even more intriguingly, in the television series the drunk is an elderly man who looks like a laborer, but in the movie he seems to be a salaryman. Dressed in a conservative black suit, he weaves around the train car like a despairing ghost who no longer knows where he belongs.

As many commentators have noted, the old notion of Japan as a nation of white-collar salarymen has increasingly come into question. Tomoko Yoda describes the "acute sense of desolation" experienced by salarymen who no longer can be sure of permanent employment at the corporations to which they were expected to give undying loyalty.[7] Indeed, these days women in particular seem to revile the salaryman, seeing them as *oyaji* (old guys) who, according to Laura Miller, present themselves as "short, stocky, dark-suited" men "with pomade-plastered hair."[8] The former symbol of Japan's postwar success has thus devolved into a creature to be ejected from contemporary Japan's more complex, postbubble society.

But who is replacing the salaryman? In some ways we can say that there is no absolute replacement, no single masculine role that embodies "Japan" the way the salaryman persona did for years. Instead, he has been replaced by a much more varied inchoate mass of personae. These include the androgynous *bishōnen* (beautiful boys), aggressive young entrepreneurs (such as the recently indicted financier Murakami), or the creative "cooking man" who has become a staple of television, manga, and anime. Among these new types, the *otaku* has been, until recently, one of the most problematic; at the same time, however, he is increasingly ubiquitous, as more people give up on making connections in an increasingly technologically dependent and depersonalized society.

Both the movie and the television series show the faces of the "new" Japanese male in the most literal sense. Since they cannot reproduce the "look" of an Internet chat room in the way that the book does so effectively, the two visual media spend a great deal of time on the appearance of 2channel members. Indeed, some of the most arresting and affecting moments in the narrative are the reaction shots of Densha's Internet supporters as they follow him along in his romantic trials, at times cheering, critiquing, commiserating, and congratulating with an intensity usually reserved for favorite sports teams. For while *Densha Otoko* is, on the one hand, a love story between two heterosexual characters, it is also a (largely) homosocial love story among the male denizens of 2channel who themselves blossom and bond along with the romance between Hermes and Densha.

As is clear in both the book and the visual versions of the story, 2channel members are a varied lot. The film and television series round up a group of memorable faces and continually flash back to them throughout the narrative. In the movie version these include three young men, obviously *otaku,* who like to play war games and see Densha's courtship of Hermes in terms of a military attack. The television series, with its longer narrative arc, has a whole array of distinctive-looking characters: a round-faced young man in a neatly fitting train conductor suit who often uses train metaphors in his postings; a glasses-wearing shut-in *(hikikomori)* who, at the beginning of the series, does not even open the door when his mother brings up his dinner tray; an ordinary-looking middle-aged man estranged from his wife; a gorgeous young artistic type who contributes the most detailed illustrations to Densha's online narrative; a middle-aged Hanshin Tigers sports fan; a military enthusiast who dresses in combat fatigues; a lecherous young man with a plethora of posters of female anime characters on his walls and some suspiciously large female dolls;

and a middle-aged professorial type with a row of books behind his computer and a penchant for wearing "I [heart] literature" bandannas around his head.

None of these characters is remotely prepossessing (with the exception of the handsome artist), but as the series and movie continue, the viewer comes to know and appreciate their goofy charms. Far from conforming to the stereotypical creepy *otaku* type, they are rendered as totally unthreatening. As their sincere enthusiasm for and desire to help in Densha's courtship becomes increasingly apparent, they also become increasingly individual. Their stories, too, become part of the narrative, as the viewer sees at least some of them become inspired by Densha's experiences and start to confront life beyond the safety of the computer screen. Their individuality, in fact, may seem almost a conscious challenge to the twenty-first-century fear that technology will render us more homogenous and increasingly anonymous. There are also a few women characters, such as a bruised wife and a young teenage idol, and even one or two characters dressed in salaryman suits. The emphasis, however, is clearly on men, and particularly on men who are *not* salarymen, or at least abandon their office persona when relaxing at home.

What they share in common is their fondness for what I call transitional or talismanic objects. All the members of Densha's 2channel group are consistently positioned with their computer screen in front of them and some kind of toy, stuffed animal, or action figure placed nearby. This is also the case with Densha himself, who, at certain moments of heightened intensity, clutches a variety of talismanic objects, ranging from his cell phone and his computer to a stuffed green creature vaguely resembling an octopus, to, most frequently, a female doll with rabbit ears and two carrots protruding from her shapely rear end, apparently named "Hina," the fictional heroine of an anime developed expressly for the television series. I have discussed the *otaku* culture's use of dolls, stuffed animals, and action figures as transitional or talismanic objects elsewhere, but for now it is worth noting that this fetishization of commercial products exists in a world where human connection is increasingly tenuous.[9]

Although it is true that samurai undoubtedly fetishized their swords, and, as Anne Allison and others have pointed out, this current techno-animism is undoubtedly related to indigenous Shinto religions,[10] few men of previous generations would have been seen hugging dolls, toys, action figures, or, for that matter, computers (the television series contains several intense scenes of the 2channelers embracing their computers while crying). This reliance on comfort objects may have trickled down from *shōjo* culture and is now ubiquitous in modern Japanese life. It should be emphasized, however, that the 2channel members seem even more addicted to these objects than the average Japanese. This may well be related to the fact that these (generally) young men are still not "grown up" in the conventional sense of being a salaryman, a responsible member of society with a wife and family, and they therefore cling to childlike objects of attachment in order to both maintain their transitional status and compensate for their lack of more conventional objects of affection. The placement of these objects in close proximity to the computer suggests techno-fetishism at its most extreme, almost as if the objects were mediators between "real" life and the world of the Internet.

This exceptional dependence on transitional/talismanic objects becomes the impetus for two of the most symbolically fraught episodes in the television series, the moments when Densha decides to abandon his *otaku*-hood, followed by his subsequent choice to reverse that decision and reveal himself as an *otaku*. By this point Densha has been going out with Hermes for some time, aided by insights and advice from his 2channel supporters, who correctly divined that when the young lady on the train sent him a thank-you gift of Hermès cups, she might be open to establishing a relationship with him. Although the initial stages of their romance have gone well (considering Densha's lack of expertise with women, dating, and small talk), Densha is haunted by fear that she may discover him to be an *otaku*. The moment comes when he feels that he has been proven correct. He has to decide between attending Comiketto, a mammoth comic market that occurs twice a year in Tokyo, and going to a play with Hermes. Densha and his friends have been officially invited to have a booth at the event, where they plan to exhibit their *dojinshi* (amateur comic books), and he believes that he cannot pass up this opportunity. When Hermes discovers him at the event and tells him that she no longer wishes to see him, he immediately assumes it must be her distaste at his *otaku* practices, something that he had hidden from her until then.

In fact, Hermes is angry only because he lied to her, but as an obsessive self-hating *otaku*, Densha cannot imagine such a reaction. When she breaks up with him, he feels that the only thing he can do is to dispense with all his *otaku* activities, to abandon everything that made up his previous identity. In a conventional American television series, this decision might well have been the emotional high point of the series. The viewers have already been thematically prepared for Densha's "graduation" by earlier scenes (all of which come directly from the book) in which Densha gets a makeover—a new haircut, contact lenses, trendy clothes—in order to succeed on his first date with Hermes. His graduation from *otaku*-hood (complete with a ceremony at an Akihabara maid café) thus seems an inevitable part of his maturation process.

But there is more. In a scene that plays out in agonizing detail, Densha packs every one of his action figures and other comfort objects, even though he finds it hard to abandon them. He holds his favorite anime doll, Hina, in his hand for a long time and stares at her intently. To the sound of the theme music from *Gundam,* a classic anime series about war in outer space beloved of *otaku,* he places his cartons on the river, a ritual gesture of renunciation. On the way back, in a moment that underlines his sacrifice, he runs into a man "cosplaying" (dressing up in costume) as Amuro, one of the major characters in *Gundam.* Upon returning home, however, he discovers that two of his boxes have been returned, including one holding Matilda, another favorite *Gundam* action figure, whom he salutes. In a final gesture of sacrifice he sells all his remaining *otaku*-related possessions in order to buy Hermes a beautiful china plate for her birthday, with the hope that she will appreciate his taste and be willing to see him again. The expensive chinaware symbolically suggests that he is moving from the childish world of the *otaku* to the elegant world that the name Hermes and its associated products emblemize. After his shopping expedition, Densha returns home to face a totally empty room, an image that could be seen as negative, indicative of his loss of identity, or as full of potential, suggesting the possibilities of his post-*otaku* life.

In fact, the series has it both ways. Densha goes beyond his *otaku* persona, but it remains a part of him as an important component of his identity. Discovering that Hermes actually broke up with him because he lied to her, Densha decides (as usual, with the aid of his 2channel friends) that the only way to reach her heart is to be himself, to "come out" to her. Although he and his friends use the term *coming out,* what they mean is not what is usually suggested by that phrase: it refers to Densha revealing himself as an *otaku.*

When Hermes unexpectedly visits him at home he tells her that he has something to show her. He first invites Hermes to stand outside his bedroom while he makes his preparations. When he finally lets her in, she sees him standing in a colorful but unattractive shirt, wearing a bandanna tied around his head, and surrounded by a huge variety of *otaku*-oriented paraphernalia, most notably action figures, stuffed toys, anime posters, and anime dolls. He then proceeds with his "coming out" speech:

> When I was in high school, I began to like anime. Then I started collecting video games and action figures. At technical school I started going to Akihabara. I'd go to [anime] voice actor and idol events. Rather than talking with people I preferred watching anime and playing games.
>
> So people started calling me an *otaku*. But I liked anime and games so much I just couldn't quit. This is the kind of person I am. I am an *otaku*. Maybe they say I'm creepy or gross, but that's just the way it is. This is the only way I can be. But I want you to see me as I am. If this is the real me, if you can accept me as I am, I hope we can be friends again.

Densha's speech has elements of a classic confession by an addict, touching on both addiction ("I just couldn't quit") and abjection (he might be called "creepy or gross"). Unlike in the addict's confession, however, Densha does not vow to change, but instead he asks Hermes to accept him as he is.

Hermes' reaction to this speech summons romance. She smiles slightly and tells him, "You were sneaky. That's just what I was going to say." Then, looking around the cluttered room, she pronounces, "This is a nice room. It's very individual. I like it." And finally, "Will you make up with me so we can be friends again?"

The scene shifts to a series of reaction shots showing the faces of all of Densha's Internet friends. It is clear that Densha has logged on and described to them the events the viewer has just seen. The screen explodes with happy faces and congratulatory messages as his various friends cheer him on. The word "Yes!" *(kita)* appears in various permutations. Others write, "Thank you for your courage" or "Go for it!" *(ganbatte)*. In the episode's last scene, Densha receives a phone call from Hermes, who thanks him for her birthday gift. We see what she is holding: it is not the expensive china plate but rather Hina, Densha's favorite anime doll. He says shyly, "Glad you like it. It's only sold in Akihabara." Densha has finally achieved the greatest wish-fulfilling fantasy of all, to be accepted, and perhaps loved, for who he is.

These two episodes, one of renunciation and the other of affirmation, contain core themes of *Densha Otoko* that might be considered illustrative of an alternative form of contemporary Japanese masculinity. I use the word "alternative" rather than "new" because, while the actual mise-en-scènes of *Densha Otoko,* from the maid cafés of Akihabara to the fancy French china with which Hermes is identified, is unique to contemporary Japan, the virtues privileged in these scenes are ones deeply identified with traditional Japanese culture, or at least the traditional Japan expressed in literature, arts, and the cult of the samurai.

Most obvious of these are the values of stoicism, sacrifice, and perseverance or endurance. Spurred by his love for Hermes, Densha is willing to give up everything that he holds most dear, everything that constitutes what he is. The camera lingers almost erotically on the many figures and toys that have been so intimately connected with him, imbuing the scene of his packing them away with an intensity worthy of a lover's renunciation or a soldier's abandonment of a treasured weapon. These implications are underlined first by the close-up of Densha staring lovingly at Hina, and then by the references to the military *Gundam* series, including the use of its theme music, the Amuro cosplayer, and finally the deeply felt salute to Matilda. Although it might be possible to see these elements (particularly the bizarre Amuro figure) through an ironic lens, their actual performance is played out in a fashion that comes across as more poignant than satiric.

When Densha discovers that he may not need to abandon his treasures, he makes another kind of sacrifice, the decision to expose himself to potential ridicule by coming out as an *otaku.* We are obviously meant to view this gesture as a genuinely brave act, underlined as it is by the admiring chorus of voices from the 2channelers, who thank him for his courage and praise him for his ability to *gambaru,* a term that connotes perseverance and endurance in the face of challenges and even potential humiliation. Densha's lengthy confession, which acknowledges his willingness to be despised as "disgusting" or "creepy," encapsulates the virtues of sincerity, endurance, and courage that a traditional heroic figure would be expected to possess.

It should be mentioned that the television series contains other scenes in which Densha displays these appealing masculine traits, episodes that are absent from both the book and the movie. The reasons behind this are partly technical: a lengthy television series requires many more scenes to fill its episodes than does a book or film. These scenes bring notes of humor, drama, and pathos that contribute to a more well-rounded view of both Densha and Hermes while adding a colorful cast of supporting characters and entertaining episodes to the overall story. Hermes, for example, is given a backstory consisting of her father's abandonment of her mother, which explains her fear of men's duplicity. The television series also adds a rival for her affections, Sakurai, a sleazy restaurateur who has a bit of an *otaku* streak himself, as is shown in his fascination with technological toys.

The most interesting scenes, however, are the ones that explore, amplify, or subtly comment on Densha's *otaku* persona. Early in his relationship with Hermes, for example, she discovers that she is being stalked. Densha not only starts escorting her home but also ultimately discovers the stalker's identity, a maintenance man at Hermes' company, and confronts him. While both the book and movie contain scenes in which Hermes becomes worried about a groper on the train, Densha's primary response is to suggest that he escort her home and give her a manual on how to avoid gropers in future. The television series intensifies the drama by depicting a genuine stalker pursuing Hermes, thus giving Densha another chance to show his heroic side. When the stalker is identified, however, Densha does not turn him over to the police but rather convinces him to "go home to the country." Perhaps even more surprisingly, the stalker gives Densha a parting gift, a photo of Densha and Hermes happily walking together.

With his toxic attitude toward women and his love of camera technology, the stalker can be seen as the dark side of the *otaku* type, Densha's alter ego. Indeed, the stalker and Densha bond over their shared love for Hermes, with the stalker pointing out the crucial difference that Densha "makes her happy" while he could only bring her grief. This scene clearly fulfills male fantasies: the potential *otaku* viewer is allowed to see that his darkest motives can be reinterpreted in the positive light of the series' upbeat outlook.

Another scene unique to the television series depicts Densha showing his courage and sincerity at an agonizing dinner with Hermes' family, which takes place at the restaurant of Densha's secret rival, Sakurai. The episode begins semicomically with Sakurai spiking Densha's food with hot sauce, causing him to make a fool of himself through most of the dinner. The mood changes abruptly to melodrama, however, when Hermes' estranged father barges in and asks her mother to sign divorce papers. Although the father abruptly dismisses Densha, the young man returns to the table and makes a speech about marriage notable more for its sincerity and genuine feeling for Hermes than for its articulateness.

This kind of stammering sincerity is precisely what makes Densha so attractive. Although his heroism is far from the conventional bravery epitomized by Watanabe Ken in *Last Samurai,* his stumbling and inarticulate sincerity combined with genuine bravery is deemed equally impressive. At the end of the scene, Hermes' mother, who had initially been so horrified by Densha's appearance that she asked her daughter if she needed contact lenses, abruptly turns to Hermes and says, "I understand why you chose him."

Densha's confession also reveals another trait that has long been associated with Japanese culture, namely masochism, which is exemplified by the "sympathy for the underdog" *(hōganbiiki)* stories in premodern

Japanese theater and literature and, more recently, by scenes of torture and humiliation popular in *yakuza* (gangster) films. The masochism in *Densha Otoko* contains elements of the underdog and of ritual humiliation, but the series plays it out in a setting strongly identified with contemporary Japanese society.

Once again, the television series strongly amplifies a trait largely implied in the book and film. Recall the opening of the series, with its paradoxical celebration of all things *otaku* combined with Styx's self-loathing lyrics that suggest the need for "somewhere to hide." The subsequent scene in which Densha is seen weeping and thinking about committing suicide is also created for television. The buildup to this scene, as the viewer later discovers, is a long series of events that place Densha in a variety of humiliating positions. These all take place on his birthday (hence the piece of cake that Densha holds as he contemplates suicide) and begin with his father and sister forgetting about his special day, underlined by the fact that they do, coincidentally, have a cake prepared for someone else, a cake that Densha at first mistakes as being intended for him. Events at the office are even worse. Densha is abused and humiliated not only by the office bully but also by an attractive female colleague who, at various points in the series, hits him, reviles him for being an *otaku,* and, on his birthday, gets so enraged with him for bringing her some papers in disorder that she asks him why he has any reason to live. The papers are disordered because Densha dropped them down a sewer shortly after being accused of being a Peeping Tom when he climbed a tree in an unsuccessful attempt to rescue a little girl's balloon.

These incidents are, of course, played for broad comedy. Densha is shown as a hapless misfit, reviled and ignored by family and friends, incapable even of rescuing a lost balloon. They connect with the opening episode in Akihabara when he tries to return the young woman's makeup brush only to be treated with panic and horror. Other scenes amplify descriptions in the book to bring out their full masochistic potential. For example, on Densha's second date with Hermes, he mentions having trouble finding the restaurant's bathroom. In the television series this incident develops into an excruciating vision of Densha wandering haplessly around the restaurant, totally lost, while being covertly observed by Hermes' best friend, who finds the whole situation extremely amusing.

Not all of these episodes are simply humorous. Another masochistic episode revolves around a more complex set of circumstances and emotions, ultimately leading to a denouement in which Densha is able to show his sincerity and ingratiate himself with Hermes. This episode reveals Densha's alternative form of masculinity since it involves a mismatch in expectations between *otaku* behavior and more glamorous forms of male activity. On an early date Hermes asks Densha what he does for fun on weekends. Frantically wracking his brains for an activity that does not sound too intensely *otaku*-ish, Densha blurts out "surfing," meaning, of course, surfing the web. Not surprisingly, Hermes interprets this as the water sport and excitedly asks Densha to let her watch him the next time he surfs. The inevitable comic complications ensue. Densha spends huge amounts of money and time trying to learn to surf, and the series shows in painful detail how he slips, falls, and crashes into the cold ocean. On the appointed day he still cannot even stand up on the board, but, at the last minute, a sudden downpour seems to save him. What follows illustrates the reward of honesty. Rather than accept his luck and hope that he can escape having to surf again, Densha finds that he must confess his duplicity. Bowing before Hermes in the sand while the drenching rain continues, he tells her of the mistake and apologizes to her for lying. Instead of being angry with him, Hermes is moved by his sincerity, exonerating him by saying that the misunderstanding was her fault as much as his.

This genuinely moving scene is echoed toward the end of the series when Densha attempts to bring Hermes her birthday present (the china plate) after she has broken up with him. Encouraged by his 2channel comrades, who tell him he must try to connect with her at least one more time, Densha sends her a message saying that he will be waiting with his present on the night of her birthday where they met for their first date. Once again it is raining, but this time he is alone as Hermes is at a fancy club celebrating with friends. The episode cuts back and forth between an increasingly sodden and sick-looking Densha pathetically clutching his birthday package and Hermes trying to enjoy her party while becoming increasingly ridden with guilt. Eventually, through a series of coincidences combined with Hermes' guilt, she finds him standing in the rain. He tries to hand her the package but faints, breaking the plate inside the box. She kneels beside him and asks anxiously if he is okay.

Both the surfing and the birthday episodes highlight a form of masculine endurance, perseverance, and sincerity expressed through suffering. Both episodes are drawn out, with many close-ups of Densha's anguished face, to the point where the viewer almost cringes at his misery. At the same time, it is clear from the many messages of praise from his 2channel friends that the audience is expected to admire his fortitude. Masochism is thus seen as the route to establishing the most sincere form of masculine identity, worthy of admiration and emulation. In these scenes Densha is far from being the classic action hero but is rather characterized by a willingness to endure pain at all costs. In this regard he epitomizes both certain classic samurai values—most notably the willingness to sacrifice for another and persevere despite humiliation—and also the values of the so-called *nimaime,* or secondary male actor in Kabuki and early Japanese films, who is seen as the softer romantic lead in comparison to the action hero, who dispenses with feminine affection entirely.

Densha Otoko's masochism, I would submit, is also related to sociocultural trends. While far from every Japanese male considers himself an *otaku,* the work's tremendous popularity suggests that, at some level, male readers and viewers indeed identify with this abject figure. The salaryman was the iconic figure of Japan from the beginnings of the postwar economic boom through the heady days of the bubble economy, a symbol of success and pride. Postbubble Japan is a different place, uncertain of its future, ambivalent about its past, lost in a transitional phase that seems to have no clear direction. The early vision of Densha Otoko as inept, bumbling, and even an object of horror can be seen to epitomize that sense of loss and uncertainty. In this regard the use of the American rock group Styx's song to introduce the television series may also be linked with masochism, a vision of a robotic, shameful Japan as seen by the rest of the world. Densha's discovery of the strength within himself and his outside affirmation, first through his 2channel friends and then through Hermes' acceptance and love for him, can be read as a national wish-fulfilling fantasy—a desire for what are believed to be basic Japanese values to still operate and be influential in a society where technology is crowding out history, culture, and community. Paradoxically, it is the Internet that allows these values to return, not only by galvanizing Densha to dig these virtues out of his own identity but also by providing a form of social community that supports him through his period of self-reconstruction.

In the book Densha shows Hermes the Densha Otoko thread and, after reading through it, she comments, "They were all really good people weren't they?" This comment is echoed at the end of the series, although in this case the conversation takes place when Hermes and Densha are on a train. In one sense the image of the train is retrograde, a long way from the instant mind travel of wired technology. But Densha himself is both a denizen of the new world and a link to the older one. By calling the book, movie, television series, and protagonist "Train Man," their creators call attention to this contradiction at the heart of Japanese society. In the feel-good world of the work, these contradictions empower rather than weaken. While the train can be seen as a liminal object, floating in a transitional space, we are meant to see by the end of *Densha Otoko* that this particular train now has a direction, one that encompasses both past and future.

NOTES

1. Prindle 1998, p. 35.

2. But see Kinsella 1995, pp. 220–54 for an equally dark view of *shōjo* culture.

3. See Bukatman 1993.

4. See, for example, Winnicott 2006, pp. 1–20.

5. It should be noted that 2channel is also known as a site for sexual fantasy and racist and nationalist propaganda. While the book *Densha Otoko* in particular contains some fairly racy postings, these are subsumed within the romantic and virtually asexual love story of Densha and Hermes. In the feel-good vision of *Densha Otoko* problematic political aspects are ignored.

6. There are, of course, women *otaku* and, from what my sources in Japan tell me, their numbers are increasing. In the television version, in particular, women members of "2-channel" play an important role in supporting and encouraging Densha on several occasions. Overall, however, the *otaku* phenomenon at this point (2008) can still be characterized as mainly male. The reasons for this male gendering are open to speculation, but they are probably connected to the fact that the earliest computer, Internet, and video game users have been largely male.

7. Yoda 2000, p. 653.

8. Miller 2004, p. 52.

9. For further discussion of the transitional object in relation to *otaku* culture, see my article, Napier 2008.

10. Allison 2006.

REFERENCES

Allison, Anne. 2006. *Millennial Monsters: Japanese Toys and the Millennial Imagination.* Berkeley: University of California Press.

Bukatman, Scott. 1993. *Terminal Identity: The Virtual Subject in Post-Modern Science Fiction.* Durham: Duke University Press.

Kinsella, Sharon. 1995. "Cuties in Japan." In *Women, Media, and Consumption in Japan,* ed. Lise Skov and Brian Moeran, 220–54. Honolulu: University of Hawai'i Press.

Miller, Laura. 2002. "Male Beauty Work in Japan." In *Men and Masculinities in Contemporary Japan.* See Roberson and Suzuki 2002.

Napier, Susan. 2008. "Lost in Transition: Train Men and Dolls in Millennial Japan." *Mechadamia* 3: 205–10.

Prindle, Tamae. 1998. "A Cocooned Identity: Japanese Girls Films: Nobuhiko

Oobayashi's *Chizuko's Younger Sister* and Jun Ishikawa's *Tsugumi*." *Post Script* 15, no. 1: 24–36.

Roberson, James E., and Suzuki Nobue, eds. 2002. *Men and Masculinities in Contemporary Japan: Dislocating the Salaryman Doxa*. London: Routledge.

Winnicott, H. D. 2006. *Playing and Reality*. New York: Routledge.

Yoda, Tomoko. 2000. "A Roadmap to Millennial Japan." *South Atlantic Quarterly* 99, no. 4: 629–68.

8 Failed Manhood on the Streets of Urban Japan

The Meanings of Self-Reliance for Homeless Men

Tom Gill

The two questions Japanese people most often ask about the homeless people they see around them are "Why are there any homeless people here in Japan?" and "Why are they nearly all men?" Answering those two simple questions will, I believe, lead us in fruitful directions for understanding both homelessness and masculinity in contemporary Japan.

The first question is not quite as naïve as it might sound. After all, Article 25 of Japan's constitution clearly promises that "All people shall have the right to maintain the minimum standards of wholesome and cultured living," and the 1952 Livelihood Protection Law is there to see that the promise is kept. For many years the government refused to address the issue of homelessness on the grounds that it was already covered by existing welfare provisions. The second question, usually based on the evidence of visual observation, may be slightly *more* naïve than it sounds, since homeless women may have good reason for staying away from areas where there are many homeless men and thus are not necessarily immediately noticeable. Nonetheless, there is abundant quantitative data suggesting that at least 95 percent of homeless people, in the narrowly defined sense of people not living in housing or shelter, are men.[1] Men are more likely than women to become homeless in all industrialized countries, but nowhere is the imbalance quite as striking as it is in Japan.[2]

Thus the two questions I raised above are closely related. Livelihood protection *(seikatsu hogo)* is designed to pay the rent on a small apartment and provide enough money to cover basic living expenses. People living on the streets, parks, and riverbanks may be assumed not to be receiving livelihood protection, which means in turn that they have not applied for it, or they have applied and been turned down, or they have been approved but then lost their eligibility. And since most of the people concerned are men, our inquiry leads us toward a consideration of Japanese men's relationship with the welfare system.

A woman at risk of homelessness is far more likely than a man to be helped by the Japanese state. To start with, there are two other welfare systems designed almost exclusively for women: support for single-parent families (frequently referred to as *boshi katei,* literally "mother-and-child households") and support for victims of domestic violence. One reason why so few women show up in homeless shelters is that many women who lose their home are housed in facilities designated for one of these other two welfare categories. But perhaps more significantly, even today in Japan, the core family unit tends to be thought of as mother and children. When families break up, children usually stay with their mother, and that group will get more help from the state than the detached father. The mostly male officials running the livelihood protection system tend to show a paternalistic sympathy for distressed women, especially if they have children, whereas distressed men are more likely to be viewed as drunkards, gamblers, or otherwise irresponsible. In child custody disputes courts usually side with the mother, and fathers often have a hard time even visiting their children since visitation rights are not established by Japanese divorce law. Endemic sexism punishes members of either sex who attempt to step outside their approved roles, including men wanting to nurture their children. But those same courts are also notoriously weak at enforcing alimony and child support payments,[3] which in a different way tends to drive a man apart from his family: if he makes a clean break, it may be relatively easy to stay in hiding and avoid payments. Thus material interests, legal systems, and cultural expectations conspire to separate men from their wives and families.

My belief is that the phenomenon of homeless men in Japan results from a gendered conception of personal autonomy that finds expression in two ways: first, in a deeply sexist welfare ideology that penalizes men for failing to maintain economic self-reliance, while at the same time largely keeping women and children off the streets because they are not expected to be self-reliant in the first place; and second, in a concern with self-reliance on the part of homeless men grounded in conceptions of manliness *(otokorashisa).*

"Self-reliance" is the usual translation of the Japanese *jiritsu,* which crops up frequently in welfare circles, notably in the name of the new law enacted in 2002 to support homeless people, the Homeless Self-Reliance Support Law (Hōmuresu Jiritsu Shien-hō), and the Disabled People Self-Reliance Support Law (Shōgaisha Jiritsu Shien-hō) enacted in 2005. It is one of a cluster of frequently used expressions—*jiritsusei* (self-reliance, independence), *jishusei* (autonomy), *shutaisei* (agency, autonomy, or, for Koschmann, "subjectivity")[4]—clustered around the theme of the individual's control over his own fate. Self-reliance, I contend, is a gendered term in a patriarchal society that has not expected women to be self-reliant, nor encouraged them to be so. All officials in local and central government would presumably like to see homeless men become self-reliant, but they define the idea in different ways and have different ideas about how to achieve it.

Here is a microlevel example of the regional variation in thinking on self-reliance. Tokyo's Ōtaryō shelter gives each man a packet of twenty Mild Seven cigarettes a day. The staff explained to me that most of the men using the shelter were smokers, and if they were not given cigarettes, they would have to go around the streets looking for cigarette butts, which would damage their self-respect. Mild Sevens, which cost 300 yen a pack, are one of the mainstream brands most often smoked by salarymen. The Hamakaze shelter in Yokohama gives each man ten Wakaba cigarettes a day. This is a rougher brand than Mild Seven, costing 190 yen a pack and smoked by those who cannot afford better. The need to supply the men's smoking habit is still recognized, but they are not to be spoiled by being given a whole pack of the same cigarettes that those who are employed smoke. The Nishinari Self-Reliance Support Center in Osaka gives its residents no cigarettes; instead the residents are made to work for fifteen minutes every day on cleaning and tidying the premises. Their wage for this labor is 300 yen, which they can feed into the cigarette vending machine in the lobby to buy a pack of twenty of their preferred brand. Here, too, the importance of maintaining the men's self-respect is emphasized, though this time the threat is seen as coming from getting something for nothing rather than from having to search for cigarette butts.

Thus, in these early days of homeless policy in Japan, it is possible to observe officials and social workers wrestling with the concept of personal self-reliance at the same time that they struggle to find effective ways of getting homeless people off the streets. In the course of these efforts, a new ideological category appears to be emerging. It used to be that people either could achieve independence (in which case they got a job and lived on their own income) or could not, in which case they would depend on another person, typically a husband or father, or, in the absence of such a person, they would receive livelihood protection. Now the new emphasis on "self-reliance support" creates an intermediate category: people who are *not* independent but with some support *could become* independent.

This may be read as an attempt to avoid creating a culture of welfare dependence by returning homeless people to productive life, or, more cynically, as a way of postponing a solution to the problem while reducing costs by marooning homeless people in a series of cut-price temporary shelters while denying them livelihood protection. Both those mind-sets are at work in the system. However, with self-reliance emerging as such an important trope in debate on homelessness and welfare, I propose in this chapter to focus on the men themselves, using the lifestyles and discourses of some homeless Japanese men known to me as a way to illuminate the meaning of "self-reliance" for homeless Japanese men.

In his study of poor black men in the Chicago projects, Alford Young notes the tendency of scholars to neglect the views and beliefs of the subjects themselves, instead depicting "traditional, often troublingly simplistic pictures of these men as either extremely passive or overly aggressive respondents to the external forces of urban poverty."[5] Researchers of marginal men in Japan face similar temptations to portray them as passive victims or as active resisters, though two recent major works in English largely succeed in steering between these two stereotypes. Hideo Aoki views underclass men as patching together improvised lives in the face of extremely difficult external circumstances.[6] That matches my own impression, though perhaps the socioeconomic environment is somewhat less brutal than Aoki suggests. Rather than simply condemning and abandoning underclass men, I would argue, the Japanese state has shown a kind of repressive tolerance, sometimes rewarding men who make an effort to conform to mainstream norms. Miki Hasegawa focuses more narrowly on resistance to the authorities by homeless men in Tokyo's Shinjuku district, emphasizing the complex relations between the men themselves and the activists who attempt to support their resistance, sometimes to the point of taking it over.[7]

Aoki and Hasegawa both provide valuable insights into the relationship between homeless men and the Japanese state. Neither of these works, however, takes a very close look at individual men, and this is what I will attempt to do here, introducing five homeless Japanese men, each unique, but each dealing with the challenge of conceptualizing self-reliance while living on the margins of Japanese society. I could not possibly claim that these five men are "representative" of the many thousands of homeless men in Japan today; I will merely state that men such as these are among that population. Each resides in a different Japanese city, and each experiences a different living situation, so at least in a small way I have attempted to reflect the variety of lives being lived by marginal Japanese men today.

OGAWA-SAN: CAN COLLECTOR

In the city of Kawasaki, between Tokyo and Yokohama, the price of scrap aluminum climbed to 185 yen per kilo in the summer of 2007, driven by soaring demand from China's quickly growing economy, strong local demand, and price competition among scrap metal dealers. Several residents of the Aiseiryō homeless shelter were making a modest income from collecting cans, and one of them, Ogawa-san, showed me the ropes. We set out at 6 A.M. for the district of Furuichiba, where local householders were due to throw out their metal waste that morning. By 6:30 there were a dozen homeless men on bicycles crisscrossing the zone, competing with us. Ogawa said the competition was tough but fair. No one would attempt to grab somebody else's cans off the sidewalk, for instance, or to muscle in on a garbage spot already being foraged by another man.

On this morning we found several large caches of beer cans, and we soon amassed thirteen kilos of cans plus two kilos of pots and pans. We sold the lot to a local scrap metal dealer for 2,800 yen. On a day like this Ogawa can make more than the minimum hourly wage (720 yen in Kawasaki), albeit for only a few hours. We took the money straight around the corner to the FamilyMart convenience store and used some of it to buy booze, which we slowly consumed lying under a tree in nearby Fujimi Park.

As Ogawa told me, a life built on collecting cans is a fragile thing: one never knows when the price of aluminum might collapse. (Indeed, scrap metal prices plummeted about 50 percent in the months following the global economic crisis of fall 2008, which had a severe impact on the lifestyles of homeless people.) On the other hand, he pointed out, high prices attract more people wanting a share of the rich pickings. Many homeless people these days are competing for cans with local residents' associations and scrap dealers as well as each other. Moreover, some local authorities have put locks on the collecting places and declared it an offense for anyone other than municipal garbage collectors to remove the contents. Kawasaki's mighty neighbor, Yokohama, has passed such an ordinance.[8] What was once viewed as trash is now widely seen as a valuable resource.

Obviously, then, collecting cans is an improvised survival aid and not an unorthodox career choice. I would nonetheless argue that the cycling recyclers of Kawasaki tell us quite a lot about homeless men in Japan. Can collecting as practiced here is an economic activity with an unpredictable outcome and plenty of room for employing personal strategies and tactics. As such, it is likely to appeal to the kind of man who likes to gamble. Consider Ogawa-san. He is a strong, stocky man of average height, with weather-tanned skin and terrible teeth. Born in 1940 on the border between Hiroshima and Shimane prefectures in western Japan, he was sixty-seven when I met him. For more than twenty years he had a cushy job working for a public corporation that supervised the Yokohama docks. He says he earned a good salary for doing little work. He was married to his second wife, the first having been a teenage adventure many years before, but he never had children. The second marriage was not a happy one. He says his wife was a depressive woman whom he saved from suicide, but he admits he treated her badly: "I never took my wife on holiday; I hardly even took her out for a meal. Any spare cash I had was used for gambling."

Ogawa's main weaknesses were bicycle racing and slots. He reckoned that nearly everyone in his shelter had a gambling problem. Maybe Kawasaki has more compulsive gamblers than the average city, with its bicycle and horse-racing tracks right in the center of town. But the slots and pachinko are worse, he says, because racing happens only at certain times of day, but there is always an open *pachisuro* place,[9] and there the money disappears faster. He can't blame his wife for leaving him after he lost his job. It was his fault. She is back in Kobe now, with her relatives. He hasn't phoned her for some years now. I asked Ogawa why he did something so self-destructive. He offered three reasons—married life was boring, he had too much free time at work, and he had easy access to gambling facilities—but he cited the first of these as the biggest factor.

Being over sixty-five, Ogawa was old enough to be approved for livelihood protection, yet he had not applied. This, he said, was not out of pride or principle, but for the pragmatic reason that he was waiting for the statute of limitations to expire on his unpaid debts. If he applied for welfare he would need to get a certificate of residence, which would expose his whereabouts to his creditors. If approved for welfare, he would have to hand over most of his monthly income to loan sharks. For now it was better to make a little cash collecting cans, keep a low profile, and stay away from the bureaucracy. He understood that under Japanese credit law his debts would be cancelled after five years of noncollection, and he had about a year to go. The homeless shelter he was staying in was scheduled for closure the following year, and he was thinking of applying for welfare shortly after that.

I believe that many homeless men in Japan are not on welfare for similarly pragmatic reasons. They are waiting, either because of some legal issue like Ogawa's, or because they are not yet over the age of sixty and expect to be turned away by welfare officials. These pragmatic types are often overlooked in the debate on welfare, which tends to polarize around the rival ideological models of the man too proud to apply and the man turned away for no good reason by prejudiced officials.

The phenomenon of can collecting by homeless men presents a tricky challenge to the Japanese authorities. On the face of it, it should be welcomed: rather than begging or passively waiting for welfare or charity, these men are getting on their bikes in search of gainful activity. Yet collecting cans is viewed as problematic. First, it is widely assumed that most of the money raised goes straight into alcohol or gambling, enabling homeless men with addictions to maintain them without feeling much pressure to reform their lifestyles. Second, as an opportunistic, unscheduled economic activity, it resembles day labor in that it does not require a regular working week. For both these reasons, can collecting is viewed by many welfare professionals as a barrier to leaving homelessness and unemployment rather than as a possible first step on the ladder out, and hence the activity is specifically prohibited in many homeless facilities.

HOTOKE: PARK LIFE RESISTANCE

In Nagoya there is a locally famous homeless man who humorously calls himself "Hotoke," a complex term that variously means "Buddha" or "spirit," usually that of a deceased person that achieved enlightenment or was unusually kind. As a matter of principle, Hotoke tells no one his real name or other personal data. He always says that he is zero years old and was born on planet Earth.

Hotoke embodies the spirit of self-reliance. I first met him in 2002, the same year that the Homeless Self-Reliance Support Law was passed. At the time there were close to a thousand homeless men living in three great parks in central Nagoya: Wakamiya Ōdori Park, Shirakawa Park, and Hisaya Park. Hotoke was living in Shirakawa Park in a large shack with a tentlike awning attached to it, with a lot of furniture, bric-a-brac, and books. The city government was building a homeless shelter in Wakamiya Ōdori Park, and officials were going around the park dwellings trying to persuade their owners to use the shelter when it opened. (Men who did not have shacks or tent dwellings were not allowed to use the shelter, a policy reflecting the shelter's objective of clearing the parks of homeless dwellings.)

Hotoke stoutly refused to leave. Two years later he was one of only eight men still living in Shirakawa Park when the city authorities and police came to forcibly expel the holdouts. Dragged from his dwelling, which was then dismantled and removed, Hotoke still refused to leave the park. While the other men went into the shelter or the hospital, Hotoke took to living under a tree (just like the original Buddha, Siddhartha Gautama).

His one-man show of resistance lasted six months, until 3 June 2005. That day two city officials interrupted Hotoke while he was cooking. In a moment of irritation, he flicked some miso soup at them. Hotoke was arrested for allegedly assaulting and injuring the two city officials. At his trial in the Nagoya District Court, true to form, Hotoke refused to give his real name, age, or date of birth. He was consequently denied bail and had to spend the seventeen months of the trial in detention. Finally he was convicted and sentenced to a fine of 300,000 yen, converted to two months' imprisonment, meaning that Hotoke was free to go since he had already served far more time than that. Hotoke appealed the decision to the Nagoya high court. In September 2007 he won a small victory when the judge upheld the assault charge but turned down the second charge of causing actual bodily injury and reduced the fine from 300,000 to 200,000 yen. Hearings in both court cases were held before courtrooms packed with Hotoke's friends and supporters.

Hotoke is an interesting case for our theme of self-reliance: stubborn as a mule, he has fought a one-man crusade against the authorities long after most men would have given up. But his self-reliance is not total: he has drawn on alternative sources of support, such as the local day-laborer union and gifts from supporters. And when he has fallen ill, Hotoke has on occasion used hospitals, where his bills were covered by the medical arm of the livelihood protection program. His powerful expression of individual resistance is made possible partly by a pragmatic willingness to accept certain forms of assistance from individuals, and even occasionally from the city of Nagoya, which he nonetheless refers to as Bullyville (Jakusha-ijime-shi).

In 2007 Hotoke was living in an ingeniously designed hut on wheels, which he could move short distances if told to do so by police. He explained that it had been built by Makiguchi-san, a former day laborer from Osaka who had built some twenty of these wheeled huts and lent or rented them to homeless people. Makiguchi had also negotiated a deal with the city government to allow homeless people in Wakamiya Park to draw water from public hydrants in the park. Makiguchi's ingenuity and stubbornness had turned him into a third force in the relations between the authorities and homeless people in Nagoya—making him another intriguing image of self-reliance.

TSUJIMOTO-SAN: WALDEN ON THE MUKO RIVER

Several homeless men have cheerfully described themselves and their friends to me as "lazy." One of those was Tsujimoto-san, who lives near Osaka, in a stout, well-constructed shack on the Muko River, on the border between Nishinomiya and Amagasaki. Born in Saitama in 1944, Tsujimoto was sixty-three when I got to know him and had lived on the Nishinomiya side of the river for a decade after many years of wandering around Japan. Thin and slight of build, he has glasses and a lined face that frequently creases further into a smile or laughter.

The riverbank lifestyle is one that appeals to homeless men in search of peace and quiet. Compared with park communities, riverside dwellings are far less likely to be removed and their residents less likely to be harassed by police or city officials. As well as having fewer passersby than city parks, riverbanks have a complex administrative structure, divided between various branches of city, prefectural, and national governments, which tends to result in administrative paralysis and the benign neglect of homeless colonies. The stretch of the Muko River where Tsujimoto lives is close to two provincial cities, and a nearby railway station provides easy access to Osaka, so it is suburban rather than rural and combines convenience with relative tranquility. On the other hand, the same relative remoteness and administrative neglect that makes riverbanks peaceful locations can be dangerous when fights break out or gangs of youths come to harass homeless men. Moreover, riverbanks are at risk of flooding, as was dramatically demonstrated in August 2007, when twenty-eight homeless men were rescued by helicopter from the Tama River between Tokyo and Kawasaki after a typhoon caused the river to burst its banks.

Tsujimoto tours neighborhoods on the day of the month when large-scale general refuse *(sodai gomi)* is being put out, and has had some success in finding jewelry, fine china, and other valuables. Even so, he estimates his average monthly income at just 15,000 to 20,000 yen. He has a sheaf of technical qualifications that permit him to work as an electrician and operator of various kinds of construction machinery. He also claims to have a second-class diploma in abacus *(soraban)* and certificates in flower arranging and tea ceremony. His neat and tidy hut does somewhat recall a tea ceremony room, and when conversing with visitors he kneels in front of it in the upright *seiza* style, which he says he finds comfortable. He says he could easily get employment, and that labor recruiters have approached him several times. But, like Melville's Bartleby, he prefers not to: "I have no appetite for work. I'm tired of worrying about what other people think, tired of boss-underling relationships. Since coming here, I've felt at ease."

Tsujimoto's lifestyle seems comfortable: he has time for hobbies such as reading historical fiction and playing *shōgi* with friends or video games on his Game Boy. He has a small TV that he runs off a car battery, which is regularly recharged for him by a friend. He has oil lamps for lighting and camping gas for cooking. About ten men live in the immediate vicinity. He says they get on very well, though he never shares food with them. To him, that is indicative of an excessively intimate friendship. Like many homeless men, including homeless author Ōyama Shiro (Ōyama 2000 and 2005), he says he deliberately avoids intimate friendships for fear of incurring obligations.[10] Occasionally he will make fishing trips, traveling vast distances on his bicycle; he says the fish in the Muko River are not worth catching. He mentioned that there were three male-female couples and one gay male couple living in the 150 to 200 dwellings on the banks of the Muko River. He once knew of a single woman, but she was long gone.

Like Ogawa, Tsujimoto had a working career that was far from that of the *lumpenproletariat*. The youngest son among seven siblings, he graduated from senior high school and started out working for a firm that maintained and repaired printing presses. He traces his wanderlust to the frequent business trips that this specialized profession required. He quit after five years and thereafter drifted from job to job. His electrician's qualifications enabled him to earn good money—indeed, sometimes he could make 10,000 yen without lifting a finger, just by allowing some maintenance company to put his name on the safety certificates for electricity substations, "which never break down anyway." A period during which he earned easy money is thus another point he shares with Ogawa.

But whereas Ogawa said he was pragmatically playing out time before applying for livelihood protection, Tsujimoto insisted that he had never applied for it and never would. When I asked him why, he said, "I don't want to live anymore," and he added that he had attempted suicide three times. He did not want or need to have his livelihood protected. When a local volunteer encouraged him to apply for welfare when he got older and weaker, he replied that he would sooner throw himself into the river than enter an apartment, or else he would hang himself from the tree under which we were sitting. He said he was tired of life and was living only by inertia, although he said it with a good-humored laugh, and I could not guess how serious his talk of suicide might be. Tsujimoto also said he had no interest in using the self-reliance support centers in nearby Osaka. He did not trust any institution set up by politicians, whom he viewed with contempt.

Figure 8.1. The view from Yoshida-san's shack on the Shōnai River in Nagoya.

It is tempting to think of Tsujimoto as a Japanese Thoreau, retreating to a semirural location, maintaining a self-reliant lifestyle, and casting a cold eye on modern society. That said, Tsujimoto is situated firmly within the cash economy, preferring to use income from his scavenging activities to buy food from a supermarket rather than farming. Indeed, I found few cases of homeless men growing vegetables or keeping chickens, though admittedly in many locations legal obstacles would have made it difficult to do so.

YOSHIDA-SAN: RAILING AT SOCIETY

The biggest riverbank settlement in Nagoya is along the Shōnai River. It was there that I found Yoshida-san living under the Shin-Taiko Bridge in a small shack by a footpath (figure 8.1). On the other side of the footpath, twenty yards away, were four more shacks surrounded by an immense quantity of stinking trash. At least two of them were clearly uninhabited and the trash had invaded them, warping the walls and spewing out from the cracks.

Yoshida-san looked to be about forty. He was a stocky man, running to fat, with an unkempt beard and wavy black hair, and he wore black shorts and a sweat-stained gray T-shirt. Initially suspicious of my presence, he became increasingly talkative, and our conversation lasted several hours. He told me that the mountain of stinking garbage on the other side of the path was the legacy of a homeless man who had been driven out with threats of violence by Yoshida and a couple of his friends. Since then, the local authorities had several times said they were going to clear away the garbage, but they had yet to do so. To Yoshida, this was absolutely typical of the rank incompetence and cynical lying of government officials in Japan.

Where Tsujimoto's view from the riverbank was one of world-weary ennui, Yoshida's was darker and more cynical. "Japan is finished," he remarked several times. He had various conspiracy theories—all the state-run gambling games were fixed, for instance, and elections likewise were decided in advance. After each rant he would raise his eyebrows, shrug his shoulders, and say, "Right?" with the bored air of one who knew the score. It was all so obvious—Japan was a society run by the rich, for the rich; it was totally corrupt and deeply unfair. Japanese society was like an army, in which lower ranks had no power over higher ranks. He knew from experience that employers would mercilessly exploit their workers. Government policies to help homeless people were a mere excuse to keep people off the welfare rolls. The state pension, just 70,000 yen a month, was tantamount to abandoning the elderly to death—and now the government had just admitted to *losing* millions of pension records.[11] For Yoshida, mainstream religion was a money-making scam with no interest in helping the weak and poor, and the fact that most of the food handouts for homeless people were provided by Japan's tiny Christian minority should make the Buddhist temples and Shinto shrines feel thoroughly ashamed of themselves.

For Yoshida, abundant evidence of the corruption and incompetence of the government and other large organizations meant that only an idiot would place any trust in the system. "In this country," he asserted, "there isn't a single person you can rely on. All you can do is live for yourself." To him, this meant taking advantage of whatever resources he could find around him. As well as scavenging for cans and other materials, which he said brought in a cash income of 20,000 to 30,000 yen a month, this also meant lining up for handouts and foraging for food. The local MacDonald's had been an excellent source for some time, as the manager had put out leftovers for homeless people every night. Now, however, due to a new city ordinance defining leftover food as industrial waste, the manager was obliged to pay good money for a company to take the leftovers away and destroy them—much to Yoshida's exasperation.

This gradual criminalization of foraging for food may be placed alongside the gradual expulsion of dwellings from parks, the tentative criminalization of can collecting, and the previous crackdown on reselling magazines picked out of trains and stations, as part of a consistent pattern whereby the state delegitimizes self-reliant activities performed by homeless people. Masculine pride, in Japan and many other parts of the world, is tied to being able to look after oneself. Yet it seems that, despite the government rhetoric of self-reliance, when a man is down on his luck, almost any attempt to look after himself without resorting to the welfare system will, one way or another, run afoul of the law. Note, incidentally, that for Yoshida, foraging for food and queuing for handouts were activities constructed differently from applying for welfare. At first glance all these activities may seem like an admission that one cannot support oneself, but to Yoshida collecting food thrown out by restaurants and shops was something requiring effort and local knowledge, and did not entail dependence on the state. The handouts, likewise, came from private citizens rather than the hated state. Meanwhile, he contended that the mountains of food destroyed each day according to government regulations amounted to yet another national disgrace.

Yoshida said he had been homeless for five years, ever since he had been laid off. He had previously worked for one of the many manufacturers of auto parts supplying Toyota Motor in nearby Toyoda city. Because of his low wages, lively social life, and keen interest in pachinko, he had no savings to tide him over when he was laid off. He had wound up spending the night in a local park, was attacked by schoolboys, and was rescued by a kindly older man who, despite being slightly mentally handicapped, showed him how to survive homelessness. He owed his life to this man.

Eventually the old man fell ill. He was hospitalized and told to apply for livelihood protection when he was discharged. But it was just before Golden Week (the series of public holidays at the start of May), and the hospital discharged him when the welfare offices were closed. Although he could barely walk, he was told to make his way to the emergency homeless shelter and stay there until the holiday ended and he could be placed in a welfare apartment. Yoshida helped him hobble to the shelter and left him there. When he returned to visit three days later, the man was gone. He'd apparently left the shelter barefoot, for he had left his shoes behind. Yoshida has never seen him since. He blames the welfare authorities. When a person is going to be put on the rolls to receive livelihood protection, the welfare office conducts extensive background checks to make sure the person really has no financial resources and nobody who might provide for him. The latter search starts with parents, siblings, and children and may extend to distant relatives or even unrelated friends. The shame of being the subject of such an investigation is a major deterrent to applying for welfare, especially for men, since, as mentioned above, self-reliance is a key part of their masculine self-image. Yoshida thinks that this is what made his friend run away.

In many parts of Japan local schoolboys will violently harass homeless men for amusement. Another informant, Hirayama-san, who lived in a large shack in Osaka Castle Park, said that if homeless men did not fight back, the schoolboys would lose interest and give up harassing them. Yoshida, however, took the opposite view. When local boys threw stones at homeless men, it was vital to resist them. He always did. The kids were all cowards at heart, he believed, so he would give their bicycles a good kicking, or frog-march them to the local police box and demand to see their parents. He said that once he had slapped one of the boys in front of his parents in order to teach the whole family a lesson. He added that every summer, just before the school holidays began, he would ask the police to issue circulars to local schools ordering pupils not to attack homeless people.

One source of Yoshida's bitterness is his sense that he has not been given a fair chance in society. One of six siblings in a poor family, he says he left school after completing junior high school because his parents could not afford to send him to senior high. He regrets that and would like to somehow catch up on his education and escape from homelessness. He struck me as a man whose cynicism and belligerence covered up an all-too-evident insecurity. Self-reliance and self-defense were obsessions for him, but he also looked to mutual assistance among homeless men as a way of remaining safe in a dangerous world. He had a good friend, a former postman, who lived in one of the shacks near the mountain of garbage. Yoshida also said that he would advise and assist newly homeless men who arrived at the riverbank, sometimes encouraging them to use the same support facilities that he himself spurned. I had just visited one of them and showed him some of their published materials. He was surprised at the range of services available, and I thought I saw his cynicism waver as I bade him farewell.

For Yoshida, informal bonds of mutual assistance between homeless men were a viable alternative to dependence on the government-run welfare system. His powerful attachment to the old man who showed him the ropes was an expression of that impulse. While Tsujimoto sought security in solitary independence, Yoshida sought it in friendship and cooperation with his peers, a set of pure autonomous relations he contrasted with the cynicism and corruption of nonhomeless society. Here we start to sense why his conception of masculinity is problematic to the state: he valorizes the free association of men who cannot be co-opted into larger social units, men who are quite unlike the stereotypical corporate warrior, whose fight for his company parallels a soldier's fight for the nation. Yoshida's vision of masculine self-reliance was specifically opposed to the state and hence liable to be stamped upon.

NISHIKAWA-SAN: THE BROADER VIEW

My final case study is of a man who got off the streets by successfully applying for welfare. For many years now Nishikawa-san has been living alone in one or another of the cheap lodging houses of Kotobuki-chō, Yokohama.[12] He used to support himself by doing day labor, but he has been living on livelihood protection for some years. Classical American definitions of homelessness[13] would include Nishikawa, since he is largely cut off from family and society, but Nishikawa draws a clear distinction between himself and men who live in the street. He sees himself as having escaped from homelessness, and he had no hesitation in applying for livelihood protection when he felt the time was ripe. For him, welfare is just another of the resources available in postmodern society. Although he sacrificed a degree of autonomy when he signed on for welfare and sometimes expresses gratitude to the Japanese nation for supporting him, it did not harm his pride much. This is because Nishikawa does not believe *anyone* is really autonomous or self-reliant. He argues that some people may appear autonomous, but in fact their lives are intertwined with broader society and their thoughts conditioned by the surrounding culture and media.

Born in 1940, Nishikawa is one of many Japanese men whose lives were decisively influenced by Japan's defeat in World War II, although he was only five years old when it happened. He says he still remembers his confusion on seeing the tall American soldiers arriving in his native Kumamoto at the start of the Occupation. As a small child he did not fully grasp the difference between these giant warriors and the Nazi storm troopers he had seen on cinema newsreels. One moment these supermen had been conquering Europe; now here they were taking charge of Japan.

After the war, Nishikawa went to high school, where many of the teachers had fought in the war and would brag about their exploits and wounds. He recalls the deep sense of disgust he felt about that: how could they brag when they had lost the war? After graduating he joined the Ground Self-Defense Force and was stationed first at Sasebo in Kyushu, and later at the Makomanai Base near Sapporo. Nishikawa enjoyed the all-male society of the military and was inclined to romanticize it as a "society of knights." He said, "It's because there are no women that such an ideal society is possible, at least for a fleeting moment. If women come in it gets dirtied immediately." He stressed that he was not talking about homosexuality, but a pure society of comrades—a common trope in prewar Japanese thinking. Yet this deeply sexist celebration of all-male society was offset by a wry awareness that the war was over and that these soldiers would likely never see action. As he said, it was more like playing at soldiers, or "being in the boy scouts or a school club." For him, it was deeply refreshing to enjoy military life safe in the knowledge that any real fighting would probably be done by the Americans.

Built by the Americans during the Occupation and recently vacated by a U.S. unit, Makomanai Base placed the military masculinity of the conqueror in another register. The facilities were bigger and better than those at Japanese bases and were built in the style of an American log cabin. Nishikawa especially admired the exceptionally large library, which seemed to speak to a superiority of intellect to match that of bodily strength and military technology already demonstrated.

By his own account, Nishikawa has never had sex without paying for it. In this he resembles homeless day laborer Ōyama Shirō (a pseudonym), whose memoir of life on the margins was translated into English as *A Man with No Talents*.[14] Intensely shy with women, Nishikawa has never been able to contemplate relations without being totally drunk. When he was in the GSDF, his fellow officers sometimes took him to the Sapporo pleasure district of Susukino. A brief session with a prostitute would cost 1,000 yen, this in an era when a soldier's pay was about 6,000 yen a month. On the rare occasions when the drunken Nishikawa managed to achieve penetration, he recalls being rewarded with a sudden sharp pain in his penis, which would somehow get pinched in the intrauterine contraceptive device favored by the Susukino women. He called this a "plastic curtain," obstructing intimacy between men and women. For him it symbolized the fundamental impossibility of true love or communication between the sexes. To Nishikawa, prostitution was not a sign of men's power over women. On the contrary, the fact that men had to pay through the nose and then experience intense pain led him to the rueful conclusion that "in a matrilineal society like Japan, men can never win out over women."

Contrary to the mainstream academic consensus, he often argued that Japan was a matrilineal society, and he even read violence and cruelty by Japanese men as expressions of their frustration at being unable to dominate women. His opinions echoed Bourdieu's observation that "manliness . . . is an eminently *relational* notion, constructed in front of and for other men and against femininity, in a kind of fear of the female, firstly in oneself."[15]

Like many *Nihonjinron* scholars, Nishikawa also sees deep significance in diet, oversimplifying Japan and the United States as fish-eating and meat-eating cultures, respectively. He attributes Japan's defeat in the war to the fact that a woman-dominated fish-eating nation was taking on the patrilineal and meat-eating Americans. Like so many Japanese men of his generation, he recalls seeing American soldiers out on dates with Japanese girls: "The men seemed so big, and the women so small. We're not meat eaters, so it can't be helped."

Spells of homelessness after he quit the GSDF brought a new twist to Nishikawa's "*gaijin* complex." In the West, he mentioned, homeless men would usually have some kind of skill: they would do conjuring tricks, or play the violin, or juggle like Peter Frankl (an eccentric Hungarian mathematician known for performing juggling shows in the streets of Tokyo—hardly a representative homeless man). Homeless Japanese men, by contrast, had no special skills and would just continue walking the streets until they keeled over and died.

As the postwar years rolled by, Nishikawa read widely and was especially influenced by Colin Wilson's *The Outsider.* Wilson's 1956 study of modern culture heroes, fictional and real, sees alienation from mainstream society as a defining feature of those who have deep insight into the human condition. From his own outsider's perspective, Nishikawa started to question his infatuation with American muscular virility, turning to what he saw as its dark side. He developed an obsessive interest in violent crime in the United States. He could name half a dozen American mass murderers, complete with the dates, locations, and circumstances of their crimes.

Nishikawa had a deep sense of shame about his failure to be a credit to his family, a sense made all the more acute because he is an oldest son, out of three brothers and one sister. On learning that one of his brothers had died in a traffic accident, he reflected, "He was only a year younger than me, but I bullied him constantly. I thought I was some kind of emperor just because I happened to be the oldest son. I was an A-class war criminal.[16] Now that he was dead, I felt personally responsible as oldest son for failing to protect him." In such ways are personal and public issues entwined in

Nishikawa's mind. His discourse is a lament for lost masculinity, in which his own life as an alcoholic day laborer, narrowly saved from death on the streets by the Japanese welfare system, becomes a microcosm of Japan's defeat in war and of an inadequacy in Japanese men that he sees as persisting despite the great economic revival of the postwar years. That lingering regret for failed manhood is a theme I often come across among homeless men, though never expressed so clearly as by Nishikawa.

That said, going on welfare does not necessarily mean abandoning all traces of self-reliance. Many Kotobuki men drink away their welfare money in the first few days of the month and are then penniless again. Nishikawa is not like that. He husbands his resources carefully, calculating each day's expenditures so that even on the last day of the month he can still purchase the four or five glasses of cheap sake that he requires to keep himself going. In the last couple of years he has even made several trips back to his native Kyushu to see his sister and look for old school friends, riding slow local trains, outrageously fare dodging, and feigning drunken unconsciousness when accosted by the authorities. His feelings of shame are focused elsewhere, on deeper matters. Self-reliance for him is an unattainable metaphysical ideal; reliance, whether on an employer or a welfare agency, is an incidental detail.

Many of the men I have studied are difficult to discuss using English-language homeless terminology, with its bipartite distinction between "street homeless" (or, in British parlance, "rough sleepers") and "sheltered homeless." Japanese shack dwellers are not exactly on the street, or in a shelter as usually conceived. Their dwellings are homemade, but they are mostly quite well built. Though most are small, some are large enough to bear comparison with a small apartment. I have observed some that have legal postal addresses and have mail delivered to them. Some have furniture; some have guard dogs or pet cats. Many have gas from camping stoves, some have water supplies from nearby fire hydrants or drinking fountains, and a few have electricity from car batteries. At least one case has been documented of a homeless man's dwelling with a solar panel supplying electricity.[17] The great majority of these dwellings are clustered in settlements, which arguably represent a kind of alternative community.

There is considerable interest in the design of Japanese homeless dwellings, including several art and photography exhibitions and at least three published collections of photos, sketches, and text: Sogi Kanta's *Asakusa Style* (2003), Sakaguchi Kyōhei's *Zero-yen House* (2004), and Nagashima Yukitoshi's *Cardboard House* (2005).[18] These books testify to the resourcefulness and skill of the men who build, maintain, decorate, and live in them. As well as admiring the skill of the design, one is also struck by the air of domesticity, the *homeliness,* of these dwellings. When large numbers of them are gathered together in villagelike communities, one begins to wonder whether "homeless" accurately describes these men.

Living without women and with little cash obliges shack dwellers to acquire skills long since lost to most Japanese men and considered the preserve of women. In a society where many men can barely peel an apple, they must cook for themselves. They also have to build, maintain, furnish, and repair their own living space, unlike most men, who will pay professionals to do these things for them. So, although they have very little by way of income or possessions, and they may on occasion join lines of people waiting for handouts of food, in some ways they actually seem *more* self-reliant than most mainstream men.

As with can collecting, so with park dwelling: Japanese cities have gradually turned the screw on this lifestyle, which is seen—not without justification, in some cases—as obstructing the use of parks by nonhomeless people. The typical approach has been to lure those living in shacks into temporary prefabricated shelters; to threaten any who refuse to go with forcible expulsion, as in Hotoke's case; and to fence off vacated areas of parks to prevent newcomers or returnees from settling there. By such methods the authorities have gradually whittled down the park populations. The elaborate homemade dwellings celebrated by Sogi, Sakaguchi, and Nagashima are becoming steadily harder to find.

The irony is that once these seemingly self-reliant men have been put through the shelter system, they will likely be either clients of the state (living on welfare) or in a more desperate homeless condition than before, expelled from their park communities and reduced to living in cardboard boxes. Hence "self-reliance support" may actually *reduce* men's degree of self-reliance. The figures published by the Ministry of Health, Labor and Welfare, which show a 51.9 percent reduction in nonsheltered homeless people, to 13,124 in January 2010, from 25,296 seven years earlier, largely reflect the gradual war of attrition on the park settlements. Some of those evicted men may well still be homeless, but they are now away from the more noticeable concentrations.

As mainstream society slowly tightens the noose on homeless settlements, repressively throwing the men onto the street or tolerantly placing them in welfare hostels and cheap apartments, how do homeless men conceptualize their place in society? Connell and Messerschmidt observe that "'masculinity' represents not a certain type of man but, rather, a way that men position themselves through discursive practices."[19] How do homeless Japanese men position themselves?

Though my informants show a tremendous variety of personalities, outlooks, and lifestyles, they have certain things in common. First, they do not beg—and this is true of most homeless Japanese in my experience. In contrast, most of them do not seem to hesitate to accept food handouts *(takidashi)* from volunteers, nonprofit organizations, and others. What is shameful is to ask for help, not to accept what is offered. This may also explain why some men who will not apply for livelihood protection will nonetheless stand in line for hours, day after day, to receive minimal emergency assistance such as Yokohama's 714-yen food vouchers *(panken)*. Some of these men have been turned down for livelihood protection; others insist that they do not want full-scale welfare, just a little help to get by. So accepting assistance entails a kind of hierarchy of shame. Begging is seen as the most abject abandonment of masculinity, and very few homeless Japanese men will do it. To beg is to openly admit one's inferiority vis-à-vis the man (or, worse still, woman) from whom you beg. It is a loss of manhood in the sense of adulthood as well as masculinity; only children beg to get something for nothing. It leaves no room for psychological maneuver. Accepting food handouts from activists or charity workers is less humiliating because at least one is not forcing one's need on other people. Those who hand out the food assuage shame by addressing the homeless men (who are typically older than themselves) as *senpai* (senior), creating an image of intergenerational cooperation rather than one-sided charity. Standing in line for food tickets is also a humiliating business, but in a sense the tiring wait at the ward office makes the activity somewhat akin to work done to get pay. Applying for livelihood protection feels to some like an admission of failed manhood comparable to begging, though others see livelihood protection as comparable to the pension they never got from their decades of insecure labor. Informal economy activities such as recycling cans fit very well with notions of masculine self-reliance, making it all the more galling when the state delegitimizes such work.

In short, each of the survival strategies available to homeless men in Japan carries different implications for masculinity, usually as constructed relative to the state or broader society. That has been the main sense in which I have used the term in this chapter. When masculinity is constructed relative to *women*, a bleaker picture emerges. None of the men discussed here has been able to sustain married life; none can expect to be looked after by a wife, daughter, or daughter-in-law in old age; none has a girlfriend or can even afford to hire prostitutes; and the best they can hope for in terms of female companionship is a friendly smile from a matronly waitress at a cheap bar. Viewed in this light, these men look much more like cases of failed manhood. Yet the way they talk positions themselves not relative to women but relative to the state or mainstream society, perhaps because they sense they are on firmer ground in the latter debate.

Along with this range of survival strategies comes a range of discursive practices open to homeless men as they seek to position themselves within Japanese society. My case studies give some indication of the options available. They include a pragmatic approach that ekes out a minimal level of survival until the welfare system kicks in (Ogawa); a radical refusal to compromise with the repressive-tolerant authorities (Hotoke); a hermit-like detachment from mainstream society (Tsujimoto); outright denunciation of mainstream society and an emphasis on camaraderie among those living on its margins (Yoshida); or a metaphysical view of human life that makes the differences between the mainstream and the margins appear trivial (Nishikawa). What these varying strategies have in common is that they soften the blow to the ideal of masculine self-reliance that comes from not being able to support oneself economically in a mainstream lifestyle.

In their various ways, these men are trying to come to terms with their failure to achieve conventional standards of manhood. As some of them point out, the stereotypical salaryman is far from self-reliant himself. He relies on his company, his boss, his wife, and others. His autonomy is also limited. Despite the language it employs, the Homeless Self-Reliance Support Law is really an exhortation to homeless men to trade in one mode of limited autonomy for another—to become self-reliant in a narrowly defined, socially sanctioned way. As the slow but steady criminalization of homeless lifeways proceeds, I anticipate that the increasingly beleaguered settlements of huts and tents may take on the character of last redoubts. As their inhabitants are gradually expelled, they will either be pushed further from mainstream society or brought into the welfare system, their masculinity further undermined by the need finally to abandon the brave image of the self-reliant man.

NOTES

1. For example, a government survey conducted in January 2009 and published on 9 March 2009 counted 495 homeless women in a total homeless population of 15,759, equivalent to 3.1 percent (www.mhlw.go.jp/bunya/seikatsuhogo/homeless09/index.html). Murayama (2004), writing specifically about homeless women in Japan, also gives a figure of about 3 percent.

2. In the United States and United Kingdom, for example, surveys have generally found homeless populations to be roughly 70 percent male.

3. Curtin 2002.

4. Koschmann 1996.

5. Young 2003, p. 6.

6. Aoki 2006.

7. Hasegawa 2006.

8. Odawara was the first city in Kanagawa prefecture to ban can collecting, in 2004. In the next couple of years, Yokohama, Zama, Kamakura, Chigasaki, Fujisawa, and Hiratsuka followed suit. Hayashi 2007, p. 20.

9. A place where you can play pachinko or slot machines.

10. Many homeless men will avoid using their surname and will also refrain from asking someone else their surname or other personal details. Patari 2008 quotes some informants in Ueno Park as describing this as "homeless etiquette."

11. In February 2007 the Social Insurance Agency admitted that it had lost track of some fifty million pension records when it changed its computer system in 1997.

12. Nishikawa-san is an intellectual day laborer who features in my book *Men of Uncertainty* (Gill 2001, pp. 168–70).

13. "Homelessness is a condition of detachment from society characterized by the absence or attenuation of the affiliative bonds that link settled persons to a network of interconnected social structures." Caplow et al. 1968, p. 494.

14. "I have never slept with a woman who was not a prostitute. I am, in short, a man with no talents who is incapable of relating to women or coping with work." Ōyama 2005, p. 128.

15. Bourdieu 2001 [1998], p. 53.

16. This is a reference to the Tokyo War Crimes Tribunal of 1946–48, in which class A ("crimes against peace") was one of three classes of crime, usually thought of as the most serious.

17. Sogi 2003, p. 19; Sakaguchi 2004, pp. 182–83.

18. Some of Sakaguchi's photos of homeless dwellings may be viewed at his home page: www.oyenhouse.com/en/Zero_Yen_House/. He published a sequel in 2008, *Zero Yen House Zero Yen Life,* focusing on a single brilliant shack architect encountered on the bank of the Sumida River in Tokyo.

19. Connell and Messerschmidt 2005, p. 841.

REFERENCES

Aoki, Hideo. 2006. *Japan's Underclass.* Melbourne: Trans Pacific Press.

Bourdieu, Pierre. 2001 [1998]. *Masculine Domination.* Stanford: Stanford University Press.

Caplow, Theodor, Howard M. Bahr, and David Sternberg. 1968. "Homelessness." In *International Encyclopedia of the Social Sciences,* ed. David Sills, 494–99. New York: Macmillan.

Connell, R. W., and James W. Messerschmidt. 2005. "Hegemonic Masculinity: Rethinking the Concept." *Gender and Society* 19: 829–59.

Curtin, Sean. 2002. "Japanese Child Support Payments in 2002." Available at www.glocom.org/special_topics/social_trends/20020909_trends_s6/index.html.

Gill, Tom. 2001. *Men of Uncertainty: The Social Organization of Day Laborers in Contemporary Japan.* Albany: State University of New York Press.

Hasegawa, Miki. 2006. *We Are Not Garbage! The Homeless Movement in Tokyo, 1994–2002.* London: Routledge.

Hayashi Mahito. 2007. "Seisei suru Chi'iki no Kyōkai: Naibuka Shita 'Hōmuresu Mondai' to Seidōka no Rōkaritii." *Soshiorojii* 52, no. 1: 53–69.

Koschmann, J. Victor. 1996. *Revolution and Subjectivity in Postwar Japan.* Chicago: University of Chicago Press.

Murayama, Satomi. 2004. "Homeless Women in Japan." *Kyōto Shakaigaku Nenpo* 157–68.

Nagashima Yukitoshi. 2005. *Danbōru Hausu.* Poplar.

Ōyama Shirō. 2000. *San'ya Gakeppuchi Nikki.* TBS Britannica.

———. 2005. *A Man with No Talents: Memoirs of a Tokyo Day Labourer.* Ithaca: Cornell University Press.

Patari, Juho. 2008. *The "Homeless Etiquette": Social Interaction and Behavior Among the Homeless Living in Taito Ward, Tokyo.* Saarbrücken: VDM Verlag.

Sakaguchi Kyōhei. 2004. *Zero-en Hausu.* Little More.

Sogi Kanta. 2003. *Asakusa Stairu.* Bungei Shunju.

Young, Alford A., Jr. 2003. *Minds of Marginalized Black Men: Making Sense of Mobility, Opportunity, and Future Life Chances.* Princeton: Princeton University Press.

PART III

Bodies and Boundaries

9 Collective Maturation

The Construction of Masculinity in Early Modern Villages

Nagano Hiroko

Translated by Anne Walthall

Early in the nineteenth century, a young man named Genzō from the region near Mashiko had sex with a widow. This by itself was not necessarily a problem—in many villages, widows were considered fair game for unmarried men. The reason why Genzō was forced to write a letter of apology and thus expose his affair to the prying eyes of later historians is that he had gone outside his own village. He apologized not to the widow, but to her village's youth group for having violated its territory.[1] At issue then and in this chapter is not Genzō's masculine identity as an individual, but the construction of masculinity structured through collective participation in the youth group and its exercise of social authority.

Among the many issues concerning masculinity in Japan's early modern farm villages that deserve scholarly attention, this essay will investigate two. The first focuses on the connection between the construction of masculinity and the formation of men's groups not necessarily connected with production and labor, such as social clubs and sports clubs monopolized by men in modern European society or the armed forces in present-day Japan (see also chapter 4 in this volume).[2] This chapter suggests that such male groups and alliances characterized Japan's early modern villages and examines their structure and functions with respect to the exercise of masculine power within the social organization of village society and in particular over female villagers' sexuality. In short, I ask how masculinity worked as a tool of social power.

The focus of this chapter is the role of collectivization and systemization in the process of constructing masculinity and its exercise of authority. I begin with childhood, when, at the level of education, ritual, or even visual symbols, gender asymmetry is not yet apparent. It only becomes obvious in the coming-of-age ceremony that marked a man's maturation and the young men's collectivization and organization into youth groups that followed. I argue that the formation of young men's masculinity was tied to their engagement in a number of social activities; various virtues fostered during this process in turn came to be seen as masculine. Both mechanisms greatly contributed to the male and masculine domination of the village as a social and public sphere. Defined in opposition to men and masculinity, women were excluded from the experiences of collective, organized social activities. Hence, women and femininity were confined to the physical, sexual, and private realms and subordinated to men and masculinity in the hierarchy of values. Youth groups that occupied a position of social authority through the construction of masculinity were permitted to exercise it in various ways. One important way was the subjugation and control of the female villagers' sexuality. In contrast to a husband's control over his wife's sexuality, the control exercised by youth groups was rigidly prescribed, limited, and fluid.

CHILDHOOD PRIOR TO GENDERED ASYMMETRY

How was masculinity constructed in early modern farm villages over the standard life course for a man? Let us begin by examining the characteristics of gendered differentiation found in infancy and from there move on to consider how boys and girls were treated up to their coming-of-age ceremonies.

The *Illustrated Guide to Agronomy (Nōgyō zue)* provides visual evidence for gender differentiation in childhood. Famous as representative of Edo-period illustrated farm manuals, it depicts the yearly cycle of agricultural work and the way the farmers lived their lives in a Hokuriku farm village near the Japan Sea.[3] Children engage in various types of work, such as cutting grass, carrying manure, transporting and spreading seedlings, weeding, and pulling oxen and horses laden with goods. Most are boys somewhat older than ten years, gauging by the bangs across their foreheads. While we cannot call it labor, children also help out by guarding against sparrows and gleaning fallen grains. Those who ward off sparrows are boys with bangs, but the gleaners appear to be about seven or eight years old. In scenes of village life, younger children are shown being carried on their mother's back, being held by the hand, playing with dogs, and talking with their mother or father on the paths between rice paddies. Mothers nurse infants on these paths during rice transplanting time. On the village's days off, children entertain themselves by instigating cockfights or arm wrestling, and during festivals for the village's tutelary deity, they enjoy all sorts of amusements. Children can also be seen behind the hearth inside the house. Many infants are depicted among the children in scenes of daily life, but it appears that in their case the artist was indifferent to sexual differences.[4] From around the age of ten, however, boys and girls are differentially depicted, as can be seen by the boys' bangs. It can be further noted that of the children depicted as ten or older and engaging in agricultural pursuits, the vast majority are adolescent boys; figures of girls are rare.

The process of differentiating gender as children get older presented visually in the *Illustrated Guide to Agronomy* can also be seen in volume five of Kaibara Ekiken's *Japan's Customary Precepts for Children (Wazoku dōjikun),* which begins with the following statement regarding children's discipline and education:

> Boys go outside, submit to a teacher, learn things, mingle with friends, and observe the correct ways of the world. They do not rely solely on their parents' teachings but experience many things beyond. Girls are always inside, with no way to go out, learn the proper way by following teacher and friends, or learn by observing social etiquette. Since they develop through nothing but their parents' teachings, they must not neglect what they are told by their parents.[5]

This text is not aimed at farm children in particular but instead deals with education and discipline for all different levels of society, from farmers to the ruling class. Still, it can be seen as representative of early modern discourse. In contrast to girls, whose opportunities to learn come only from their parents, boys learn both from their parents and from the experiences they have beyond family boundaries. In other words, if boys are the sex that goes outside and girls are the sex that stays indoors, then social experience is indispensable for the former but unavailable to the latter.

Despite these strictures, both girls and boys were encouraged to acquire an education. In the so-called temple schools *(terakoya)* that provided instruction for commoner children, it was thought that "from the age of seven boys and girls should not sit together in pursuing their studies," but this did not imply the exclusion of girls from the school entirely.[6] According to *Multiplication Tables for Girls (Onna kuku no koe),* "Children learn good and bad from the teachings they follow . . . regardless of whether they are boys or girls."[7] Kaibara Ekiken emphasized an early start to education, claiming, "According to people of old, children should start being taught as soon as they can eat well and speak clearly." This is because "if instruction does not begin early, the child will absorb bad habits." Nevertheless, what draws our attention is his statement that "in the beginning in raising a daughter, there is no great difference with a boy." What is noteworthy is that one sex is not described as more important than the other, but boys and girls are treated more or less similarly.

Rites of passage performed for boys and girls between birth and childhood point to a similar symmetry. The *Treasury for Women (Onna chōhōki),* a life course manual first published in the Genroku era (1688–1703) that remained popular throughout the Edo period, gives detailed instructions for marking milestones.[8] According to it, a boy puts on his clothing with the left arm first, a girl with the right; a boy makes his first temple visit on the thirty-second day of his life, a girl on the thirty-third. For the ceremony at which a child eats food for the first time, a boy sits on the left knee, a girl on the right. For ceremonies related to giving a child a name, fixing the hair, and wearing a divided skirt *(hakama),* the records concern both boys and girls without distinction. Nevertheless, the names chosen on the seventh night of a child's life made it easy to tell whether the infant was a girl or a boy, and wearing the divided skirt tended to be limited to boys only.

The performance of rites of passage for children depended as much upon the family's status as on the child's biological sex. Families belonging to the village's upper class received congratulatory gifts and distributed red bean rice. It is probable that as the social status of the family dropped, these rites of passage were abbreviated or perhaps even omitted. Still, to the extent that they did not cause an economic burden, they were considered necessary and were punctiliously performed. From this survey we see that in early modern farm villages gender functioned as technology that gave meaning to physical difference from the moment of birth. At the same time, the way it functioned had characteristics peculiar to childhood. That is, gendered differentiation appeared in both norms and practice requiring that boys behave like boys and girls behave like girls. Even though only boys were to amass social experience as the sex that goes outside, there were not yet exclusionary groups formed for that purpose. As Ekiken says, they were still at the stage at which "in raising a girl . . . there is not much difference from boys." This line of reasoning is backed up by visual representations that do not discriminate between girls and boys in infancy. In rites of passage as well, gendered differences in infancy were formal, symbolic, and symmetrical.

THE PROCESS OF CONSTRUCTING MASCULINITY

When did divergence in gender differentiation first occur in early modern farm villages? I argue that various village activities afforded a systematic organization for village youth. These, together with the coming-of-age ceremonies that marked the maturation of boys, triggered the process of gender differentiation and masculinization.

Ethnologist Segawa Kiyoko draws the following conclusions from her analysis of folk customs related to youths and maidens, an analysis that investigates coming-of-age ceremonies in each region in Japan (see also chapter 5 in this volume):

> In the past, village youths and maidens performed the loincloth celebration around the age of thirteen *sai* to mark their natural maturation, and then around fifteen, seventeen, or nineteen *sai* they performed the coming-of-age ceremony. Concrete expressions of coming-of-age included designating a name-giving parent, changing the name, shaving the bangs, or putting on a tall cap *[eboshi]*. Girls blackened their teeth and made themselves look like adults. This was a significant occasion because from this time forward they would be treated as full-fledged villagers with an adult's competence in terms of work and marriage.[9]

Segawa notes that the first maturation ceremony, the loincloth celebration, is associated with the physical development of both boys and girls. In many cases, it was the occasion for boys to receive loincloths and for girls to receive underskirts as symbols of their sexual maturation, thus maintaining the male/female symmetry I have described as a core characteristic of childhood.

In the second stage, the coming-of-age ceremony, the male/female symmetry in rites of passage breaks down. The coming-of-age ceremony for boys required preparation. This was an important ceremony for the household, conducted with blood and marital relatives in attendance. Once the name-giving parent, usually a socially prominent relative, had been designated, a name different from the childhood name was revealed. A few cases from the Edo period shed light on concrete procedures. For example, in the first month of 1850, Taguchi Tokunosuke from Machikata village in Hida province came of age and changed his name to Kosaburō. To celebrate Kosaburō's coming-of-age, the Taguchi family held a celebration with coins, a divided skirt made with cloth from Kokura, fans, paper, writing brushes, sake, and wheat meal.[10] On 1848/10/14, the Kusakabe house in Hida-Takayama performed the coming-of-age ceremony for Hidenosuke.

Early that morning it offered sacred sake and other gifts to the tutelary Hachiman shrine along with his forelock wrapped in paper stating that "this is the forelock for a man born in the year of the ox, Kusakabe Hidenosuke, now known as Yasubei." The name-giving parent was Kyūbei from the Kusakabe main house, who participated in an exchange of sake cups.[11] These ceremonies disclose expectations for social maturation apart from sexual maturation.

For young women, by contrast, there were no ceremonies that implied an expectation of social maturation such as we see in boys' coming-of-age ceremonies. According to Segawa, the second stage in coming-of-age ceremonies for girls consisted of blackening the teeth for the first time. In the Edo period, blackening the teeth was a practice that a woman began upon her engagement or from the day of her nuptials. Thus, it functioned as the physical mark of a woman's subordination to her husband, his exclusive right to her sexuality, and her enclosure in the physical, sexual, and private realm centered on reproductive ability in the absence of social organization. The hurdles lying in wait in the interval between coming-of-age and marriage for men, by contrast, marked their path to social maturation and, by implication, to the construction of ideal masculinity in early modern farm villages. For men, the coming-of-age ceremony was only the first step, a caveat that needs to be attached to Segawa's claim that it marked the transition to becoming "a full-fledged villager with adult competencies."[12] To sum up, sexual and social maturation were expected of men whereas only sexual maturation was anticipated for women.

Although the marks of coming-of-age varied—putting on a tall cap *(eboshi)* or cutting the forelock, for example—in almost all cases a man in an early modern farm village who had completed this ritual joined a young man's association.[13] Since before World War II, Japan's ethnographers have been accumulating research on these associations.[14] In recent years, on the historiographical side, a chiefly social history approach has appeared.[15] Based on these perspectives, let me sketch the concrete features of these organizations.

First, let's look at one example of how young men were collectivized and organized.

> Item: Every year on the second night of the first month for the first song fest of the new year, we will ascertain who has entered or left the young men's group, we will discuss all matters, and we will decide what is to be forbidden.
>
> Item: Men above the age of fifteen *sai* are to join the association of young men and serve until they are forty *sai*. It is also decided that each house should have one man apiece in the organization.

> Item: In case of a household with either many old people or many children in such extreme poverty that it is difficult to perform the duties of the youth group associates, it will be exempted from participation in the youth group for a set number of years determined by the youth group's agent.
>
> Item: When a man over twenty *sai* joins the youth group, he should serve in it for twenty years.
>
> Item: Those whose status is worker or who go to reside in some other place will be forgiven the youth group dues for that period.
>
> Item: Select the youth group agent from among the associates for his good character. He must be honest first of all with a big heart, deeply compassionate, possessed of discernment without bias or partiality, frugal, not addicted to drink or sex. The individuals who fit these qualifications will be voted on by ballot to decide who will be the agent. Since such individuals are rare, if someone lacks a little in any of these qualifications, we should put up with it.[16]

As we see here, in the latter half of the early modern period the rules to be followed by the youth group tended to be codified as "youth group regulations." They typically stipulated qualifications for membership in the organization. One basic principle was that men join at age fifteen *sai* and serve until they were forty. Another rule prescribed that there should be one member per household, and not every man in the village between the ages of fifteen and forty qualified for membership. Men could be exempted for economic reasons. We also know that the youth group's agent was chosen by ballot from among the members.

There were, of course, numerous regional variations in the qualifications for joining the youth group and the point at which men withdrew. Hirayama Kazuhiko classifies youth groups into two structural types.[17] In the first, which was most prevalent in western Japan, all the men join and then leave when they marry. In the second, more often found in the east, one man, usually the oldest son, joins from each household, and withdrawal is determined by age, not marriage. What this means is that we cannot say it was possible for every young man in the village to join the youth group. In both kinds of youth group, however, unmarried men who were to succeed to their natal house inevitably became members of the youth group upon coming-of-age. Let us keep in mind two characteristics: the nucleus of unmarried men who were to succeed to house head and the numerous variations in other qualifications.

An age-rank system structured youth groups. In almost all cases men joined at fifteen *sai*, a moment that coincided with the coming-of-age ceremony as a rite of passage. This held true regardless of regional variations, as described above. Various stipulations prescribed rank-consistent behavior, for example, "men who have just joined the association must behave courteously to senior members," or "senior members must treat the new members with compassion in giving them orders."[18] The "agent" *(sewanin)* took the lead in the youth group and managed its affairs. Men who had been adopted from other villages or who married into the village were also added to the youth group members. The regulation that in this village "all over the age of twenty *sai* are to be enrolled in the youth group" had probably been crafted in anticipation of such circumstances.

Youth groups took the lead in entertainment and cultural activities performed within the confines of village society. Having their own funds, youth groups often put on plays. In the second month of 1833, for instance, the youth associates of Sakurano village in Shimotsuke province (present-day Tochigi prefecture) held a meeting and drew up a protocol promising that "we will without fail cover the production costs."[19] Everyone sealed the protocol with fingernail prints rather than using seals, which would have been the way of their farmer fathers. On the night of 1798/8/12, the eighteen youths in Toyazuka village in Kōzuke (now Gumma prefecture) framed a similar protocol sealed in a circle with fingernail prints.[20] Signing the document in a circle shows that the youths assumed equal collective responsibility. They took responsibility for everything, including negotiations with the producer in Edo and the finances.

Youths were able to stage performances of plays and other events because they had their own sources of funds. For example, accounts showing income and expenditures in 1863 for the youths of Karino village in Sagami (present-day Kanagawa prefecture) display a total of 7 *ryō*, and of that more than 80 percent had been assessed on and collected from the youth group members themselves. There is also a notation—"revolving credit association; dependent"—that can be interpreted to mean that the youths as an organization participated in a revolving credit association.[21] In the protocol from Gotanda village mentioned above, it is specified that "turns for collecting needed funds from the youths will revolve among the associates; the agent will keep one set of ledgers showing all the youth group's income and costs, and one will be written down for the youth group; the expenses for each meeting will be clearly recorded; a grand reconciliation of the accounts will be held on the night of the first day of the last month of the year; and on that occasion, every member of the group is to verify the accounts."[22] In addition, youth groups probably owned drums, lanterns, livery coats, and other items.

Youth groups often organized plays, sumo tournaments, puppet theater performances, and other events arranged in conjunction with festivals for the village's tutelary deity. In festivals, however, the shrine priest, village officials, and the farmer heads of houses who constituted village assemblies took the chief roles. They participated in rituals at the small shrine at the core of the festival, leaving the youth group only a subsidiary role. Nevertheless, it was indispensable in that the tutelary shrine festival as a public event served as a spiritual bond for village society.

In many cases the youth groups provided essential services by carrying portable shrines, running horses, and so forth. The festival at the Toride post station in Shimōsa province (now Ibaraki prefecture) was "held to offer prayers for a bountiful harvest of the five grains and for peace under heaven." During the festival for the ox-headed heavenly king, all the village youths performed a dance, and the porters who carried the portable shrine were decided a year in advance. This, too, was their duty.[23] The following statement describes the roles for youths in the Hachiman shrine festival at Tamamura post station in Kōzuke province (now Gumma prefecture) at which they were expected to run horses.

> The festival for the Hachiman shrine in Tamamura post station is performed every year by a league of seven villages, but at the time for running horses on the sixteenth day of the eighth month of this year, everyone in the seven villages acted disorderly, and the situation was completely untenable. As a consequence, the seven villages have met and decided on a protocol that henceforth when running the horses during the festival, in accordance with precedent, the horses will be lined up at the watering hole, a village official will accompany each horse from his village holding the bridle, and he will give instructions to the youths. The horses will proceed in order down to the viewing stands. Once they have arrived at the command post and observation stand, they will perform the festival rites together.[24]

Whether by participating in shrine festivals or doing village work assigned by the village and domain authorities, young men obtained a place in the public sphere by providing labor power. Their actual contributions were spelled out as follows:

> Take the fire watch especially seriously, and if you see anything suspicious, go there at once.
>
> When laborers are needed for official boats in the inlet, take the work seriously, and be careful not to act rudely.
>
> Should you see a boat unable to handle a strong wind, help it immediately.[25]

Sometimes regulations spelled out the behavior expected of youth groups at weddings:

> When sending sake to celebrate a wedding, go estimate the number of youths. When going to the house, perform the rites and celebratory greetings correctly. When treated to sake, receive it without being rude. In no way should you be even the least impolite to a host who does not like to drink a lot. If you keep all this in mind, even if the host forgets something, the assembly will end beautifully. You should ask how things are a few days later.[26]

> In providing sake to celebrate a marriage adoption, it is decided that the adopted son is to provide thirty-two *mon* and the bride is to provide sixteen *mon*.[27]

> When tips are distributed to the youth group at a wedding, everyone should arrive together early in accordance with precedence.[28]

> All celebrations for bringing in a son-in-law or a bride or for coming-of-age should be performed correctly based on consultation with the chief of the youth group.[29]

Conforming to these regulations signaled the youth group's consent to the marriage.

Comprised chiefly of unmarried men, the youth group performed roles that were central to a village's entertainment and cultural activities; it played an indispensable if subsidiary role in the tutelary deity festivals, which promoted village society's spiritual bonds; and it did village work assessed by the domain authorities and the village. All of these constituted hurdles for the village man between coming-of-age and getting married, and engagement in these social activities molded these men's manhood. The skills necessary for these social activities gelled as masculine virtues, including loyalty to youth group and village, a sense of mission, feelings of solidarity, bravery, energy, and a sense of cooperation. At the same time, the social and public space of the village became masculinized—controlled by men and these "masculine" ideals.

SEXUALITY AND THE OPERATION OF MASCULINE AUTHORITY

As we have seen, young men performed social and public activities as a group, and as a matter of course, such activities required regulations whose violation resulted in various forms of punishment and sometimes sanctions. In addition to containing notations explaining each prohibition, documents, especially letters of apology, speak to the various ways in which masculine authority was exercised over village women. Possibly because youthful behavior had come to be seen as deviant, extensive regulations set standards of conduct, presents, and the treatment of guests at weddings and celebrations and delineated formalities for conducting rituals and festivals, the supervision of the youth group's assets, and stipulations for everyday behavior. Quarrelling, arguing, gambling, games of chance, entertainments with serving girls, drinking at commercial establishments, and consorting with vagrants were forbidden. At a meeting held on 1866/1/2, the youths of Karino village in Sagami province, for instance, presented the following agreement to the village officials.

> Illicit sex—Men who commit this are to suffer permanent ostracism.[30]
>
> Gambling—Men who commit this are to be fined 3 *kanmon.*
>
> Lottery—Men who participate in this are to be fined 5 *kanmon.*
>
> Winking at [misdeeds]—The fine is 1.5 *kanmon.*
>
> Robbery—Men who commit this will be beaten with a club.
>
> Conspiracy—Men who commit this are to suffer permanent ostracism.
>
> Drinking—Aside from sacred sake, do not drink for no reason. Naturally if people drink within the village, but even if it should become known through indirect means that people are sneaking off to neighboring villages to break this prohibition, they shall be punished immediately in accordance with the law.
>
> At this time, so that not even parents shall have cause to harbor resentment, elders and juniors, including the entire group of dependents, affix their fingernail prints as a sign that no one has any intention of behaving contrary to what is stated above.
>
> 1866/1/2, Managers: Ichitarō, Kitarō, Denjirō
>
> Agents: Genjirō, Isaburō, Shichinosuke[31]

Other documents show how youth groups extended their authority over men outside their organizations. In 1816, Ume'emon wrote a letter of apology to the "honorable members of the youth group" in Ōsawa village. The content was as follows:

> I am thankful that through mediation by shrine and temple priests in this area as well as by Yoheita and Shūzō, agents for the youth group in this village, the youth group has accepted my apology for my outrageous behavior. Hereafter I will endeavor to keep this in mind. If by any chance I should be recalcitrant, the members of the youth group may do whatever they like, and I will not say a word. Hereafter I will follow the customs of this area and obey the agents' commands. For the sake of the future I have made this statement.

1816/3, The man himself: Ume'emon
Agents: Hyōemon, Yoheita, Shūzō[32]

Another document from a different village provides more details regarding the circumstances under which youth groups had the customary right to sanction outsiders. It, too, ends in an apology directed at the youth group associates.

> This concerns Genzō, a dependent of Tomikichi in the neighboring village of Nanai Shinden who visited Tsubonouchi Shino. Since he snuck into Shino's and committed outrageous deeds, he has been placed with the youth group of this village for censure, and no words can excuse his behavior. We settled the matter by leaving it up to the person in charge to handle at his discretion. But then again Mohachi had relations with her and committed outrageous deeds without any compunction. This, too, is inexcusable.[33]

Genzō and Mohachi had consummated a sexual relationship with a woman who was likely to have been a widow, and that is probably the reason they were forced to write a letter of apology. In this case youth group members exercised their social authority by carrying out sanctions against a deed committed by men outside their organization.

The approved way for a youth to have sexual relations with someone outside his village was for him first to talk with the youths of that village and gain their consent. This procedure reconfirms the voicelessness of the woman in question and the kind of social authority that allowed youth groups control over the sexuality of servants and other women caught up in this network of male power.[34] Regulations clearly defined the exact shape of that authority as well:

> You must take strict precautions to avoid the appearance of illicit behavior. For example, if you are visiting a house for the first time and the master is absent, you must not enjoy yourself there even for a moment. If you are there on business, state the nature of the business to the mistress of the household truthfully. Once you have finished your greetings, you should leave at once. Furthermore, even if you are having an affair with a servant woman, you should not act as you please by entering the house without permission and without scruple for the master's good name. Whether it is a question of a man's daughter or his daughter-in-law, it goes without saying that you should avoid the appearance of illicit behavior nor should you even jest with them.[35]

The intent of such clauses must have been to prevent deviant sexual behavior on the part of youths before it could happen, but these regulations also suggest that so long as young men were members of a youth group, they were forbidden individual control or dominance over a woman as a sexual subject. Here we see that the nuances of youths' control over female sexuality was completely different from a man's monopolistic control over his wife's sexuality within marriage.

Let us examine the youth group's collective exercise of masculine authority over widows a little further. In *A Record of the Yearly Ceremonies in a Farm Family (Nōka nenjū gyōji ki)*, the rural entrepreneur Ōdaira Yohei, from Echigo, on the Japan Sea, provides the following story:

> The period from the last ten days of this month through the middle of the tenth month is called *kakusechi,* when all the men in the prime of life in what is known as the youth group pay out rice and money to rent a temple or house where they gather to eat and drink as they please. For their guests they summon mature women who are without husbands for not less than two days and two nights and not more than three days and three nights. Although their licentious conduct is beyond words, since any refusal or remonstrance brings immediate reprisals, masters and parents do not forbid this regrettable evil practice.[36]

In other words, the youth group summoned widows for an orgy. Out of fear of immediate reprisals, the women could not refuse. Neither was it possible for older men to protest. At the same time, let us not overlook how the author denigrated this behavior. His criticism implies that the youth group as a social power, which is to say its collective masculinity, confronted a crisis.

The process of constructing masculinity in early modern farm villages took place within specific operations of power exercised through the male youth group. In contrast to childhood, during which gender asymmetry was not yet apparent, coming-of-age ceremonies for young men and their inclusion in organized groups brought gender asymmetry to the fore. Youths constructed their masculinity through social activities on behalf of the village, the virtues that these activities fostered came to be seen as attributes of masculinity, and organizations designated for men controlled the village's social and public space. Defined as masculinity's polar opposite, femininity was excluded from the experiences of being organized, collectivized, or engaged in socially public activities, confined to the physical, sexual, and private realm, and placed beneath masculinity in the hierarchy of values. Youth groups that occupied a position of social authority in the construction of masculinity were permitted to exercise power in various spheres, in particular the control of female sexuality. As we have seen, however, this control differed in kind from that of a husband over his wife. By the early nineteenth century, criticisms of male group behavior had begun to challenge this particular type of collectively constructed masculinity.

This chapter has provided an analysis of how youth groups exercised masculine authority within the rigidly gendered realm of village society, but several issues remain to be addressed. Masculinity in early modern farm villages cannot be defined as one size fits all. Dominant and subordinate forms of masculinity can be assumed to have existed even within youth organizations. Second is the problem of masculinity and collectivization. Apart from youth group organizations, various other types of collectivized masculine domains did not allow the assimilation of femininity. It is vital to study these domains as well. Third, if masculinity is constructed historically and socially, we must interrogate its variability. In other words, we must ask what can break down specific forms of masculinity once they are constructed, and under what circumstances this becomes possible.

NOTES

Titled "Nihon kinsei nōson ni okeru masukyurinitei no kōchiku to jendaa: shūdanka, sōshikika to kenryoku sayō o megutte," this essay first appeared in a slightly different version in Sakurai Yuki, Sugano Noriko, and Nagano Hiroko, eds., *Jendaa de yomitoku Edo jidai* (Tokyo: Sanshōdō, 2001).

1. Mashiko Chōshi Hensan Iinkai 1985–91, vol. 3, pp. 744–45.
2. Holt 1989; Hargreaves 1994; Parker 1996.
3. Nōsangyoson Bunka Kyōkai 1983a. Authored, published, and illustrated in 1717 by Tsuchiya Matasaburō, also author of *Agricultural Work from Spring to Fall (Kōka shunjū)*. Nagashima Atsuko has examined the actual conditions of women's work in early modern farm villages through *Nōgyō zue*. See Nagashima 1993.
4. Other illustrations—such as those found in *Night Talks by an Old Farmer (Rōnō yawa)*, which depict the conditions of general agricultural enterprises throughout the four seasons (*Nihon nōsho zenshū*, vol. 71), or those in *The Secrets of Sericulture (Yōsan hiro)*, the representative sericulture manual from the Edo period (*Nihon nōsho zenshū*, vol. 35)—exhibit the same tendencies as those seen in *Nōgyō zue*. .
5. Kurokawa Mamichi 1977, p. 495.
6. Kurokawa Mamichi 1977, p. 471.
7. Emori 1993–94, vol. 7, p. 21.
8. Nagatomo 1993.

9. Segawa 1972, p. 47.
10. Gifu-ken 1971–87, vol. 8, pp. 239–41.
11. Gifu-ken 1971–87, vol. 8, p. 238.
12. According to Segawa, depending on region and period, the two stages in the coming-of-age ceremonies might be combined and performed only once. Even in that case, the structure of coming-of-age ceremonies that predicated both sexual and social maturation for men but only sexual maturation for women remained the same.
13. According to ethnographers, at one time unmarried village women also formed groups. These differed from male youth groups in that they had no age-rank order, nor were they systematically organized. Furthermore, they performed none of the public social practices done by youth groups. Instead, their chief function was to gain sexual knowledge and to select spouses under the control of the young men's groups. (Both Segawa and Hirayama make this point.) I argue that the male youth group controlled the sexuality of unmarried women, the youth group took the initiative, and it was in this sense that women were organized.
14. The chief ethnographic texts are: Nakayama 1930; DaiNihon Rengō Seinendan 1936; Sakurai 1962; Satō Mamoru 1970; Segawa 1972; Mogami 1978; Inoguchi 1978; Amano 1980; Tsuboi 1984; Sakaguchi 1985; Hirayama 1988; Yamaoka 1993. In English, see Varner 1997.
15. Yasumaru 1974; Takahashi 1978; Tani 1984; Furukawa 1986; Ujiie 1989; Mega 1995; Takahashi 1997.
16. This is an agreement decided by the youth group from Gotanda village in Musashi province in the first month of 1847. See Kawasaki-shi 1988, vol. 2, pp. 233–34.
17. Hirayama 1988; and Tsuboi 1984, chapter 2.
18. Shizuoka-ken 1986–96, vol. 12, p. 609.
19. Tochigi Kenshi Hensan Iinkai 1974–, vol. 4, pp. 828–29.
20. Gunma Kenshi Hensan Iinkai 1977–, vol. 14, p. 842.
21. Minami Ashigara 1988–2001, vol. 2, pp. 124–26.
22. Kawasaki-shi 1988, vol. 2, p. 234.
23. Toride Shishi Hensan Iinkai 1982–89, vol. 3, p. 792.
24. Gunma Kenshi Hensan Iinkai 1977–, vol. 14, p. 843.
25. Shizuoka-ken 1986–96, vol. 12, p. 609.
26. DaiNihon Rengō Seinendan, p. 324.
27. Kawasaki-shi 1988, vol. 2, p. 234.
28. DaiNihon Rengō Seinendan, p. 324.
29. DaiNihon Rengō Seinendan, p. 324.
30. Shogunal and domain law detailed punishments for the criminal offense of illicit sex. This does not mean that they were always strictly applied. Therefore, it sometimes happened, as we can see here, that punishments were inserted into youth group regulations. In this period male and female sexual relations outside marriage or publicly approved prostitution were considered illicit. See Nagano 1982 and Ujiie 1996.

31. Minami Ashigara 1988–2001, vol. 2, pp. 132–33.
32. Mashiko Chōshi Hensan Iinkai 1985–91, vol. 3, p. 745.
33. Mashiko Chōshi Hensan Iinkai 1985–91, vol. 3, pp. 744–45.
34. According to Weeks 1989 (the Japanese translation was published in 1996), sexuality involves not simply sexual acts and sex consciousness, but also knowledge concerning sex bestowed with social meaning through discourse. Weeks places family and kin systems, economic and political organizations, social norms, political intervention, and the culture of resistance in the domain of the social construction of sexuality. It is also necessary to take such a multidimensional approach to the control of youth groups over sexuality, but that is beyond the scope of this chapter.
35. DaiNihon Rengō Seinendan, p. 319.
36. Nōsangyoson Bunka Kyōkai 1980, vol. 25, p. 283.

REFERENCES

Amano Takeshi. 1980. *Wakamono no minzoku*. Perikansha.
DaiNihon Rengō Seinendan, ed. 1936. *Wakamono seido no kenkyū*. Nihon Seinenkan.
Emori Ichirō, ed. 1993–94. *Edo Jidai josei seikatsu ezu daijiten*, vols. 1–10. Ōzorasha.
Furukawa Sadao. 1986. *Mura no asobi-kyūjitsu to wakamono no shakaishi*. Heibonsha.
Gifu-ken. 1971–87. *Gifu kenshi: shiryōhen*, vol. 8. Gannandō Shoten.
Gunma Kenshi Hensan Iinkai. 1977–. *Gunma kenshi shiryōhen*, vol. 14. Maebashi: Gunma-ken.
Hargreaves, Jennifer. 1994. *Sporting Females: Critical Issues in the History and Sociology of Women's Sports*. London: Routledge.
Hirayama Kazuhito. 1988. *Gōhon seinen shūdanshi kenkyū josetsu*. Shinsensha.
Holt, Richard. 1989. *Sport and the British: A Modern History*. Oxford: Clarendon.
Inoguchi Shōji, ed. 1978. *Kōza: Nihon no minzoku*, vol. 3, *Jinsei girei*. Yūseidō.
Kawasaki-shi. 1988. *Kawasaki shishi: Shiryōhen*, vol. 2. Kawasaki-shi: Kawasaki.
Kurokawa Mamichi, ed. 1977. *Nihon kyōiku bunko: gakkōhen*. Nihon Tosho Sentā.
Mashiko Chōshi Hensan Iinkai. 1985–91. *Mashiko chōshi*, vol. 3. Mashiko-chō: Mashiko-chō.
Mega Atsuko. 1995. *Hankachō no naka no onnatachi*. Heibonsha.
Minami Ashigara. 1988–2001. *Minami Ashigara shishi shiryōhen: Kinsei*, vol. 2. Minami Ashigara: Minami Ashigara.
Mogami Kōkei, ed. 1978. *Kōza: Nihon no minzoku*, vol. 2, *Shakai kōsei*. Yūseidō.

Nagano Hiroko. 1982. "Bakuhan hō to josei." In *Nihon joseishi,* ed. Joseishi Sōgō Kenkyūkai, vol. 3. Tōkyō Daigaku Shuppankai.

Nagashima Atsuko. 1993. "Hataraku nōson no onnatachi: Kaga *Nōgyō zue* o yomu." In *Nihon no Kinsei,* vol. 15, *Josei no Kinsei,* ed Hayashi Reiko, 227–60. Chūō Kōronsha.

Nagatomo Chiyoji, ed. 1993. *Onna chōhōki: Otoko chōhōki.* Shakai Shisōsha.

Nakayama Tarō. 1930. *Nihon wakamono shi.* Shun'yōdō.

Nōsangyoson Bunka Kyōkai, ed. 1980. *Nihon nōsho zenshū,* vol. 25. Nōsangyoson Bunka Kyōkai.

———, ed. 1981. *Nihon nōsho zenshū,* vol. 35. Nōsangyoson Bunka Kyōkai.

———, ed. 1983a. *Nihon nōsho zenshū,* vol. 26. Nōsangyoson Bunka Kyōkai.

———, ed. 1983b. *Nihon nōsho zenshū,* vol. 71. Nōsangyoson Bunka Kyōkai.

Parker, Andrew A. 1996. "Sporting Masculinities: Gender Relations and the Body." In *Understanding Masculinities: Social Relations and Cultural Arenas,* ed. Mairtin Mac an Ghaill. Philadelphia: Open University Press.

Sakaguchi Kazuo. 1985. *Izu shotō no wakamonogumi to musumegumi.* Miraisha.

Sakurai Tokutarō. 1962. *Kō shūdan seiritsu katei no kenkyū.* Yoshikawa Kōbunkan.

Satō Mamoru. 1970. *Kindai Nihon seinen shūdanshi kenkyū.* Ochanomizu Shobō.

Segawa Kiyoko. 1972. *Wakamono to musume o meguru minzoku.* Miraisha.

Shizuoka-ken. 1986–96. *Shizuoka kenshi: shiryōhen,* vol. 12. Shizuoka-shi: Shizuoka-ken.

Takahashi Satoshi. 1978. *Nihon Minshū Kyōikushi kenkyū.* Miraisha.

———. 1997. *Kazoku to kodomo no Edo jidai.* Asahi Shinbunsha.

Tani Teruhiro. 1984. *Wakamono nakama no Rekishi.* Nihon Seinenkan.

Tochigi Kenshi Hensan Iinkai. 1974–. *Tochigi kenshi shiryōhen: Kinsei,* vol. 4. Utsunomiya: Tochigi-ken.

Toride Shishi Hensan Iinkai. 1982–89. *Toride shishi: Kinsei shiryōhen,* vol. 3. Toride-shi: Toride-shi Shomuka.

Tsuboi Hirofumi, ed. 1984. *Mura to murabito: kyōdōtai no seikatsu to girei.* Shogakkan.

Ujiie Mikito. 1989. *Edo no shōnen.* Heibonsha.

Varner, Richard E. 1997. "The Organized Peasant: The Wakamonogumi in the Edo Period." *Monumenta Nipponica* 32, no. 4: 459–83.

Weeks, Jeffrey. 1989. *Sexuality.* London, New York: Routledge.

Yamaoka Ken. 1993. *Nenrei kaiteisei no kenkyū.* Hokki Shuppan.

Yasumaru Yoshio. 1974. *Nihon no kindaika to minshū shisō.* Aoki Shoten.

10 Climbing Walls

Dismantling Hegemonic Masculinity in a Japanese Sport Subculture

Wolfram Manzenreiter

Free-climbing is a sporting activity that encourages a range of behavior potentially subversive of both male and female socialization. Appreciation of the climbing body draws from the registers of both aesthetics and athletics, particularly when the climber's body is on display as an object of (mostly other climbers') gaze. With the interchanging roles of lead- and second- and teamwork-based belay techniques to reduce the risk of fall and injury, free-climbing depends on shared responsibilities, mutual trust and support, understanding, and caring—all characteristics stereotypically associated with femininity. Many other modern sports, by contrast, as sports historians and sociologists frequently note, tend to prioritize attitudes and behavior patterns that resonate with stock images of masculinity, including combative competitiveness, physical aggression, and mental toughness.[1] A large body of academic work has deconstructed the complexities of historicity, class, power, and discourse that are conflated in gender stereotyping in sports. Yet it must be noted that the impact of this work on mainstream perceptions of the boundaries between essentialized gender categories has remained weak, particularly in relation to sports. Thus, at first sight, free-climbing appears to have the potential to transgress the stereotypical gender binaries of active/passive, strong/weak, independent/dependent.

"Androgyny" has only recently been introduced to debates about gender in sports. It is associated with those sports that lack a clear-cut gender identity in that they are embedded in alternative visions of gender images transgressing essentializing categories. A sport is thought of as androgynous, for example, when physical strength or competitiveness is no more or less important than flexibility and sociability, thus inviting the participation of men and women on equal footing. Free-climbing shares these androgynous qualities with other "lifestyle sports" such as surfing, skating, or snowboarding, which emerged as an alternative to the highly formalized and organized patterns of "achievement sports" in the context of the North American counterculture movement of the 1960s and subsequently spread globally. While each lifestyle sport possesses its own distinctive history, localities, and objectives, they all share a number of "commonalities in their ethos, ideologies, and increasingly the national and transnational consumer industries that produce the commodities that underpin their cultures."[2] Lifestyle sports are more about participation than about spectatorship. They tend to disregard competition, though they appreciate both excellence and development; they tend to rely on fewer formal rules and regulations for membership. Participating in lifestyle sports usually exceeds the act of onsite performance, which provides just the pivotal point for the constitution of a larger subculture with core members and regulars ("locals") plus occasional visitors and sympathizers ("tourists"). The more committed members tend to regard themselves as unconventional, adventurous, and explorative in the creation of new spaces and values and thus invite researchers to consider their potential to rewrite the scripts of male and female physicality.[3]

In this chapter I explore the potential of alternative sports for the creation of new or alternative masculinities in Japan. I will argue that despite its inherent androgynous characteristics, the practice of free-climbing and other alternative sports is highly gendered in conventional ways. While heteronormative ideas of a natural or naturalized gender order persist, not least because of appropriation by consumer industries and the difficulties in aligning different ideas of masculinity according to the demand of different lifeworlds and social settings, alternative sports and similar countercultures provide opportunities for popularizing new and alternative masculinities. Subcultural spheres allow some men to develop new and alternative masculinities and some women to challenge or convert established hierarchies of gender relations. But not all men and women are equally able to undermine a gendered hierarchy or to question each and any stock image and representation of heteronormativity.

Social scientific research on the gendered nature of sport provides ample evidence that in Japan as well the same institutions and ideologies that shape national sport cultures elsewhere have successfully achieved and maintained the construction of sport as a male institution: cultural patriarchy,[4] consumer capitalism,[5] the educational system,[6] and the media.[7] However, ethnographic research on "masculinity rites" that are of crucial importance for negotiating gender relations and gendered identities has so far only been done on sports within highly formalized, competitive, and organized settings, such as martial arts training centers (dōjōs),[8] boxing gyms,[9] and extracurricular sport clubs at schools and universities.[10]

My research data are based on extensive participant observation among two different groups of free climbers from western Japan in the years 1995 and 1996. All names appearing in the following field notes and transcripts are pseudonyms crafted to guarantee anonymity to informants and climbing buddies. The historical context of the 1990s, which saw conventional assumptions about the gendered order of private and public lives increasingly undermined, is relevant for explaining the complexities of change and perseverance I noted in the subculture of climbers. Yet the literature on alternative sports in Japan and elsewhere suggests that the underlying principles reproducing a gendered hierarchy and sporting masculinities within the subworld of alternative sports have hardly changed since then. I start with a short introduction to free-climbing in Japan. Subsequent sections examine mechanisms of inclusion and exclusion, the significance of the body, and various markers of status differentiation and status inversion within the subculture. My conclusions interrogate the appropriateness of androgyny as a concept in sports and comment on the variability and plurality of masculine identities among Japan's free climbers.

FREE-CLIMBING IN JAPAN

Free-climbing is a specific variant of climbing. It emerged in the 1960s as a distinctive subculture as a response to the unease among climbers about the technological suppression of nature through the excessive use of artificial climbing aids. Free climbers restrict their ambitions to mastering the technical challenges of climbing routes of limited height but increasing difficulty through a reliance on physical strength and skill alone. The rejection of unnatural climbing aids initiated a sportification process that curtailed the climber's exposure to jeopardy and risk taking. First the traditional placement of protection while leading was replaced with fixed protection that allowed climbers to concentrate on the move instead of wasting scarce energy and strength on placing bolts or nuts. In a second step, the manufacturing of handholds, artificial walls, and entire indoor climbing centers enabled climbers to develop their abilities all year round unhampered by weather conditions.

As in many other places, free-climbing became popular in Japan when it was transplanted from its original mountainous environment to urban training facilities. Japan's topography has abundant mountains, crags, and cliffs, but the rock is often of poor quality, brittle, or covered with moss. Indoor climbing gyms not only solved this problem, but they also eliminated the time required to travel from urban areas to climbing sites. When Osaka City Rock opened in 1989, it was the first indoor training facility of its kind in the country. Similar commercial climbing gyms followed first in other metropolitan areas and later throughout the country. Nowadays more than two hundred private climbing facilities operate throughout Japan. Some of the newer gyms are colossal, even by Japanese standards, at three stories high with hundreds of climbing routes. The largest of them offer space for up to more than a hundred climbers simultaneously at various bouldering areas and diverse walls with inclined faces, chimneys, noses, and roofs.

Most of Japan's climbing gyms are open to the public. They usually operate according to a membership system that provides members with hefty discounts and prime access to the facilities. At Pinnacles Gym, one of my regular training hangouts, which took its name from the climbing towers in front of the main entrance, I was greeted with a membership form on which I waived any right for compensation claims in the case of injury during use of the facility. In exchange for a small registration fee I received a membership card that authorized me to make full use of the climbing area, including the forty-foot-high outdoor pinnacles and the locker rooms, but not the fitness and power training equipment that generated the fitness club's main source of income. As a limited member, I was granted access to the climbing area at any time during the opening hours for an entrance fee of half the price that one-time visitors were expected to pay. Many climbers are satisfied with what they find at places like Pinnacles Gym, which has long climbing routes and a dense bouldering area. For some it provides a substitute for the real thing, while for others it operates as a perfect supplement to natural rock, allowing them to concentrate on solving various climbing problems, memorizing technical moves, and working on particular body parts.

In the gym alpine climbers mingle with "cracksmen" (alpine-style climbers preparing for their next big-wall ascent), amateur boulderers concentrating on powerful and dynamic moves to master shorter routes of limited height, and competitive free climbers. The Japan Free Climbing Association (JFA) and traditional mountaineering federations regularly hold competitions. The Japan Mountaineering Association (JMA) and its regional branches are officially in charge of hosting national and international tournaments. The national federation is affiliated with the semipublic Japan Amateur Sports Association (JASA) as well as the International Federation of Sports Climbing, a recent offshoot of the International Mountaineering and Climbing Federation (UIAA). Established in 1989, the JFA numbered about 1,100 individual and institutional members in 2007, though it is safe to assume that some ten thousand Japanese are frequently and continuously involved in free-climbing. In contrast to traditional mainstream sports, climbing is usually performed outside the institutional framework of special clubs and organizations. The attraction of lifestyle sports is based in part on its countercultural appearance and informal structures of enclosure and belonging. Without membership registration systems, however, making reliable estimates of participation rates is difficult. Both golf and swimming draw an estimated 10 million frequent practitioners, while baseball and soccer attract 4.6 million and 3.8 million, respectively.[11] In that sense, climbing is a minority sport.

Climbing walls or rocks is the core activity through which regular members of the free-climbing subculture express their way of life. It serves as the main site for them to develop a sense of their individuality, but it is not just the physical act of climbing that provides climbers with a special sense of identity. Climbing takes center stage in their conversations and their shopping and traveling preferences, as well as in their choice of reading material. The colorful advertisements for climbing gear, clothes, travel equipment, and other paraphernalia on the pages of special interest magazines feature a universe of commodities available for conspicuous consumption. Climbers often wear gear or clothes from relevant brands in settings not necessarily related to climbing. Media consumption is also of great significance for their identity. The JFA publishes a membership magazine that features articles primarily on climbing spots in Japan, domestic competitions, and outstanding athletes. The JFA heralds its *Free Fan* as "Japan's best Free Climbing Magazine," which is probably true, since it is the only magazine on the market with that focus.[12] On the commercial side, Japan's leading outdoor publishing house relaunched its temporarily halted magazine *Iwa to Yuki* in 1997 under the corresponding English title *Rock and Snow.* Catering to the needs of the avant-garde of high-altitude climbers and advanced free climbers alike, this stylish quarterly records major advances in domestic and international climbing and offers training tips, travel suggestions, and information on new gear, clothes, and publications. In recent years the Internet has also established itself as a prominent resource for communicative and representational purposes, yet it is impossible to be a climber without engaging in climbing.

INCLUSION/EXCLUSION: BREAKING INTO A MEN'S WORLD

Men outnumber women in free-climbing, just as they do in most other sports in Japan. At Pinnacles Gym, the members and visitors included both men and women and varied considerably in age. Given the constant coming and going, keeping a record of all the club members, either at one time or throughout the year, was impossible. My guess, however, is that the number of regular subscribers was no higher than two hundred. Only on very rare occasions were there more than forty climbers in the gym at the same time. The more avid members were in their twenties, followed by those in their forties and fifties. I spotted very few teenagers and no older climbers at Pinnacles Gym. On weekdays female climbers were fairly underrepresented. On no occasion did I notice that fewer than seven out of ten climbers were male. On Sundays the ratio of female climbers tended to increase because many more couples came accompanied by children. At Yamanaka High, where some of my climbing mates had rented the school gymnasium, including its movable climbing wall, for two training sessions of three hours a week, only two women belonged to the intimate network of twelve or thirteen members. In their late twenties and early thirties, they were considerably younger than the men, who were between thirty-four and forty-five years of age. The quantitative marginalization of women should not tempt us to jump to the conclusion that free-climbing is not androgynous. To some degree, the underrepresentation of women is simply a lasting legacy of the mountain-climbing world from which free-climbing originated. Due to its potentially dangerous and occasionally life-threatening environment, mountain climbing has long been deemed an activity inappropriate for women. Even before the "Westernization of the Japanese landscape," which turned mountains into desired objects of leisure activities, and the worship of death-defying heroism established a male-only club membership system during the early twentieth century, native belief in the sacredness of mountains and (probably Buddhist) misogynist concerns with the impurity of the female body had banned women from many mountainous regions *(nyonin kinsei)*.[13] Perhaps appropriating these older beliefs, climbing clubs of the early and mid-twentieth century that saw themselves as pioneers of mountaineering, and those that emulated the front-runners explicitly recruited male rookies only, claiming that women lacked the necessary physical and mental strength. The sportification of climbing after the 1960s decreased the impact of natural hazards and human errors and subsequently eroded overt gender discrimination. With a reduced risk of death or serious injury, contemporary urban free-climbing no longer feeds into older hypermasculine fantasies. Thus, the overrepresentation of men in climbing today is at odds with the central requirements of a sport that does not necessarily disadvantage female bodies. As Shira, a forty-year-old bachelor and artisan with a long climbing history and probably the most talented climber at Yamanaka High, noticed, "On first sight this appears to be a sport that requires muscular strength, but in principle women can easily outdo physically stronger men. In climbing, balance is much more important, so in my opinion it may be better suited for women than men."

In fact, many of the qualities of a good climber suggest the suitability of female bodies: flexibility, a good sense of balance, stamina, rhythm, a favorable strength-weight ratio, and a high degree of bodily control. Commanding a great deal of physical strength is helpful, though it is far from sufficient. Kita, a twenty-four-year-old graduate student I knew from Pinnacles Gym, regularly observed that at the climbing gym where he worked part-time as an instructor, the male bias toward physical strength could even be detrimental. According to Kita, "Men coming to the gym for the first time are full of confidence in their strength, and they think that's all it takes to climb up the wall. But as beginners, they can't climb very well. They push too hard and soon run out of power. Women don't have physical strength but a good sense of balance, so they rely on that, try a bit here and there, little by little, and in the end, it works out well."

Access to the free-climbing scene is conditioned by social forces that contribute to the overrepresentation of men. As a commercial club, Pinnacles Gym is open to anyone willing to join and able to pay. Since climbing is a collaborative activity, customers usually come in groups or pairs, though the staff at Pinnacles Gym was always ready to belay the occasional solitary visitor. During my first visits to the gym I often relied on this service, until I had the confidence to ask people for a helping hand and ultimately established my own network of climbers. Suki, the young female club attendant who introduced me to the place, confirmed that the relative absence of larger groups of female climbers is quite common.

> Here at Pinnacles Gym, we have many female members, but not in climbing. Don't you think it's hard *[kitsui]* for girls? Maybe they don't like the rental shoes. . . . Certainly it's not as fashionable as aerobics or jazz dance or the like. Of course, like Aiko-san [a woman in her thirties who was halfway through a moderate route, tied by a rope to her male companion], a few come here quite often. But most show up only once or twice, and then they give up.

Over the year I visited Pinnacles, I also very rarely encountered groups of climbers made exclusively of women, thus confirming Suki's point. Often it is a relationship with a climbing husband or boyfriend that brings women into the climbing gym and keeps them coming. Similarly, starting a serious relationship with a boyfriend who is not part of the scene often causes women to drop out, a phenomenon that Mizuno has observed among surfers as well.[14] Thus, even though market mechanisms provide easy access to lifestyle sports to both men and women, and there is nothing intrinsically gendered about the physical suitability of those participating in the sport, the participation of women is effectively limited by other social and cultural factors, which will be explored in the following sections.

Climbers at Pinnacles Gym were allowed to come and go as they pleased, but I could be fairly certain of meeting certain people at certain times. On Tuesday nights, when I regularly visited, I often joined a group of students whom I had approached during the first month of my membership. Ken (twenty-two), Taka (twenty-two), and Hiro (twenty) had climbing experience of two to four years each, during which they had reached an advanced level. Only the part-time instructor Kita, whom the bunch knew from courses at his fancier workplace in the metropolis nearby, had the climbing competency necessary to participate in national tournaments. On his motivation to start climbing, Kita remembered, "One day, there was this competition on TV, the Rock Masters maybe? I saw all these guys climbing up the wall like Spiderman, doing such and such, and I thought 'That is cool!' I thought why not give it a try, and looked up one of these climbing magazines for a place to learn climbing. Finally I ended up at H Gym." His students Ken and Taka, who moved into the area when they enrolled at university, had both been attracted by the reputation of the mountaineering club at their university. Taka said,

> During high school, I was a member of the mountaineering club, but we hardly did the real stuff. The school was afraid of accidents, so it was only camping and hiking. I had heard about the university club and what they achieved in the past. They had even climbed in the Himalayas and the Andes, so I was really hot for it. But then it was all disappointing; there were just Ken and I joining that year, and only three advanced *senpai* students who sometimes came to the weekly meetings, sometimes not. And these guys had no idea of climbing! Seeing how they even struggled at the slope of Konpira-san [a mediocre rock garden northeast of the city] was really frightening . . . so we thought we better arrange things by ourselves.

Hiro was also attracted by images of climbing, but his job at a convenience store ultimately led him to practice: "I usually skipped through the pages of *Iwa to Yuki*, *Gakujin*, or *Yamakei* as soon as the new numbers were in the racks. One day this guy, Taka, who was doing shifts with me, happened to notice this and asked me, 'Do you do any climbing?' I said no but would like to, and then he offered to let me join him sometimes if I wanted."

The importance of male-male relationships for gaining access to free-climbing is even more pronounced in the case of voluntary associations like the Yamanaka High Club. In contrast to the market-mediated membership system at the gym, entrance to the club relies solely on personal contacts and individual gatekeepers. I was invited to join the group by Fuji, who recognized me as a neighbor living in the same ward and one day approached me at Pinnacles Gym. Fuji, a forty-two-year-old telecommunications engineer who was married and had two children, was the strongest climber of the group and spent more time and energy on the sport than anyone else. Like Tarō (a forty-three-year-old public employee) and Mori (a forty-year-old shop owner), he developed his interest in climbing during his years at university. Fuji related:

> About a year before I started at the company, I went to Mount Yari for the first time, together with some fellow students from the lab who belonged to the student mountaineering club. One of them also introduced me later to the climbing spots at Ogawayama. For some years I did alpine climbing, ice climbing, winter climbing, and canyoning *[sawanobori]*, all that stuff, but my passion waned when the children were born. About ten years ago I started rock climbing again north of here. That's when I met Shira-kun.

Male-dominated social and business networks fostered the recruitment of other members. Forty-five years old, married with two children, and working as a salesperson at a local bookshop, Yama started climbing in the late 1980s, when he accepted the invitation of a local branch of the Japan Workers Alpine Federation (JWAF) to a climbing day at the local rocks and fell in love with the sport. Tarō, the only other member besides Fuji and Shira who had been with the group for the entire five years of its existence, was a JWAF board member and one of the belay persons on that particular day. He invited Yama to get in touch with the people who later founded the Yamanaka High Club. Tarō later channelled into the club more recruits from the JAWF such as Yūji, a thirty-five-year-old junior high school teacher. Similarly, colleagues, neighbors, and customers introduced the other members (The company Matsu worked for was the main supplier for Mori's shop). One of two women in the group, Miho, a thirty-one-year-old office worker at a local newspaper, had joined the group three years earlier with her husband Yūji. Since Yūji was often too busy to attend the Thursday-night training sessions, Miho persuaded her friend Takako (a thirty-year-old sales assistant) to accompany her. Takako was not as enthusiastic about climbing as her friend and came infrequently.

The same pattern of networks funnelling male members into male groups has been observed for other subcultures. Studying a group of regulars at the surf shop where she was working, Mizuno noted how word-of-mouth recommendation *(kuchikomi)* smoothed the transfer of male-dominated relations from the public into the surfing scene.[15] The skateboarding subculture observed by Tanaka was also born and reproduced through *kuchikomi* and personal relations.[16] Such basic patterns are barriers preventing many women from gaining access to male-dominated worlds.

GENDER RELATIONS

As we have seen above, women are not entirely excluded from the world of climbing. Rather, they are granted a kind of transitory membership status. Their peripheral position is often caused by an implicit desire of the core members to remain among themselves. Performing manhood in front of men reconstructs a homosocial environment, providing in turn ritualized markers for men to express their identity and status. In mainstream society, markers of manhood include occupational success, wealth, power and status, physical prowess, and sexual achievement.[17] Within sporting subcultures, women are permitted to confirm the status and identity of male members, so long as they conform to expectations. Surf magazines such as *Beach Combing,* which list tide charts, also occasionally feature "flirt sections" that describe spots where one's chances are best for "chatting up chicks" *(nanpa)* and where to find commercial sex services in case this strategy does not work out. Beach jamborees or parties *(konpa)* are integral to the surfers' lifestyle, and they offer plenty of opportunities for the men to demonstrate their "masculine qualities," both as womanizers and as heavy drinkers. Mizuno also observed that married men are usually excluded from the beach parties, though her notes indicate that the strict rules of married life might be bent when surfers go rambling abroad.[18]

Perhaps because most of the climbers at Yamanaka High were married, talk about sexual prowess played no role in their expression of their masculine identities. Conversations in the locker room and during the rare drinking sessions tended to deal with the awkwardness of professional life or the demands of family life *(katei sābisu)*. It is important to note that none of the older climbers held career positions. Most of the men I encountered were employed in ordinary white-collar, middle-class jobs, and, with the exception of Matsu (a thirty-four-year-old career-track sales manager who was not married), none seemed to have particular career aspirations or saw opportunities for advancement. Rather than devoting their lives to their work, they appeared to focus on what they gained from practicing a sport they loved and the affiliation to a specific social group and a larger subculture. The valorization of relationships around climbing and the prioritization of climbing over work suggest a transformation of masculine identities in the world of leisure and consumption.

Among the younger men at Pinnacles Gym, women were slightly more often a topic of conversation, though the men usually refrained from more explicit sexist comments. Their self-restraint did not prevent them from peeping through the windows into the Tuesday-night aerobics course (exclaiming "Sugē!" [Cool!]) or pointing out women they found particularly attractive, saying, "Are mite mite, ii mune da nē!" (Oh look, nice tits!) followed by "E, dotchi?" (Wait, which?). I am also certain that my presence as the thirty-year-old father of two young boys must have hampered such conversations despite the casual and direct conversational style we shared otherwise.

Due to the remote location of Yamanaka High, everybody arrived by either car or motorbike, and the group usually dispersed as soon as the training was over. Occasionally, however, a group of three or four agreed to go out for a drink on the way home. Heavy drinking occurred only at scheduled events, such as at the regular year-end parties or when the group would meet at a downtown bar to celebrate a birthday. Miho and Takako filled the glasses for the men as if it were quite natural for them, though this action was also performed by anyone interested in refilling his own glass as well. Tidying up the gymnasium after the training session was another routine that tended to reinforce gender-specific role patterns. Even though this task was always collectively managed, Miho or Takako was usually the first to start moving the pads back to the storage rooms and the last to put away the broom. Sometimes the advanced climbers, lost in an argument about how to solve a climbing problem, missed the sweeping session, whereas the women, if they were around, never failed to complete their share of the work.

BODIES AND BODY TALK

The body is of crucial significance for the cultural construction of gendered identities. Before and after climbing the participants regularly discussed the appearance and performance levels of their bodies and those of others. Climbers complained about excessive weight or injuries, or they mildly criticized each other for "stupid" or "wrong" moves. Body talk among the younger climbers frequently touched upon the climbing-specific functionality of various body parts, but it also focused on their bodies' shape, development, and appeal.

While the body is significant for the cultural construction of masculinity within any sport, and the ideal of hard, muscular male bodies persists in sports sociologists' narrow vision of gendered bodies as well as in ordinary practitioners' minds,[19] climbers' actual bodies as well as their ideas about ideal bodies vary considerably in accordance with age and group norms. The bodies of the older climbers at Yamanaka High did not resemble any mediated image of male physical strength. Some were basically flesh and bones, some were fleshier, and some were quite muscular though still rather small and thin. All in all, their bodies were not outstanding in shape or size, with the notable exception of Matsu, who had been on his university's rugby team. Matsu's position in the sales department of a major household appliance maker did not leave him much time for the gym, and thus he had started to put on weight. Tarō had the fleshy appearance of an overweight white-collar employee who ate too much and did not exercise enough. Along with Matsu, he was a mediocre climber. Yama weighed about as much as Tarō, but because of his height and broad shoulders, he was better proportioned, and, not least because of his dedication to training regularly, he was a much more proficient climber. Fuji, by contrast, was short and slim even by Japanese standards but extraordinarily strong at the wall. Thin and of average size, Shira excelled in flexibility and balance even though he did not train as much. Despite his apparent disinterest in honing his climbing skills, he competed on a fairly equal level with Fuji.

I could not discern any status-related stratification of body shapes. The clothing the climbers wore, however, was more telling. In contrast to the casually dressed climbers at Yamanaka High, where floppy T-shirts and shorts were worn in summer, and sweaters and track pants in winter, the climbers at Pinnacles Gym sported revealing tank tops and tight-fitting pants from popular brands. Often their clothing sported tribal designs, images or phrases referring to climbing, or logos of companies specializing in climbing gear.

Body consciousness was openly expressed by a stylish and brand-conscious appearance and by showing off physical strength. Occasionally climbers demonstrated their strength to each other and to bystanders by performing one-handed pull-ups or by speeding up inclining routes without using their feet, moving hand over hand from one big hold *(yatsu)* to another. Though these impressive displays of strength were meant to show off the muscles on one's arms, shoulders, and back, they were actually counterproductive for climbing, since they wasted energy, and recovery from them could take an untrained climber a full day.

STATUS AND HIERARCHY

A friendly, open-minded, and warm-hearted atmosphere of mutual trust, support, and sympathy characterized my climbing experience at both gyms. Most climbers considered themselves egalitarian, informal, and easygoing. However, I also observed certain status differences and an awareness of those differences among the climbers. Status differentiation in the climbing subculture is first rooted in one's climbing ability, followed by length of membership in the group, and, to a lesser degree, experience and overall knowledge about climbing. Whereas Mizuno observed that surfing skills, length of group membership, and age were the variables defining the hierarchical relationships within the surfing subculture, age did not play a discernible role in climbing culture since it usually coincided with years of experience or length of membership.[20] It was impossible to observe what role gender might play in status differentiation. Both women at Yamanaka High climbed at a lower level than all the other members, while the student group at Pinnacles Gym consisted of men only.

Length of membership seems to correlate to the processes of status differentiation for male climbers. Fuji was the most powerful climber, had been a member of the group the longest, and had a long history of climbing experience. He belonged to the group's founding generation and was tacitly accepted as its leader, largely because he managed the rental contract with the gymnasium's owner and collected monthly fees from the group. Tarō also belonged to the same age group and was a member of the founding generation. In contrast to Fuji, he was inferior to most others as a climber, and his overall experience as a free climber was limited, notwithstanding his responsibilities in the JWAF. Yama joined the group slightly later but had a more prominent position since he was a markedly better climber. He was also acknowledged for his distinctive experience abroad, where he had visited famous climbing spots such as Yosemite National

Park and Joshua Tree in the United States, Arco in northern Italy, and Krabi in southern Thailand.

Status differences had an impact on the climbing itself. The order of succession at the wall and the choice of the person holding the rope are two examples. The climbing wall at Yamanaka High offered space for up to four parties at a time, but the less skilled climbers usually stayed back until the expert climbers had finished their first round or they were explicitly invited to go ahead. Climbers at the same level automatically teamed up, since belaying was often reciprocal, but sometimes it was necessary to ask someone else to hold the rope. Although the members of the top group did not mind asking anyone to belay them, the other climbers tended to ask someone further down in the hierarchy or someone at a similar level first. If Miho and Takako were around, they would usually build a rope team on their own.

When addressing each other the climbers usually used nicknames, though not everyone seemed to have one; the women, for example, were addressed by their name and the diminutive suffix *-chan*. Status markers such as the honorific *-san* (as in Shira-san) or the *masu* forms of verbs were used by the women and some of the younger and peripheral male members when talking to Shira or Fuji. Plain Japanese was spoken among people of the same age group. Fuji, Yama, and Shira used a plain colloquial style in nearly all instances, both when talking with each other and when talking to the rest of the group. When I was introduced to the group they would use honorific Japanese, which corresponded with my outsider status as a foreigner and my affiliation with a prestigious university but not with my age or climbing skills. This changed when I took the initiative to switch gradually to more neutral speech conventions.

Everyone used polite language when about to start a route, such as "Onegai shimasu" (I beg for your help) or "Hajimemasu!" (Starting!) to indicate that from that moment onward, the primary responsibility for the climber's physical safety was entrusted to the belayer feeding the rope. The formula reversing the status level belongs to a ritual device framing the climbing activity itself and is in marked contrast to the conventional phrasing of the proceeding invitation, such as "Yama, chotto birei shite kurehen no?" (Yama, can you feed me the rope?) followed by "Ii yo" (Okay, will do). The end of the ritual frame was usually announced by a phrase like "O-tsukare sama deshita" or "Arigatō gozaimashita," by which the climber expressed his gratitude to the belayer, though at this time the more advanced climbers tended again to fall back on plain forms ("Go-kurō san").

During the ascent another ritualistic inversion of the social order often occurred. When a climber encountered difficulty moving ahead because of a lack of stamina or technical knowledge, the belayer or someone else watching from below would usually start shouting encouragement, such as "Ganbare!" (Hang in there!), "Faito!" (Fight!), or "Akirameru na!" (Don't give up!), followed by similar cheering from more members until the entire group had joined the choir. Since the pain and struggle the climber was going through at this moment were deeply engraved into the memory of every climber's body, they were all free to invert the usual communication codes in order to express their sympathy. This demonstration of collective suffering and support is surprisingly effective. No matter how much the muscles of the forearm are trembling, the legs shaking, or the finger joints hurting, you simply can't give up when your comrades are doing their best to motivate you to stick it out a bit longer, to go for one more move, to give it one more try. I personally experienced how my initial distaste for the noisy and importunate intrusion from the ground into my private struggle on the wall slowly changed into an appreciation for this demonstration of caring and inclusion and how it actually filled me with strength and confidence, if only for a short period. Similar patterns of mutual surveillance and supportiveness based on shared experiences discipline surfers' behavior when they are shivering with cold or struggling with the waves on their way out to the lineup.[21]

NO PAIN, NO GAIN: BODY AND MIND CONTROL

Long and exhausting training routines are a central element of traditional approaches in sport education in general and in the martial arts in particular. The endless repetition of exercises helps athletes internalize bodily movements until they can be performed without conscious effort. At the same time, by enduring the arduous repetitions the athletes acquire certain dispositions esteemed by Japanese society in general. Willpower *(seishinryoku)* is the underlying capacity that enables athletes to endure *(gaman)* hardship *(kurō)* and to overcome psychological strain. Writing about school and university rugby in Japan, Light concludes that the ability to endure discomfort, frustration, pain, and labor is an indication of "a particular form of masculinity shaped by *seishin* and the associated cultural concept of *gaman*."[22] Chapman describes how a Japanese karate athlete positively reframed the severe beating he received from his master for more than thirty minutes as a valuable lesson in hardship, which is "the tool by which a craft apprentice is fashioned into a skilled practitioner and, in a wider Japanese social context, how the youth is seen to mature into a man of-the-world."[23] McDonald and Hallinan even argue that the practice of rowing at the university level is actually about accumulating *seishin* capital, or a body-mind disposition revolving around hierarchical relationships, self-sacrifice, learning through hardship, the concepts of harmony and cooperation, and the qualities of patience, endurance, perseverance, and discipline.[24]

Climbing, too, resonates with these features of the dominant sport ideology. Climbing requires a lot of practice and repetitious exercise to acquire a kind of somatic intelligence, which consists of a stock repertoire of basic moves, grip techniques, and body postures that can be applied quickly, efficiently, and naturally in accordance with the demands of a line. The accumulated experience of successful climbs translates into what are deemed "manly" qualities of courage and endurance. The differences in climbing skills stockpiled in practice and experience become evident when climbers are in action. While all group members acknowledge individual effort and progress, the rank order is ultimately based on the question "Who is able to climb the most difficult route?" All climbing scales lack precision and objectivity to some degree, but a comparison of those climbing the same route in front of the group answers all questions. On-sight climbing (lead ascents without any prior information about the route, its problems, and its solutions) is generally valued more highly than redpoint ascents (leading the entire route without a fall or rest). Climbs at the upper limit of a climber's ability usually need more than one push to be completed, and climbers must often make more than one attempt to finally achieve a redpoint ascent.

Less difficult because the assurance of a rope fixed from above reduces the fear of a fall since the climber can simply sag onto the rope, top-rope climbs are clearly frowned upon, particularly among advanced free climbers. When I asked students at Pinnacles Gym why they always wanted to lead, Ken answered, "I don't need a rope hauling me up the wall." Hiro agreed, stating, "That sissy *[nanpa-na]* style of climbing is embarrassing." Everyone at Yamanaka High except for the top climbers, however, occasionally or even frequently enjoyed the comfortable safety of this belaying style. Even though they naturally would resort to it when following as the second climber in multipitch climbing, some men commonly perceived top-rope climbing as a style acceptable for women only, and particularly not suitable for the "hard guys faction" *(kōha)* of climbing.

Constant training is needed to build the physical strength, stamina, techniques, and knowledge required to lead in climbing. Experience is also needed to cope mentally with the inherent risk of falling and the lurking fear of pain. Rephrasing the famous statement used by the legendary U.S. football coach Vince Lombardi, "Winning isn't everything, it's the only thing," Fuji explained, "In climbing, mental power is not everything, it's the only thing. . . . No matter how strong your body is, no matter how far you have developed your climbing technique and ability to read the line, when you're scared of falling, no chance to move . . . if you don't know what to do next, how to make the next step, and you become frightened, then you can't do anything at all."

Climbing at the edge of one's abilities always necessitates the risk of a fall. Since protections in free-climbing are set at short intervals (on average about every three or four feet), a fall is usually stopped quickly if the belaying second reacts appropriately. However, even an uncontrolled fall of just a few feet may cause severe pain and injuries, and all advanced climbers have stories to tell about skin abrasions, contusions, sprains, or broken bones. As Shira said, "What worries me most in climbing is injury, of course. No one wants to get injured, but to a certain degree risk taking is unavoidable; otherwise you can't improve your skills." For some the fear is reason enough to quit the sport. Kita said, "I know of people who stopped climbing because they were always thinking about what will happen to my job if I am injured, or what will come next, after I recovered, will it happen again. . . . But what I am more afraid of is becoming a man that is too scared to extend his limits." For these reasons it is not overall climbing capacity but the ability to lead that is most closely associated with masculinity in this subculture: having courage *(gattsu),* the mental as well as the physical strength to move on. The key concept of *seishin* generally operates at the subconscious level, though it occasionally appeared in conversations with the climbers as well.

Yet in one regard the free climbers differed markedly from the widely accepted image of male stoicism among athletes. According to Yama, "Sometimes you meet people at the rocks acting like ascetic monks. Objectively seen, they don't seem to enjoy themselves . . . there is something dreary about their style. When you say hello or talk to them, no reaction comes back." This description resonates with the stock image of the "lone wolf," the man of the mountains *(yama otoko),* who is seen as strong, stoic, self-reliant, experienced, and skilled in all alpine techniques. But the ideal representation of masculinity in mountain climbing discourse is not a role model for the free climbers. Said Fuji, "There is nothing wrong with being stoic or concentrated during climbing, but afterwards people should be relaxed and cheerful." Similarly, Kita claimed that "free climbing will stay a minor sport if the public continues to associate it with maniacs. I want people who know nothing about free-climbing to think climbing is fun and stylish when they happen to watch climbers in action."

At Yamanaka High and Pinnacles Gym, one could not help but hear how cheerful the atmosphere was. In addition to the chatting by resting climbers and cheering calls, there was also a constant sound layer of moaning and groaning by the climbers at the wall, who seemed to use their voices as a device to amplify their power.

REPRESENTATIONS OF MASCULINITY IN LIFESTYLE SPORTS

This discussion of two free-climbing settings—one a public climbing gym, the other a small network of dedicated climbers—has shown that subcultural formations are tied into the social and psychosomatic construction of masculinity to a degree similar to mainstream sports. The free-climbing subculture is shaped by values and performance patterns such as dominance, hierarchical relations, toughness, perseverance, and mental strength, which resonate with conventional ideas of hegemonic masculinity. Because men have long appropriated climbing as a male activity, homosociality, ideas of domination, and the ethical appreciation of pain work toward the reproduction of a hegemonic sporting masculinity. Even though there is nothing inherently male or female about free-climbing, the experience of climbing with male and female climbers in Japan has shown that its practice and discourse are not androgynous but conventionally gendered.

Nevertheless, the variation of attitudes and norms within the Yamanaka High group and between the different clubs shows that sporting masculinities in lifestyle sports are not fixed and essentialized entities but are subject to change and variation over the life course. Younger climbers with able and powerful bodies expressed their maleness through heteronormativity and hegemonic masculinity, whereas older men had a wider array of socioeconomic resources such as work or family from which to draw their identities. Alternative sports do not produce only hegemonic but also subordinated, compliant, and alternative forms of masculinity. Free-climbing thus continues to be an arena of hypermasculinity for some men, while for others it offers the opportunity to enact and represent alternative images of masculinity that place more emphasis on the social and emotional amenities to be gained from participation in this sport.

NOTES

1. Wōrsching 2007, p. 203. See also Messner and Sabo 1990; Hargreaves 1994.
2. Wheaton 2004b, p. 140.
3. Wheaton 2004a, p. 16.
4. Edwards 2007; Manzenreiter 2008.
5. Spielvogel 2003; Manzenreiter 2004.
6. Itō 2001; Sekiguchi 2001; Itani 2003; Light 2003; Manzenreiter 2007.
7. Hirakawa 2002; Iida 2002 and 2003.
8. Chapman 2004.
9. Ikemoto 2006.
10. Cave 2004; Dalla Chiesa 2002; Light 2000a, 2000b; McDonald and Hallinan 2005; Vincenti 1997.
11. Sasakawa Sports Foundation 2004, p. 24.
12. The cover of *Free Fan*, no. 56.
13. Manzenreiter 2000, pp. 45–48.
14. Mizuno 2002, p. 52.
15. Mizuno 2002, p. 45.
16. Tanaka 2003, pp. 54–56.
17. Kimmel 1994, pp. 128–29.
18. Mizuno 2002, p. 48.
19. Adams 2005, p. 64.
20. Mizuno 2002, p. 45.
21. Mizuno 2002, pp. 52–53.
22. Light 2000b, p. 99.
23. Chapman 2004, p. 329.
24. McDonald and Hallinan 2005, p. 194.

REFERENCES

Adams, Mary Douglas. 2005. "'Death to the Prancing Prince': Effeminacy, Sport Discourses and the Salvation of Men's Dancing." *Body & Society* 11, no. 4: 63–86.

Cave, Peter. 2004. "*Bukatsudō:* The Educational Role of Japanese School Sport Clubs." *Journal of Japanese Studies* 30, no. 2: 383–415.

Chapman, Kris. 2004. "*Ossu!* Sporting Masculinities in a Japanese Karate *Dōjō*." *Japan Forum* 16, no. 2: 315–35.

Dalla Chiesa, Simone. 2002. "When the Goal is Not the Goal: Japanese School Football Players Working Hard at Their Game." In *Japan at Play: The Ludic and the Logic of Power,* ed. Joy Hendry and Massimo Raveri, 186–98. London: Routledge.

Edwards, Elise M. 2007. "Gender Lessons on the Field in Contemporary Japan: The Female Athlete in Coaching Discourses." In *This Sporting Life: Sports*

and Body Culture in Modern Japan, ed. William W. Kelly with Sugimoto Atsuo, 211–28. New Haven: Yale CEAS.
Hargreaves, Jennifer. 1994. *Sporting Females: Critical Issues in the History and Sociology of Women's Sports.* London: Routledge.
Hirakawa Sumiko. 2002. "Supōtsu, jendā, media imēji. Supōtsu CF ni egakareru jendā." In *Gendai media supōtsu ron*, ed. Hashimoto Junichi, 91–115. Kyōto: Sekai Shisō Sha.
Iida Takako. 2002. "Media supōtsu to feminizumu." In *Gendai media supōtsu ron*, ed. Hashimoto Junichi, 71–90. Kyōto: Sekai Shisō Sha.
———. 2003. "Shinbun hōdō ni okeru josei kyōgisha no kendō-ka. Sugawara Kyōko kara Narazaki Noriko e." *Journal of Sport and Gender Studies* 1: 4–14.
Ikemoto Junichi. 2006. "Nihon bokushingu no esunogurafii. Shakai hendō ni ikiru wakamono no aidentiti kōchiku to sabukaruchā jissen no shiten kara." *Shakaigaku Hyōron* 58, no. 1: 21–39.
Itani Keiko. 2003. "Josei taiiku kyōshi e no mensetsu chōsa kara mita gakkō taiiku no jendā sabukaruchō." *Journal of Sport and Gender Studies* 1: 27–38.
Itō Kimio. 2001. "Supōtsu kyōiku to jendā." In *Taiiku kyōiku o manabu hito no tame ni*, ed. Sugimoto Atsuo, 124–41. Kyōto: Sekai Shisō Sha.
Kimmel, Michael. 1994. "Masculinity as Homophobia: Fear, Shame and Silence in the Construction of Gender Identity." In *Theorizing Masculinities*, ed. Harry Brod and Michael Kaufman, 119–41. London: Sage.
Light, Richard. 2000a. "Culture at Play: A Comparative Study of Masculinity and Game Style in Japanese and Australian School Rugby." *International Sports Studies* 22, no. 2: 26–41.
———. 2000b. "A Centenary of Rugby and Masculinity in Japanese Schools and Universities: Continuity and Change." *Sporting Traditions* 16, no. 2: 87–104.
———. 2003. "Sport and the Construction of Masculinity in the Japanese Education System." In *Asian Masculinities*. See Louie and Low 2003.
Louie, Kam, and Morris Low, eds. 2003. *Asian Masculinities: The Meaning and Practice of Manhood in China and Japan.* London: Routledge.
Manzenreiter, Wolfram. 2000. *Die soziale Konstruktion des japanischen Alpinismus. Kultur, Ideologie und Sport im modernen Bergsteigen.* Wien: Institut für Ostasienwissenschaften, University of Vienna (Beiträge zur Japanologie 36).
———. 2004. "Her Place in the 'House of Football': Globalisation, Sexism and Women's Football in East Asian Societies." In *Football Goes East: Business, Culture and the People's Game in East Asia*, ed. Wolfram Manzenreiter and John Horne, 197–221. London: Routledge.
———. 2007. "Physical Education and the Curriculum of Gender Reproduction in Japan." In *Gender Dynamics and Globalization: Perspectives on Japan within Asia*, ed. Claudia Derichs and Susanne Kreitz-Sandberg, 123–42. Berlin: LIT Verlag.

———. 2008. "Football in the Reconstruction of the Gender Order in Japan." *Soccer and Society* 9, no. 1: 244–58.

McDonald, Brent, and Chris Hallinan. 2005. "*Seishin* Habitus: Spiritual Capital and Japanese Rowing." *International Review for the Sociology of Sport* 40, no. 2: 187–200.

Messner, Michael, and Donald Sabo, eds. 1990. *Sport, Gender, Men and the Social Order: Critical Feminist Perspectives.* Champaign: Human Kinetics.

Mizuno Eri. 2002. "Supōtsu to kai bunka ni tsuite no ikkōsatsu. X sōfu shoppu ni mirareru 'dansei bunka.'" *Kyōto Shakaigaku Nenpō* 10: 35–60.

Sasakawa Sports Foundation (SSF). 2004. *Supōtsu raifu dēta 2004. Supōtsu raifu ni kan suru chōsa hōkokusho.* Sasakawa Sports Foundation.

Sekiguchi Hisashi. 2001. "Taiiku supōtsu ni miru 'otokorashisa' baiyō no rekishi." In *Nihon no otoko wa doko kara kite doko e iku no ka,* ed. Asai Haruo et al., 204–21. Seiunsha.

Spielvogel, Laura. 2003. *Working Out in Japan. Shaping the Female Body in Tokyo Fitness Clubs.* Durham: Duke University Press.

Tanaka Kennosuke. 2003. "Toshi kūkan to wakamono no 'zoku' bunka." *Supōtsu Shakaigaku Kenkyū* 11: 46–61.

Vincenti, James J. 1997. "The Relationship between Female Status and Physical Strength in a Japanese University Athletic Club." *Journal of Sport and Social Issues* 21: 189–210.

Wheaton, Belinda. 2004a. "Introduction: Mapping the Lifestyle Sport-Scape." In *Understanding Lifestyle Sports: Consumption, Identity and Difference,* ed. Belinda Wheaton, 1–28. London: Routledge.

———. 2004b. "Selling Out? The Commercialisation and Globalisation of Lifestyle Sport." In *The Global Politics of Sport: The Role of Global Institutions in Sport,* ed. Lincoln Allison, 140–61. London: Routledge.

Wōrsching, Martha. 2007. "Race to the Top: Masculinity, Sport, and Nature in German Magazine Advertising." *Men and Masculinities* 10: 197–221.

11 Not Suitable as a Man?

Conscription, Masculinity, and Hermaphroditism in Early Twentieth-Century Japan

Teresa A. Algoso

When thirty-year-old Otsuju was arrested in Dalian, Manchuria, he turned out to be far more riveting than the common thief he appeared to be at first glance. It soon became apparent that Otsuju was "a cripple" *(fugusha)*, part male and part female. Calling him a "strange double-sexed person," government officials probed into his past, only to discover that Otsuju had been born with the name Fuji—and as a woman. The story of Otsuju/Fuji first appeared in 1906, in a *Far East News* article entitled "A Woman Found to Have Testicles."[1] It is but one of a number of stories that point to the construction and fortification of a new male-female dichotomy in the early twentieth century.

Whereas sex and status had been inseparable social identifiers during preindustrial times, reforms and discourses during the Meiji era (1868–1912) had created "a category of 'woman' that cut across all classes and that was set in opposition to 'man'".[2] As a state-bolstered system of rights and obligations came into existence in Meiji Japan, it had become crucial to determine who qualified for which privileges and their attendant responsibilities. Because one of the key determinants in this context was an individual's sex, the discipline of medical jurisprudence played a major role, particularly when an individual's sex could not be definitively ascertained.

From the early Meiji era, the discipline of medical jurisprudence had turned its sights to a newly named phenomenon: *han'in'yō*. *Han'in'yō* was used to refer to those individuals who could not be unproblematically assigned either female or male status. The early twenty-first-century English terms that most closely approximate the meaning of *han'in'yō* are "intersexuality" and "disorder of sex development" (DSD).[3] I have chosen to avoid these terms and instead use the seemingly antiquated "hermaphroditism" for three reasons. First, DSD and intersexuality have, respectively, strong medical and political connotations that were not inherently present in discourse on *han'in'yō*. Second, the breakdown of the word "hermaphroditism" into "Hermes" and "Aphrodite" mirrors the literal translation of *han'in'yō* as half "yin," half "yang." Finally, the frequent reference by early twentieth-century Japanese writers to the English word "hermaphroditism" and to its Indo-European language variations indicates that this term was culturally intelligible to the authors of these texts.

Hermaphroditism is an ideal site at which to investigate anxiety about ambiguous sex because it becomes a nexus for debates regarding what is feminine and what is masculine. The concept of hermaphroditism as pathology is valid theoretically only within a system that differentiates individuals into male and female; Stephan Hirschauer calls such processes of pathologization "medical personifications of cultural troubles."[4] In the case of early twentieth-century Japan, images of a "modern girl" whose economic self-sufficiency "positioned her beyond the reach of state and family,"[5] of a new "manhood fraught with anxiety, indecision, nervousness, and a susceptibility to falling in love,"[6] and of a "proliferation of 'perversions'"[7] all contributed to an increasing uneasiness about the boundaries between male and female.

Donald Roden has shown that by the 1910s there was widespread fascination with "gender ambivalence," accompanied by an oftentimes panicked concern about the erosion of the categories of masculine and feminine. Sex distinctions were increasingly seen as blurred, and many perceived this increasing ambivalence as standing in the way of Japan's progress. In 1921, General Ugaki Kazushige, who was soon to become Japan's minister of war, stated that the "feminization of men and the masculinization of women and the neutered gender that results is a modernistic tendency that makes it impossible for the individual, the society, or the nation to achieve great progress."[8] Such concerns increased attention to individuals who might challenge, or even transcend, the very categories of male and female.

Similar to the way that the appearance of the concept of homosexuality has been shown to have created heterosexuality, the delineation of hermaphroditism can be shown to be instrumental in strictly delineating male from female.[9] Just as the existence of the categories male and female necessitates the existence of the hermaphrodite—a category that embraces all bodies that do not fit the standards of the other two—the classification of hermaphrodite also creates and solidifies the boundaries of those very categories by cordoning off ambiguous bodies, leaving as legitimate only those that reinforce the normative definitions of male and female.

Scientists, doctors, bureaucrats, and others in positions of societal authority are then free to sort out and decide which sex to assign the bodies in the remainder category, thereby accomplishing two things. First, they take socially inexplicable bodies and, through discourse and surgery, force them to become intelligible within a dichotomous sex system. Second, with every pronouncement and with every cut of the surgical knife, they define the meaning of the two socially and medically prescribed categories of male and female. The very resistance of hermaphroditic bodies to classification is magnified back in defining these two categories. By declaring, for instance, that breasts do not belong on a body that has been declared male and that testicles do, a female body is concurrently constituted as its opposite—that is, as a body that possesses breasts and does not possess testicles. While such declarations explicitly define male and female bodies, they simultaneously and implicitly define hermaphroditic bodies as any that do not fit into one of these two mutually exclusive categories. The male-female dichotomy and the remainder category of hermaphrodite endlessly reinforce each other, each by defining what the other is not.[10]

In this chapter I examine how medical jurisprudence discourse on hermaphroditism supported the role of the conscription exam in defining a new ideal of masculinity. Because the rights and responsibilities of citizenship were assigned based on a scientifically measurable masculinity—a masculinity defined in accordance with military requirements—individuals with bodies that did not conform to this new definition of masculinity were legally or socially marginalized.

HERMAPHRODITISM AND MEDICAL JURISPRUDENCE

In the late nineteenth century, cross-dressing was an object of legislation because it inhibited the state's abilities to track and regulate its citizens.[11] Hermaphroditism caused similar problems because the law required the division of all people into two sexed types for purposes as varied as education, marriage, military service, succession, inheritance, voting, and other civil rights.[12] Issues involving ambiguous sex were typically difficult to resolve, a situation that necessitated a system for determining whether any particular individual was male or female. The courts and practitioners of forensic medicine had to be able to pass judgment on what was to be done about the individual who turned into a man after marrying as a woman, the recruit who was male in the family register but had become pregnant during service, or the male head of a family who was found to be a woman after succession.[13]

Within both medical and legal contexts, hermaphroditism was broadly, and seemingly universally, understood to be of primarily two types: "true" and "pseudo." "True hermaphroditism" *(shin-han'in'yō)* indicated the presence of both ovaries and testicles. The logic behind this taxonomy coincided with the European paradigm that was prevalent at the time. In both locations it was the possession or absence of ovaries and of testicles that was the key to determining sex, so those who possessed both ovaries and testicles were considered to truly straddle the boundary line between male and female.[14] Though other individuals might qualify as hermaphrodites, the true hermaphrodite—as the name suggests—was the only one seen to be so ambiguous as to be entirely outside the categories of male and female. It is noteworthy that virtually all of the Meiji- and Taisho-era texts that address hermaphroditism make a point of saying that true hermaphroditism is extremely rare, "with only two or three cases ever being reported."[15] This is perhaps because all but the true hermaphrodite can be seen to possess an essential *(honrai)* sex that is either male or female. In line with a contemporary tendency toward intricate classification, these authors also frequently classified true hermaphroditism into double-sided compound (ovaries and testes on both left and right sides of the body), single-sided compound (both ovaries and testes on one side, but only either an ovary or a testis on the other side), and single-sided singular (an ovary on one side and a testis on the other).

Whereas the puzzle of true hermaphroditism was usually put aside after a few obligatory sentences, "pseudohermaphroditism" *(ka-han'in'yō)* generally garnered much more attention, perhaps because it was seen as more frequently necessitating legal and medical intervention—or perhaps because it was more readily identified. Pseudohermaphroditism was invariably divided into two types: masculine and feminine. Two texts from the late 1890s, for example, both define a masculine pseudohermaphrodite as an individual who "is actually male, but whose outer sexual organs appear female," while a feminine pseudohermaphrodite is an individual who "is actually female, but whose outer sexual organs appear male."[16]

In Meiji and Taishō Japan, the field of medical jurisprudence focused less on using medical methods to resolve legal issues (as it would later in the century), and more on issues that were simultaneously both medical and legal in nature. It is therefore unsurprising that the majority of medical jurisprudence texts included a section on hermaphroditism, the resolution of which required the input of medical experts yet had legal consequences. Although some authors focused primarily on the medical dimension of hermaphroditism, providing complex taxonomies and delving into possible causes, virtually all authors discussed, at least briefly, three issues: marriage, inheritance, and the granting of rights reserved for men.

In this context, the story of seventeen-year-old Shinjirō, which originally appeared in a newspaper article in 1909, is illustrative. Shinjirō had always worn men's clothes and spent his time with male friends, with whom he gossiped about girls, talked big, and told jokes. His friends were unaware that he had a "freakish" aspect, that he possessed both male and female reproductive organs. Shinjirō's deformed status was divulged when he suddenly discharged menstrual blood while having abdominal pains. He was hospitalized by the examining physician to undergo treatment because parts of him were discovered to be "completely female." People at the hospital spoke of Shinjirō as having been cursed by fate. To have always thought oneself a man and then suddenly to have to come to grips with being a woman: was it any wonder, they asked, that, despite her complete "recovery," she attempted suicide?[17] When Shinjirō was declared to be female, she lost more than her lifelong conception of herself as male; she also lost all of the male privileges that she had previously enjoyed.

The issue of sex-determined privileges and obligations had been highlighted as early as 1886 in the text *Trial Medicine (Saiban Igaku)*, which defined the primary goal of medical jurisprudence with respect to hermaphroditism as the determination of whether an individual should be classified as male or female. This differentiation into female and male, the text explained, was necessary for determining issues of inheritance, for confirming whether the examinee "should be married out as a bride or should take a wife," and for deciding whether male administrative rights should be granted.[18] A year later another medical jurisprudence authority published similar words: "Generally, the essential point of hermaphrodite-related examination is to judge whether an individual should be married out as a bride or should be the heir . . . and to decide whether or not that individual should have the administrative rights of a man."[19]

An archetypal example commonly cited in medical jurisprudence texts was that of "the hermaphrodite who, mistakenly believing oneself male, or believing oneself female, marries and is then sued for divorce by his or her spouse because he or she is unable to perform sexual intercourse."[20] Some suggested that discovery of hermaphroditism most commonly occurred when a male pseudohermaphrodite, after having been raised as a girl, was "discovered upon the marriage bed to be unable to have intercourse."[21]

These authors generally saw European countries as being more advanced in dealing with the legal problems that could occur as a result of ambiguous sex, stating that they expected hermaphroditism to be at the center of "a trend toward increasingly frequent battles over inheritance rights or voting rights" in Japan.[22] Various authors also cited the existence of Prussian laws to deal with problems arising from ambiguously sexed individuals, while bemoaning the fact that hermaphroditism was "insufficiently addressed in our country's civil law."[23]

A number of these medical jurisprudence authors explicitly linked the idea of the nation-state to forensic examination's primary goal of "deciding whether a given individual is male or female, in order to determine that individual's social position."[24] The author of the 1917 text *Medical Jurisprudence (Hōigaku),* for example, stated, "An individual's rights and obligations greatly differ based on whether that individual's sex is male or female. On the level of the individual, there are, for instance, matters such as succession and inheritance. When talking on the level of the community or of the nation, there are issues such as enfranchisement versus disenfranchisement and military service."[25] More explicitly, regarding those "ambiguous humans" called hermaphrodites, the 1928 *Synopsis of Medical Jurisprudence (Hōigaku taii)* stated that "when such individuals reach a certain age, as a member of the nation *[kokka],* a decision must be made as to whether they are male or female."[26]

DEFINING A NEW KIND OF MASCULINITY

The military took a leading role in urging the necessity for determining new standards for the masculine body. In her examination of "the construction and normalization of Japanese sexuality," Sabine Frühstück shows how "the modern national military was . . . one of the core organizations for the development of hygienic thought and practice."[27] This process can be seen particularly clearly in the debate about the "decline of young men's physiques" in the late 1930s.[28] Led by Koizumi Chikahiko, head of the Army Bureau of Medical Affairs, this was only one in a long line of debates on the Japanese national physique. Takaoka Hiroyuki looks at what he terms "physical strength" ideology in this context and suggests that it is best to think of the debate as an instance of the army using its increasingly influential voice to construct a totalitarian system of management based on the perceived need for increased "human war potential"—a strategy set up by the army to create the soldier-equals-citizen ideal toward which it was aiming.[29] Because the Japanese state first deployed statistical methods on a large scale in the quest for a potent, modern military, and because the military was responsible for the production of the only countrywide physical exam statistics in pre–World War II Japan—via the conscription examination system—it was therefore in a position, as Japan headed into all-out war, to initiate debate about the state of the physical strength of the nation's youth.[30]

Koizumi and others expressed a sense of crisis that the social changes accompanying increased industrialization, urbanization, and education had produced a citizenry with bodies and spirits that were too far from what the military demanded. Although Koizumi bemoaned the deterioration of the Japanese male physique *(taii)*, Takaoka suggests that for Koizumi, this is merely shorthand for physical standards *(taikaku tōi)* as measured via the conscription exam: "The declining physique being problematized was not the Japanese physique in general, but rather the perceived increase of feeble *[kinkotsu hakujaku]* recruits."[31] Though Takaoka focuses on a later time period, the points that he makes about the ability of military policy and rhetoric to make physical strength into a social issue are relevant to the early 1900s as well. Under the "physical strength" ideology, "various domains of citizen's lives were checked from the perspective of physical strength." This was a central axis of the "healthy soldier, healthy citizen" strategy founded upon the needs of the military.[32]

Frühstück argues that statistical methods not only played administrative roles but "also created new categories of people."[33] For example, the National Physical Strength Management Law (Kokumin tairyoku kanri hō) of 1937 established an annual physical for all minors, with the results being recorded in a "citizen's physique notebook." The system fulfilled a need for objective criteria by creating measurable standards. Measurements of height, weight, and chest circumference allowed masculinity to be expressed purely in terms of numbers and reflected an example of the army's "human scientific management," the aim of which was the development of human resources, or "human war potential," for use by the nation-state. By separating male youth into the "healthy" and the "weak-bodied," these wartime social strategies erased the boundary between society and the barracks, resulting in the permeation into civilian society of the military's norms and systems of management.[34] As Takaoka points out, one could look at this law as simply establishing an innocuous system of health examinations, except for the fact that the physical exertion portions of the exam coincided too closely with the military's needs—and that the government used the results of the physicals as justification to embark upon the improvement of citizen's physiques.[35]

The citizenry in general was managed to a certain extent via the family registration and tax systems, but those who entered the military were subjected to a level of personal information acquisition and management that, according to Arakawa Shōji, was not experienced by women.[36] Rather than utilizing the categories of male and female, however, it is perhaps more useful to think of this system as one that divided the citizenry into those who were fit for duty and those who were not. Those deemed fit for duty entered into a highly rigid system of bodily management and control, one that offered status and career prospects as compensation, while those disqualified from service escaped incorporation into this system of management while simultaneously losing access to its concomitant rewards.[37]

The importance of this development is not merely that military service became a prerequisite for full manhood, but also that the conscription examination and military service defined a specific kind of manhood. The examination created a new standard, a new method of evaluating masculinity that could not have existed in preconscription society, one that proffered the possibility of sorting and evaluating all males based primarily on bodily criteria. For the first time, in a society that placed an increasing "premium . . . on scientific-mindedness," ideal masculinity could be defined through the use of numbers.[38] The era had arrived in which the evaluation of individuals "as men" would result in the degradation of various body types: the short, the sick, those lacking the endurance to march long distances, and those judged to have physical or mental disabilities that precluded training for battle were all denied full manhood.[39] In particular, to be classified as Class D, which signified a "physical or psychic functional impediment," meant having one's body and/or psyche declared unfit under the modern nation-state.[40] To be recognized as a man, one had to have the physique and robustness necessary to endure military training. Physical criterion began to hold substantial meaning in the context of the conscription exam and, as a result, height, for example, began to be seen as "an orthodox measure of the worth of a man."[41]

Enforcement of the conscription system spread an image of masculinity based on bodily criteria beyond the military context. Richard Smethurst demonstrates that diffusion of the "soldier's ethos" into civilian society was in fact one of the goals of the creators of the conscription system, who "saw the draft as a way of building unity and commitment to national goals through the education of civilians in military values."[42] They hoped "to send [draftees] back to civilian society to serve as community examples . . . [and to] be like soldiers all of the time."[43]

Because those who rose through the ranks during military service were then recognized as being capable men once they had returned to civilian life, and because, even after being discharged from service, such men were expected to maintain the military spirit and to perform their obligations to society through activities such as involvement in their local reservist associations and as youth group leaders, a new axis for evaluating masculinity rapidly formed.[44] As more and more men returned from military service, this new image of masculinity was distilled and strengthened throughout Japanese society.[45]

HERMAPHRODITISM AND THE CONSCRIPTION EXAM

The implementation of the conscription exam not only demeaned the masculinity of the short or the sick, but it also led to the "discovery" of individuals with sexual characteristics perceived as abnormal. The 1937 text *The Latest in Medical Jurisprudence (Saishin hōigaku)* stated that "at every year's conscription examinations, there are instances of an individual who had been raised male, turning out to in truth be female, and being disqualified as a result."[46] Established by the Conscription Law of 1873, the exam itself consisted of: the measurement of height, weight, and chest circumference; an examination of eyesight (including checking for color blindness) and hearing; an internal organ examination by means of a stethoscope and palpation; confirmation that all one's limbs moved properly; and an examination of fingers, eyes, nose, ears, the anal cavity (including noting the existence of hemorrhoids), and the sex organs (which included checking for the presence of venereal disease).[47]

One interviewee noted that the examiners "of course also looked under the *fundoshi* or loincloth . . . in part to check for venereal diseases."[48] Venereal disease was a matter of concern to the medical examiners, but it was only one of the reasons for checking the examinees' genitals. A 1912 Ministry of Defense document entitled "Revising Procedure for Army Physical Checkup" made explicit what else was being checked. It delineated sixty specific conditions that would result in not passing the exam, including conditions such as chronic lung disease, excess body fat, feebleness, and stuttering. Condition number forty-eight was "serious urethral deformity, hermaphroditism, or urinary fistula."[49]

For specific examples of hermaphroditism in the context of the conscription exam, we must turn to sources outside the field of jurisprudence. For this purpose, the 1922 book *Thoughts on Hermaphroditism (Hannannyokō)*, edited by the prominent journalist and social critic Miyatake Gaikotsu (1867–1955), is particularly useful. Gaikotsu, a pioneer independent publisher, provides a compilation of recorded instances of hermaphroditism from the early eighteenth to the early twentieth century. The twentieth-century depictions, which make up the bulk of the stories, were culled mostly from newspaper articles.[50] For instance, Gaikotsu provides the text of a 1907 newspaper article relating the story of a Gunma youth who appeared one evening at the inn of the conscription officers who were conducting local examinations.[51] He had come to ask for a special examination because he was disfigured, which made being examined along with the other youths embarrassing. When asked the nature of his disability, he explained that he possessed both female and male reproductive organs. The physical examiners found that the potential recruit, who in all respects had appeared a man when clothed, had female breasts and looked "just like a woman" when naked—until one noticed the existence of testicles and a penis. As the youth was "on the verge of tears at the humiliation of being exposed in public with such a strange body," the examiners expressed sympathy and allowed him to wrap his breasts and conceal his genitalia "like a woman" when he appeared at the exam location the following day. After a cursory examination the youth was immediately disqualified from conscription, labeled—in all likelihood—as belonging to Class D, a classification that encompassed "the 'physically or mentally deficient,' or those regarded as unsuitable for becoming a soldier, including criminals and dwarfs."[52]

As a site for evaluating masculinity, the conscription examination system played a key role in the "discovery" of hermaphroditism. The frequency of reports in *Hannannyokō* that revolve around the conscription exam casting doubt upon the prior sex classification of an individual reveals a state-sponsored concern with definitions of masculinity. Another case from 1907 is that of twenty-one-year-old Mankichi, the eldest son of an Awaji fisherman. Because he had been engaged in the fishing industry since early childhood, Mankichi possessed an extremely well developed "masculine" physique, and the exposed portions of his body were colored bronze from the sea and sun: he was "in no way inferior to a man." But when the conscription examination physicians caught sight of the parts of Mankichi's body that had been protected from the sun and sea, they became suspicious, for he had the "whiteness of a woman." Further examination revealed breasts like those of an eighteen-year-old girl. Yet even this discovery did not resolve matters, because Mankichi reported that he was unable to urinate except by standing like a man. Out of amazement, the examination officials tried to photograph Mankichi, but he adamantly refused their request. Though the article does not explicitly state the outcome of Mankichi's exam, it seems reasonable to assume that he did not pass—for if he had, he would not have been in a position to refuse the officials' efforts to photographically document his strangeness.[53] In the case of another youth who was discovered to be hermaphroditic, the reader is explicitly told "because he was not suitable as a man for conscription, he did not pass."[54]

Another revealing case from 1921 is that of an individual raised as a girl and then later granted malehood. As second daughter Tetsuko grew up, it became clear that there was something unusual about her. When she was a third-year elementary school student, an Imperial University surgeon declared it impossible to determine whether she was male or female and suggested that such a determination wait until she had further developed. After graduation she apprenticed at a clothing shop, did up her hair and wore makeup, and excited the neighborhood boys with her beauty. But when she was twenty-three years old, Tetsuko and her parents became concerned when she sprouted hair from her chest to her shins and her physique turned into that of a man. Another trip to a physician resulted in surgery that revealed her to be "a splendid young man." Tetsuko's name was changed to the masculine Tetsuo, and the physician's report was submitted to the Tokyo regional court, along with "pictures from when she was a woman and pictures after he became a man." Upon being declared legally male, Tetsuo went for his conscription exam but was exempted based on his height and weight.[55]

It is noteworthy that Tetsuo felt compelled to proffer himself for the exam. Smethurst explains that a villager who did not join the local military reserve association would be perceived as effectively "proclaim[ing] that he as an individual stood outside the collective hamlet membership."[56] Similarly, those who did not pass, or did not participate in, the yearly conscription examination failed a crucial rite of passage into manhood: "Passing as Class A was equivalent to becoming a full-fledged member of society *[ichininmae]*. . . . Those not picked to serve were deemed unworthy in some way—their weight or their height or something else about them was insufficient."[57] Participating in the local reserve association, attending the conscription examination, fulfilling military duty—all of these were essential for an individual to enter into male adulthood.[58] Tetsuo's experience shows that being granted the privileges of malehood necessitated taking up the attendant legal obligations as well. Perhaps Tetsuo could truly feel himself to be a man only by undergoing this essential coming-of-age ritual of masculinity.

UNEASY SEXUALITIES

Let us return to the story of Otsuju/Fuji and to the legal discourse on masculinity in which hermaphroditism played a part. In her youth, Fuji was a renowned beauty and the recipient of many amorous advances. Despite these affirmations of her femininity and her desirability as a woman, Fuji sought medical advice because she did not "feel like a woman." The examining physicians found it impossible to declare her either male or female and eventually resorted to surgery in order to solve the puzzle that Fuji presented. When surgical examination revealed the existence of testicles it was decided that she was male, and Fuji took the name Otsuju.

Now a twenty-one-year-old man, Otsuju cut his hair, discarded his skirts, and began drinking and being physically active. "A previously gentle woman, he completely transformed into a man of sturdy physique." Yet despite his marriage and successful transformation, Otsuju left his birth town, driven by the gossip surrounding his metamorphosis. After a decade of wandering, Otsuju arrived in Manchuria and—destitute and desperate—he turned to thievery. After the arrest in Dalian, an examining physician found that Otsuju had only "a superficial penis" and that no other male anatomy was present. It turned out that he was a woman after all—or, rather, "exactly like a woman." The reporter who publicized the story observed how strange it was that this person who had once been a woman now had a wife, and suggested that the reader feel pity for an individual whose engagement in crime was likely the result of such a bizarre disability.

The above account demonstrates three points related to the idea that sexual ambiguity precluded the ability to live in accord with societal strictures. First, it is noteworthy that hermaphroditism comes up a number of times in Gaikotsu's text in the context of criminality and prostitution. In the case above, the reporter explicitly linked Otsuju/Fuji's hermaphroditism with descent into a life of crime. In other cases the link is less explicit.

Both criminality and hermaphroditism could be seen as inexorably leading to a life outside respectable society and, once exposed, both therefore came under the purview of the state. In one case from 1919, Yuki, who was imprisoned on charges of larceny, fell in love with another female inmate, Haru, during her prison sentence. Upon her release, Yuki cut her hair, began dressing as a man, and took on the name Yukio. Yukio and Haru lived together as man and wife until Yukio was again arrested for thievery. Yukio's hermaphroditism was discovered when his "small stature and gentleness" made the authorities suspicious.[59] A 1907 account related the discovery that a geisha, although a "girl in appearance," possessed testicles instead of ovaries and a vagina but no uterus.[60] Yet another account from 1910 centers on the prostitution by Gen of his common-law wife, Chiyo, to a farmer. Upon arrest it was discovered that, "despite being a woman," forty-six-year-old Gen had cut off all her hair and had starting dressing in men's clothing about thirty years earlier.[61] Though this last story might, by early twenty-first-century standards, be seen as a case of transgenderism, in the early twentieth century it was classified as quasi-hermaphroditism *(jun-han'in'yō).*

The second point to note is that, in the case of individuals raised as women, their extraordinary beauty is often remarked upon when their hermaphroditism is discovered, as it was in the story of Otsuju/Fuji. It is clear that the authors wondered how someone so attractive to members of the "opposite" sex could turn out to be sexually ambiguous, particularly since such ambiguity led to the fearsome prospect that even the most beautiful of women could turn out to be male. A 1921 article told the story of a girl named Tomie who became a woman through surgery. Although Tomie was loved by all the youth of the village, when she was eighteen word got out that she possessed both male and female genitalia. Given the choice to become either a man or a woman through surgery, upon reflecting on her beauty, Tomie chose to become a woman.[62]

The final and most important point to be made is that a clear anxiety over nonsanctioned sexualities underlay a large number of these reports. The most obvious concern was that an individual living as a wife could turn out to be a man, therefore rendering the relationship homosexual. But there is also the question of how to determine whether a relationship is heterosexual or homosexual when one of the partners is neither male nor female.

Just as the writer of "A Woman Found to Have Testicles" remarks upon the oddity that Otsuju/Fuji had once been a woman but now had a wife, so too did the writer of "Prison Romance" comment that Yukio/Yuki had had the experiences of both being a wife and of having a wife. In two other cases reported above—those of Mankichi and of the Gunma youth—the reporter emphasized that the individual's genitalia had never been used for anything other than urination. In other words, the fact that Mankichi and the Gunma youth were both ambiguous was rendered a bit more palatable by making it clear that they had never had sexual intercourse—a possibility fraught with the potential for same-sex relations. One woman who, via surgery, was in the end able to become "truly female," had previously divorced her husband when she began to grow male parts. Though her anxiety over this sudden transformation would likely have been part of the decision to leave her husband, the divorce once again guarded against the possibility that two sets of male genitalia might come into contact.

Within his taxonomy, Gaikotsu's initial division was between psychic *(seishinteki* or *shinriteki)* and physiological *(seiriteki)* hermaphroditism. Although his stated purpose was to focus exclusively on physiological hermaphroditism, his category of quasi-hermaphroditism *(jun-han'in'yō)* included "masculine women" and "feminine men."[63] This interest in individuals whose reproductive anatomy was, to Gaikotsu, unproblematic indicates that, just as male and female were not clearly differentiable categories, neither were psychic and physiological. An excellent source for explaining this relationship and better placing it in the context of the issue of sexuality is the 1919 book *Research on Sexual Desire and the Study of Psychoanalysis,* written by Kyūshū Imperial University professor and medical scientist Sakaki Yasusaburō.

Like Gaikotsu, Sakaki suggested that psychic hermaphroditism belonged to a completely different category than "ordinary" hermaphroditism.[64] Sakaki's description of psychic hermaphroditism shared with its physiological counterpart a concept of entwined maleness and femaleness: he gave, as an example of psychic hermaphroditism, the young man who has "fallen into sexual perversion and who, even while being a man, senses 'mightn't I be a woman?'" His description is of individuals who perceive themselves as being the sex that is the "opposite" of their essential sex. Sakaki further cited the fact that male prostitutes *(kagema)* generally imitated women's taste in clothing and in posture. Rather than having the ambivalent anatomy of a physiological hermaphrodite, the ambivalence of psychic hermaphrodites was in the relationship between their "anatomical" sex and what they feel to be their "true" sex.

Sakaki claimed that male psychic hermaphrodites—who "think of themselves as women"—desired masculine men and that female psychic hermaphrodites desired gentle women. It is telling that the men who loved *kagema*—or any male psychic hermaphrodites—"did not lose their masculine souls." The reason that these men desired *kagema* and other feminine men was precisely for their resemblance to beautiful women. In other words, because the objects of their affections were not masculine men, but rather men who resembled women in physique and in behavior, the lovers of *kagema* were not considered hermaphroditic in any way.[65]

Sakaki clearly associated psychic hermaphroditism with same-sex desire; that is, with the case in which someone desired an individual of the sex they should only desire if they were of the "opposite" physiological sex. This perception of same-sex desire as signifying hermaphroditism is clear in the case of Etsu, the fourth daughter of a family in Saitama prefecture. Sixteen-year-old Etsu had been apprenticed at a temple since a young age. Though she had always had female genitalia, she also acquired a penis at puberty. When the doctor examining her learned that the "structure of her sexual desire was that of a man," Etsu was immediately diagnosed as male. Fourth-born daughter Etsu had the fortune to become second son Eppei; the local court was petitioned and the family register was altered.[66]

As Etsu/Eppei's case makes abundantly clear, there were multiple methods of classification available and in competition for predominance. Neither doctors, families, nor bureaucrats viewed psychic and physiological hermaphroditism as mutually exclusive; nor did they believe hermaphroditism to be as stable and as clearly delineated as Gaikotsu suggested. Etsu/Eppei was a hermaphrodite as much for a masculine desire for female sex partners as for ambiguous genitalia.

Gregory Pflugfelder has shown how various conceptualizations of psychic hermaphroditism were frequently used to explain same-sex desire. According to the trope of compound sex *(fukusei)*—one of several frameworks used by early twentieth-century Japanese sexologists to explain same-sex desire—all individuals were a composite of male and female; the designation "woman," for instance, signified a predominance of the feminine over the masculine rather than an exclusion of the masculine. A second strategy used to explain same-sex desire was that of inversion *(tōsaku)*, which posited that a man who, like women, was attracted to men was necessarily like a woman in other ways, both psychological and physiological. All such strategies endeavored to fit same-sex desire within the modern scientific two-sex paradigm of heterosexual attraction.[67] This was accomplished by rendering the couple as psychological, or even physiological, opposites on an uncompromisingly polarized male-female dichotomy.

Attempts to utilize the concept of hermaphroditism to explicate same-sex desire are well demonstrated in Pflugfelder's example of the case of a twenty-six-year-old male prosecuted in 1881 for seducing another man to act as the penetrator in anal intercourse. Rumors circulated that the young man was a male hermaphrodite because he passed as a woman and enjoyed being anally penetrated. Both he and his critics associated his role as the penetrated not with age, which was the standard under the older Edo aesthetics of *shudō*, but with his "feminine" identity. It was common that males perceived as feminine were the subject of speculation about hermaphroditism, as in the popular imagination, a feminine psyche in a presumably male body suggested that such a body might also be partially feminine.[68]

There are two articles on hermaphroditism in particular that I would like to address in this context. In the story of Gen, described briefly above, not one word is said about his physiology. We are merely told that Gen, "despite being a woman," had cut off all her hair and started dressing in men's clothing about thirty years earlier. Gaikotsu's commentary on the article that Gen was a male quasi-hermaphrodite seems to be based primarily on the fact that his sexual partners—his wife as well as various geisha—were all female. Some used the term "quasi-hermaphrodite" to reference individuals who, in our modern schema, would not fall into the category of "hermaphrodite," that is, individuals whose inner and outer organs are of the "same sex." What differentiated a quasi-hermaphrodite from a single-sexed person was discord between the sex of the reproductive organs and the outward appearance of the individual—for instance, masculine women and feminine men.[69] In other words, an individual who had both vagina and ovaries and who had neither penis nor testicles could still be classified as a hermaphrodite if he was read by the casual observer as being male—if the "ideal mode or model of existence" that he approximated was closer to the male than to the female.[70]

Even more revealing is the 1916 excerpt "A Factory Girl Has a Wife." Eight years after eldest daughter Fuji had left her village to work at a factory in Kyōto, she returned with short hair and Western-style clothing, accompanied by a young woman. The news that "Fuji had turned into a man and returned with his wife" soon became the talk of the town. What is notable here is Gaikotsu's commentary on this article: "As long as we assume that this is not a case of homosexuality, then [Fuji's] is a case of male pseudohermaphroditism."[71] However, because there is nothing in the article to indicate that Fuji is hermaphroditic rather than homosexual, this assumption makes sense only if hermaphroditism were *easier to accept* than same-sex desire.

At the same time that the military was engaged in defining a new masculinity for the battlefield, the medical jurisprudence profession was endeavoring to lay out ground rules for the very delineation of male from female. In both cases, judgment was being passed on the examinees as to their suitableness as men; in both cases, being declared "unsuitable" as a man cut off an individual from the full status, rights, and obligations that accompanied male citizenship.

This newly idealized masculinity would appear at first glance to be one based solely upon the form of the body. Yet medical jurisprudence discourse on hermaphroditism makes it clear that the body was not easily extricable from the psyche. Hermaphroditism was sufficient grounds to be declared unfit for duty—but what we might call same-sex desire was, ironically, sufficient grounds to be declared hermaphroditic—ironic because this very declaration served the purpose of redefining that desire as no longer "same-sex."

Because this chapter has examined normative sex in the context of the conscription exam, what has been primarily revealed is a concern about insufficient masculinity. Many early twentieth-century cultural commentators, however, expressed anxiety that *both* male and female were edging perilously close to one another. In a 1920 *Kaizō* (Reconstruction) article entitled "Contemporary Society and the Convergence of the Sexes," Nogami Toshio lamented the blurring of biological "distinctions . . . ordained by nature" and chastised those who argued that "the former spiritual and physical differences between the sexes no longer existed, and that men and women should proceed henceforth as one and the same entity."[72] Two years later, General Ugaki Kazushige proclaimed that men should be thoroughly masculine, that women should be thoroughly feminine, and that it was "imperative that we not allow the rise of neutered people who defy nature's grace."[73] Miyatake Gaikotsu, on the other hand, applauded as positive progress the fact that women and men were becoming more alike. Not only were men gradually softening and coming to resemble women, but women had become more spiritually and physically robust, "yielding mostly individuals who were close to men."[74]

Though cultural commentators may have debated the merits and demerits of ambiguously sexed individuals, the Japanese state apparatuses worked on the premise that rights and responsibilities were to be assigned based on a two-sex system. Asymmetrical attribution of those rights and responsibilities was justified via a rhetoric that afforded authentic citizenship only to those on the male side, based on presumed military service. This was accomplished by defining manhood as the scientifically quantifiable ability to engage in military service. This definition required, of course, the exclusion of all individuals who could not properly be classified as men. The Meiji state's use of scientific methods to determine who was fit for service led to the creation of new categories of people: the feeble, the physically deficient, the hermaphroditic. It is precisely because masculinity was in the process of being so strictly defined that such ambiguous entities became subjects of debate.

NOTES

1. Gaikotsu 1922, pp. 369–70.
2. Kano 2001, p. 30.
3. Lee et al. 2006, pp. 488–89.

4. Hirschauer 1997.
5. Silverberg 1991, p. 247.
6. Roden 1990, p. 43.
7. Pflugfelder 1999, p. 289.
8. Roden 1990, pp. 42–43; the Ugaki quotation is on p. 52.
9. Katz 1995.
10. Charlotte Furth notes a similar phenomenon in her discussion of gender anomalies in late Ming China. She suggests, "Gender transgression often merely serves to reinforce accepted social hierarchies by a controlled display of their inversion" (Furth 1988, p. 24).
11. Pflugfelder 1999, p. 151.
12. Gaikotsu 1922, p. 334; Robertson 2001 [1998], p. 50.
13. Gaikotsu 1922, p. 334.
14. Dreger 1998, p. 29.
15. For examples, see Kominami 1918, p. 493; Hiraga 1899, pp. 249–50; Sawada 1909, p. 184; Tanaka 1902, pp. 222–23.
16. Katayama 1897, pp. 144–46; Hiraga 1899.
17. "A Man with Menses" ("Gekkei arishi otoko") was originally published in the *Shizuoka Bulletin (Shizuoka kōhō)* in June of 1909 (Gaikotsu 1922, p. 373).
18. Yamamoto 1886, p. 125.
19. Yoshii 1887, p. 26.
20. Tanaka 1902, p. 229.
21. Hiraga 1899, p. 253.
22. Tanaka 1902, pp. 220.
23. Ishikawa 1900, pp. 380–81; Asada 1937, p. 414; Tanaka 1902, pp. 220–21.
24. Hiraga 1899, p. 251.
25. Takada 1917, p. 174.
26. Mita 1928, p. 264.
27. Frühstück 2003, pp. 3, 26.
28. Takaoka 2006.
29. Takaoka 2006, pp. 181–82.
30. Takaoka 2006, pp. 178–79.
31. Takaoka 2006, pp. 180–81.
32. Takaoka 2006, p. 178.
33. Frühstück 2003, p. 6.
34. Takaoka 2006, pp. 191, 178, 200.
35. Takaoka 2006, p. 186–87.
36. Arakawa 2006, pp. 17–18.
37. Smethurst 1974, pp. 92–94.
38. Frühstück 2003, p. 5.
39. Arakawa 2006, pp. 15–16; Takaoka 2006, p. 185.
40. Kitani 2003, pp. 4–5.
41. Arakawa 2006, p. 23.
42. Smethurst 1974, p. 5.

43. Smethurst 1974, pp. 5–6.
44. Smethurst 1974, pp. 8, 89–90.
45. Arakawa 2006, pp. 16–18, 30.
46. Asada 1937, p. 409.
47. Katō 1996, p. 15; Kitani 2003, p. 4.
48. Kuroda 1988.
49. Beishō Bōei Kenkyūjo 1912.
50. See Tanizawa and Yoshino 1986.
51. Gaikotsu 1922, pp. 371–72.
52. Frühstück 2003, p. 28. "Wearing an Underskirt to the Youth Inspection" ("Koshimaki o shite sōtei kensa") was initially published in various Tokyo newspapers in October of 1907.
53. "A Man Who Urinates Through a Vulva" ("Inmon yori hō'nyō suru otoko") was originally published in the *Osaka Report (Ōsaka Shinpō)* in May of 1907 (Gaikotsu 1922, pp. 370–71).
54. "A Man with Two Urethras" ("Futatsu no nyōdō aru otoko") was originally published in Gaikotsu's 1914 book *Curiosities (Ki).*
55. His height measured four *shaku,* six *sun* (Gaikotsu 1922, pp. 382–83). According to the 1873 Conscription Law, anyone whose height was under five *shaku,* one *sun* automatically failed the physical exam (Katō 1996, 46). "A Man Goes as a Bride ("Otoko ga oyome ni yukimasu") was originally published in the *Tōkyō Daily Newspaper (Tōkyō Nichinichi Shinbun)* in May of 1921.
56. Smethurst 1974, pp. 81–83.
57. Kitamura 1999, pp. 109–10.
58. Yamasaki 2001, p. 51; Kitamura 1999, p. 116; Kuroda 1988.
59. "Prison Romance" ("Gokuchō romansu") was originally published in the *Osaka Daily Newspaper* in February of 1919 (Gaikotsu 1922, pp. 381–82).
60. "A Male Geisha" ("Otoko no jo-geigi") was originally published in the *Osaka Daily Newspaper* in November of 1907 (Gaikotsu 1922, p. 372).
61. "A Woman Who Is a Common-law Husband" ("Naien no otto-taru onna") was originally published in the *Kobe Newspaper* in November of 1910 (Gaikotsu 1922, p. 374).
62. "A Woman Without a Uterus" ("Shikyū no naki onna") was originally published in the *Tōkyō Asahi Newspaper* in October of 1921 (Gaikotsu 1922, p. 383).
63. Gaikotsu 1922, p. 333.
64. Sakaki 1919, p. 182.
65. Sakaki 1919, pp. 187–88.
66. "From Nun to Monk" ("Ama yori sō e") was originally published in the *Osaka Asahi Newspaper* in October of 1908 (Gaikotsu 1922, 372).
67. Pflugfelder 1999, pp. 255–61.
68. Pflugfelder 1999, pp. 166, 167.
69. Gaikotsu 1922, pp. 332–33.
70. Robertson 1991, p. 89.

71. "A Factory Girl Has a Wife" ("Kōjo ga tsuma o motsu") was originally published in the *Osaka Daily Newspaper* in September of 1916 (Gaikotsu 1922, p. 375).

72. Roden 1990, p. 44; Nogami 1920, pp. 195, 204.

73. Roden 1990, p. 52; Ugaki 1968, p. 363.

74. Gaikotsu 1922, p. 388.

REFERENCES

Arakawa Shōji. 2006. "Heishi to kyōshi to seito." In *Dansei-shi 1: Otoko-tachi no kindai*, ed. Abe Tsunehisa, Obinata Sumio, and Amano Masako, 13–46. Nihon Keizai Hyōronsha.

Asada Hajime. 1937. *Saishin hōigaku*. Chūō Kōronsha.

Beishō Bōei Kenkyūjo. 1912. *Rikugun shintai kensa tetsuzuki chōkaisei no ken*. Beishō Bōei Kenkyūjo.

Dreger, Alice Domurat. 1998. *Hermaphrodites and the Medical Invention of Sex*. Cambridge, MA: Harvard University Press.

Frühstück, Sabine. 2003. *Colonizing Sex: Sexology and Social Control in Modern Japan*. Berkeley: University of California Press.

Furth, Charlotte. 1988. "Androgynous Males and Deficient Females: Biology and Gender Boundaries in Sixteenth- and Seventeenth-Century China." *Late Imperial China* 9, no. 2: 1–31.

Gaikotsu Miyatake. 1922. *Hannannyōkō*. In *Miyatake Gaikotsu Chosakushū*, vol. 5, ed. Tanizawa Eiichi and Yoshino Takao. Kawade Shobō Shinsha, 1986.

Hiraga Seijirō. 1899. *Kanmei hōigaku*. Kanehara Iseki.

Hirschauer, Stefan. 1997. "The Medicalization of Gender Migration." *International Journal of Transgenderism* 1, no. 1. Available at www.symposium.com/ijt/ijtc0104.htm.

Ishikawa Kiyotada. 1900. *Jitsuyuō hōigaku*. Nankōdō Shoten.

Kano, Ayako. 2001. *Acting Like a Woman in Modern Japan: Theater, Gender, and Nationalism*. New York: Palgrave.

Katayama Kunika. 1897. *Hōigaku teikō, zōho kaitei*. Shōnan Shoin.

Katō Akiko. 1996. *Heiekisei to kindai nihon—1868–1945*. Yoshikawa Kōbunkan.

Katz, Jonathon. 1995. *The Invention of Heterosexuality*. New York: Dutton.

Kitamura Riko. 1999. *Chōhei/sensō to minshū*. Yoshikawa Kōbunkan.

Kitani Toshio. 2003. *Shiryō: Chōhei shintai kensa kisoku: Chōhei to chōhei kensa*. Kitani Toshio.

Kominami Mataichirō. 1918. *Jitsuyō hōigaku*. Nankōdō Shoten.

Kuroda Toshio, ed. 1988. *Mura to sensō: Heijikei no shōgen*. Katsura Shobō.

Lee, Peter A., Christopher P. Houk, S. Faisal Ahmed, and Ieuan A. Hughes. 2006. "Consensus Statement on Management of Intersex Disorders." *Pediatrics* 118: 488–500.

Mita Sadanori. 1928. *Hōigaku taii*. Shōkadō Shoten.

Nogami Toshio. 1920. "Gendai seikatsu to danjo ryōsei no sekkin." *Kaizō* 3, no. 4: 185–204.
Pflugfelder, Gregory M. 1999. *Cartographies of Desire: Male-Male Sexuality in Japanese Discourse, 1600–1950*. Berkeley: University of California Press.
Robertson, Jennifer. 1991. "The Shingaku Woman: Straight from the Heart." In *Recreating Japanese Women, 1600–1945*, ed. Gail Lee Bernstein, 88–107. Berkeley: University of California Press.
———. 2001 [1998]. *Takarazuka: Sexual Politics and Popular Culture in Modern Japan*. Berkeley: University of California Press.
Roden, Donald. 1990. "Taishō Culture and the Problem of Gender Ambivalence." In *Culture and Identity: Japanese Intellectuals During the Interwar Years*, ed. J. Thomas Rimer, 37–55. Princeton: Princeton University Press.
Sakaki Yasusaburō. 1919. *Seiyoku kenkyū to seishin bunsekigaku*. Jitsugyō no Nihon Sha.
Sawada Junjirō. 1909. *Taiji ni okeru shiyō bunsei no genri oyobi yō*. Kōbundō.
Silverberg, Miriam. 1991. "The Modern Girl as Militant." In *Recreating Japanese Women, 1600–1945*, ed. Gail Lee Bernstein, 239–66. Berkeley: University of California Press.
Smethurst, Richard J. 1974. *A Social Basis for Prewar Japanese Militarism: The Army and the Rural Community*. Berkeley: University of California Press.
Takada Giichirō. 1917. *Hōigaku*. Kokuseidō Shoten.
Takaoka Hiroyuki. 2006. "Sensō to 'tairyoku': Senji kōsei gyōsei to seinen danshi." In *Dansei-shi 2: Modanizumu kara sōryokusen e*, ed. Abe Tsunehisa, Obinata Sumio, and Amano Masako, 176–202. Nihon Keizai Hyōronsha.
Tanaka Kōgai, with Sata Yoshihiko. 1902. *Iji danpen, zōtei 3 han*. Handaya Iseki.
Tanizawa Eiichi and Yoshino Takao, eds. 1986. *Miyatake Gaikotsu Chosakushū*, vol. 5. Kawade Shobō.
Ugaki Kazushige. 1968. *Ugaki Kazushige Nikki*, vol. 1. Misuzu Shobō.
Yamamoto Yoshio. 1886. *Saiban igaku*. Shimamura Risuke.
Yamasaki Hiroshi. 2001. "Kindai dansei no tanjō." In *Nihon no otoko wa doko kara kite, doko e yuku no ka?*, ed. Asai Haruo, Itō Satoru, and Murase Yukihiro, 32–53. Jūgatsusha.
Yoshii Iwatarō. 1887. *Saiban igaku ron*. Taihōkan.

12 Love Revolution

Anime, Masculinity, and the Future

Ian Condry

On 22 October 2008 a Japanese man by the name of Takashita Taichi set up an online petition to call for legal recognition of the right to marry an anime character. He offered the following explanation: "Nowadays, we have no interest in the three-dimensional world. If it were possible, I think I'd rather live in a two-dimensional world. But this doesn't seem likely with today's technology. So can't we at least have marriage to a two-dimensional character legally recognized? If that happens, my plan is to marry Asahina Mikuru."[1]

Within a week, roughly a thousand people had expressed their support for this unlikely project, and more than three thousand had done so by two months later. Many people mentioned the character they'd marry. Other signers took it as a curious joke. "I'd like to meet you distributing this petition in person," said one. A number of journalists and bloggers outside Japan picked up on the story, mostly with a tone of joking about "those wacky Japanese," but also with a hint of sociological wonderment. Given the tendency for young Japanese nowadays to delay marriage, doesn't this signify more trouble in the future? One online commentator even speculated on possible legal ramifications: "Will Mr. Takashita be paying royalties to comic book creators? Or does he consider copyright protection a form of 2D slavery?"[2]

The idea of developing relationships, or even falling in love, with characters in virtual worlds is not especially new, nor is it unique to anime (Japanese animated films and TV shows). Yet the debates surrounding Japan's obsessive fans, often identified as *otaku,* and their self-involved attachments are interesting for the ways they constitute a particular kind of argument about the future of masculinity and love. I am interested in the ways these debates revolve around a question of the value of private, inconspicuous consumption as a legitimate expression of manhood. Might this also reframe the ways we envision the politics of working toward a better future?

Part of what gives the debate about Japanese men and anime characters cultural specificity is not only the strange category of men known as otaku but also the notion of *moe*, loosely, a term for affectionate longing for 2-D characters, or, more accurately, a reference to an internalized emotional response to something, generally with no hope for a reciprocal emotional response.[3] In discussions about the cultural significance of anime in Japan, the idea of *moe* is also associated with larger questions about the ways fans relate to virtual characters and worlds, and in turn about the power of media producers vis-à-vis consumers. As we will see, for some writers, *moe* constitutes a "love revolution," that is, an example of pure love and a logical extension of the shift from analog to digital technology. For another theorist, *moe* symbolizes a postmodern, "database" form of consumption, whereby today's otaku reject the experience of the larger stories of anime and favor instead the piecemeal sampling of elements of 2-D characters.

What I find most provocative about the notion of *moe* is the assertion of the value of an internalized consumption. In this chapter I will map some of the ways this value is described as a means to think about whether it might point toward a new kind of politics. It at least offers an intriguing alternative to a focus on productivity as the measure of a man. Otaku raise the question, what kind of value arises from consumption, especially if that consumption is immaterial, a kind of affective attachment, simply, in a word, love?

OTAKU VERSUS SALARYMAN

In some ways, the image of the Japanese otaku as a geeky, obsessive, socially inept, technologically fluent nerd represents the polar opposite of the image of the gregarious, socializing breadwinner, the salaryman. If the salaryman is measured by his productivity, then the loner otaku, with his comic book collections, expensive figurines, and encyclopedic knowledge of trivia, can be viewed as a puzzle of rampant, asocial consumerism. Anthropologists James Roberson and Nobue Suzuki argue that until recently the dominant image of men and masculinity has been the "middle-class, heterosexual, married salaryman considered as responsible for and representative of 'Japan.'"[4] Their volume aims to dislocate the taken-for-granted salaryman image of manhood by providing instead a variety of "ethnographically-based understandings, which are sensitive to the reflexivities of the lived, constructed and embedded . . . diversity of masculinities in contemporary Japan."[5] Arguably, otaku represent part of that diversity, all the more so with their widening presence as a stock figure in Japanese popular culture, as portrayed, for example, in the film *Otaku no Video* (1991), directed by Mori; in the TV series *Paranoia Agent* (2004), directed by Kon; and in the Train Man phenomenon. Yet the discourses around *moe* and otaku aim not only to illustrate variety but also to establish different grounds for evaluating masculinity.

In the United States, the word *otaku* is often used simply to mean "serious anime fan" (with a fairly positive connotation), but in Japan the term carries a more complex range of meanings. In general, the word indicates people with an obsession for "geeky" realms of knowledge and activity, such as cult anime, manga (comic books), computer games, and military trivia. Images of the otaku in Japan tend to oscillate between negative portrayals focusing on antisocial behavior and potentially dangerous habits on one hand, or, on the other, positive portrayals of future-oriented, postindustrial sensibilities that contribute to the global strength of "cool Japan" products in popular culture. Of course, delving below the surface reveals that the debates surrounding otaku for the past twenty years complicate such a simple binary opposition. Scholars in Japan distinguish sharp generational differences among otaku-type cultures, and there are gender differences as well. Indeed, even the word *otaku* is a slight misnomer in the sense that people who identify as these kinds of devoted fans today tend to self-identify using the shortened version "ota" (katakana "wo" and "ta"), in part as a way of distinguishing themselves from older generations of otaku. Moreover, though the stereotypical gender of an otaku is male, there are also female otaku, who are sometimes called *fujoshi* (literally, "rotten girls"), a term commonly used for the young women devotees of "boys love" comic books, which portray beautiful boys in romantic relationships with each other. A friend of mine who organizes a club event for women obsessed with eyeglasses *(megane moe)* uses another term, noting that she is too old to be a rotten *girl,* and so prefers the term *kifujin,* a pun on "aristocratic lady" with the "woman" *(fu)* kanji character replaced with "rotten."

Given these variations, anime scholar Thomas Lamarre cautions against looking at otaku as a "bounded culture, psychology, or identity" and proposes instead that it makes the most sense to look at otaku activities in terms of labor.[6] The question for him is not who is or is not an otaku, but rather, what types of activities do otaku do, and do these activities constitute a kind of labor that can subvert, or provide an alternative to, capitalist control? In an analogous way, my look at discourses surrounding otaku is not meant to describe a bounded culture, identity, or psychology, but rather aims to explore the meanings of consuming the virtual and to see what this might reveal about how we tend to judge masculinity.

I would point out that many interpretations of otaku masculinity share a common assumption with salaryman masculinity, namely, that value (a man's worth) tends to be grounded in productivity. If we consider some examples of "bad otaku" and "good otaku," we can see that they are deemed significant because of what they produce. Some "bad otaku" are notable for producing violence or disturbing, sexualized media. In 1988, the term *otaku* gained notoriety after the arrest of a serial killer named Miyazaki Tsutomu, who was accused of being an avid consumer of slasher kiddie porn manga, though this turned out to be an exaggeration. Less extreme but more widespread are fans who produce their own comic books *(dōjinshi)*, many of which explore varieties of transgressive eroticism, as discussed by sociologist Sharon Kinsella.[7] More recently, in June 2008, a deranged twenty-five-year-old man attacked random people in the Akihabara section of Tokyo, killing seventeen, an act that, according to one commentator, "condenses the whole of the present" as a representative incident, in part because the murderer declared his intentions online prior to the act.[8]

In contrast, "good otaku" have been recuperated as leaders in the new information society, again because of what they produce. Self-proclaimed otaku Tajiri Satoshi, for example, developed the Pokémon handheld video game, which eventually led to a global media bonanza, including an animated TV series that airs in more than sixty countries and mountains of licensed merchandise.[9] As anthropologist Anne Allison describes, Tajiri's desire to use virtual worlds as a way to reconnect with other (living) people was part of what drove fascination with the Pokémon game, in which players could not complete their collections unless they communicated with others.[10] More recently, as Susan Napier discusses in this volume, the example of the Train Man *(Densha Otoko)* phenomenon shows how otaku can also be portrayed as sensitive diamonds in the rough, whose nerdiness can disguise a more generous manhood than that of drunken and emotionally distant salarymen. In each case, however, the measure of the man is his productivity: making a video game, producing animated films, or, in the case of Train Man, remaking himself. "Bad otaku," too, are evaluated based on what they make, whether it is violence or homemade media. Although a focus on otaku-type masculinities can help complicate the too-simple equation of manhood in Japan with the salaryman, we still remain wedded to a notion of manhood centered around productivity. But, of course, what makes otaku interesting and distinctive is their approach to consumption. Currently, an important way of talking about otaku consumption is to focus on their attraction to virtual characters.

CHARACTER *MOE*

The debates surrounding anime and otaku often revolve around the elusive concept of the "character" *(kyarakutaa)* as something that exists beyond its particular media instantiations. Takashita, the petitioner above, for example, does not say he wishes to marry "anime characters" per se, but rather 2-D *(nijigen)* characters. This is partly because many of these characters move fluidly across media. For example, the character he mentions, Asahina Mikuru, was introduced in a serialized "light novel" (i.e., young adult fiction) called *The Melancholy of Haruhi Suzumiya,* by Tanigawa Nagaru (2003), then remade as an anime TV series in 2006 by Kyoto Animation.

In other words, 2-D characters can originate in manga, anime, video games, light novels, drama CDs, toys, or figurines, then move across media over time; they tend not to be defined by a single medium. Characters not only move across media, but they also help explain the logic of a variety of activities related to anime. At anime conventions, many fans dress as their favorite characters in a practice known as "cosplay" (short for "costume play"). Fanzine artists reimagine their favorite characters in new, at times erotic, situations in their homemade works. In fact, Tokyo's fan-made manga convention called Comic Market is the largest annual event held in all of Japan, drawing almost half a million visitors over three days each August. Toy companies take advantage of the fans' love for characters by marketing all manner of figurines and other licensed merchandise. In short, characters move across media and even beyond media, and in this circulation they tend to develop an internal coherence despite being a fiction of virtuality. Anime as a cultural phenomenon derives much of its power from this circular motion of characters. In some ways, the concept of *moe* can be seen as an attempt to substantiate this reality of the virtual in terms of an emotional response.

Moe is the noun form of the verb *moeru,* "to burst into sprout, to bud," as a ripening green plant does as it develops into maturity. The kanji is written with the grass *(kusa)* radical on top and the character for "bright, cheerful" underneath (i.e., the sun and moon together). The kanji character thus acts as a visual reference to the fact that the *moe* attraction is often bestowed upon 2-D characters who are on the verge of maturing into young women. *Moe* does not refer to girls per se, but to the yearning desire to care for, or nurture, them. In this sense it is also a pun on *moeru* ("to boil, to burn," written with a different kanji), which can be viewed as a reference to a heated sensual desire as well. The term *moe* is troubling to some in Japan, because it apparently centers on the inappropriate desire by relatively grown men for (imaginary) immature girls.[11]

Yet others argue that *moe* should be seen in terms of purity, and that the characters' youth evokes innocence, not depravity. As one Japanese college student explained to me, *moe* isn't about sex; rather, it's a light, warm, pleasant emotional response, "feeling strawberry," he proposed, using pseudo-English. Media studies professor Okuno Takuji describes it thus:

> Originally, *moe* referred to the affectionate feelings *[renjō]* that today's otaku held for female manga and anime characters. The objects of that affection were generally beautiful young girls *[bishōjo]*, but the roots were in sisterlike characters, for example, Maetel in *Galaxy Express 999*, or Mine Fujiko from Monkey Punch's *Lupin III*. Although these characters were always intimates, their positions were quite separate, which meant that affection could not be expressed directly. *Moe*, then, was that hazy *[moyamoya]* feeling. Now, men with that *moe* feeling collect posters and doll figures as the object of their affection. In other words, they take that 2-D desire for the opposite sex and bring it into the 3-D world (or, sometimes, they confuse the two worlds).[12]

Okuno points to the complexity of yearnings even within the virtual worlds, such that attraction was often balanced with a sense that the characters needed to be protected and cared for. The group of otaku who founded the anime studio Gainax, for example, also produced a video game with precisely this theme of nurturing, whereby the goal of the game was to raise a young princess to maturity.[13] Yet I argue that the *moe* feeling should not be seen as a confusion of the virtual worlds and real worlds, but rather a questioning of the relationship between the two, or perhaps whether there really is a distinction between virtual and real.

A book called *Hating the Otaku Wave*, a published conversation between otaku defenders and detractors, extends the discussion of *moe* and love. In one section they debate the idea that what *moe* offers is "pure love" *(jun'ai)* that exceeds what can be experienced with a real woman. One skeptic notes that when you type *moe* into an Internet search engine, most of the hits are pornographic. Doesn't that mean that *moe* is mostly a euphemism for pornography? Otaku writer Uminekozawa Melon says no.

> Even within pure love, can't there be an element of eroticism? . . . It's absolutely possible to feel pure love for a 2-D character. I've had 2-D characters that I'd think about, and like so much, that I couldn't escape from their spell. . . . Inside me, that character was god. I really believe that's true *moe*. I might even be considered a *moe* fundamentalist. . . . The feeling of *moe* is exactly the same as love *[koi]*.[14]

The writer justifies the legitimacy of this kind of love in terms of a deep inner feeling. In many ways this echoes a statement by the famed anime director Miyazaki Hayao, who recalled seeing the anime feature film *Legend of the White Serpent* in 1958, when he was a senior in high school.

> I have to make an embarrassing confession. I fell in love with the heroine of a cartoon movie. My soul was moved. . . . Maybe I was in a depressed state of mind because of the [university] entrance exams, or [maybe the cause was] my undeveloped adolescence, or cheap melodrama—it's easy to analyze and dismiss it, but the meeting with *Legend of the White Serpent* left a strong impression on my immature self.[15]

Put this way, the desire for an animated character seems quite reasonable. Anime scholar Helen McCarthy, who translated Miyazaki's quotation above, even argues that this moment was instrumental in shifting the director's attention away from manga and toward anime. Yet we can also hear in Miyazaki an element of embarrassment. He fears he was "immature," his feeling may have been a symptom of a larger distress (depression), or perhaps it was simply something "cheap" and therefore superficial. Nevertheless, the feeling made a deep impression on him. If one's relationship with virtual characters is deeply moving, and if it can influence the course of people's careers, why should there be any prejudice against this kind of attachment? One reason is that it seems to propose a rejection of society and more traditional measures of manhood.

RADIOWAVE MAN (DENPA OTOKO)

A writer who uses the pen name Honda Tōru takes the idea of *moe* farther than most. He proclaims that *moe* represents nothing less than the dawning of a love revolution. Taking the title Radiowave Man (Denpa Otoko), he deliberately positions himself in contrast to the cultural phenomenon of Train Man, another popular image of contemporary otaku manhood. In the *Train Man* story, the otaku becomes a man by shedding his otaku awkwardness and getting the girl in real life. Honda argues in his book *Radiowave Man* that Train Man is a travesty.[16]

According to Honda, otaku should not be ashamed of their alternative standards of manhood. An otaku should be proud of his masculinity, even if he is enamored only of fictional 2-D characters with big eyes, beribboned hair, and short skirts. Indeed, Honda views young men's fascination with 2-D characters as the natural evolution of mankind. He even declares it a revolution comparable to that of the Meiji Restoration in 1868, when America's "black ships" forced the opening of Japan to foreign trade and led to the downfall of the military government and to the restoration of imperial rule.

> For people who have grown up with the "common sense" that love equals the 3-D world, it may be impossible to convey the point I'd like to make: 3-D love is like the Edo era's shogunate government. Throughout that period, everyone thought that the shogunate would continue forever. It was almost impossible to imagine another kind of government, and floating in this vague understanding, all of a sudden, the black ships appeared. . . . Now, the love revolution *[ren'ai kakumei]* expanding in Japan is easiest to understand in terms of the Meiji Restoration. For a long time, everyone expected the commonsense belief that "love = 3-D world" would continue, but it has begun to be destroyed by the appearance of the *moe* phenomenon.[17]

Honda adds that people who do not fall for 2-D characters are behind the times. He makes his case by construing history as a linear evolution defined by technology—a point regarding otaku discourses that Lamarre notes as well.[18] According to Honda, digital technologies such as cameras and plasma screen TVs were initially regarded as lacking "warmth" and "reality"; professional photographers, for example, found fault with digital photos, and some nightclub DJs rejected CDs in favor of vinyl records. In the end, Honda reminds us, everyone came to embrace the digital, and, he says, the same thing will happen with love. Just as VCRs (analog) gave way to DVD players (digital), so too will men give up on the analog world of real women in favor of the digital world of characters. While it might be easy to dismiss such proclamations, I would argue that unpacking some of these notions of manliness may be helpful for seeing the contours of normative masculinity. Certainly, *moe* masculinity runs afoul of the society's standards of measuring men by their productivity, but *Radiowave Man* speaks to a broader concern among men generally.

FORGIVING UNSUCCESSFUL MEN

One way to read Radiowave Man's manifesto is not primarily as a rejection of relationships with real women, but perhaps more importantly as a defense of failed men. This echoes what Michael Kimmel calls a "two-sided posture" necessary for masculinity studies: "One must engage masculinity critically as ideology, as institutionally embedded within a field of power, as a set of practices engaged in by groups of men. And yet given the contradictory locations experienced by most men, men not privileged by class, race, ethnicity, sexuality, age, physical abilities, one must also consider a certain forgiveness for actual embodied men as they attempt to construct lives of some coherence and integrity in a world of clashing and contradictory filaments of power and privilege."[19] This helps explain why so much otaku-oriented anime contains characters who suggest a problematization of masculinity, for example, the many troubled male protagonists who essentially reimagine the hero as vulnerable, conflicted, and anything but all-powerful. Susan Napier sees this in the fourteen-year-old character Shinji, a boy in the mid-1990s *mecha* (giant robot) TV series *Neon Genesis Evangelion:* "His conflict with his father, issues with women, and generally antiheroic attitude toward saving the Earth lead up to the rich portrait of full-fledged neurosis."[20] Ultimately, however, Shinji is the hero of the series, and his weaknesses prove instrumental in reshaping the destiny of mankind, partly through passive acquiescence, but also with a sense that developing a new future requires alternative styles of heroic action. Even passive, insecure, dubiously virile warriors have a place in saving the world in many anime series.

In other words, if the salaryman stood for one model of Japan's economic productivity, I would argue that otaku represent a new form of manhood through consumption that offers an alternative vision of value, one that can provide new insight into the contemporary era. For example, an otaku perspective on masculinity reminds us of the vulnerability experienced by many men who live outside the dominant ideal of male success. Not all men get the good education, the good job (and salary), the loving wife and children. What then? It makes sense to find alternative sources of value in one's life, to rationalize alternative modes of existence as engaged, rewarding, and meaningful. Otaku are by no means unique in this regard. In her book on Japan's military, Sabine Frühstück notes that for many male service members, "joining the Self-Defense Forces is marked by a sense of defeat in some area of their lives," a failed college entrance exam, a low-income background that precludes costly training at technical schools, a feeling of disappointment in one's job situation, or an inability to find meaningful work. Joining the SDF offers a new chance. But because SDF soldiers are prohibited from engaging in combat missions, the men are also closed off from a sense of accomplishment that might come with valor on the battlefield, the traditional measure of value for the military man. Frühstück shows how, nevertheless, the service uses gender politics to create "true men" and a new kind of "postwarrior heroism" that does not depend on courageous action in battle, but rather places value in individual sacrifice and personal betterment through training.[21]

Similarly, otaku may be unsuccessful in the salaryman's world, but the public discussion of the legitimacy of love for anime characters also points to realms in which actively debating which character you would marry is of real value. The online petition created a space for many to make similar claims of love and commitment to virtual characters. Other online message boards facilitate a similar kind of community building around emotions evoked by 2-D characters. In other words, what makes the debate about otaku masculinity interesting is not only the expansion of varieties of manhood, but the challenge of rethinking how productivity and consumption offer alternative modes for evaluating contemporary men.

CONSUMING THE POSTMODERN DATABASE

We can extend our consideration of *moe* consumption through a look at philosopher Azuma Hiroki's claim that new otaku-type cultures *(otakukei bunka)* reflect a new orientation toward viewing the world as a large database. He contrasts his perspective with that of manga artist and critic Ōtsuka Eiji, who argues that what fans consume when they buy merchandise related to an anime or manga is a piece of "grand narrative" *(ōki na monogatari).*[22] According to Ōtsuka in 2004, revisiting an argument he made years earlier, stories have replaced ideologies in guiding our understanding of social action.[23] For Ōtsuka, the power of media arises from the productivity of creators, and when fans relate to characters they are engrossing themselves in pieces of a larger narrative world in which the characters live. Clearly, however, when otaku fans express a desire to marry the anime character they love, they are making a bid to recontextualize the worlds in which they exist. Azuma theorizes this as a shift away from consuming a "story" and toward dipping into a "database."

We might view this debate in terms of the different kinds of value that arise from productivity versus consumption. Ōtsuka recognizes the central place of characters in understanding contemporary anime fandom, but, as a writer himself, he emphasizes the critical judgment of producers in developing characters with a breath of life and stories that evoke a contemporary urgency. Azuma, by contrast, notes that otaku tend to be fascinated by small details, diverse elements of overall projects, regardless of their connection to the internal logic of anime stories. Azuma offers a diagram to clarify the distinction between himself and Ōtsuka. For Ōtsuka, a "tree model" represents the relationship between original story and consumer. The deep level of the "grand narrative" can be expressed on the surface through a variety of media ("small stories," e.g., specific manga, anime, games, and novels) that leads to the consumer's eye. As Azuma says in the diagram, the subjectivity of the "I" is "determined by going through the story." This is similar to how Susan Napier uses the story of Evangelion as a way of grasping the leading male character Shinji's commentary on masculinity. Napier draws a conclusion about Shinji based on how he develops through the whole story in order to interpret the anime series' larger messages.

In contrast, Azuma proposes a "database model" of consumption, whereby individual consumers actively choose elements of the anime that they feel are most important, regardless of whether they are central to the overall "story" designed by the producers. Azuma views the subjectivity of the "I" (and eye) as determinant. "The 'I' extracts the story," he says, and the arrow of causality runs from the eye to the deeper database. In this regard, Azuma takes a different lesson from the anime series *Neon Genesis Evangelion*. He says that the series was important not because of its narrative but because of the database of elements it presented.[24] His use of the term "database" is meant to highlight the diversity of elements that comprise the different characters (e.g., the neurotic and inarticulate Shinji, the brash and self-assertive Asuka, or the affectless but powerful Rei) and the world setting in which they interact. Audience members frustrated by the inconsistencies of the narrative may be missing the larger point, Azuma implies, by not focusing on the details and relating to them individually. As proof of this kind of consumption, which Azuma relates to *moe*, he describes the sensation that arose around another character that became popular before even having a story.

According to Azuma, the appearance of a character called DiGiCharat (Dejikyaratto) marked a symbolic moment in the development of the *moe* phenomenon; it exposed the new modes of masculinity arising from this database style of otaku consumption. The character's name combines "digital," "character," and "cat," though it is more commonly referred to as Dejiko.

Dejiko was created in 1998 to be the mascot for a video game magazine.[25] This character had absolutely no story and no background associated with it—I mean, her. Gradually, her popularity increased. She got her big break when she appeared in a TV commercial in 1999. By 2000 she had her own anime series, and she later appeared in novels and merchandise. Azuma says that her character elements, not the story behind her, are what led to her popularity. The proof is that she grew popular before a story was created. Dejiko's elements include a maid outfit, cat ears, mittens, a tail, and bells in her hair. Azuma relates the rise of Dejiko to a larger phenomenon, that of otaku who compile online databases of imaginary characters from anime, manga, video games, and other media, using keywords to identify different elements of each character.

One thing that makes the *moe* debates about anime instructive is that they locate the value of characters not in the producer's intentions but in the consumers' uptake. The importance of understanding varieties of consumption, and the ways these interpretive fan practices may speak more broadly to gender, can be seen in a consideration of Judith Butler's notion of performativity. She says her notion of performativity grew from thinking about Franz Kafka's short story "Before the Law": "There the one who waits for the law, sits before the door of the law, attributes a certain force to the law for which one waits." Her point is that in this situation the law gains its force not from an external authority but from an internal anticipation. By extension she asks, "whether we do not labor under a similar expectation concerning gender, that it operates as an interior essence that might be disclosed, an expectation that ends up producing the very phenomenon it anticipates."[26] Performativity locates the source of power in gender relations at least partly in our suppositions about what the future might hold. This brings into focus the importance of subjective analytics, which through recursive actions reinforce (or subvert) gendered patterns. This offers one way of understanding the value of internalized consumption.

Yet Butler also draws attention to the need to link this internal anticipation back to the public world. We have to ask, how does this reframe the contexts in which we imagine social action? Azuma's database idea explains why DiGiCharat is a pivotal example for contemporary shifts in viewing masculinity and value in terms of consumption rather than production. DiGiCharat was created by combining elements of *moe*—cat ears, mittens, bells, maid outfit—in a way that drew attention, not to some underlying original story, but to a sense of attraction within the consumer. But the consequences for a performativity that acts in some way on the larger social world seems only weakly defined in Azuma's model. The consequences of consumption seem to vanish into a dark well of otaku emotionality, with little impact on the real world of women and men. This is related more broadly to otaku theorizing regarding the aesthetics of the anime image.

Thomas Lamarre offers a helpful discussion of Azuma's emphasis on image and information over narrative. In considering several otaku commentators, including the neo-pop artist Murakami Takashi, the Gainax founder Okada Toshio (the self-proclaimed "otaking"), Azuma, and others, Lamarre identifies common threads through what he calls the "Gainax discourse," such as a shared sense of the operation of the anime image and of anime aesthetics. When otaku go frame by frame to observe the jet trails of missiles or the space battles of giant robots, their obsessive attention to detail, with little regard to the overall story, is representative of a particular approach to aesthetics in which the anime image becomes "a non-hierarchized field of information": "In other words, the distributive visual field involves a breakdown in perceptual distance, which results in a purely affective relation to the image. Anime breaks out of its television frame, and the distance between viewer and image collapses into a moment of affect."[27] The Gainax discourse argues for a breakdown in the guiding power of the narrative, as well as a parallel breakdown in the hierarchy of producers (there is no single creator), a breakdown in the hierarchies between fan and producer, and a radical break with definable subject positions.[28] This relates to our original question about otaku and modes of masculinity by locating the power of the character not in the vision of the creators—that is, as arising from productivity—but rather in the ex post facto consumption by, and devotion of, fans. Yet this is where the emotion seems to end, namely, in the eye ("I") of the otaku interpreter. But if there is no connection back into the story, and the meaning of the character is embodied only in the feelings of individual otaku who have an affective response, we reach a theoretical dead end, a *moe* cul-de-sac.

REDISCOVERING SOCIAL CONTEXT

A path out of this emotional never-never land comes from attending to some of the ways the social context is present, but insufficiently attended to, by those who analyze *moe* as a purely internalized response. By explaining consumption in terms of a disembodied eye, Azuma loses sight of the embeddedness of the "database" in larger social worlds. Azuma might have a better argument about the radical subjectivity arising from otaku love for characters if otaku were to fall in love with characters they created themselves. But the objects of *moe* fascination are public, and usually well-known, characters, at least within particular communities of fans. Among those who signed the petition calling for the legal recognition of marriage to anime characters, the many people who mentioned the character they'd marry drew from well-known examples. *Moe* is not just a feeling, it is also a way of talking about one's feelings, and, without having to give much explanation, sharing the glow of affection with others who might have similar feelings. So, too, with Dejiko. One could argue that she had a "story" of sorts before the development of her anime and manga serials. When fans became interested in Dejiko, they inserted her into their own personal histories of caring for, or at least being interested in, characters. The growth of her popularity is the story, the background, the lived presence that gives the *moe* feeling substance as a social phenomenon.

In addition, the theory of otaku consumption makes it easy to conclude that tuning in to the details of the anime results in tuning out society, whether in the form of real women or in the broader, shared narratives aimed for by producers. Takashita (the marriage petitioner) and Radiowave Man both give that impression by saying that they have no interest in the 3-D world and real women. This is the common image of the otaku as withdrawing from society into a world of affective consumption. But Takashita and Radiowave Man are also making their arguments publicly to a broader social world. Takashita did not only want to instigate a legal change; he wanted to announce the name of the character he would marry. (I suspect the latter motive was the greater impetus for his petition.) "Individual" *moe* feeling is debated in many online realms in which fans can discuss the merits of different characters. The message board 2channel (*nichan,* 2ch.net), the social networking site Mixi, and video sharing sites are just a few examples of places where various flavors of affective 2-D desire can be discussed. To say that this is somehow separate from the "3-D world" makes no sense.

Consider, for example, the video sharing site Nico Nico Dōga (www.nicovideo.jp), which in June 2008 was at the center of a minor *moe*-related scandal. Japan's Imperial Household Agency expressed dismay when a video clip showing fan-made images of the current seventeen-year-old princess Mako starting gaining attention online.[29] Amateur artists had transformed her into an anime character, complete with music videos. Significantly, what makes Nico Nico Dōga a huge phenomenon in Japan is that it combines the accessibility of YouTube with the public commentary of an online message board. Visitors can add their comments to low-resolution user-uploaded videos, and the comments scroll by as the video plays. The adoring messages posted by some users were then reported on in Japan as an example of "Princess Mako *moe*" (Mako-sama *moe*).

Although this can be read as creating a 2-D image detached from the real-world princess, one can find an alternative reading by attending to the commentary that scrolls by as the "*moe* images" appear. At one point in the video, the user commentary scrolling by roughly translates as: "This is trouble for the Imperial Household Agency . . . A recommendation from Central Office of Moe . . . To the Emperor, banzai!" with ASCII art too (crying? laughing? both?). It is the urge toward public display among a community of peers who care that makes the *moe* phenomenon significant.

In sum, although the *moe* feeling may be internalized, it is connected to a broader range of politics and social settings. The arguments of Radiowave Man for his preference for 2-D characters over 3-D women and Azuma's emphasis on the radical immanence of the anime image can both be seen as gambits for encouraging society to respect the depth of otaku emotionality and to grant their consumption some respect. With the marriage petition as well, what may be most striking is not the desire to move into a 2-D world, but rather the desire to have love for 2-D characters *legally* recognized by broader society. After all, it is difficult to imagine that much would change in a relationship between an otaku and a 2-D character if they could somehow be married. What might change is that people who fall in love with characters could gain a measure of societal acceptance. This alters the way we should interpret the debates about otaku and masculinity. Rather than seeing the assertions of the value of *moe* affect as a rejection of real women and the 3-D world, we should view it instead as a plea for accepting a new kind of relationship between consumption as feeling (as love) and society. This gesture toward a new kind of politics may well extend beyond the world of otaku as well, as we will see in the final example.

MASCULINE CONSUMPTION IN *THE GIRL WHO LEAPT THROUGH TIME*

The anime director Hosoda Mamoru is not an otaku, nor does he make films aimed at otaku, yet one of his recent feature films offers a portrait of masculinity with intriguing parallels to the discourses surrounding *moe*. These parallels point toward the usefulness of seeing otaku discourses, and discourses about audiences more generally, as potentially revealing of larger trends in society. We can see this in Hosoda's rationale for reinterpreting a classic sci-fi story (and live-action film) as an anime for today's youth.

When I asked Hosoda what he thought of the discussions of *moe* and otaku sensibilities, he was dismissive. He viewed *moe* as a rationalization used by otaku to willfully misunderstand what a creator is aiming for and to value instead their own misinterpretations.[30] He sees the storytelling of his films as the opposite of otaku "database" consumption. Even so, over the course of several interviews with Hosoda, I was struck by something. Although Hosoda rejects the value of *moe,* he nevertheless relies on a strikingly similar logic for understanding contemporary Japanese youth culture. This parallel logic outside the realm of otaku suggests that *moe* may reflect something characteristic of broader society. Specifically, when Hosoda updated and reinterpreted the sci-fi story from the 1960s, he altered the motivation of the leading male character in a way that depends on recognizing the value of a personal, internalized consumption. Yet the movie as a whole also works its way out of the *moe* cul-de-sac by balancing this urge toward consumption with a recognition of the importance of broader social relationships.

In an interview I conducted on 30 March 2006, at Madhouse anime studios not far from Ogikubo Station in Tokyo, Hosoda discussed his forthcoming film, *The Girl Who Leapt Through Time (Toki o kakeru shōjo).* In particular he noted the challenges of reinterpreting a story that had already been remade seven times since the 1960s. The story originated as a novella by Tsutsui Yasutaka, one of the "three greats" in Japanese science fiction.[31] It revolves around three characters: a high school girl and her two male friends. The premise is this. While cleaning up the science lab after school, the girl hears a strange sound and then discovers a broken beaker. Suddenly, mysterious smoke causes her to lose consciousness. She awakes unharmed but soon notices a change. She finds herself leaping backward through time, reliving the previous day and its dangerous, though ultimately harmless, events (earthquake, fire, and car accident, for example). With the help of the two boys, she gradually unravels the mystery, discovering that one of her male friends is in fact a time traveler from the future who mistakenly gave her the power to leap through time. The 1967 short story, the well-known 1983 live-action film version, and Hosoda's 2006 anime version all share an emphasis on the anxieties associated with high school crushes, the love triangle between the girl and two boys, and the sadness surrounding the boy's inevitable return to the future.

How did Hosoda change the characters? In Tsutsui's original story, the boy from the future travels to the present to collect plants that no longer exist in his time and to help society as whole. We learn that although the boy is young, he is also a PhD scientist who needs the plants to make medicines. As such, the original character reflects early postwar Japan's anxieties concerning environmental degradation. By the late 1960s, the awareness of mercury poisoning in Minamata was just one example of the ways economic growth seemed to be producing a variety of ecological and health threats.[32] Tsutsui's story portrays youth as instrumental in tackling societal problems. We can also note in the original story that manliness arises from the youth's productivity, specifically his creation of medicines from specific material resources.

What makes Hosoda's time traveling boy different is that he comes from the future not because he is on a quest to help society, but rather to consume something. This attitude has strong parallels to the otaku notion of *moe*. Hosoda constructs an alternative vision of the future, one that hinges on a different understanding of the sources of social change. Hosoda explained,

> My idea was this. For people like us, born in the '60s and '70s, the future was going to go on and improve, if not by us, then by people around us, like the Apollo Mission group. The idea of the tube going through the air is about infrastructure and the way an organized society is necessary to accomplish that. It is a picture of a big society working together, and how that will happen. But today, it's more like young people have individual pictures of the future, not collective visions of the future.
>
> If today's young people have much more individual pictures of the future, how would that affect the reason the boy came back? He won't come back for plants. I imagine that he will come back for a more individual reason, something to do with his inner self *[kokoro]*. So, in this version of *The Girl Who Leapt Through Time*, why did the boy from the future come back? To see a painting.

Intriguingly, the painting itself was not designed for public display, but rather was made as an object for personal reflection. In particular, Hosoda imagined the painting as a Buddhist picture painted "perhaps four hundred or five hundred years ago, say in the Muromachi period, though it really isn't specified in the film."

Such Buddhist paintings are not meant to be shown in public. Rather, their purpose is to be an object of meditative reflection, to soothe the heart during troubled times. Notably, in the Muromachi period, the country was torn by ongoing wars. "The boy comes back to see a painting as a way to overcome the horror of his times." What makes the boy in Hosoda's films a particular kind of man, and thereby a particular model of masculinity, is not that he produces something, but that he consumes something in a way that will make him a better person, more at ease in his heart, even though he faces a world filled with trouble. In some ways this seems a tragic way to view the future (and the present), because it implies that there is no hope of making the world a better place. But perhaps there is another perspective.

Remember that the latter half of the twentieth century brought the triumph of technology in the moon shot missions, but also the potential for global nuclear annihilation. In addition, neoliberalism, which holds the free market as the best arbiter of value and productive efficiency, promises economic growth for all, yet it also explains away current suffering for an anticipated greater good. In both we can see a potentially dangerous paternalism in the desire to control society's future direction. In contrast, might it not make sense that each individual imagines his or her own future and seeks out those moments and spaces of aesthetic satisfaction that can calm the troubles within his or her own heart? I would argue that there is something potentially heroic in the conscientious consumer, such as the boy who travels to see a painting that can soothe his heart, because this consumer rejects a paternalistic, and potentially devastating, self-righteousness embedded in the desire to make the world as a whole a better place. If so, perhaps the masculine sensibility described by Hosoda, which from one perspective emphasizes a narcissistic worldview, might well entail a positive, even progressive, politics. At least we can note that this logic reframes the meaning of politics away from the top-down forces of governmental control toward a more distributed, self-guided notion of easing the heart's troubles as a means to making a better world. Even so—and this is an important point—for all the film's emphasis on finding one's own path and controlling one's own destiny, ultimately the boy from the future finds solace not in the painting but in the friendships he develops with the girl and the other boy. The enduring commitment to a community of peers soothes the pain in his heart and makes the trip to our present worthwhile. In this sense, Hosoda's film works its way out of the *moe* cul-de-sac by incorporating a logic of social context, and the value of social relationships with small groups of friends is part of what adds value to a kind of internalized, affective consumption.

It is easy to dismiss as ludicrous a petition calling on society to legally recognize marriage to an anime character. One can see it as a joke, as some signers did, or one might express concern for men who are so pathetic that they can only hope to have relationships with virtual characters. What is lost in such reactions, however, is a recognition that the range of discussions about otaku and *moe* attractions provides a perspective on thinking more generally about the impacts of virtual worlds and the value of an internalized, immaterial consumption. For one thing, we can observe how evaluating masculinity tends to emphasize men's productive capacities rather than their consumer experiences. Even when we evaluate consumerism, we tend to emphasize the ways it may contribute to economic growth; our spending is seen as productive in the sense that it enables businesses to keep investing, furthering the cycle of market expansion. The online commenter who wondered whether marriage to a 2-D character would require royalties to be paid to its creator is a perfect example of the urge to translate immaterial, internalized consumption into something outwardly productive. This is just one of many examples of the ways the standards for evaluating manhood depend on a logic of productivity. Otaku may offer an alternative style of manhood compared to salarymen, yet both "good otaku" and "bad otaku" tend to be held up to standards of creating things, whether commodifiable goods or havoc. The idea of relating to anime primarily in terms of "love" can be aptly be viewed as a gesture toward a different basis for understanding value, consumerism, and media. So, too, the debate between Ōtsuka and Azuma can be interpreted as a way of wrestling with divergent understandings of how people should relate to media content. In some ways their debate reproduces this conflict between valuing producers' grand narratives and consumers' piecemeal sampling. Both, however, might be faulted for construing their conclusions too narrowly, that is, seeing them primarily as saying something about anime, manga, and otaku.

Hosoda's *The Girl Who Leapt Through Time* shows that a larger process may be at work, and we can catch a glimpse of this process by considering the transformative power of art. Art's power is not aimed at building better bridges or rocket ships, but rather pointed inward to ease the conflicts within our hearts, and to overcome the horror of our times by giving us objects upon which to reflect. This is media as meditative tool, not potential investment. Put that way, we can see parallels between Radiowave Man, Azuma, and the boy Hosoda creates in his film. Their sense of themselves lacks a feeling—a *moe* "strawberry" feeling, perhaps— that might make them more whole. For us to recognize the varieties of masculinities, we may also need to recognize the varieties of masculine failures. In this respect, theories of otaku's emotional attachments to virtual objects are useful for proposing an alternative to thinking about manhood in terms of productivity.

But one of the things that makes looking at otaku important, even for those of us who do not consider ourselves otaku, is that it offers a means of seeing the variety of ways consumption of the "virtual" has real-world substance. It is the desire for public recognition and acceptance that is shared across Takashita, Radiowave Man, Azuma, and others. Quite the opposite of a rejection of society, this is rather an affirmation of the importance of social acceptance. In this, our otaku brethren may not be so different from the rest of us. Or perhaps there is a little bit of otaku in all of us. In any case, the tendency to view otaku as separate, wacky, or simply weird tends to obfuscate the ways otaku attitudes can reveal ourselves. In our rush to ridicule those pathetic fans who would rather marry an anime character than go through the trouble of relating to real others, we risk reinforcing a too simple naturalness of social mores. In this respect, the workings of anime and masculinity can best be understood if we move beyond thinking of otaku as a bounded culture or identity, to think more deeply instead about the ways *moe* consumption may be part of a broader range of social transformations. More personal understanding of (possible) futures (rather than one future for us all) combined with a variety of proposals supporting the value of affective consumption as a legitimate expression of masculinity offer the chance to reframe political action away from centralized governance toward a more distributed and networked understanding of power and social change. To me, this is the fascinating lesson of the otaku love revolution.

NOTES

1. All translations are by the author unless otherwise noted. See "Nijigen kyara to no kekkon o hōteki ni mitomete kudasai—Shomei katsudō nara *'Shomei TV'*" (Please legally recognize marriage to a two-dimensional character—If it's a petition campaign, use "Shomei TV") at www.shomei.tv/project-213.html (accessed 3 December 2008). The Shomei TV website is designed to encourage people to set up online petitions for any kind of movement, and people can do so anonymously or with fictitious names.

2. Posted in English at www.news.com.au/comments/0,23600,24576437-5014239,00.html. Posted by TP, 30 October 2008 (accessed 8 December 2008).

3. The question of reciprocity in *moe* desire is complicated. At one level, people who feel a *moe* response to inanimate objects can hardly expect those objects to reciprocate. This is certainly the case with *moe* for industrial factories, for example, as evidenced in the publication of several "factory *moe*" *(kōjō moe)* photography books and websites (see, e.g., "Daily Factory Moe" at http://d.hatena.ne.jp/wami/ [accessed 17 December 2008]). But at a deeper level, I argue that *moe* implies a desire for reciprocity in the sense that those who feel *moe* hope for public recognition that such desires for inanimate or virtual objects are viewed as worthwhile. In other words, there is a desire for reciprocity in terms of a community response, though this is generally undertheorized by *otaku* commentators themselves.

4. Roberson and Suzuki 2002, p. 1.

5. Roberson and Suzuki 2002, p. 5.
6. Lamarre 2006.
7. Kinsella 1998.
8. Ōsawa 2008, p. v.
9. Allison 2006.
10. Allison 2006.
11. The term is used in many more innocuous ways as well, sometimes simply as a reference to anything related to manga or anime. The magazine *Pia,* a weekly entertainment guide, devotes the section of its website "MoePia" to a list of voice actor performances, theme song bands, and other live events related to anime (http://t.pia.co.jp/moe/moe.html [accessed 3 December 2007]).
12. Okuno 2007, p. 168.
13. Takeda 2005.
14. Nakahara et al. 2006, pp. 61–63.
15. McCarthy 1999, p. 28.
16. Honda 2005.
17. Honda 2005, p. 142.
18. Lamarre 2006.
19. Kimmel 2002.
20. Napier 2005, p. 123.
21. Frühstück 2007, p. 12.
22. Azuma 2001, pp. 42–52.
23. Ōtsuka 2004.
24. Azuma 2001, p. 62.
25. Azuma 2001, pp. 63–66.
26. Butler 1999, p. xv.
27. Lamarre 2006, p. 368.
28. Lamarre 2006.
29. Netallica 2008. The article, "'Princess Mako *Moe*' Is a Big Hit Online; Imperial Household Dismayed," prompted readers online to post comments questioning whether it was actually "a big hit," noting that adoring fans of the princess had emerged four years earlier, after pictures of her in a junior high school uniform appeared in the press. Regardless of its popularity level, it represents an example of *moe* as part of a public debate about proper manhood. The videos can be seen at www.nicovideo.jp if you search for "Mako sama" in Japanese (accessed 2 July 2008).
30. Interview with Hosoda Mamoru in July 2007.
31. Tsutsui 2003 [1967]; for a discussion, see Bolton et al. 2007.
32. George 2001.

REFERENCES

Allison, Anne. 2006. *Millennial Monsters: Japanese Toys and the Millennial Imagination.* Berkeley: University of California Press.

Azuma Hiroki. 2001. *Dōbutsuka suru posuto modan.* Kōdansha gendai shinsho.

Bolton, Christopher, Istvan Csicsery-Ronay Jr., and Takayuki Tatsumi. 2007. *Robot Ghosts and Wired Dreams: Japanese Science Fiction from Origins to Anime.* Minneapolis: University of Minnesota Press.

Butler, Judith. 1999. "Preface." In *Gender Trouble: Feminism and the Subversion of Identity.* New York: Routledge.

Frühstück, Sabine. 2007. *Uneasy Warriors: Gender, Memory, and Popular Culture in the Japanese Army.* Berkeley: University of California Press.

George, Timothy S. 2001. *Minamata: Pollution and the Struggle for Democracy in Postwar Japan.* Cambridge, MA: Harvard University Asia Center.

Honda Toru. 2005. *Denpa otoko.* Sansai Books.

Kimmel, Michael. 2002. "Foreword." In *Masculinity Studies & Feminist Theory: New Directions,* ed. J.K. Gardiner, ix–xi. New York: Columbia University Press.

Kinsella, Sharon. 1998. "Japanese Subculture in the 1990s: Otaku and the Amateur Manga Movement." *Journal of Japanese Studies* 24, no. 2: 289–316.

Lamarre, Thomas. 2006. "Otaku Movement." In *Japan after Japan: Social and Cultural Life from the Recessionary 1990s to the Present,* ed. T. Yoda and H.D. Harootunian, 358–94. Durham: Duke University Press.

McCarthy, Helen. 1999. *Hayao Miyazaki: Master of Japanese Animation: Films, Themes, Artistry.* Berkeley: Stone Bridge Press.

Nakahara Masaya, Takahashi Yoshiki, Uminekozawa Melon, and Sarashina Shūichirō. 2006. *Ken otaku ryu.* Ohta Shuppan.

Napier, Susan. 2005. *Anime: From Akira to Howl's Moving Castle.* New York: Palgrave Macmillan.

Netallica (Yahoo Japan News). 2008. "Netto de daininki 'Mako sama moe'! Kannaichō konwaku gimi." In *Nikkan Saizō.* Available at http://netallica.yahoo.co.jp/news/37946 (accessed 7 July 2008).

Okuno Takuji. 2007. *Japan kūru to Edo bunka.* Iwanami Shoten.

Ōsawa, Masachi. 2008. *Akihabara hatsu: 00 nendai e no toi.* Iwanami Shoten.

Ōtsuka Eiji. 2004. *Monogatari Shōmetsu ron: Kyarakutaaka suru "watashi," ideorogii ka suru "monogatari."* Kadokawa Shoten.

Roberson, James E., and Suzuki Nobue, eds. 2002. *Men and Masculinities in Contemporary Japan: Dislocating the Salaryman Doxa.* London: Routledge.

Takeda Yasuhiro. 2005. *The Notenki Memoirs: Studio Gainax and the Men Who Created Evangelion.* ADV Manga.

Tsutsui Yasutaka. 2003 [1967]. *Toki o kakeru shōjo.* Kadokawa Bunko.

13 Gendering Robots

Posthuman Traditionalism in Japan

Jennifer Robertson

Even Triumph Japan, the maker of intimate apparel, has joined in [the celebration of Astro Boy's fifty-second birthday on 7 April 2003]. As part of its program of one-off theme items, it has produced the Astro Boy bra, with the cups in the shape of Astro Boy's head. For what it is worth, he faces away from the wearer, and unfortunately, his facial features have been omitted. This may have been the moment Astro Boy became Astro Man, but we will never know.

SHANE GREEN, "Astroboy Still on the Go"

The construction of gender is both the product and the process of its representation.

TERESA DE LAURETIS, *Technologies of Gender*

We need to recognize that robot design is not simply the design of an object but the design of a whole range of dynamics.

MATSUI TATSUYA

Many Japanese roboticists, almost all of whom are male, have either a picture or a figurine of Tetsuwan Atomu ("Mighty Atom," better known to English speakers as Astro Boy) in their laboratory, and most acknowledge the boy robot as a childhood inspiration, as the reason for their interest in building sociable robots. Atomu (figure 13.1) played a key role in fostering among postwar Japanese an image of robots as cute, friendly, and humanlike, characteristics that currently inform the thriving humanoid robotics industry. In this chapter, I will analyze the gendering of "real" humanoid robots designed to coexist and interact with human beings in the home and workplace. Among the questions informing my analysis are how do robots embody notions of the relationship in humans between sex, gender, and sexuality, and how do (the mostly male) roboticists design and attribute the female or male gender of humanoid robots? As I will

Figure 13.1. Tetsuwan Atomu (Astro Boy). Available at http://connect.in.com/serie-rubi/photos-1-1-1-b4f674a411e7df7cbe0d399191253d21.html.

show, the gendering of humanoid robots draws from domains of gendering practices contingent upon shape, color, function, and sociolinguistic convention. Most of the humanoids developed over the past two decades are gendered, if sometimes ambiguously, and the recent trend is toward distinctly feminine/female and masculine/male robots.

Atomu's origin story is in part a case study, albeit a fictional one, of gender fluidity. Created in 1951 by the physician-cum-cartoonist Osamu Tezuka (1928–89), Atomu is Japan's most famous robot. A nostalgia-fueled revival of things Astro Boy peaked in 2003 when a new television anime series was broadcast to mark both the fortieth anniversary of the first series and Atomu's birthday. The story of Atomu, described by Tezuka as a "reverse Pinocchio," begins in the Ministry of Science, which is headed by one Professor Tenma, who has been trying to create a robot capable of human emotions. His son Tobio suggests that he build a boy robot. Ironically, Tenma's obsession with his quest keeps him from giving Tobio fatherly love. The son runs away from home and is killed in an automobile accident, whereupon the grieving professor creates a boy robot in Tobio's likeness.

In actuality, Tezuka's prototype for Atomu was the "girl robot" in his own comic "Metropolis" ("Daitokai"), which is not to be confused with Fritz Lang's film *Metropolis,* a movie that also featured a gynomorphous robot.[1] The girl robot in Tezuka's "Doctor Mars" ("Kasei Hakase") was also a precursor to Atomu. In other words, in a reversal to the epigraph, the "Astro Boy bra" might be understood figuratively as acknowledging and confirming Atomu's originary femininity and not his emergent manhood. An enthusiastic fan of the all-female Takarazuka Revue, in which females assume men's roles, Tezuka also created a number of tomboy characters in his comics, such as Sapphire, the protagonist in "Princess Knight" ("Ribon no Kishi"), who alternates genders, living as both a prince and a princess.[2]

I should note at the outset that there are two key cultural factors that influence the generally positive view of robots in Japan. First and foremost is Shinto, the native animistic beliefs about life and death. Unlike the three major monotheisms that have never had a home in Japan, Shinto lacks complex metaphysical and theological theories and is primarily concerned with notions of purity and pollution. Shinto holds that vital energies or forces called *kami* are present in all aspects of the world and universe. Some *kami* are cosmic and others infuse trees, streams, rocks, insects, animals, and humans, as well as human creations such as dolls, cars, and robots.[3]

The second factor concerns the meanings of life and living; life and fertility are especially celebrated in Shinto. *Inochi* is the Japanese word for "life." It encompasses three basic, seemingly contradictory, but interarticulated meanings: it is a power that infuses sentient beings from generation to generation; a period between birth and death; and the most essential quality of something, whether a living being or a made object such as a car or a puppet.[4] Thus robots, humanoid and otherwise, are "living" things within the Shinto universe, and in that sense they are part of both the natural world and human society. And, as we shall see, it is as gendered members of a household or workplace that humanoid robots are being conceived and marketed.

GENDER AND CONTINGENCY

In humans, gender is both a concept and a performance embodied by females and males, a corporeal technology produced dialectically. The process of gendering robots makes especially clear that gender belongs both to the order of the material body and to the social and discursive or semiotic systems within which bodies are embedded.[5] Teresa de Lauretis's enduring insights into the "technology of gender" are especially relevant to the exploration of robot gender. To paraphrase her argument, the construction of gender goes on through the various technologies of gender (such as robotics) and institutional discourses (such as nationalism and pronatalism) with "power to control the field of social meaning" (value, prestige, kinship location, and status, for example) and thus "produce, promote, and 'implant' representations of gender." As she observes astutely, if gender representations are "social positions which carry differential meanings," then for someone or something—such as a humanoid robot—to be represented as female or male "implies the assumption of the whole of those meaning effects."[6] However, the assumption of those "meaning effects" is not necessarily conceived as part of a bigger picture. My aim in this chapter is to make visible that bigger picture and to show how its constituent components effectively, if not necessarily intentionally, reproduce a sexist division of gendered labor among humans and humanoids alike.

Much of what roboticists take for granted in their own gendered socialization and quotidian lives is reproduced and reified in the robots they design. In short, gender for them constitutes commonsense knowledge, or a cognitive style through which they experience the social world as a factual object. The practice of attributing gender to robots is not only a manifestation of roboticists' commonsense knowledge, or habitus, but it is also an application of this knowledge to create and sustain, or to leave self-evident, the facticity of their social world.[7]

Gender attribution is a process of reality construction. In my investigation of the criteria by which roboticists assign gender, it became clear that their naïve and unreflexive assumptions about humans' differences informed how they imagined both the bodies and the social performances of their creations. Unlike human infants, robots lack "naturally occurring" genitals, which therefore play no role in their initial gender assignment.[8] However, as explained by Suzanne Kessler and Wendy McKenna, in the absence of visible physical genitalia—which is usually the case among humans, who are usually clothed in public settings—"cultural genitals" are invoked in attributing gender: "The relationship between cultural genitals and gender attribution is reflexive. The reality of a gender is 'proved' by the genital, which is attributed, and, at the same time, the attributed genital only has meaning through the socially shared construction of the gender attribution process."[9]

Euro-American feminists were instrumental in establishing the now accepted view that bodies are not simply given or neutral. There are at least two kinds of bodies: the male and the female. That said, male and female bodies themselves are distinguished by a great deal of biological variability, from phenotype to physiology. Corporeal variability is also expressed in the form of intersexed bodies with genitals and reproductive organs neither clearly male nor clearly female. Suzanne Kessler details how this natural "variability"—a word she uses deliberately instead of the medical referent "ambiguity"—both confounds and underscores the dominance of sociocultural constructions (and medical reconstructions) of the sex/gender dichotomy.[10]

Gender is not simply a feature or characteristic of a given female body or a given male body. Examining the processes whereby Japanese roboticists assign gender to humanoids necessarily involves looking closely at the sociohistorical particularities of the sex-gender system in Japan. In Japan past and present, for example, femininity and masculinity have been enacted or lived by *both* female *and* male bodies as epitomized by the four-hundred-year-old all-male Kabuki theater and the all-female Takarazuka Revue, founded in 1913. Nevertheless, both theaters continue to reproduce not alternative but dominant stereotypes of femininity and masculinity. Moreover, there is a qualitative, socially reinforced—and socially sanctioned—difference between the kind of femininity performed and lived by male bodies and the kind of masculinity performed and lived by female bodies, whether on or off stage.[11] In short, the kind of body matters in the meaning and function of gender that emerges in practice. The point to remember here is that the relationship between human bodies and genders is *contingent.*[12] Whereas human female and male bodies are distinguished by a great deal of variability, humanoid robot bodies are effectively used as platforms for reducing the relationship between bodies and genders from a contingent relationship to a fixed and *necessary* one.

Roboticists may perceive female and male bodies as "specific forms of livability in the world," but they do not interrogate them as feminists especially have done.[13] Rather, they tend to uncritically reproduce and reinforce dominant stereotypes (or archetypes) attached to female and male bodies. I came to realize, over the course of my fieldwork, that in their theorizing about human-robot relations, roboticists in general treat humans and robots as if they were gender-neutral categories, despite all evidence to the contrary. Like the average person, robot designers and engineers take for granted their habitual, everyday behavior, which is resistant to change and thus reproduced in the stereotypic forms they give, and the activities they assign, to their humanoid creations.

ROBOTS AND INNOVATION

Up until now, I have referred to (humanoid) robots as self-evident things. But what exactly is a robot? Coined by his artist brother Josef from *robota,* or "forced labor," the term was first used by Czech playwright Karel Čapek in his play *R.U.R., Rossum's Universal Robots. R.U.R.,* which premiered in Prague in 1921, was about a factory in the near future where synthetic humans, or robots, were mass-produced as tireless laborers for export all over the world. Performed in Tokyo in 1924 under the title *Artificial*

Human (Jinzō ningen), it sparked a "robot boom" in Japanese popular culture that has continued to this day, from Atomu to the androids and cyborgs that dominate anime (animated films).

In practical usage, a robot is a device that performs its tasks either under direct human control, under partial control with human supervision, or completely autonomously.[14] A robot is an aggregation of different technologies—sensors, software, telecommunications tools, motors, and batteries—that make it capable of interacting with its environment. Industrial robots look like pieces of machinery, whereas to be called a humanoid, a robot must meet two criteria: it has to have a body that resembles a human (head, arms, torso, legs) and it must act like a human in environments designed for the capabilities of the human body, such as an office, hospital, or house. There are basically two categories of humanoid robots with respect to their gendered embodiment: those designed to "pass" as human and those whose overall shape bears some resemblance to human morphology.

The five-year Humanoid Robotics Project (HRP), launched in 1998 by the Japanese Ministry of Economy, Trade and Industry (METI), gave a consortium of twelve corporations and ten universities a mandate to develop first-generation intelligent humanoid robots able to use hand tools and work in human environments, including hospitals, offices, and households. This project established the groundwork for *Innovation 25*, the central government's manifesto or visionary blueprint for revitalizing Japanese society by 2025. First introduced online in February 2007 by former prime minister Abe Shinzō, and apparently supported by the current prime minister, *Innovation 25* promotes a "robotic lifestyle" epitomized by security and convenience. Robot technology is widely thought to be the industry that will "rescue" the Japanese economy from an ongoing recession. Robotics is also promoted as the means to secure the revival and stability of Japanese social institutions, such as the traditional extended family, by paving the way to "a life that will become so much more convenient, safe, and comfortable."[15] No other country as yet attributes to robotics such powerful agency and efficacy.

More than 75 percent of Japanese families live in nuclear households. How will robots and robotics revitalize the traditional extended family? One section in *Innovation 25* provides us with a clue. A detailed illustrated sketch of a day in the life of the "Inobe family," it introduces the typical Japanese extended household of the future, that is, fifteen years from now. Their fabricated last name is a shortened form of *inobēshon* (innovation). The family consists of a heterosexual married couple, Naoyuki and Yumiko, their daughter Misaki and son Taiki, the husband's parents Ichiro and Masako, and Inobē-*kun,* a male-gendered robot. The newest member of the household, Inobē-*kun* is five years old and the size of an elementary school student. He is connected to the household's many electronic gadgets and the family's own and regional wireless networks, and he can "converse" to an "impressive extent" with family members.[16]

Following the introduction of the Inobe family, the fictional ethnography records each member's daily routine, beginning at 6:30 A.M., when the elderly couple arises, and ending at 11 P.M., when LED lights in the house dim and then turn off automatically.

> At 7:00, Yumiko, Naoki and Taiki arise. [The elderly couple is already up.] The extended family eats breakfast together in front of a 103-inch flat-screen display, which is actually a composite of many different screens, enabling each person to watch their preferred program wearing headphones. But this morning they are all watching Misaki in a broadcast from Beijing [where she is an exchange student], and they talk and laugh among themselves.

The kitchen-table-cum-home-entertainment-center around which the Inobes gather in the morning is described in the popular robotics literature as the contemporary equivalent of yesterday's *irori,* or hearth, around which a family would gather for meals and socializing.[17] Yumiko, in a pink apron, is busy preparing a meal, her normative gender role of "good wife, wise mother" *[ryōsai kenbo]* intact.

Yumiko has the closest relationship with Inobē-*kun.* This is not surprising, since household robots (regardless of their attributed gender) are imagined to serve as surrogate housewives, that is, as devices through which a human housewife distributes her personal agency,[18] a point clearly illustrated in *Innovation 25* by a cartoon of a multiarmed pink humanoid fembot simultaneously holding a basket of clothes to be ironed, doing laundry, rocking and bottle feeding an infant, and helping a young girl with her geometry homework. Implicit in *Innovation 25* is the notion that a married woman who is relieved by advances in Internet technology and robot labor of housekeeping, caretaking, and child-raising chores will be free not only to maintain a career, but also to have more children. This is an especially important development given the static birthrate and rapidly aging population. The use of the suffix *-kun* to indicate a male person, the boybot's use of familiar kinship terms, and references to his ability to think make clear that the Inobe's household robot is regarded as a living member of the corporate household.

> At 17:00 Yumiko finishes "teleworking" in her home office and has a conversation with Inobē-*kun*. She asks the robot: "Have you finished cleaning the house?" "Are there any messages?" "Have you started preparing the bath?" Inobē answers, "The whole house is clean except for mama's [Yumiko's] office. Grandpa will be home at around 18:00, and there was a message from Grandma saying that she would be home at 17:00 so she should be here any minute now. I'm thinking of preparing the bath at 18:00. Papa said he would be home at 19:00.[19]

Innovation 25 has provoked a number of criticisms on Japanese blogs. As one critic, a housewife and mother of two who manages a website on social issues, fumed: "There's absolutely no reality to the image of everyday life [in the proposal]. It reads like a twenty-year-old science fiction novel! Am I the only person who doesn't share [*Innovation 25*'s] view of an ideal future? If the Japanese have become spiritually and intellectually impoverished it's because they leave things up to machines in the name of convenience; they've lost the ability to gain knowledge from the natural environment."[20]

However much its vision of the future reads like blog-worthy if dated science fiction, *Innovation 25* is *the* platform on which the state has based the national budget. Twenty-six billion dollars have been earmarked for distribution over the next ten years to promote robot technology. METI set aside more than $17.5 million in its 2007 budget to support the development within eight years of intelligent robots that rely on their own decision-making skills in the workplace.[21]

EMBODIED INTELLIGENCE

What has distinguished Japanese robotics—although now robotics in almost all other countries has followed suit—is the concept of embodied intelligence or embodied cognition. Roboticists point out that intelligence cannot merely exist in the form of an abstract algorithm but requires physical instantiation, that is, a material body. "Embodiment" in this sense follows a phenomenological paradigm in recognizing that the body (whether human or robotic) is actively and continually in touch with its surroundings. Moreover, cognitive processes originate in an organism's sensory-motor experience. Dynamic interaction between a robot and its environment generates emergent autonomous behavior, as opposed to behavior initiated by some external control system. Advances in nanotechnology and artificial life (or alife), including self-evolving genetic algorithms,[22] have led to the development of new sensory, actuation, and locomotion

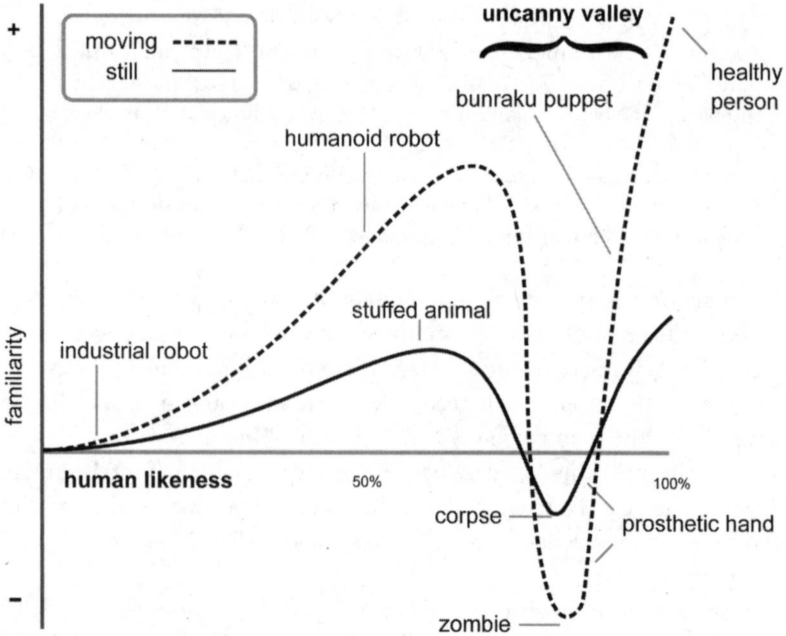

Figure 13.2. A diagram of Mori's theory of the uncanny valley. Available at http://en.wikipedia.org/wiki/Uncanny_valley.

components that enable the actualization of embodied (artificial) cognition. Also contributing to the refinement of the concept of embodied intelligence are new robot designs based on a deeper understanding of the role of form and material properties in shaping the physical, behavioral and overall performance characteristics and capacities of robots.[23] These new designs along with recent discoveries in neurophysiology have confirmed the relationship between the "motor system" and the "cognition system."[24]

Central to the emphasis in robotics on embodied intelligence has been qualitative research in the field of child development. Data from studies of infants are also used dialectically. In June 2007, the Japanese Science and Technology Agency unveiled the Child Robot with Biomimetic Body, or CB2, which will teach researchers about sensory-motor development in human children. CB2 moves like a human child between the ages of one and three years old, although it is disproportionately large and heavy at 1.2 meters tall and 33 kilograms. The humanoid has neither genitals nor an attributed gender identity—yet. Its 56 actuators take the place of muscles, and it has 197 sensors for touch, small cameras working as eyes, and an audio sensor. CB2 can also speak through a set of artificial vocal

Figure 13.3. Wakamaru. Photograph by the author at TEPIA, Tokyo, August 2009.

chords. With this robot, researchers hope to "study human recognition development," such as language acquisition and communication skills. Left unaddressed is how gender identity is formed, inasmuch as the gender attribution process and the performance of gender roles alike are premised on language and communication. Roboticists involved with CB2 are keen on the eventual creation of a new intelligent "robo species."[25]

CB2 and other humanoids notwithstanding, there is considerable debate among roboticists about what embodiment entails: how humanlike—how femalelike or malelike—should or should not humanoid robots look? How should their bodies be proportioned? Should they be bipedal or move about on wheels? Germane here is Mori Masahiro's theory of the uncanny valley, or *bukimi no tani* (figure 13.2). A roboticist who focuses on humans' emotional response to nonhuman entities, Mori argues that a thing, such as a prosthetic hand, that looks real but lacks the feel and temperature of a living hand creates a sense of the uncanny or sudden unfamiliarity. Conversely, wheeled robots such as Wakamaru (figure 13.3), which resembles the human body in only a general way but speaks and gestures as humans do, generates a sense of familiarity. Mori thus recommends that engineers retain the metallic and synthetic properties of robots so as to avoid the creepiness factor and forestall any cognitive-emotional confusion among humans.[26] Incidentally, Wakamaru, created by Mitsubishi

Heavy Industries, was assigned male gender, although at first glance the banana-colored humanoid seems to be wearing a petticoat. This is actually a body shape that combines the look of samurai armor with that of the *hakama,* or pleated "skirt" worn over a man's kimono. Wakamaru is named after the immortalized twelfth-century samurai Minamoto Yoshitsune, whose childhood name was Ushiwaka.

Among the roboticists who have not followed Mori's advice are Hara Fumio and Ishiguro Hiroshi. They create "face robots" and androids that can "pass" as humans. Whereas Hara is working on facilitating emotional interactions between humans and humanoids (or "morpho-functional machines"), Ishiguro believes that android and gynoid twins offer an improvement on teleconferencing because they project the physical presence of particular humans and not just their video images and voices.[27] Ishiguro is among those who reason that the creation of "soft-bodied systems" will facilitate human-machine communication and interaction and will stimulate the development of new biocompatible materials, including artificial muscles, tendons, and tissues, as well as biosensors.[28] Whereas both Hara and Ishiguro are intent on creating female and male proxies, Cynthia Breazeal, an MIT roboticist, eschews anatomically realistic sociable robots. Kismet, Breazeal's first, somewhat cartoonish sociable robot, was purposively designed as a gender-neutral creature ("kismet" is Turkish for "fate").[29] In contrast, the majority of Japanese roboticists designing humanoids that will interact with humans in everyday living and working environments proceed with an idea of the gender of their creation in mind.

GENDERING HUMANOIDS

Because face robots are designed to pass as humans, roboticists either model them after specific females or males or resort to giving them standardized and stereotypically gendered features. Ishiguro's first adult gynoid, Actroid Repliee Q1, covered in skinlike silicone, was modeled after Fujii Ayako, a newscaster at NHK (Japan Broadcasting Corporation). She was debuted at the 2005 World Expo in Aichi prefecture. Sophisticated actuators made it possible for her to mimic Fujii's facial and upper body movements. Moreover, internal sensors enabled her to make subtle "natural" movements that simulated breathing, blinking, and shifting her weight from one side to the other.[30] Unlike bipedal humanoids such as Honda's Asimo (figure 13.4), she cannot walk.

Ishiguro created a second Actroid, which he also debuted at Expo 2005. Instead of appropriating the face of an actual model, Actroid Repliee Q2's

Figure 13.4. Honda's Asimo (Advance Step in Innovative Mobility) with author, Honda Laboratory, Wako City, February 2007. Photograph by Jack Yamaguchi.

face was a composite of that of the "average" Japanese female (figure 13.5). To create it, the faces of several young Japanese women were scanned and the images combined to derive a statistically average composite face. The result is a female face that is both anonymous and singularly *Japanese*. In short, for Ishiguro a face, as a constellation of features, is not just "a unique three-dimensional barcode" of a particular individual's gender identity, but also a topographical map of and for a national ethnic identity.[31]

Actroid Repliee Q2's Japaneseness was further underscored by her voice, which was "high-pitched" and "girlish."[32] Her male designers clearly correlated gender (femininity) *and* nationality (and/or ethnicity) with voice. Even if they were not intending to reify a pernicious stereotype, they nevertheless reinforced Japanese "men's language" and "women's language" as essentialized and essentializing performances. As feminist linguists argue compellingly, in reality, Japanese women's speech is a prescribed norm that *does not* reflect how most women actually speak. High voice pitch is a feminine ideal and a cultural constraint promoted in

Figure 13.5. Actroid Repliee Q2, a composite of the "average" Japanese female. Image adapted from *Robocon* 60 (2008): 8.

recent history by the government in collusion with the popular media and reinforced today by robot designers.[33]

Numerous YouTube videos of Actroid Repliee versions can be viewed to corroborate my point. The gynoid featured in the video at www.youtube.com/watch?v=4sjV_lxSVQo&feature=related, for example, is overdeterminedly feminine, from her breathy, high-pitched, girlish voice to her fashionably shaggy brown hair and manicured nails. She is dressed in an

"I ❤ Hello Kitty/official cheerleader" white sweatshirt, a black miniskirt hemmed with white lace, and chartreuse pumps festooned with a large bow of the same color. In the YouTube spot, Actroid Repliee Q2 protectively covers her chest with her right arm and, in a teasingly cute voice, warns (presumably male) visitors to the robot expo that touching her bosom constitutes "sexual harassment."

Will human females be replaced by their humanoid counterparts within decades? It was not an accident that Actroid Repliee was named after the French *répliquer,* to replicate. Takahashi Tomotaka, a leading robot designer and founder of Robo Garage, who is committed to creating "feminine female" robots, predicts that half all the humanoids created in the future will be fembots.[34] Already the many uses (male) roboticists imagine for the Actroid Repliee gynoids include their employment "in upmarket coffee shops, bars, information booths, office complexes, and museums to greet customers and to give directions." An advertising poster also suggests the use of Actroid Repliee as an ambassador, a spiritual leader, and a nurse. No further details of these applications are provided, although the nurse Actroid is shown presumably interacting with a patient. Clearly she cannot yet perform any nursing task—or any other such task for that matter—except perhaps formulaic interviews, but it is conceivable that even this may be of some value in situations where there are staff shortages and long waiting times. Rentals currently cost about $4,000 for a five-day period, plus charges to choreograph the humanoids' software.[35]

Meanwhile, in July 2006 Ishiguro's lab built a robot clone of Ishiguro himself named Geminoid HI-1, "H" and "I" being the roboticist's initials. The android was purposively created by Ishiguro as his doppelgänger through which he aims to "tele-presence" his unique personhood.[36] Its silicone-and-steel body was made from casts taken from Ishiguro's body. Controlled by a motion-capture interface, Geminoid HI-1 can imitate Ishiguro's singular body and facial movements, and it can reproduce Ishiguro's voice in synchronization with his posture and movements. The android not only wears his maker's clothing, but the android's hairpiece was fashioned from hair plucked from Ishiguro's head (figure 13.6). Ishiguro is keen on tele-lecturing from home to his students at Osaka University through Geminoid HI-1, who would substitute for its maker in the classroom.[37] To summarize from a limited sample based on Ishiguro's precedent-setting creations, whereas gynoids have been designed to replace flesh-and-blood females, androids—and Geminoid HI-1 is the only example thus far—are designed to augment and multiply the agency of a particular human male, in this case, Ishiguro.

Figure 13.6. Ishiguro Hiroshi and his robot double, Geminoid HI-1. Available at http://sankei.jp.msn.com/photos/etc/080514/etc0805142251000-p1.htm.

Enter HRP-4C, a new-generation gynoid unveiled in the spring of 2009 as a body double of and for (or to replace?) the average human female. Her "name" is an acronym for Humanoid Robotics Project–4th Cyborg, and she sports a silicone face—framed by shoulder-length black hair in a page-boy—fashioned from a composite photograph of five female employees at the Advanced Institute of Science and Technology (AIST), where she was created. HRP-4C's dimensions are based on the averages for Japanese women recorded in the Japanese Body Dimension Database (1997–98): she is 158 centimeters tall and weighs forty-three kilograms (including the battery). Her height is average, but she is about ten kilograms lighter than the average woman in her twenties. Like her face, her hands are also covered in a silicone skin. The rest of her anthropometrically calibrated body consists of silver and black plastic molded to resemble a Barbarella-like costume, which accentuates the ample "breasts" and shapely "buttocks." The fembot's movements were part of an algorithm developed by motion capturing those of human females and then mimicking them. Similarly, the robo-Barbarella's interactions with humans are enabled through speech and gesture recognition.[38] HRP-4C debuted at a fashion show held during the Eighth Japan Fashion Week in Tokyo, which opened on 23 March 2009. As explained somewhat tautologically on the AIST website, "HRP-4C is expected to pave the way for the early practical application of humanoid robots by utilizing the key characteristic of humanoid robots, namely a human appearance."[39]

Whereas human female and male bodies are distinguished by a great deal of variability, humanoid robot bodies are effectively used as platforms for reducing the relationship between bodies and genders from a contingent relationship to a fixed and necessary one. This is obvious in the case of gynoids and androids and is evident even in the case of nonface robots. In April 2006, Takahashi unveiled the bipedal FT *(efutei)*, for Female Type, his first fembot. Up until that time, he explained, "the great majority of robots were either machinelike, malelike, or childlike for the reasons that not only are virtually all roboticists male, but also that fembots posed greater technical difficulties. Not only did the servo motor and platform have to be 'interiorized' *[naizōsuru]*, but the body [of the fembot] needed to be slender, both extremely difficult undertakings."[40] Technical difficulties aside, Takahashi—and my research suggests that he is representative of Japanese roboticists in this regard—invokes, in no uncertain terms, his commonsense view that an attribution of female gender requires an interiorized, slender body, and male gender an exteriorized, stocky body. Takahashi has not been consistent in equating the interiorization of body parts per se with a female-gendered body as his very first robot, the Astro Boy–inspired Neon, was specifically assembled so as "not to have any of its mechanical components visible."[41] Thus, in order to feminize FT over and beyond her interiorized body, Takahashi consulted with a number of professional fashion models in developing an algorithm enabling the thirty-three-centimeter diva-bot to "perform a graceful catwalk with all the twists, turns and poses of a supermodel" (figure 13.7).[42]

FT, HRP-4C, Geminoids, and Actroids point to roboticists' interest in the correspondence of sex, gender, and anthropometrics; face robots in particular are a product of "facial studies," an interdisciplinary and thriving field in Japan. One of the main activities of the Japan Academy of Facial Studies, established in March 1995 by anthropologist Kohara Yukinari, is to determine the link between faces and (gendered) professions. In an exhibition sponsored by the Academy at the National Science Museum in 1999, photographs of males, from the Meiji period (1868–1912) and the present, employed variously as bankers, professional wrestlers, politicians, and students were compiled and processed by a computer, producing a composite "typical" face for each category.[43] As Kohara notes, the "results reveal that the characteristic features vary from one group to another and inspire the question: Do those with similar faces join the same profession, or does working in a particular field change one's face?"[44]

Figure 13.7. The FT (Female Type) "performing a graceful catwalk." Available at www.rawfish.com.au/ft-robot.

Significant here with respect to the technology of gender is the conflation of sex (*qua* anatomical body) and profession and the conflation of face and profession. In the former, biological maleness is the universal qualification for a career in finance, spectator sports, politics, and academia, whereas in the latter, a particular *kind* of masculine appearance seems to qualify one for a particular *kind* of career for males.

It is clear that face robots are also designed with particular professions in mind. The gender of humanoid robots that do not pass as actual humans is less literal and in many cases unclear, even if a humanoid is given a gendered name and referred to by a gendered suffix, such as *-kun* (for boy). Instead, the assignment of a gendered identity in such robots seems to be contingent upon their function or "profession" (whether security guard or catwalk model) and constructed character.

Several years before FT's debut, Matsui Tatsuya, Takahashi's contemporary and the founder of Flower Robotics, created Pino and Posy (figures 13.8 and 13.9), two bipedal humanoids that typify the commonsense attributes of female and male gender noted above. For Matsui, aesthetics is a "technological issue . . . inseparable from [a] robot's primary mechanical functions." Although he does not use the word "gender," his allusions

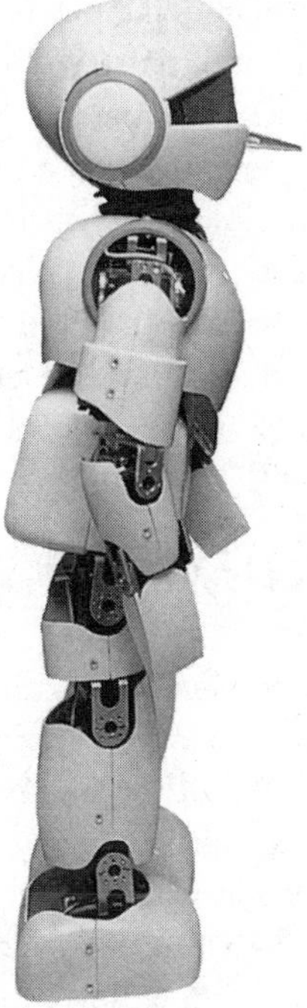

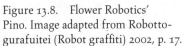

Figure 13.8. Flower Robotics' Pino. Image adapted from Robottogurafuitei (Robot graffiti) 2002, p. 17.

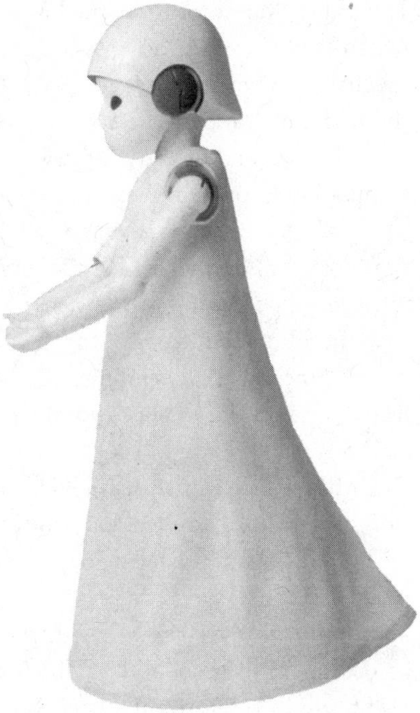

Figure 13.9. Flower Robotics' Posy. Image adapted from Robottogurafuitei (Robot graffiti) 2002, p. 36.

to the gendered character of his technological creations are numerous and striking. Matsui emphasizes that in designing humanoid robots, he (and other roboticists) are also "design[ing] the relationship between the human and the robot." Moreover, he continues, the exterior design of the robot "subverts" the privileged gaze of the human by enabling the robot to look back at the human, "thus creating . . . a spatial dimension previously unexplored in the research of humanoid robot design":

> The relationship between robots and humans is a factor that designers have to explore more deeply for the successful integration of one into the society of the other. Indeed, the mere inclusion of the robot in society in this century is not enough to sustain a lasting or particularly harmonious relationship between the two. For the robot to evolve from object to entity we need to address its genesis in purely human terms as we did with PINO *[sic]*, the humanoid robot who shares an ancestral link with Pinocchio, the puppet who aspired, through artificial means to be a boy, or more specifically, human.[45]

The pointy-nosed Pino, named after his Italian namesake, was therefore scaled to the size of "a one-year-old child taking its first steps," or about seventy-five centimeters tall. According to Matsui, invoking the theory of the uncanny valley, "the scale of a fully grown adult pose[s] a threatening presence and would . . . cause a general sense of unease, being less a companion than a cumbersome and overpowering mechanical object."[46]

Pino's masculinity is suggested through the incorporation of conventionalized masculine gender markers, such as a squarish head, angular jaw, well-developed chin, sturdy neck, and straight shoulders. Matsui claims that the humanoid's body was inspired by the lithe muscularity of male ballet dancers, and, echoing Takahashi's notion of exteriorized masculinity, he left the boybot's internal machinery visible to underscore his anatomy.[47]

Unlike Pino, whose segmented body is "incomplete" or "unfinished" *(mikansei)*, Posy's veiled body conveys a sense of modesty and innocence. Although Matsui modeled Posy after a flower girl at a church wedding, he imagines her serving as a receptionist.[48] Posy's expressive almond-shaped, and feminine, eyes stand in contrast to Pino's visor, which changes color according to his mood. Like Hello Kitty, Posy lacks a mouth (as does Pino). Her head, in the form of a pageboy haircut, sits atop a willowy neck, and her puffy cheeks recall cherubic young girls. A sleeveless gossamer dress simultaneously gives Posy an angelic appearance, highlights her smooth anthropomorphic arms and hands, and covers ("interiorizes") the unfeminine network of wires and metal plates forming her body.

ROBO-IMAGINEERS

Let us return again to the relationship between robotics and Japanese society. The Humanoid Robotics Project was spurred by demographic problems facing Japan, namely the looming population crisis caused by a declining birthrate coupled with a rapidly aging society. The birthrate presently stands at about 1.3 children per married woman, and more than 21 percent of the population of 127.8 million people (which includes permanent foreign residents) is over sixty-five years of age. That percentage is expected to increase to over 40 percent by 2050. The latest estimates produced by the health ministry project that the population will shrink to less than 111 million in 2035 and to less than 90 million in 2055.[49] Moreover, demographic estimates made back in 1995 indicated that more than 600,000 immigrants a year for the next fifty years would be needed to keep the labor force at its 1995 level of 87.2 million persons.[50] Former prime minister Koizumi Junichirō chose to ignore these estimates, and he responded to the question of how widely Japan should open its domestic labor market to foreign workers as follows: "If [foreign workers] exceed a certain level, it is bound to cause a clash. . . . Just because there is a labor shortage does not mean we should readily allow [foreign workers] coming in."[51]

How will robots change these disturbing trends? Most roboticists, I realized from their writings and my interviews, have a conservative, if not reactionary, sociocultural agenda for their high-tech creations. This is blatantly evident in the image of the kind of household robots will share with humans, namely, a traditional extended, patriarchal family model imagined to secure a stable society.[52] This timeless ideal-type model, reified in *Innovation 25,* serves as a foil against which to measure demographic trends. These trends are not contextualized or analyzed in terms of the constellation of historical, political, and socioeconomic conditions that occasioned their emergence. Rather, they are treated simply as surface abnormalities rather than indicative of a deeper malaise within the society itself. Women who choose not to marry or to give birth, for example, are disparaged as "selfish" or "parasites." What is missing in the sociocultural applications of robotics is any sense of how real women and men struggle with the trials and tribulations that confront them on a daily basis.

In a commentary that can be applied to robotics, critical theorist Manuela Rossini notes that "the inventors and scientific users of biomedical technologies are also *imagineers,* not just of bodies but of cultural configurations and social arrangements as well."[53] But the act of imagining per se does not necessarily yield fresh or progressive results. *Innovation 25* and the Japanese humanoid robot industry exemplify "retro-tech," or advanced technology in the service of traditionalism. A vision of and for new technologies that facilitate the transcendence of ethnocentrism, paternalism, and sexism, and their associated power relations, apparently is shared by neither roboticists nor the government committee and planners responsible for *Innovation 25*.

In my view, robotics in Japan today represents an ethos of technological progress conjoined with an ethos of revanchism. Or, put differently, robots (and robotics) are being enlisted to perform a kind of technologically sophisticated salvage anthropology that can be used to mobilize ethnic-national sentiments and to revivify the traditional patriarchal family as a microcosm of Japanese society. I describe this complex of motives as "reactionary postmodernism," in which images and forms of the past, including invented traditions, are mined for their nostalgic and novel impact. My use of "reactionary postmodernism" is informed by the insightful and prescient analyses of Hal Foster and Susan Foster.[54] According to them, reactionary postmodernism stands in contrast to "resistant postmodernism." Whereas the former is "an instrumental pastiche of pop- or pseudo-historical forms," the latter "is concerned with a critical deconstruction of tradition." And whereas reactionary postmodernism exploits cultural codes and conceals social and political affiliations, resistant postmodernism questions cultural codes and explores social and political affiliations.[55]

Innovation 25 develops a view of the Japanese family and its members as "posthuman," a term that generally refers to humans whose capacities are radically enhanced by biotechnological means so that they surpass those of "ordinary—or unenhanced—humans." The posthuman condition is already a staple of Japanese manga (comics) and anime. Of course, posthumanism as I have just defined it is nothing new: human bodies today have prosthetic limbs, immune system "reprogrammers," artificial hearts, titanium bones, and a whole host of inserts and implants. We are all dependent on technology and converging with machines, but perhaps this trend is actualizing more explicitly and relentlessly—and is even more desired—in Japan. The Japanese state is the first to attempt to organize and orchestrate society around robot technology and the advent of humanoid robots that will both compensate for the declining and aging population and make replacement migration less necessary (or even unnecessary).

Complementing the technological enhancement of humans is the perception of humanoid robots as, effectively, living persons. Nearly twenty years ago, feminist sage Donna Haraway envisioned a posthuman future as liberating. Her symbol of freedom was the cyborg, an individual who is neither entirely technological nor totally biological, and neither male nor female in any absolute sense.[56] As eulogized in *Innovation 25*, posthumanism may offer unprecedented convenience, safety, and ontological security to the majority of Japanese, but those "benefits" are accompanied by entrenchment in, and not liberation from, conventionally embodied male and female gender roles and the patriarchal family.

NOTES

I would like to thank my colleagues at the University of Tel Aviv, Princeton University, and the University of Maryland, where I presented different versions of this chapter, for their astute and helpful comments. Research for this article was supported by a 2007 fellowship from the NEH (Advanced Research in the Social Sciences on Japan) and a 2008 faculty research grant from the Center for Japanese Studies, University of Michigan. A longer, revised version of this chapter is "Gendering Humanoid Robots: Robo-Sexism in Japan," *Body & Society* 16, no. 2 (2010): 1–36.

1. "Gynomorphous" and "andromorphous" are the adjectives describing an automaton resembling a woman and man, respectively. Similarly, I distinguish between gynoids and androids.

2. Tezuka's "Princess Knight" (1953) inspired comic book artist Ikeda Riyoko's "Berysaiyu no bara" (The rose of Versailles, 1972–74), performed at regular intervals by the Takarazuka Revue as one of its most successful postwar productions. For detailed information on the revue, see Robertson 2001 [1998].

3. Many journalists, roboticists, and scholars writing about the friendliness ascribed to robots by the Japanese cite Shinto as an important factor.

4. Adapted from Morioka 1991, pp. 85–87.

5. De Lauretis 1987, p. 18.

6. De Lauretis 1987, p. 5.

7. I made a similar argument with reference to the practice in the Edo period of attributing gender to plants and seeds based solely on aesthetic criteria (Robertson 1984). "Habitus" is a mindless or unconscious orchestration of actions that do not presuppose agency and intentionality. It is a set of internalized predispositions that enable people to cope with unexpected situations and improvise (see Bourdieu 1977).

8. Sex robots, which are fitted with humanlike genitalia but are without "intelligence," as defined in this chapter, are an exception. I do not deal here with these sex toys (see www.ananova.com/news/story/sm_1361247.html, http://kafee.wordpress.com/2007/10/28/sex-dolls-robots-love-and-marriage/; Dorfman 2005; Levy 2007). As Kessler and McKenna argue, physical genitals play little role in gender attribution among humans, except at the moment of gender assignment at birth, when a newborn is determined to either have or lack a penis. Those infants whose genitalia are ambiguous are often "corrected" surgically and, later, hormonally (Kessler and McKenna 1985, pp. 58–59; also Kessler 1998). See also chapter 11 in this volume. Having followed the scholarly feminist literature on gender for decades, and having explored the operations of the sex-gender system in Japan and elsewhere, I continue to find Kessler and McKenna's pathbreaking work on the gender-attribution process and on the phenomenon of "cultural genitals" salient. It is misleading to assume a theoretical teleology in gender studies—that the most recent publications are the most cutting edge. The relentless presentism of a good deal of contemporary scholarship on the relationship of sex, gender, and sexuality conjures the image of a reinvented wheel.

9. Kessler and McKenna 1985, p. 155.

10. Kessler 1998.

11. Robertson 1991 and 2001 [1998]

12. Cf. Bloodsworth-Lugo 2007, pp. 18–19; Grosz 1994, p. 58.

13. See, e.g., Sheets-Johnstone 1992. This is true of male and (the comparatively few) female roboticists.

14. Autonomous (or semiautonomous) robots did not become possible until the 1950s and 1960s, with the invention of transistors and integrated circuits. Compact, reliable electronics and a growing computer industry were also critical to the development of robots. In the computing world, having more transistors on a chip means more speed and possibly more functions. Moreover, as the component density of chips radically increases, the chips themselves become smaller and thinner, which has enabled developments in humanoid robotics in the area of emergent and embodied intelligence.

15. See www.kantei.go.jp/jp/innovation/chukan/inobeke.html.

16. All material on the Inobe family is from *Innovation 25* unless otherwise noted.

17. Kanemori 2007, p. 16.

18. See, for example, Yamato 2006.

19. Inobē-*kun*'s use of kin terms underscores his membership in the Inobe household.

20. See http://studiom.at.webry.info/200703/article_2.html.

21. See www.pinktentacle.com/2006/08/intelligent-robots-by-2015-says-meti/.

22. The term *artificial life* (or *alife*) describes research into human-made systems that possess some of the essential properties of life. This interdisciplinary effort runs the gamut from biology, chemistry, and physics to computer science, robotics, and engineering (adapted from www.alife7.alife.org/whatis.shtml).

23. Inman 2006.

24. Adenzato and Garbarini 2006, p. 749.

25. It is in this context that I came up with the title of an earlier article, *Robo sapiens japanicus* (Robertson 2007). See also http://forum.ebaumsworld.com/archive/index.php/t-206094.html; www.pinktentacle.com/2007/06/cb2-baby-humanoid-robot/; www.engadget.com/2009/04/06/cb2-child-robot-returns-smarter-creepier-than-ever/.

26. Mori 1970.

27. Ishiguro's research team has found that whereas his realistic child-type Geminoid quickly precipitates uncanniness, an adult humanoid seems to provoke less eeriness and more familiarity. See www.engadget.com/2006/07/21/hiroshi-ishiguro-builds-his-evil-android-twin-geminoid-hi-1/ and www.ed.ams.eng.osaka.ac.jp/research/Android_BehavAppear_e.html.

28. Hara and Pfeifer 2003. Whereas both Hara and Ishiguro are intent on creating female and male proxies, Cynthia Breazeal, an MIT (and rare female) roboticist, eschews anatomically realistic sociable robots and has created a gender-neutral "metal bust" called Kismet with an expressive, cartoonlike face consisting of round eyeballs with blue irises, metallic eyelids, pinkish cone-shaped ears, fuzzy ochre eyebrows, and thick red cablelike lips. See Breazeal 2002, p. 48.

29. Although she provides an incisive reading of the interactive relationship between (the now mothballed) Kismet and Breazeal that occasions the robot's sociability, Lucy Suchman does not address the gendered (or not) com-

ponent of actual (as opposed to fictional) humanoids in general. See Suchman 2007, pp. 235–38, 245–46; Breazeal 2002, p. 48.

30. See http://news.nationalgeographic.com/news/2005/06/0610_050610_robot.html.

31. See de Lauretis 1987; www.wellcome.ac.uk/doc_wtx023405.html.

32. Wood 2005.

33. Shibamoto 1985.

34. See www.luxurylaunches.com/auctions/tomotaka_takahashis_ft_female_bot_to_be_auctioned.php.

35. See http://en.wikipedia.org/wiki/Actroid.

36. "Distributed personhood" refers to the ability of human actors intentionally to relocate some of their agency into things beyond the body boundary. To borrow from Alfred Gell, Geminoid HI-1 is an objective embodiment of *"the power or capacity to will* [its/his] *use"* (Gell 1998, p. 21).

37. See http://en.wikipedia.org/wiki/Actroid.

38. HRP-4C was developed as part of the User Centered Robot Open Architecture (UCROA), one of the projects under the Industrial Transformation Research Initiative, a three-year industry-academia joint project implemented by AIST in 2006 with intended applications in the entertainment industry.

39. See www.aist.go.jp/aist_e/latest_research/2009/20090513/20090513.html.

40. Takahashi 2006, p. 194.

41. Takahashi 2006, p. 67.

42. See www.luxurylaunches.com/auctions/tomotaka_takahashis_ft_female_bot_to_be_auctioned.php; http://cgullworld.blogspot.com/2007/06/ft-female-robot-does-catwalk.html.

43. The exhibition was titled "Daikaoten" (Great exhibition of faces).

44. See http://web-japan.org/trends00/honbun/tj990918.html.

45. Matsui 2000.

46. Matsui 2000.

47. Burein Nabi 2002, p. 83.

48. Burein Nabi 2002, pp. 83–84.

49. "19 prefectures to see 20% population drops by '35" 2007.

50. Kondo 2000.

51. Kashiwazaki and Akaha 2006.

52. See also Ambo 2007.

53. Rossini 2003, p. 1.

54. Foster 1983; Foster 1985.

55. Potter 1996, p. 7.

56. Haraway 1991, p. 181.

REFERENCES

"19 prefectures to see 20% population drops by '35." 2007. *Japan Times*. 30 May.

Adenzato, Mauro, and Francesca Garbarini. 2006. "The *As If* in Cognitive Science, Neuroscience and Anthropology." *Theory & Psychology* 16, no. 6: 747–59.

Ambo, Phie. 2007. *Mechanical Love.* Documentary film/DVD. Danish Documentary.

Bloodsworth-Lugo, Mary. 2007. *In-between Bodies: Sexual Difference, Race and Sexuality.* Albany: State University of New York Press.

Bourdieu, Pierre. 1977. *Outline of a Theory of Practice,* trans. Richard Nice. Cambridge: Cambridge University Press.

Breazeal, Cynthia. 2002. *Designing Sociable Robots.* Cambridge, MA: MIT Press.

Burein Nabi (Brain Navi[gation]). 2002. *Robotto gurafuitei.* Ohmsha.

De Lauretis, Teresa. 1987. *Technologies of Gender: Essays on Theory, Film and Fiction.* Bloomington: Indiana University Press.

Dorfman, Elena. 2005. *Still Lovers.* New York: Channel Photographics.

Foster, Hal. 1983. "Postmodernism: A Preface." In *The Anti-aesthetic: Essays on Postmodern Culture,* ed. Hal Foster, ix–xvi. Port Townsend: Bay Press.

Foster, Susan (Leigh). 1985. "The Signifying Body: Reaction and Resistance in Postmodern Dance." *Theatre Journal* 37, no. 1: 4–64.

Gell, Alfred. 1998. *Art and Agency: An Anthropological Theory.* Oxford: Clarendon Press.

Green, Shane. 2003. "Astroboy Still on the Go." Available at www.smh.com.au/articles/2003/03/07/1046826533340.html.

Grosz, Elizabeth. 1994. *Volatile Bodies: Toward a Corporeal Feminism.* Bloomington: Indiana University Press.

Hara, Fumio, and Rolf Pfeifer, eds. 2003. *Morpho-functional Machines: The New Species: Designing Embodied Intelligence.* Berlin: Springer.

Haraway, Donna. 1991. "A Cyborg Manifesto: Science, Technology, and Socialist-feminism in the Late Twentieth Century." In *Simians, Cyborgs and Women: The Reinvention of Nature,* ed. Donna Haraway, 149–81. London: Routledge.

Inman, Harvey. 2006. "Embodied Intelligence." Available at http://ec.europa.eu/information_society/istevent/2006/cf/document.cfm?doc_id=2570.

Kanemori Yuki. 2007. *Seikatsu yōshiki o enshutsu suru kūkan: Wabotto no hon* 7: 16–17. Chūō Kōron Shinsha.

Kashiwazaki, Chikako, and Tsuneo Akaha. 2006. "Japanese Immigration Policy: Responding to Conflicting Pressures." Available at www.migrationinformation.org/Profiles/print.cfm?ID=487.

Kessler, Suzanne. 1998. *Lessons from the Intersexed.* New Brunswick: Rutgers University Press.

Kessler, Suzanne, and Wendy McKenna. 1985. *Gender: An Ethnomethodological Approach.* Chicago: University of Chicago Press.

Kondo, Atsushi. 2000. "Development of Immigration Policy in Japan." Available at www.ip.kyusan-u.ac.jp/keizai-kiyo/dp12.pdf.

Levy, David. 2007. *Love and Sex with Robots: The Evolution of Human-Robot Relationships.* New York: Harper.

Matsui Tatsuya. 2000. "Pino Design." Available at www.plasticpals.com/?p=956.

Mori Masahiro. 1970. "Bukimi no tani." *Energy* 74: 33–35.

Morioka, Masahiro. 1991. "The Concept of Inochi: A Philosophical Perspective on the Study of Life." *Japan Review* 2: 83–115. Available at www.lifestudies.org/inochi.html.

Potter, Keith. 1996. "The Pursuit of the Unimaginable by the Unnarratable, or Some Potentially Telling Developments in Non-developmental Music." *Contemporary Music Review* 15 (3/4): 3–11.

Robertson, Jennifer. 1984. "Sexy Rice: Plant Gender, Farm Manuals, and Grass-Roots Nativism." *Monumenta Nipponica* 39, no. 3: 233–60.

———. 1991. "The Shingaku Woman: Straight from the Heart." In *Recreating Japanese Women, 1600–1945*, ed. Gail Lee Bernstein, 88–107. Berkeley: University of California Press.

———. 2001 [1998]. *Takarazuka: Sexual Politics and Popular Culture in Modern Japan*. Berkeley: University of California Press.

———. 2007. "*Robo sapiens japanicus:* Humanoid Robots and the Posthuman Family." *Critical Asian Studies* 39, no. 3: 369–98.

Rossini, Manuela. 2003. "Science/Fiction: Imagineering Posthuman Bodies." Paper presented at Gender and Power in the New Europe, the 5th European Feminist Research Conference. Available at www.iiav.nl/epublications/2003/Gender_and_power/5thfeminist/paper_709.pdf.

Sheets-Johnstone, Maxine. 1992. "Corporeal Archetypes and Power: Preliminary Clarifications and Considerations of Sex." *Hypatia* 7: 39–76.

Shibamoto, Janet. 1985. *Japanese Women's Language*. New York: Academic Press.

Suchman, Lucy A. 2007. "Human-Machine Reconfigurations: Plans and Situated Actions." Cambridge: Cambridge University Press.

Takahashi Tomotaka. 2006. *Robotto no tensai (He Is the Genius Makes a Robot [sic])*. Media Factory Inc. / Robo Garage.

Wood, Molly. 2005. "Enter the Robots." Available at www.cnet.com/4520–6033_1–6061591–1.html.

Yamato Nobuo. 2006. Robotto to kurasu: kateiyō robotto saizensen: Sofutobanku shinsho 10. Sofutobanku Kurieteibu.

Bibliography

Unless otherwise noted, Japanese books are published in Tokyo.

"19 prefectures to see 20% population drops by '35." 2007. *Japan Times*. 30 May.

Abe Ikuo. 2006. "Muscular Christianity in Japan: The Growth of a Hybrid." *International Journal of the History of Sport* 23, no. 5: 714–38.

Adams, Mary Douglas. 2005. "'Death to the Prancing Prince': Effeminacy, Sport Discourses and the Salvation of Men's Dancing." *Body & Society* 11, no. 4: 63–86.

Adenzato, Mauro, and Francesca Garbarini. 2006. "The *As If* in Cognitive Science, Neuroscience and Anthropology." *Theory & Psychology* 16, no. 6: 747–59.

Allen, Judith A. 2002. "Men Interminably in Crisis? Historians on Masculinity, Sexual Boundaries, and Manhood." *Radical History Review* 82: 191–207.

"All GSDF Troops Safely Home from Historic Mission to Iraq." *The Japan Times*, 26 January 2006.

Allison, Anne. 2006. *Millennial Monsters: Japanese Toys and the Millennial Imagination*. Berkeley: University of California Press.

Allsen, Thomas T. 2006. *The Royal Hunt in Eurasian History*. Philadelphia: University of Pennsylvania Press.

Amano Takeshi. 1980. *Wakamono no minzoku*. Perikansha.

Ambo, Phie. 2007. *Mechanical Love*. Documentary film/DVD. Danish Documentary.

Ames, Roger T. 1995. "*Bushidō:* Mode or Ethic." In *Japanese Aesthetics and Culture: A Reader*, ed. Nancy G. Hume, 279–94. Albany: State University of New York Press.

Andaya, Barbara. 2008. "Women and the Performance of Power in Early Modern Southeast Asia." In *Servants of the Dynasty: Palace Women in World History*, ed. Anne Walthall, 22–44. Berkeley: University of California Press.

Angst, Linda Isako. 2003. "The Rape of a Schoolgirl: Discourses of Power and Gendered National Identity in Okinawa." In *Islands of Discontent: Okinawan Responses to Japanese and American Power,* ed. Laura Hein and Mark Selden, 135–57. Lanham: Rowman & Littlefield.

Aoki, Hideo. 2006. *Japan's Underclass.* Melbourne: Trans Pacific Press.

Aoyama Tomoko. 2003. "The Cooking Man in Modern Japanese Literature." In *Asian Masculinities.* See Louie and Low 2003.

Arai Hakuseki. 1993. *Honchō gunki kō.* In *Kojitsu sōsho,* vol. 21, ed. Kojitsu Sōsho Hensanbu. Meiji Tosho Shuppan Kabushiki Kaisha.

Arakawa Shōji. 2006. "Heishi to kyōshi to seito." In *Dansei-shi 1: Otoko-tachi no kindai,* ed. Abe Tsunehisa, Obinata Sumio, and Amano Masako, 13–46. Nihon Keizai Hyōronsha.

Armitage, John. 2003. "Militarized Bodies: An Introduction." *Body & Society* 9, no. 4: 1–12.

Asada Hajime. 1937. *Saishin hōigaku.* Chūō kōronsha.

Asai Haruo, Itō Satoru, and Murase Yukihiro. 2001. *Nihon no otoko wa doko kara kite, doko e iku no ka?* Jūgatsusha.

Asai Junko, ed. 1992. *Kurashi no naka no komonjo.* Yoshikawa Kōbunkan.

Azuma Hiroki. 2001. *Dōbutsuka suru posuto modan.* Kōdansha gendai shinsho.

———. 2007. *Gēmuteki riarizumu no tanjō: Dōbutsuka suru posuto modan 2.* Kōdansha.

———. 2009 [2001]. *Otaku: Japan's Database Animals,* trans. Jonathan E. Abel and Shion Kono. Minneapolis: University of Minnesota Press.

Badiou, Alain. 2007. "The Contemporary Figure of the Soldier in Politics." Talk presented at the UCLA Art Center in Pasadena, California. Available at www.lacan.com/badsold.htm.

Baer, Marc David. 2008. *Honored by the Glory of Islam: Conversion and Conquest in Ottoman Europe.* Oxford: Oxford University Press.

Barshay, Andrew. 2007. *The Social Sciences in Modern Japan: The Marxian and Modernist Traditions.* Berkeley: University of California Press.

Bederman, Gail. 1995. *Manliness and Civilization: A Cultural History of Gender and Race in the United States, 1880–1917.* Chicago: University of Chicago Press.

Beishō Bōei Kenkyūjo. 1912. *Rikugun shintai kensa tetsuzuki chōkaisei no ken.* Beishō Bōei Kenkyūjo.

Ben-Ari, Eyal, and Sabine Frühstück. 2007. "The Celebration of Violence: A Live Fire Demonstration Carried out by Japan's Contemporary Military." In *Open Fire: Understanding Global Gun Cultures,* ed. Charles Fruehling Springwood, 178–98. Oxford: Berg.

Berry, Mary Elizabeth. 2006. *Japan in Print: Information and Nation in the Early Modern Period.* Berkeley: University of California Press.

Bloodsworth-Lugo, Mary. 2007. *In-between Bodies: Sexual Difference, Race and Sexuality.* Albany: State University of New York Press.

Bodart-Bailey, Beatrice M. 2006. *The Dog Shogun: The Personality and Policies of Tokugawa Tsunayoshi.* Honolulu: University of Hawai'i Press.

Bolton, Christopher, Istvan Csicsery-Ronay Jr., and Takayuki Tatsumi. 2007. *Robot Ghosts and Wired Dreams: Japanese Science Fiction from Origins to Anime.* Minneapolis: University of Minnesota Press.

Bourdieu, Pierre. 1977. *Outline of a Theory of Practice,* trans. Richard Nice. Cambridge: Cambridge University Press.

———. 2001 [1998]. *Masculine Domination.* Stanford: Stanford University Press.

Breazeal, Cynthia. 2002. *Designing Sociable Robots.* Cambridge, MA: MIT Press.

Browder, Laura. 2006. *Her Best Shot: Women and Guns in America.* Chapel Hill: University of North Carolina Press.

Brownell, Susan, and Jeffrey N. Wasserstrom, eds. 2002. *Chinese Femininities / Chinese Masculinities: A Reader.* Berkeley: University of California Press.

Bukatman, Scott. 1993. *Terminal Identity: The Virtual Subject in Post-Modern Science Fiction.* Durham: Duke University Press.

Burein Nabi (Brain Navi). 2002. *Robotto gurafuitei.* Ohmsha.

Burkman, Thomas. 2003. "Nationalist Actors in the Internationalist Theater: Nitobe Inazō and Ishii Kikujirō and the League of Nations." In *Nationalism and Internationalism in Imperial Japan: Autonomy, Asian Brotherhood, or World Citizenship,* ed. Dick Stegewerns, 89–113. London: Routledge.

Butler, Judith. 1995. "Melancholy Gender—Refused Identification." *Psychoanalytical Dialogue* 5: 165–80.

———. 1999. "Preface." *In Gender Trouble: Feminism and the Subversion of Identity.* London: Routledge.

Caplow, Theodor, Howard M. Bahr, and David Sternberg. 1968. "Homelessness." In *International Encyclopedia of the Social Sciences,* ed. David Sills, 494–99. New York: Macmillan.

Carlile, Lonny E. 2005. *Divisions of Labor: Globality, Ideology, and War in the Shaping of the Japanese Labor Movement.* Honolulu: University of Hawai'i Press.

Cave, Peter. 2004. "*Bukatsudō:* The Educational Role of Japanese School Sport Clubs." *Journal of Japanese Studies* 30, no. 2: 383–415.

Chapman, Kris. 2004. "*Ossu!* Sporting Masculinities in a Japanese Karate *Dōjō.*" *Japan Forum* 16, no. 2: 315–35.

Chase, Kenneth. 2003. *Firearms: A Global History to 1700.* Cambridge: Cambridge University Press.

Chew, I.K.H., and J. Putti. 1995. "Relationship on Work–Related Values of Singaporean and Japanese Managers in Singapore." *Human Relations* 48, no. 10: 1149–70.

Cipolla, Carlo M. 1965. *Guns, Sails, and Empires: Technological Innovation and the Early Phases of European Expansion 1400–1700.* New York: Pantheon Books.

Cohn, Carol. 1987. "Sex and Death in the Rational World of Defense Intellectuals." *Signs* 12, no. 4: 687–728.

Conlan, Thomas. 2003. *State of War: The Violent Order of Fourteenth-Century Japan.* Ann Arbor: Center of Japanese Studies, University of Michigan.

Connell, R. W. 1995. *Masculinities.* Berkeley: University of California Press.

———. 2005. *Masculinities.* 2d ed. Cambridge: Polity Press.

Connell, R. W., and James W. Messerschmidt. 2005. "Hegemonic Masculinity: Rethinking the Concept." *Gender and Society* 19: 829–59.

Cook, Theodore F. 2005. "Making 'Soldiers': The Imperial Army and the Japanese Man in Meiji Society and State." In *Gendering Modern Japanese History.* See Molony and Uno 2005.

Cox, Amy Ann. 2007. "Arming for Manhood: The Transformation of Guns into Objects of American Masculinity." In *Open Fire: Understanding Global Gun Cultures,* ed. Charles Fruehling Springwood, 141–52. Oxford: Berg.

Craft, Lucy. 2003. "Humanoid Robots Speak to the Soul." Available at http://int.kateigaho.com/apr03/robots.html.

Cross, Gary. 2008. *Men to Boys: The Making of Modern Immaturity.* New York: Columbia University Press.

Crossley, Nick. 2005. "Mapping Reflexive Body Techniques: On Body Modification and Maintenance." *Body & Society* 11 (March): 1–35.

Curtin, Sean. 2002. "Japanese Child Support Payments in 2002." Available at www.glocom.org/special_topics/social_trends/20020909_trends_s6/index.html.

DaiNihon Rengō Seinendan, ed. 1936. *Wakamono seido no kenkyū.* Nihon Seinenkan.

Dai-Tokugawa-ten Shusai Jimukyoku, ed. 2007. *Dai-Tokugawa-ten.* Dai-Tokugawa-ten Shusai Jimukyoku.

Dalla Chiesa, Simone. 2002. "When the Goal is Not the Goal: Japanese School Football Players Working Hard at Their Game." In *Japan at Play: The Ludic and the Logic of Power,* ed. Joy Hendry and Massimo Raveri, 186–98. London: Routledge.

Darling-Wolf, F. 2004. "Women and New Men: Negotiating Masculinity in the Japanese Media." *The Communication Review* 7, no. 3: 285–303.

Dasgupta, Romit. 2000. "Performing Masculinities? The 'Salaryman' at Work and Play." *Japanese Studies* 20, no. 2: 189–200.

———. 2003. "Creating Corporate Warriors: The 'Salaryman' and Masculinity in Japan." In *Asian Masculinities.* See Louie and Low 2003.

Digital Content Association of Japan (DCAJ) and Ministry of Economy Trade and Industry (METI). 2005. *Dejitaru kontentsu hakushō 2005.* METI.

De Lauretis, Teresa. 1987. *Technologies of Gender: Essays on Theory, Film and Fiction.* Bloomington: Indiana University Press.

Der Derian, James. 2009. *Virtuous War: Mapping the Military-Industrial Media-Entertainment Network.* London: Routledge.

Dorfman, Elena. 2005. *Still Lovers.* New York: Channel Photographics.

Dreger, Alice Domurat. 1998. *Hermaphrodites and the Medical Invention of Sex.* Cambridge, MA: Harvard University Press.

Ebara Yumiko. 1995. *Sōchi toshite no sei shihai.* Keisō Shobō.

Edwards, Elise M. 2000. "Gender Lessons on the Field in Contemporary Japan: The Female Athlete in Coaching Discourses." In *This Sporting Life: Sports and Body Culture in Modern Japan,* ed. William W. Kelly with Sugimoto Atsuo, 211–28. New Haven: Yale CEAS.

Emori Ichirō, ed. 1993–94. *Edo Jidai josei seikatsu ezu daijiten,* vols. 1–10. Ōzorasha.

Enda Genzō. 1968. "Seinen rōdōsha to shaseidō no tachiba." *Gekkan Sōhyō* 4: 28–38.

Endō Kimio. 1994. *Morioka han onkari nikki: Edo jidai no yasei dōbutsushi.* Kōdansha.

Enomoto Yazaemon (Ōno Mitsuo, ed.). 2001. *Enomoto Yazaemon oboegaki: Kinsei shoki shōnin no kiroku.* Heibonsha.

Faison, Elyssa. 2007. *Managing Women: Disciplining Labor in Modern Japan.* Berkeley: University of California Press.

Fausto-Sterling, Anne. 2000. *Sexing the Body: Gender Politics and the Construction of Sexuality.* New York: Basic Books.

Flood, Michael, Judith Kegan Gardiner, Bob Pease, and Keith Pringle, eds. 2007. *International Encyclopedia of Men and Masculinities.* London: Routledge.

Foster, Hal. 1983. "Postmodernism: A Preface." In *The Anti-aesthetic: Essays on Postmodern Culture,* ed. Hal Foster, ix–xvi. Port Townsend: Bay Press.

Foster, Susan (Leigh). 1985. "The Signifying Body: Reaction and Resistance in Postmodern Dance." *Theatre Journal* 37, no. 1: 4–64.

Foucault, Michel. 2007 [1997]. *The Politics of Truth,* trans. Lysa Ochroth and Catherine Porter, ed. Sylvère Lotringer. Los Angeles: Semiotext(e).

Frevert, Ute. 2001. *Die kasernierte Nation: Militärdienst und Zivilgesellschaft in Deutschland.* Munich: Verlag C. H. Beck.

Frühstück, Sabine. 2003. *Colonizing Sex: Sexology and Social Control in Modern Japan.* Berkeley: University of California Press.

———. 2005. "Genders and Sexualities." In *Companion to the Anthropology of Japan,* ed. Jennifer Robertson, 167–82. London: Blackwell.

———. 2007a. *Uneasy Warriors: Gender, Memory, and Popular Culture in the Japanese Army.* Berkeley: University of California Press.

———. 2007b. "De la militarisation de la culture impériale." In *La societé japonaise devant la montée du militarisme: Culture populaire et contrōle social dans les années 1930,* ed. Jean-Jacques Tschudin and Claude Hammon, 109–22. Arles: Editions Picquier.

Fujiwara, Masahiko. 2005. *Kokka no hinkaku.* Shinchōsha.

Furth, Charlotte. 1988. "Androgynous Males and Deficient Females: Biology and Gender Boundaries in Sixteenth- and Seventeenth-Century China." *Late Imperial China* 9, no. 2: 1–31.

Furukawa Sadao. 1986. *Mura no asobi-kyūjitsu to wakamono no shakaishi.* Heibonsha.

Fussell, Paul. 2002. *Uniforms and Why We Are What We Wear.* Boston: Houghton Mifflin.

Gaikotsu Miyatake. 1922. *Hannannyōkō*. In *Miyatake Gaikotsu Chosakushū*, vol. 5, ed. Tanizawa Eiichi and Yoshino Takao. Kawade Shobō Shinsha, 1986.

Geertz, Clifford. 1973 [1972]. "Deep Play: Notes on the Balinese Cockfight." In *The Interpretation of Cultures*. New York: Basic Books.

Gell, Alfred. 1998. *Art and Agency: An Anthropological Theory*. Oxford: Clarendon Press.

George, Timothy S. 2001. *Minamata: Pollution and the Struggle for Democracy in Postwar Japan*. Cambridge, MA: Harvard University Asia Center.

Gerteis, Christopher. 2009. *Gender Struggles: Wage-Earning Women and Male-Dominant Unions in Postwar Japan*. Cambridge, MA: Harvard University Asia Center.

Gibbs, Michael H. 2000. *Struggle and Purpose in Postwar Japanese Unionism*. Berkeley: Institute of East Asian Studies.

Gibson, James William. 1994. *Warrior Dreams: Paramilitary Culture in Post-Vietnam America*. New York: Hill and Wang.

Gifu-ken. 1971–87. *Gifu kenshi: shiryōhen*, vol. 8. Gannandō Shoten.

Gill, Rosalind, Karen Henwood, and Carl McLean. 2005. "Body Projects and the Regulation of Normative Masculinity." *Body & Society* 11 (March): 37–62.

Gill, Tom. 2001. *Men of Uncertainty: The Social Organization of Day Laborers in Contemporary Japan*. Albany: State University of New York Press.

———. 2002. "When Pillars Evaporate: Structuring Masculinity on the Japanese Margins." In *Men and Masculinities in Contemporary Japan*. See Roberson and Suzuki 2002a.

Goffman, Erving. 1961. *Encounters: Two Studies in the Sociology of Interaction*. Indianapolis: Bobbs-Merrill.

Gordon, Andrew. 1998. *The Wages of Affluence: Labor and Management in Postwar Japan*. Cambridge, MA: Harvard University Press.

Gray, Chris Hables. 2003. "Posthuman Soldiers in Postmodern War." *Body & Society* 9, no. 4: 215–26.

Green, Shane. 2003. "Astroboy Still on the Go." Available at www.smh.com.au/articles/2003/03/07/1046826533340.html.

Griffin, Emma. 2007. *Blood Sport: Hunting in Britain since 1066*. New Haven: Yale University Press.

Grosz, Elizabeth. 1994. *Volatile Bodies: Toward a Corporeal Feminism*. Bloomington: Indiana University Press.

"A Grown-up Nation? The Hostage Crisis in Iraq Sharpens Debate over Japan's Proper Role on the International Stage." 2004. *Financial Times*, 14 April.

Gunma Kenshi Hensan Iinkai. 1977–. *Gunma kenshi shiryōhen*, vol. 14. Maebashi: Gunma-ken.

Hara, Fumio, and Rolf Pfeifer, eds. 2003. *Morpho-functional Machines: The New Species: Designing Embodied Intelligence*. Berlin: Springer.

Haraway, Donna. 1991. "A Cyborg Manifesto: Science, Technology, and Socialist-feminism in the Late Twentieth Century." In *Simians, Cyborgs and Women: The Reinvention of Nature*, ed. Donna Haraway, 149–81. London: Routledge.

Hargreaves, Jennifer. 1994. *Sporting Females: Critical Issues in the History and Sociology of Women's Sports*. London: Routledge.

Hasegawa, Miki. 2006. *We Are Not Garbage! The Homeless Movement in Tokyo, 1994–2002*. London: Routledge.

Havens, Thomas R. H. 1987. *Fire Across the Sea: the Vietnam War and Japan, 1965–1975*. Princeton: Princeton University Press.

———. 1974. *Farm and Nation in Modern Japan: Agrarian Nationalism 1879–1940*. Princeton: Princeton University Press.

Hayashi Mahito. 2007. "Seisei suru Chi'iki no Kyōkai: Naibuka Shita 'Hōmuresu Mondai' to Seidōka no Rōkaritii." *Soshiorojii* 52, no. 1: 53–69.

Hayashi Reiko. 1982. *Edodana hankachō*. Yoshikawa Kōbunkan.

———. 1983. "Ryōgaeten no hōkōnin." In *Mitsui ryōgaeshi*. Kabushiki Kaisha Mitsui Ginkō.

———. 2003. *Edodana no akekure*. Yoshikawa Kōbunkan.

———, ed. 1992. *Nihon no kinsei 5 Shōnin no katsudō*. Chūo Kōronsha.

Hein, Laura. 2005. *Reasonable Men, Powerful Words: Political Culture and Expertise in Twentieth-Century Japan*. Berkeley: University of California Press.

Herman, Vivian. 1993. "Phallus, Image, Other: Reading Masculine Desire from Japanese Representations of Asia." In *Translations/Transformations: Gender and Culture in Film and Literature, East and West: Selected Conference Papers*, ed. V. Wayne and C. N. Moore, 82–98. Honolulu: University of Hawai'i and the East–West Center.

Hidaka Tomoko. 2006. "Corporate Warriors or Company Animals? An Investigation of Japanese Salaryman Masculinities across Three Generations." Ph.D. diss., Adelaide University.

"High Court: ASDF Mission to Iraq Illegal." 2008. *Japan Times*, 18 April. Available at http://search.japantimes.co.jp/mail/nn20080418a1.html.

Hiraga Seijirō. 1899. *Kanmei hōigaku*. Kanehara Iseki.

Hirakawa Sumiko. 2002. "Supōtsu, jendā, media imēji. Supōtsu CF ni egakareru jendā." In *Gendai media supōtsu ron*, ed. Hashimoto Junichi, 91–115. Kyōto: Sekai Shisō Sha.

Hirayama Kazuhito. 1988. *Gōhon seinen shūdanshi kenkyū josetsu*. Shinsensha.

Hirschauer, Stefan. 1997. "The Medicalization of Gender Migration." *International Journal of Transgenderism* 1, no. 1. Available at www.symposium.com/ijt/ijtc0104.htm.

———. 1998. "Performing Sexes and Genders in Medical Practices." In *Differences in Medicine: Unraveling Practices, Techniques, and Bodies*, ed. Marc Berg and Annemarie Mol, 13–27. Durham: Duke University Press.

Holt, Richard. 1989. *Sport and the British: A Modern History*. Oxford: Clarendon.

Honda Toru. 2005. *Denpa otoko*. Sansai Books.

Howell, David L. 2009. "The Social Life of Firearms in Tokugawa Japan." *Japanese Studies* 20, no. 1: 65–80.

Hyōdō Nisohachi. 2004. *Atarashii Bushidō*. Shinkigensha.

Iida Takako. 2002. "Media supōtsu to feminizumu." In *Gendai media supōtsu ron*, ed. Hashimoto Junichi, 71–90. Kyōto: Sekai Shisō Sha.

———. 2003. "Shinbun hōdō ni okeru josei kyōgisha no kendō-ka. Sugawara Kyōko kara Narazaki Noriko e." *Journal of Sport and Gender Studies* 1: 4–14.

Ikegami, Eiko. 1995. *The Taming of the Samurai: Honorific Individualism and the Making of Modern Japan*. Cambridge, MA: Harvard University Press.

Ikemoto Junichi. 2006. "Nihon bokushingu no esunogurafii. Shakai hendō ni ikiru wakamono no aidentiti kōchiku to sabukaruchā jissen no shiten kara." *Shakaigaku Hyōron* 58, no. 1: 21–39.

Inman, Harvey. 2006. "Embodied Intelligence." Available at http://ec.europa.eu/information_society/istevent/2006/cf/document.cfm?doc_id=2570.

Inoguchi Shōji, ed. 1978. *Kōza: Nihon no minzoku*, vol. 3, *Jinsei girei*. Yūseidō.

Inoue Kyoko. 1991. *MacArthur's Japanese Constitution*. Chicago: University of Chicago Press.

Inoue Tetsujirō and Arima Sukemasa, eds. 1905. *Bushidō sōsho*, vol. 1. Hakubunkan.

Ion, A. Hamish. 1995. "Japan Watchers 1903–1931." In *Nitobe Inazō: Japan's Bridge across the Pacific*, ed. John F. Howes, 79–106. Boulder: Westview Press.

Ishikawa Kiyotada. 1900. *Jitsuyuō hōigaku*. Nankōdō Shoten.

Ishii-Kuntz, Masako. 2002. "Balancing Fatherhood and Work: Emergence of Diverse Masculinities in Contemporary Japan." In *Men and Masculinities in Japan*. See Robertson and Suzuki, 2002a

Itani Keiko. 2003. "Josei taiiku kyōshi e no mensetsu chōsa kara mita gakkō taiiku no jendā sabukaruchō." *Journal of Sport and Gender Studies* 1: 27–38.

Itō Kimio. 1993. *"Otokorashisa" no yukue: Dansei bunka no bunka shakaigaku*. Shinyōsha.

———. 1994. "Images of Women in Weekly Male Comic Magazines in Japan." *Journal of Popular Culture* 27, no. 4: 81–96.

———. 1996. *Danseigaku nyūmon*. Sakuhinsha.

———. 2001. "Supōtsu kyōiku to jendā." In *Taiiku kyōiku o manabu hito no tame ni*, ed. Sugimoto Atsuo, 124–41. Kyōto: Sekai Shisō Sha.

Jameson, Fredric. 1984. "Postmodernism, or the Cultural Logic of Late Capitalism." *New Left Review* 146 (July–August): 53–92.

Janssen, Diederik F. 2008. *International Guide to Literature on Masculinity: A Bibliography*. Harriman: Men's Studies Press.

Kamakura Takao and Sakai Ichizō. 1975. "Infure to tatakau." *Kokurō Bunka* 1: 8–19.

Kanemori Yuki. 2007. *Seikatsu yōshiki o enshutsu suru kūkan: Wabotto no hon* 7: 16–17. Chūō Kōron Shinsha.

Kano, Ayako. 2001. *Acting Like a Woman in Modern Japan: Theater, Gender, and Nationalism.* New York: Palgrave.

Karlin, Jason G. 2002. "The Gender of Nationalism: Competing Masculinities in Meiji Japan." *Journal of Japanese Studies* 28, no. 1: 41–77.

Kasaya Kazuhiko. 1993. *Samurai no shisō: Nihongata sōshiki, tsuyosa no kōzo.* Nihon Keizai Shinbunsha.

Kashiwazaki, Chikako, and Tsuneo Akaha. 2006. "Japanese Immigration Policy: Responding to Conflicting Pressures." Available at www.migration information.org/Profiles/print.cfm?ID=487.

Katagiri Shigeo. 2007. "Mogami Yoshiaki no gassen: kenkyū saizensen." *Rekishi dokuhon* 817 (August): 74–83.

Katayama Kunika. 1897. *Hōigaku teikō, zōho kaitei.* Shōnan Shoin.

Katō Akiko. 1996. *Heiekisei to kindai nihon—1868–1945.* Yoshikawa Kōbunkan.

Katz, Jonathon. 1995. *The Invention of Heterosexuality.* New York: Dutton.

Kawai Takao. 1994. *Kindai Nihon shakai chōsashi.* 3 vols. Keiō tsūshin.

Kawasaki-shi. 1988. *Kawasaki shishi: Shiryōhen,* vol. 2. Kawasaki-shi: Kawasaki.

Kelsky, Karen. 2001. *Women on the Verge: Japanese Women, Western Dreams.* Durham: Duke University Press.

Kessler, Suzanne. 1998. *Lessons from the Intersexed.* New Brunswick: Rutgers University Press.

Kessler, Suzanne, and Wendy McKenna. 1985. *Gender: An Ethnomethodological Approach.* Chicago: University of Chicago Press.

Kessler-Harris, Alice. 2005. "The Wages of Patriarchy: Some Thoughts about the Continuing Relevance of Class and Gender." *Labor: Studies in Working-Class History of the Americas* 3, no. 3: 13–15.

Kimmel, Michael. 1994. "Masculinity as Homophobia: Fear, Shame and Silence in the Construction of Gender Identity." In *Theorizing Masculinities,* ed. Harry Brod and Michael Kaufman, 119–41. London: Sage.

———. 2002. "Foreword." In *Masculinity Studies & Feminist Theory: New Directions,* ed. J.K. Gardiner, ix–xi. New York: Columbia University Press.

Kinmonth, Earl H. 1981. *The Self-Made Man in Meiji Japanese Thought: From Samurai to Salary Man.* Berkeley: University of California Press.

Kinsella, Sharon. 1995. "Cuties in Japan." In *Women, Media, and Consumption in Japan,* ed. Lise Skov and Brian Moeran, 220–54. Honolulu: University of Hawai'i Press.

———. 1998. "Japanese Subculture in the 1990s: Otaku and the Amateur Manga Movement." *Journal of Japanese Studies* 24, no. 2: 289–316.

Kitamura Riko. 1999. *Chōhei/sensō to minshū.* Yoshikawa Kōbunkan.

Kitani Toshio. 2003. *Shiryō: Chōhei shintai kensa kisoku: Chōhei to chōhei kensa.* Kitani Toshio.

Kokumin Bunka Kaigi. 1995. *Kokumin bunka kaigi no yonjūnen.* Kokumin Bunka Kaigi.

Kokuritsu Rekishi Minzoku Hakubutsukan, ed. 2006. *Rekishi no naka no teppō denrai: Tanegashima kara Bōshin sensō made.* Sakura: Kokuritsu Rekishi Minzoku Hakubutsukan.

Kokusho Kankōkai. 1974. *Shiseki zassan,* vol. 2, *Sunpuki,* 215–318. Zoku Gunsho Ruijū Kanseikai.

Kokutetsu Rōdō Kumiai Seinenkyōiku. 1956. "Rabururetaa konkuru." *Kokutetsu Bunka* 4: 26–28.

Kokutetsu Rōdō Kumiai Seinenkyōiku. 1956. "Watashitachi no kantana kekkonshiki." *Kokutetsu Bunka* 4: 30–34.

Kokutetsu Rōdō Kumiai. 1986. *Kokutetsu Rōdō Kumiai 40-nenshi.* Rōdō Junpōsha.

Kominami Mataichirō. 1918. *Jitsuyō hōigaku.* Nankōdō Shoten.

Kondo, Atsushi. 2000. "Development of Immigration Policy in Japan." Available at www.ip.kyusan-u.ac.jp/keizai-kiyo/dp12.pdf.

Konishi Makoto, Watanabe Nobutaka, and Yabuki Takashi. 2004. *Jieitai no Iraku hahei.* Shakai Hihyōsha.

Koschmann, J. Victor. 1996. *Revolution and Subjectivity in Postwar Japan.* Chicago: University of Chicago Press.

Kumazawa, Makoto. 1996. *Portraits of the Japanese Workplace: Labor Movements, Workers, and Managers.* Boulder: Westview Press.

Kume, Ikuo. 1998. *Disparaged Success: Labor Politics in Postwar Japan.* Ithaca: Cornell University Press.

Kuroda Toshio, ed. 1988. *Mura to sensō: Heijikei no shōgen.* Katsura Shobō.

Kuroita Katsumi, ed. 1931. *Shintei zōho kokushi taikei,* vols. 38–47: *Tokugawa jikki,* vols. 1–10. Yoshikawa Kōbunkan, 1931.

Kurokawa Mamichi, ed. 1977. *Nihon kyōiku bunko: gakkōhen.* Nihon Tosho Sentā.

Kurushima Hiroshi. 1986. "Kinsei no gun'yaku to hyakushō." In *Nihon no shakaishi* 4, ed. Yamaguchi Keiji, 273–317. Iwanami Shoten.

Lamarre, Thomas. 2006. "Otaku Movement." In *Japan after Japan: Social and Cultural Life from the Recessionary 1990s to the Present, ed. T.* Yoda and H.D. Harootunian, 358–94. Durham: Duke University Press.

LeBlanc, Robin. 2009. *The Art of the Gut: Manhood, Power, and Ethics in Japanese Politics.* Berkeley: University of California Press.

Lee, Peter A., Christopher P. Houk, S. Faisal Ahmed, and Ieuan A. Hughes. 2006. "Consensus Statement on Management of Intersex Disorders." *Pediatrics* 118: 488–500.

Levy, David. 2007. *Love and Sex with Robots: The Evolution of Human-Robot Relationships.* New York: Harper.

Lidin, Olof G. 2002. *Tanegashima: The Arrival of Europe in Japan.* Copenhagen: Nias Press.

Light, Richard. 1999a. "High School Rugby and the Construction of Masculinity in Japan." In *Making the Rugby World: Race, Gender, Commerce,* ed. T.J.L. Chandler and J. Nauright. London: F. Cass.

———. 1999b. "Learning to Be a Rugger Man: High School Rugby and Media Constructions of Masculinity in Japan." *Football Studies* 2, no. 1: 74–89.

———. 2000a. "Culture at Play: A Comparative Study of Masculinity and Game Style in Japanese and Australian School Rugby." *International Sports Studies* 22, no. 2: 26–41.

———. 2000b. "A Centenary of Rugby and Masculinity in Japanese Schools and Universities: Continuity and Change." *Sporting Traditions* 16, no. 2: 87–104.

———. 2003. "Sport and the Construction of Masculinity in the Japanese Education System." In *Asian Masculinities.* See Louie and Low 2003.

Looser, Thomas. 2006. "Superflat and the Layers of Image and History in 1990s Japan." In *Mechademia,* vol. 1., ed. F. Lunning, 92–110. Minneapolis: University of Minnesota Press.

Louie, Kam. 2003. "Chinese, Japanese and Global Masculine Identities." In *Asian Masculinities.* See Louie and Low 2003.

Louie, Kam, and Morris Low, eds. 2003. *Asian Masculinities: The Meaning and Practice of Manhood in China and Japan.* London: Routledge.

Low, Morris. 2003. "The Emperor's Sons Go to War: Competing Masculinities in Modern Japan." In *Asian Masculinities.* See Louie and Low 2003.

Mackie, Vera C. 1997. *Creating Socialist Women in Japan: Gender, Labour, and Activism, 1900–1937.* Cambridge: Cambridge University Press.

Mackintosh, Jonathan D. 2008. *Homosexuality and Manliness in Postwar Japan.* London: Routledge.

Mangan, J.A. and T. Komagome. 1999. "Militarism, Sacrifice and Emperor Worship: The Expendable Male Body in Fascist Japanese Martial Culture." *International Journal of the History of Sport* 16, no. 4: 181–204.

Manzenreiter, Wolfram. 2000. *Die soziale Konstruktion des japanischen Alpinismus. Kultur, Ideologie und Sport im modernen Bergsteigen.* Wien: Institut für Ostasienwissenschaften, University of Vienna (Beiträge zur Japanologie 36).

———. 2004. "Her Place in the 'House of Football': Globalisation, Sexism and Women's Football in East Asian Societies." In *Football Goes East: Business, Culture and the People's Game in East Asia,* ed. Wolfram Manzenreiter and John Horne, 197–221. London: Routledge.

———. 2006. "Fussball und die Krise der Männlichkeit in Japan." In *Arena der Männlichkeit: Über das Verhältnis von Fußball und Geschlecht,* ed. Eva Kreisky and Georg Spitaler, 296–313. Frankfurt: Campus.

———. 2007. "Physical Education and the Curriculum of Gender Reproduction in Japan." In *Gender Dynamics and Globalization: Perspectives on Japan within Asia,* ed. Claudia Derichs and Susanne Kreitz-Sandberg, 123–42. Berlin: LIT Verlag.

———. 2008. "Football in the Reconstruction of the Gender Order in Japan." *Soccer and Society* 9, no. 1: 244–58.

Marotti, William. 2006. "Political Aesthetics: Activism, Everyday Life, and Art's Object in 1960s' Japan." *Inter Asia Cultural Studies* 7, no. 4: 606–18.

Martin, F., ed. 2008. *AsiaPacifiQueer: Rethinking Genders and Sexualities.* Urbana: University of Illinois Press.

Mashiko Chōshi Hensan Iinkai. 1985–91. *Mashiko chōshi*, vol. 3. Mashiko-chō: Mashiko-chō.

Mason, Michele M. 2005. "Manly Narratives: Writing Hokkaido into the Political and Cultural Landscape of Imperial Japan." Ph.D. diss., East Asian Languages and Literatures, University of California, Irvine.

Matsugu, Y. 2007. "Cosmo Girls and Playboys: Japanese Femininity and Masculinity in Gendered Magazines." Ph.D. diss., University of Arizona, Tucson.

Matsui Tatsuya. 2000a. "Pino Design." Available at www.symbio.jst.go.jp/~tmatsui/~tmatui.htm.

———. 2000b. "Pino—A Retrospective." Available at www.symbio.jst.go.jp/~tmatsui/pinodesign.htm.

Matsumoto Shirō. 1980. *Mitsui Jigyōshi*, vol. 1. Mitsui Bunko.

———. 1983. "Ryōgaeten no hōkōnin to seikatsu." In *Mitsui ryōgaeshi*. Kabushiki Kaisha Mitsui Ginkō.

McCarthy, Helen. 1999. *Hayao Miyazaki: Master of Japanese Animation: Films, Themes, Artistry*. Berkeley: Stone Bridge Press.

McDonald, Brent, and Chris Hallinan. 2005. "*Seishin* Habitus: Spiritual Capital and Japanese Rowing." *International Review for the Sociology of Sport* 40, no. 2: 187–200.

McLelland, Mark. 2003. "Gay Men, Masculinity and the Media in Japan." In *Asian Masculinities*. See Louie and Low 2003.

McNicol, Tony. 2003. "'Shut-ins' Turn Backs on Japan: 'Hikikomori' Make a Fresh Start in Foreign Climes." *Japan Times*, December 16.

Mead, Margaret. 1940. "Warfare Is Only an Invention—Not a Biological Necessity." *Asia XL*, 402–5.

Mega Atsuko. 1995. *Hankachō no naka no onnatachi*. Heibonsha.

Messner, Michael, and Donald Sabo, eds. 1990. *Sport, Gender, Men and the Social Order: Critical Feminist Perspectives*. Champaign: Human Kinetics.

Meyer, John W., John Boli, George M. Thomas, and Francisco O. Ramirez. 1997. "World Society and the Nation-state." *American Journal of Sociology* 103, no. 1: 144–81.

Miller, Laura. 2002. "Male Beauty Work in Japan." In *Men and Masculinities in Contemporary Japan*. See Roberson and Suzuki 2002a.

———. 2006. *Beauty Up: Exploring Contemporary Body Aesthetics*. Berkeley: University of California Press.

Minami Ashigara. 1988–2001. *Minami Ashigara shishi shiryōhen: Kinsei*, vol. 2. Minami Ashigara: Minami Ashigara.

Misaki Ryūichirō. 2000. *Ima, naze "bushidō" ka*. Chichi Shuppansha.

Mishima, Yukio. 1978. *Yukio Mishima on Hagakure: The Samurai Ethic and Modern Japan*, trans. Kathryn Sparling. Tokyo: Charles E Tuttle.

Mita Sadanori. 1928. *Hōigaku taii*. Shōkadō Shoten.

Miyamoto Mataji. 1977 [1941]. *Kinsei shōnin ishiki no kenkyū*. Kōdansha.

———. 1982. *Nihon chōnindō no kenkyū: Akinaigokoro no genten o saguru*. Kyoto: PHP Kenkyūjo.

Mizuno Aki. 2002. *Ōta Kaoru to sono jidai: "Sōhyō" rōdō undō no eikō to haitai.* Dōmei Shuppan Sābisu.

Mizuno Eri. 2002. "Supōtsu to kai bunka ni tsuite no ikkōsatsu. X sōfu shoppu ni mirareru 'dansei bunka.'" *Kyōto Shakaigaku Nenpō* 10: 35–60.

Mizushima Asaho. 1994. "Heiwa kenpō to Jieitai no shōrai." *Gunshuku Mondai Shiryō* 9, no. 166: 16–21.

Mogami Kōkei, ed. 1978. *Kōza: Nihon no minzoku,* vol. 2, *Shakai kōsei.* Yūseidō.

Molony, Barbara, and Kathleen Uno, eds. 2005. *Gendering Modern Japanese History.* Cambridge, MA: Harvard University Press.

Mori Masahiro. 1970. "Bukimi no tani." *Energy* 74: 33–35.

Morioka, Masahiro. 1991. "The Concept of Inochi: A Philosophical Perspective on the Study of Life." *Japan Review* 2: 83–115. Available at www.lifestudies.org/inochi.html.

Mosse, George L. 1996. *The Image of Man: The Creation of Modern Masculinity.* New York: Oxford University Press.

Murakami Takashi. 2000. *Superflat.* MADRA Publishing.

———. 2005a. "Superflat Trilogy: Greetings, You Are Alive." In *Little Boy: The Arts of Japan's Exploding Subculture,* ed. Murakami Takashi, 150–63. New York: Japan Society.

———. 2005b. *Little Boy: The Arts of Japan's Exploding Subculture.* New Haven: Yale University Press.

Murayama, Satomi. 2004. "Homeless Women in Japan." *Kyōto Shakaigaku Nenpo* 157–68.

Nagano Hiroko. 1982. "Bakuhan hō to josei." In *Nihon joseishi,* ed. Joseishi Sōgō Kenkyūkai, vol. 3. Tōkyō Daigaku Shuppankai.

Nagashima Atsuko. 1993. "Hataraku nōson no onnatachi: Kaga *Nōgyō zue* o yomu." In *Nihon no Kinsei,* vol. 15, *Josei no Kinsei,* ed Hayashi Reiko, 227–60. Chūō Kōronsha.

Nagashima Yukitoshi. 2005. *Danbōru Hausu.* Poplar.

Nagatomo Chiyoji, ed. 1993. *Onna chōhōki: Otoko chōhōki.* Shakai Shisōsha.

Nagura Tetsuzō. 1980. "Shōninteki 'ie' ideorogii no keisei to kōzō: Enomoto Yazaemon Oboegaki ni tsuite." *Nihonshi kenkyū* 209: 30–68.

Nakahara Masaya, Takahashi Yoshiki, Uminekozawa Melon, and Sarashina Shūichirō. 2006. *Ken otaku ryu.* Ohta Shuppan.

Nakamaki Hirochika and Hioki Koichirō, eds. 1997. *Keiei jinruigaku kotohajime: Kaisha to sarariiman.* Osaka: Tōhō shuppan.

Nakamura, Karen, and Hisako Matsuo. 2003. "Female Masculinity and Fantasy Spaces: Transcending Genders in the Takarazuka Theatre and Japanese Popular Culture." In *Men and Masculinities in Contemporary Japan.* See Roberson and Suzuki 2002a.

Nakano Hitori. 2004. *Densha otoko.* Shinchōsha.

Nakayama Tarō. 1930. *Nihon wakamono shi.* Shun'yōdō.

Napier, Susan. 2005. *Anime: From Akira to Howl's Moving Castle.* New York: Palgrave Macmillan.

———. 2008. "Lost in Transition: Train Men and Dolls in Millennial Japan." *Mechadamia* 3: 205–10.
Netallica (Yahoo Japan News). 2008. "Netto de daininki 'Mako sama moe'! Kannaichō konwaku gimi." In *Nikkan Saizō.* Available at http://netallica.yahoo.co.jp/news/37946.
Nihon Rōdō Kumiai Sōhyōgikai. 1964. *Sōhyō jūnen-shi.* Rōdōjunpōsha.
Nihon shomin seikatsu shiryō shūsei. 1968–84. 30 vols. San'ichi Shobō.
Nihon Tōkei Kyōkai. 1949–. *Nihon tōkei nenkan* (Japan statistical yearbook). Nihon Tōkei Kyōkai.
Nihon toshi seikatsu shiryō shūsei. 1975–77. 10 vols. Gakushū Kenkyūsha.
Nishikawa Yūko and Ogino Miho. 1999. *Kyōdō kenkyū: Danseiron.* Kyōto: Jimbun Shoin.
Nishizaka Yasushi. 2008. *Mitsui Echigoya hōkōnin no kenkyū.* Tōkyō Daigaku Shuppankai.
Nitobe, Inazō. 1909. *Thoughts and Essays.* Teibeisha.
———. 1969. *Bushido: The Soul of Japan.* Tokyo: Charles E. Tuttle.
Nogami Toshio. 1920. "Gendai seikatsu to danjo ryōsei no sekkin." *Kaizō* 3, no. 4: 185–204.
Nōsangyoson Bunka Kyōkai, ed. 1980. *Nihon nōsho zenshū,* vol. 25. Nōsangyoson Bunka Kyōkai.
———, ed. 1981. *Nihon nōsho zenshū,* vol. 35. Nōsangyoson Bunka Kyōkai.
———, ed. 1983a. *Nihon nōsho zenshū,* vol. 26. Nōsangyoson Bunka Kyōkai.
———, ed. 1983b. *Nihon nōsho zenshū,* vol. 71. Nōsangyoson Bunka Kyōkai.
Nye, Robert A. 2000. "Kinship, Male Bonds, and Masculinity in Comparative Perspective." *American Historical Review* 105, no. 5: 1656–66.
———. 2007. Review Essay: "Western Masculinities in War and Peace." *American Historical Review* 112, no. 2: 417–38.
Ohnuki-Tierney, Emiko. 2002. *Kamikaze, Cherry Blossoms, and Nationalisms: The Militarization of Aesthetics in Japanese History.* Chicago: University of Chicago Press.
Ōki Kiyoshi. 1975. "'Chōmirai' no sukōbai." *Kokurō Bunka* 1: 4–5.
Okuno Takuji. 2007. *Japan kūru to Edo bunka.* Iwanami Shoten.
Ōmachi Keisuke. 1964. "Seinen wo gisei to shite keizai ha seichō shita—kōdo-seichō to teichingin." *Gekkan Sōhyō* 3: 65–73.
Onimaru Hiroyuki. 1975. "Roppyaku nen to yonhyaku nen." *Kokurō Bunka* 1: 2–3.
Onishi Norimitsu. 2004. "Mission to Iraq Eases Japan Toward a True Military." *New York Times,* 16 January.
Ōno Mitsuo. 1969. "*Enomoto Yazaemon oboegaki* ni tsuite: Sono shōkai to kare no shōgyō katsudō yori mita kinsei zenki no shijo kōzō no kentō." *Shiryōkan kenkyū kiyō* 2: 59–132.
Ortner, Sherry. 1997. *Making Gender: The Politics and Erotics of Culture.* Boston: Beacon Press.
———. 2006. *Anthropology and Social Theory: Culture, Power and the Acting Subject.* Durham: Duke University Press.

Osawa Mari. 1994. "Bye-bye Corporate Warriors: The Formation of a Corporate-centered Society and Gender-biased Social Policies in Japan." *Annals of the Institute of Social Science* 19: 157–94.

———. 2007. "The Livelihood Security System and Social Exclusion: The Male Breadwinner Model Revisited." In *Gender Orders Unbound: Globalisation, Restructuring and Reciprocity,* ed. Ilse Lenz, C. Ulrich, and B. Fersch. Opladen: Barbara Budrich.

Oshiro, George M. 2004. "Nitobe Inazō and Japanese Nationalism." In *Japanese Cultural Nationalism: At Home and in the Asia Pacific,* ed. Roy Starrs, 61–79. Folkestone: Kent Global Oriental.

Ōtake Hideo. 1974. "Nihon." In *Kōza kazoku,* vol. 5, *Sōzoku to keishō,* ed. Aoyama Michio et al. Kōbundō.

Ōtsuka Eiji. 2004. *Monogatari Shōmetsu ron: Kyarakutaaka suru "watashi," ideorogii ka suru "monogatari."* Kadokawa Shoten.

Oyama Chōshi Hensan Iinkai. 1990. *Oyama chōshi.* Oyama-chō: Oyama.

Ōyama Shirō. 2000. *San'ya Gakeppuchi Nikk.* TBS Britannica.

———. 2005. *A Man with No Talents: Memoirs of a Tokyo Day Labourer.* Ithaca: Cornell University Press.

Parker, Andrew A. 1996. "Sporting Masculinities: Gender Relations and the Body." In *Understanding Masculinities: Social Relations and Cultural Arenas,* ed. Mairtin Mac an Ghaill. Philadelphia: Open University Press.

Partner, Simon. 1999. *Assembled in Japan: Electrical Goods and the Making of the Japanese Consumer.* Berkeley: University of California Press.

Patari, Juho. 2008. *The "Homeless Etiquette": Social Interaction and Behavior Among the Homeless Living in Taito Ward, Tokyo.* Saarbrücken: VDM Verlag.

Pflugfelder, Gregory M. 1999. *Cartographies of Desire: Male-Male Sexuality in Japanese Discourse, 1600–1950.* Berkeley: University of California Press.

Potter, Keith. 1996. "The Pursuit of the Unimaginable by the Unnarratable, or Some Potentially Telling Developments in Non-developmental Music." *Contemporary Music Review* 15 (3/4): 3–11.

Powles, Cyril H. 1995. "Bushido: Its Admirers and Critics." In *Nitobe Inazō: Japan's Bridge Across the Pacific,* ed. John F. Howes, 107–18. Boulder: Westview Press.

Prindle, Tamae. 1998. "A Cocooned Identity: Japanese Girls Films: Nobuhiko Oobayashi's *Chizuko's Younger Sister* and Jun Ishikawa's *Tsugumi.*" *Post Script* 15, no. 1: 24–36.

Pyle, Kenneth. 2007. *Japan Rising: The Resurgence of Japanese Power and Purpose.* New York: Public Affairs.

Rabinbach, Anson. 1990. *The Human Motor: Energy, Fatigue, and the Origins of Modernity.* Berkeley: University of California Press.

Roberson, James E., and Suzuki Nobue, eds. 2002a. *Men and Masculinities in Contemporary Japan: Dislocating the Salaryman Doxa.* London: Routledge.

———. 2002b. Introduction to *Men and Masculinities in Contemporary Japan*. See Roberson and Suzuki 2002a.

Roberts, Luke S. 1998. *Mercantilism in a Japanese Domain: The Merchant Origins of Economic Nationalism in 18th-Century Tosa*. New York: Cambridge University Press.

Robertson, Jennifer. 1984. "Sexy Rice: Plant Gender, Farm Manuals, and Grass-Roots Nativism." *Monumenta Nipponica* 39, no. 3: 233–60.

———. 1991. "The Shingaku Woman: Straight from the Heart." In *Recreating Japanese Women, 1600–1945*, ed. Gail Lee Bernstein, 88–107. Berkeley: University of California Press.

———. 2001 [1998]. *Takarazuka: Sexual Politics and Popular Culture in Modern Japan*. Berkeley: University of California Press.

———. 2007. "*Robo sapiens japanicus:* Humanoid Robots and the Posthuman Family." *Critical Asian Studies* 39, no. 3: 369–98.

———. 2008. "Aging, Trauma, and Robotherapy in Japan." Paper delivered at Psychology on the Couch, Van Leer Institute, 29–30 June, Jerusalem.

Roden, Donald. 1980a. "Baseball and the Quest for National Identity in Meiji Japan." *American Historical Review* 85, no. 3: 511–34.

———. 1980b. *Schooldays in Imperial Japan: A Study in the Culture of a Student Elite*. Berkeley: University of California Press.

———. 1990. "Taishō Culture and the Problem of Gender Ambivalence." In *Culture and Identity: Japanese Intellectuals During the Interwar Years*, ed. J. Thomas Rimer, 37–55. Princeton: Princeton University Press.

———. 2005. "Thoughts on the Early Meiji Gentleman." In *Gendering Modern Japanese History*. See Molony and Uno 2005.

Rogers, John Michael. 1998. "The Development of the Military Profession in Tokugawa Japan." Ph.D. diss., Harvard University.

Rossini, Manuela. 2003. "Science/Fiction: Imagineering Posthuman Bodies." Paper presented at Gender and Power in the New Europe, the 5th European Feminist Research Conference. Available at www.iiav.nl/epublications/2003/Gender_and_power/5thfeminist/paper_709.pdf.

Sadler, A. L. 1978 [1937]. *The Maker of Modern Japan: The Life of Tokugawa Ieyasu*. Rutland: Charles E. Ţuttle Company.

Saiki Kazuma, Okayama Taiji, and Sagara Tōru, eds. 1974. *Mikawa monogatari, Hagakure*. Iwanami Shoten.

Sakaguchi Kazuo. 1985. *Izu shotō no wakamonogumi to musumegumi*. Miraisha.

Sakaguchi Kyōhei. 2004. *Zero-en Hausu*. Little More.

———. 2008. *Zero-en Hausu Zero-en Seikatsu*. Daiwa Shobō.

Sakaki Yasusaburō. 1919. *Seiyoku kenkyū to seishin bunsekigaku* .Jitsugyō no Nihon Sha.

Sakata Kiyo. 2002 [1942]. *Onna no mita senjo*. Nagoya: Arumu.

Sakurai Tokutarō. 1962. *Kō shūdan seiritsu katei no kenkyū*. Yoshikawa Kōbunkan.

Sasakawa Sports Foundation (SSF). 2004. *Supōtsu raifu dēta 2004. Supōtsu raifu ni kan suru chōsa hōkokusho.* Sasakawa Sports Foundation.

Sasaki-Uemura, Wesley Makoto. 2001. *Organizing the Spontaneous: Citizen Protest in Postwar Japan.* Honolulu: University of Hawai'i Press.

Sassa Atsuyuki. 1999. *Rengō Sekigun "Asama sansō" jiken.* Bungei Shunjū.

Satō Mamoru. 1970. *Kindai Nihon seinen shūdanshi kenkyū.* Ochanomizu Shobō.

Sato, Masahiro. 2000. *Bushidō.* Kyōbunkan.

Sawada Junjirō. 1909. *Taiji ni okeru shiyō bunsei no genri oyobi yō.* Kōbundō.

Schad–Seifert, Annette. 2001. "Samurai and Sarariiman: The Discourse on Masculinity in Modern Japan." In *Can Japan Globalize? Studies on Japan's Changing Political Economy and the Process of Globalization,* ed. Sung–Jo Park and Arne Holzhausen, 119–212. Heidelberg: Physica Verlag.

———. 2007. "Dynamics of Masculinities in Japan—Comparative Perspectives on Men's Studies." *Gender Dynamics and Globalisation: Perspectives from Japan within Asia,* ed. Claudia Derichs and Susanne Kreitz-Sandberg, 33–44. Münster: LIT.

Schmitt, Eric, and Thom Shankar. 2005. "Military May Propose an Active-duty Force for Relief Efforts." *New York Times,* 11 October.

Segawa Kiyoko. 1972. *Wakamono to musume o meguru minzoku.* Miraisha.

Sekiguchi Hisashi. 2001. "Taiiku supōtsu ni miru 'otokorashisa' baiyō no rekishi." In *Nihon no otoko wa doko kara kite doko e iku no ka,* ed. Asai Haruo et al., 204–21. Seiunsha.

Sennett, Richard. 1992. *The Fall of Public Man.* New York: W. W. Norton & Co.

Sheehan, James J. 2003. "What It Means to Be a State: States and Violence in Twentieth-century Europe." *Journal of Modern European* History 1, no. 1: 11–23.

———. 2009. *Where Have All the Soldiers Gone? The Transformation of Modern Europe.* New York: Mariner Books.

Sheets-Johnstone, Maxine. 1992. "Corporeal Archetypes and Power: Preliminary Clarifications and Considerations of Sex." *Hypatia* 7: 39–76.

Shibamoto, Janet. 1985. *Japanese Women's Language.* New York: Academic Press.

Shilling, Chris. 2003. *The Body and Social Theory.* 2d ed. London: Sage.

Shinoda Toru. 2005a. "'Kigyōbetsu kumiai o chūshin toshita mindō kumai to ha' (jo)." *Ōhara Shakai Mondai Kenyūjo Zasshi* 561: 1–16.

———. 2005b. "'Kigyōbetsu kumiai wo chūshin toshita mindō kumai to ha' (ge)." *Ōhara Shakai Mondai Kenyūjo Zasshi* 565: 13–31.

Shizuoka-ken. 1986–96. *Shizuoka kenshi: shiryōhen,* vol. 12. Shizuoka-shi: Shizuoka-ken.

Silverberg, Miriam. 1991. "The Modern Girl as Militant." In *Recreating Japanese Women, 1600–1945,* ed. Gail Lee Bernstein, 239–66. Berkeley: University of California Press.

Smethurst, Richard J. 1974. *A Social Basis for Prewar Japanese Militarism: The Army and the Rural Community.* Berkeley: University of California Press.

Smith, Henry Dewitt II. 2003. "The Capacity of Chūshingura." *Monumenta Nipponica* 58, no. 1: 1–42.

———. 1972. *Japan's First Student Radicals.* Cambridge, MA: Harvard University Press.

Sogi Kanta. 2003. *Asakusa Stairu.* Bungei Shunju.

Sōhyō Seinenbu. 1968. "Seinenbu katsudō no genjō to mondaiten: zadankai." *Gekkan Sōhyō* 4: 39–71.

Sōhyō Seitai Iinkai. 1968. "Hansen tōsō to seinen rōdōsha no yakuwari." *Gekkan Sōhyō* 4: 18–27.

Solomon-Godeau, Abigail. 1995. "Male Trouble." In *Constructing Masculinity,* ed. Maurice Berger, Brian Wallis and Simon Watson, 69–76. London: Routledge.

Spielvogel, Laura. 2003. *Working Out in Japan. Shaping the Female Body in Tokyo Fitness Clubs.* Durham: Duke University Press.

Sreetharan, C. S. 2004. "Students, Sarariiman (pl.), and Seniors: Japanese Men's Use of 'Manly' Speech Register." *Language in Society* 33, no. 1: 81–107.

Standish, Isolde. 2000. *Myth and Masculinity in the Japanese Cinema: Towards a Political Reading of the "Tragic Hero."* Richmond: Curzon.

Suchman, Lucy A. 2007. "Human-Machine Reconfigurations: Plans and Situated Actions." Cambridge: Cambridge University Press.

Sugawa Shigeo. 1991. *The Japanese Matchlock: A Story of the Tanegashima.* Published by the author in Tokyo; distributed by Kogei Shuppan.

Sunpuki. See Kokusho Kankōkai.

Suyama Ken'ichi. 1969. *Hansenha rōdō undō: shichijūnen tōsō no shūten.* Aki Shobō.

Suzuki Masaya. 2007. *Sengoku jidai no daigokai.* PHP Kenkyūjo.

Taga Futoshi. 2001. *Dansei no jenda keisei: "Otokorashisa" no yuragi no naka de.* Tōyōkan Shuppansha.

———. 2003. "Rethinking Male Socialisation: Life Histories of Japanese Male Youth." In *Asian Masculinities.* See Louie and Low 2003.

———. 2005. "Rethinking Japanese Masculinities: Recent Research Trends." In *Genders, Transgenders, and Sexualities in Japan,* ed. Mark McLelland and Romit Dasgupta. London: Routledge.

Takada Giichirō. 1917. *Hōigaku.* Kokuseidō Shoten.

Takagi Masayuki. 1985. *Zengakuren to Zenkyōtō.* Kōdansha.

Takahashi Satoshi. 1978. *Nihon Minshū Kyōikushi kenkyū.* Miraisha.

———. 1997. *Kazoku to kodomo no Edo jidai.* Asahi Shinbunsha.

Takahashi Tomotaka. 2006. *Robotto no tensai (He Is the Genius Makes a Robot [sic]).* Media Factory Inc. / Robo Garage.

Takami Keishi. 1968. *Hansen Seinen Iinkai.* San'ichi Shobō.

Takaoka Hiroyuki. 2006. "Sensō to 'tairyoku': Senji kōsei gyōsei to seinen danshi." In *Dansei-shi 2: Modanizumu kara sōryokusen e*, ed. Abe Tsunehisa, Obinata Sumio, and Amano Masako, 176–202. Nihon Keizai Hyōronsha.

Takeda Yasuhiro. 2005. *The Notenki Memoirs: Studio Gainax and the Men Who Created Evangelion*. ADV Manga.

Tanaka Kennosuke. 2003. "Toshi kūkan to wakamono no 'zoku' bunka." *Supōtsu Shakaigaku Kenkyū* 11: 46–61.

Tanaka Kōgai, with Sata Yoshihiko. 1902. *Iji danpen, zōtei 3 han*. Handaya Iseki.

Tani Teruhiro. 1984. *Wakamono nakama no Rekishi*. Nihon Seinenkan.

Tanizawa Eiichi and Yoshino Takao, eds. 1986. *Miyatake Gaikotsu Chosakushū*, vol. 5. Kawade Shobō.

Tochigi Kenshi Hensan Iinkai. 1974–. *Tochigi kenshi shiryōhen: Kinsei*, vol. 4. Utsunomiya: Tochigi-ken.

Tokugawa Jikki. See Kuroita Katsumi.

Tōkyō Chihō Rōdō Kumiai Hyōgikai. 1980. *Sengo Tōkyō rōdō undō shi: Tōkyō chihyō nijūgonen.* Rōdō Junpōsha.

Toride Shishi Hensan Iinkai. 1982–89. *Toride shishi: Kinsei shiryōhen*, vol. 3. Toride-shi: Toride-shi Shomuka.

Totman, Conrad. 1983. *Tokugawa Ieyasu: Shogun*. San Francisco: Heian International.

Tsuboi Hirofumi, ed. 1984. *Mura to murabito:kyōdōtai no seikatsu to girei*. Shogakkan.

Tsukamoto Manabu. 1993 [1983]. *Shōrui o meguru seiji: Genroku no fōkuroa*. Heibonsha.

Tsutsui Yasutaka. 2003 [1967]. *Toki o kakeru shōjo*. Kadokawa Bunko.

Udagawa Takehisa. 2006. "Tōkoku e no teppō denpa to Kishinowada ryū: hōjutsu no ryūkō." In *Sengoku shikihō-ki no shakai to girei*, ed. Futaki Ken'ichi, 212–38. Yoshikawa Kōbunkan.

———. 2007. "Teppō denrai no jitsuzō." In *Teppō denrai no Nihonshi: Hinawajū kara raifurujū made*, ed. Udagawa Takehisa, 2–27. Yoshikawa Kōbunkan.

———. N.d. Available at www.rekihaku.ac.jp/e-rekihaku/126/rekishi.html.

Ugaki Kazushige. 1968. *Ugaki Kazushige Nikki*, vol. 1. Misuzu Shobō.

Ujiie Mikito. 1989. *Edo no shōnen*. Heibonsha.

———. 1996. *Fugi mittsū*. Kōdansha.

Urquhart, Brian. 2004. "The Good General: Tom Clancy, with General Tony Zinni (Ret.) and Tony Koltz. Battle Ready. New York: Putnam." *New York Review of Books*, 23 September.

Ushiku Shishi Hensan Iinkai. 2001–. *Ushiku shishiryō: Kinsei*, vol. 2. Ushiku: Ushiku-shi.

Vaporis, Constantine Nomikos. 2008. *Tour of Duty: Samurai, Military Service in Edo, and the Culture of Early Modern Japan*. Honolulu: University of Hawai'i Press.

Varner, Richard E. 1997. "The Organized Peasant: The Wakamonogumi in the Edo Period." *Monumenta Nipponica* 32, no. 4: 459–83.

Vincenti, James J. 1997. "The Relationship between Female Status and Physical Strength in a Japanese University Athletic Club." *Journal of Sport and Social Issues* 21: 189–210.

Vogel, Ezra. 1963. *Japan's New Middle Class: The Salary Man and His Family in a Tokyo Suburb.* Berkeley: University of California Press.

Wacquant, Loïc J. D. 1995. "Review Article: Why Men Desire Muscles." *Body & Society* 1: 163–79.

Walby, Sylvia S. 1990. *Theorizing Patriarchy.* Oxford: Basil Blackwell.

Walker, Brett L. 2001. "Commercial Growth and Environmental Change in Early Modern Japan: Hachinohe's Wild Boar Famine of 1749." *Journal of Asian Studies* 60, no. 2: 329–51.

Walthall, Anne. 1998. *The Weak Body of a Useless Woman: Matsuo Taseko and the Meiji Restoration.* Chicago: University of Chicago Press.

———. 2007. "Histories Official, Unofficial, and Popular: Shogunal Favorites in the Genroku Era." In *Writing Histories in Japan: Texts and their Transformations from Ancient Times through the Meiji Era,* ed. James C. Baxter and Joshua A. Fogel, 175–99, Kyoto: International Research Center for Japanese Studies.

Weathers, Charles. 1994. "Reconstructing of Labor-management Relations in Japan's National Railways." *Asian Survey* 34, no. 7: 621–33.

———. 2008. "Shunto and the Shackles of Competitiveness." *Labor History* 49, no. 2: 177–97.

Weeks, Jeffrey. 1989. *Sexuality.* London: Routledge.

Wheaton, Belinda. 2004a. "Introduction: Mapping the Lifestyle Sport-Scape." In *Understanding Lifestyle Sports: Consumption, Identity and Difference,* ed. Belinda Wheaton, 1–28. London: Routledge.

———. 2004b. "Selling Out? The Commercialisation and Globalisation of Lifestyle Sport." In *The Global Politics of Sport: The Role of Global Institutions in Sport,* ed. Lincoln Allison, 140–61. London: Routledge.

Winnicott, H. D. 2006. *Playing and Reality.* London: Routledge.

Wood, Molly. 2005. "Enter the Robots." Available at www.cnet.com/4520-6033_1-6061591-1.html.

Wōrsching, Martha. 2007. "Race to the Top: Masculinity, Sport, and Nature in German Magazine Advertising." *Men and Masculinities* 10: 197–221.

Yamada Akihiko. 1975. "Kōsekishō." *Kokurō Bunka* 1: 3–4.

Yamada Kazuyo. 2000. "Rōdō kumiai no shufusoshiki to 'naishiki mondai'—1960 nendai 'Sōhyō shufu no kai' no katsudo kara." *Tsukuba daigaku keizaigaku ronshū* 3: 1–48.

Yamaguchi Tomomi. 2006. "Jendaa furii ronsō to feminizumu undo no ushinarawareta jūnen." In *Bakkurashu! Naze jendaa furii wa tatakareta no ka,* ed. Ueno Chizuko et al., 244–82. Sofusha.

Yamamoto Tsunetomo. 1979. *Hagakure: The Book of the Samurai,* trans. William Scott Wilson. Kodansha International.

Yamamoto Yoshio. 1886. *Saiban igaku.* Shimamura Risuke.

Yamaoka Ken. 1993. *Nenrei kaiteisei no kenkyū.* Hokki Shuppan.

Yamasaki Hiroshi. 2001. "Kindai dansei no tanjō." In *Nihon no otoko wa doko kara kite, doko e yuku no ka?*, ed. Asai Haruo, Itō Satoru, and Murase Yukihiro, 32–53. Jūgatsusha.

Yamato Nobuo. 2006. *Robotto to kurasu: kateiyō robotto saizensen: Sofutobanku shinsho 10*. Sofutobanku Kurieteibu.

Yano, Christine R. 2002. "The Burning of Men: Masculinities and the Nation in Japanese Popular Song." In *Men and Masculinities in Contemporary Japan*. See Roberson and Suzuki 2002a.

Yasumaru Yoshio. 1974. *Nihon no kindaika to minshū shisō*. Aoki Shoten.

Yoda, Tomoko. 2000. "A Roadmap to Millennial Japan." *South Atlantic Quarterly* 99, no. 4: 629–68.

Yoshii Iwatarō. 1887. *Saiban igaku ron*. Taihōkan.

Yoshinaga, S. 2002. "Masculinist Identifications with 'Woman': Gender Politics in Postwar Japanese Literary Debates." *US-Japan Women's Journal* 22: 32–63.

Young, Alford A., Jr. 2003. *Minds of Marginalized Black Men: Making Sense of Mobility, Opportunity, and Future Life Chances*. Princeton: Princeton University Press.

Contributors

Teresa A. Algoso is a Fulbright scholar and a doctoral candidate in the Department of History at the University of California, Santa Barbara. Her article "Thoughts on Hermaphroditism: Miyatake Gaikotsu and the Convergence of the Sexes in Taishō Japan" appeared in the *Journal of Asian Studies* (August 2006). In her dissertation she uses hermaphroditism as a lens to explore the processes in Meiji Japan through which male and female came to be seen as rooted in the body.

Ian Condry is a cultural anthropologist and associate professor in comparative media studies at MIT. He is the author of *Hip-Hop Japan* (Duke University Press, 2006), published in Japanese as *Nihon no Hip-Hop* (NTT, 2009). His chapter here is related to his forthcoming book, *The Soul of Anime: Collaborative Creativity and Japan's Media Success Story*, which is based on fieldwork research in Tokyo animation studios.

Sabine Frühstück is a professor of modern Japanese cultural studies at the University of California, Santa Barbara. She is the author of *Colonizing Sex: Sexology and Social Control in Modern Japan* (UC Press, 2003) and *Uneasy Warriors: Gender, Memory, and Popular Culture in the Japanese Army* (UC Press, 2007), which was translated into Japanese as *Fuan na heishitachi: Nippon Jieitai Kenkyū* (Hara shobō, 2008). Currently, Frühstück pursues a transnational, multidisciplinary analysis of varying configurations of infantilism and militarism, roughly between the Russo-Japanese War of 1904–5 and the ongoing war in Iraq, tentatively titled "Playing War: On the Militarization of Childhood in the Twentieth Century."

Christopher Gerteis is lecturer in the history of contemporary Japan at the School of Oriental and African Studies, University of London. His first book, *Gender Struggles: Wage-earning Women and Male Dominant Unions in Postwar Japan* (Harvard University Asia Center, 2009) examines the extent to which customary notions of work, gender, and ethnicity influenced the formation of the socialist labor movement in postwar Japan. Gerteis's current work explores the intersection of consumer capitalism, social history, and the politics of culture and identity in contemporary Japan.

TOM GILL is a professor of social anthropology in the Faculty of International Studies at Meiji Gakuin University's Yokohama campus. He writes mainly on the lives of underclass men in urban Japan and has published a book, *Men of Uncertainty: The Social Organization of Day Laborers in Contemporary Japan* (SUNY Press, 2001), and many papers in English and Japanese on the subject. In his current research he is looking at comparative studies in the United States and Britain, along with gambling as practiced by Japanese men.

WOLFRAM MANZENREITER teaches on modern Japanese society in the Department of East Asian Studies at Vienna University. His research is mostly concerned with social and anthropological aspects of sports, popular culture, technology, and labor in a globalizing world. The author of several books and articles on sport, popular culture, and leisure in Japan, he is currently working on a new monograph entitled *Sport and the Political Economy of the Body in Japan* and a coedited volume, *The Production of EURO™pe: Football Spectacles and European Identities.*

MICHELE M. MASON is an assistant professor at the University of Maryland, College Park whose interests include modern Japanese literature and history, colonial and postcolonial studies, gender, and feminist studies. Also engaged in the study of the U.S. atomic bombings of Hiroshima and Nagasaki, she has published the article "Writing Hiroshima and Nagasaki in the 21st Century: A New Generation of Historical Manga" (*The Asia-Pacific Journal: Japan Focus*, November 2009) and coproduced a short dual-language documentary film entitled *Witness to Hiroshima* (2010) (see www.witnesstohiroshima.com). She is currently writing about representations of Hokkaido in modern Japan.

NAGANO HIROKO is a professor of economic history at Chūō University. She is author of *Jendā-shi o manabu* (Learning from gender history; Yoshikawa Kōbunkan, 2006), *Nihon kinsei jendā-ron* (Gender in early modern Japan; Yoshikawa Kōbunkan, 2003), and *Bakuhan-sei kokka no keizai kōzō* (The economic structure of the Bakuhan state; Yoshikawa Kōbunkan, 1987), and coeditor of *Keizai to shōhi shakai* (Economics and consumer society, Gender history series, vol. 6; Akashi Shoten, 2009), *Nihon kindai kokka no seiritsu to jendā* (Gender and the establishment of Japan as a modern nation; Kashiwa Shobō, 2003), *Esunishiti, jendā kara miru Nihon no rekishi* (Histories of Japan from the perspectives of ethnicity and gender; Yoshikawa Kōbunkan, 2002), *Jendā de dokkaku Edo jidai* (The Edo period understood through gender; Sanseido, 2001), *Josei no kurashi to rōdō* (Women's work and living, Japanese women's history collective, vol. 6; Yoshikawa Kōbunkan, 1998), and *Seiji to josei* (Politics and women, Japanese women's history collective, vol. 2; Yoshikawa Kōbunkan, 1997).

SUSAN NAPIER is professor of Japanese studies at Tufts University. She has taught at University of Texas, Harvard, and Princeton and was recently visiting professor of Animation Studies at the University of Pennsylvania. Her most recent books include *Anime from Akira to Howl's Moving Castle* and *From Impressionism to Anime: Japan as Fantasy and Fan Cult in the Mind of the West.*

Luke Roberts is a professor of early modern Japanese history at the University of California at Santa Barbara. He is the author of *Mercantilism in a Japanese Domain: The Merchant Origins of Economic Nationalism in Eighteenth-Century Tosa* (1998) and coauthor with Sharon Takeda of *Japanese Fisherman's Coats from Awaji Island* (2001). Currently he is wrapping up a book on political culture entitled *Performing The Great Peace: Political Space and Open Secrets in Tokugawa Japan,* to be published by the University of Hawai'i Press in 2011. His next project is a samurai social history pursued through the biography of an Edo-era samurai, Mori Yoshiki, based on diaries and memoirs of Yoshiki, his family, and friends.

Jennifer Robertson is professor of anthropology and the history of art at the University of Michigan. Among her books are *Native and Newcomer: Making and Remaking a Japanese City, Takarazuka: Sexual Politics and Popular Culture in Modern Japan* (edited), *Same-Sex Cultures and Sexualities: An Anthropological Reader* (edited), and *A Companion to the Anthropology of Japan* (edited by Blackwell). Robertson's most recent articles focus on art, eugenics, the politics of "blood," and humanoid robots.

Sakurai Yuki is an independent scholar. For more than twenty years she has been employed by the Society for Research on Women's History (Sōgō Josei-shi Kenkyūkai), and in that role she has contributed to women's historiography and assisted scholars of women's issues. Sakurai is the author of the articles "Mabiki to datai" (Infanticide and abortion), "Kinsei nōmin kokka no okeru rōjin no chii" (The status of the elderly within the early modern rural state), "Kinsei ni okeru ninshin, shussan gensetsu" (The debates about pregnancy and birth during the early modern era), and "Edo jidai chūgoku no nōmin kazoku" (Rural families in the latter half of the Edo period), among others. Currently she is researching gender as it relates to funeral ceremonies among rural families.

Anne Walthall is professor of Japanese history at the University of California, Irvine. Among her publications are *The Weak Body of a Useless Women: Matsuo Taseko and the Meiji Restoration, Servants of the Dynasty: Palace Women in World History* (edited), and *East Asia: A Cultural, Social, and Political History* (coauthored with Patricia Ebrey and James Palais). She is currently researching the history of Hirata Atsutane and his descendants from the perspectives of faith and family.

Index

Text	10/13 Aldus
Display	Aldus
Compositor	BookMatters, Berkeley
Printer and binder	Sheridan Books, Inc.